Robert Accinelli examines in comprehensive detail the making of the American military and political commitment to Taiwan during the first half of the 1950s. Starting with President Truman's declaration in January 1950 that the United States would not militarily assist Taiwan's Nationalist Chinese government, he shows why the United States subsequently reversed this position and ultimately chose to embrace Taiwan as a highly valued ally. In addition to describing the growth of a close but uneasy association between the United States and the Nationalist regime, he focuses on the importance of the Taiwan issue in America's relations with the People's Republic of China and Great Britain.

According to Accinelli, U.S. policy developed within the context of shifting international circumstances and domestic developments such as McCarthyism and the Truman-MacArthur controversy. National security interests were the decisive factor in the emergence of the commitment to Taiwan, as American leaders reacted to a succession of Asian crises, particularly the Korean War and Communist Chinese intervention in it but also the chilling nine-month confrontation that began in September

United States
Policy toward
Taiwan,
1950–1955

CRISIS

and Commitment

The University of North Carolina Press   Chapel Hill and London

Manufactured in the United
States of America

The paper in this book meets the
guidelines for permanence and
durability of the Committee on
Production Guidelines for Book
Longevity of the Council on
Library Resources.

Library of Congress
Cataloging-in-Publication Data
Accinelli, Robert. Crisis and
commitment: United States
policy toward Taiwan, 1950–1955
/ by Robert Accinelli.   p.   cm.
Includes bibliographical refer-
ences and index.
ISBN 0-8078-2259-0 (alk. paper)
1. United States — Foreign
relations — Taiwan. 2. Taiwan
— Foreign relations — United
States. I. Title.
E183.8.TA33   1996
327.7305124'9 — dc20
95-22269   CIP

Portions of Chapter 9 appeared
previously, in somewhat different
form, in "Eisenhower, Congress,
and the 1954–55 Offshore Islands
Crisis," *Presidential Studies Quarterly* 20 (Spring 1990): 29–48, and
are reproduced here with permission of the Center for the Study of
the Presidency.

00 99 98 97 96   5 4 3 2 1

For Nancy

Among the proliferation of foreign commitments by the United States during the early cold war, one of the most fateful was to the exiled Chinese Nationalist government on Taiwan (Formosa). The defeated Republic of China (ROC), seemingly orphaned by the United States in early 1950 after fleeing from the mainland of China to its island haven, gained a new lease on life as a result of the intervention of the U.S. Seventh Fleet in the Taiwan Strait in June 1950. Subsequently the ROC became first a de facto, then in 1955 a formal, American ally. By extending military protection to Taiwan and once again becoming the patron of the Kuomintang (KMT) regime of Chiang Kai-shek, the United States contributed measurably to the animosity between it and the People's Republic of China (PRC) that congealed during this half decade. In 1954–55, Sino-American differences over Taiwan, which had come to encompass the Nationalist-occupied offshore islands, resulted in one of the most threatening confrontations of the entire cold war.

No issue, not Korea, not Vietnam, divided the United States and China more fundamentally during this period, none was a greater source of contention between them during the remaining years of intense Sino-American rivalry, and none posed a bigger roadblock to their eventual reconciliation and to the normalization of relations in 1979. The United States, despite the severance of formal political and military ties with Taiwan that accompanied the establishment of diplomatic relations with China, has maintained important economic, military, and unofficial connections with its onetime ally. And Taiwan itself has undergone a heralded transition from underdeveloped country to economic dynamo and from an authoritarian state to an emerging democracy. Although the Taiwan issue has been less conspicuous and grating in Sino-American relations since the early 1980s, it still possesses a destabilizing potential. In June 1995 this potential was vividly demonstrated by Peking's white-hot anger over Washington's decision to permit Taiwan's president Lee Teng-hui to make a brief private trip to his alma mater, Cornell University, the first visit by a Taiwanese leader to the United States since the termination of diplomatic relations.

Despite the undeniably far-reaching significance of the political and military commitment to Taiwan molded in Washington between 1950 and 1955, no historian has yet given this pivotal development the comprehensive and detailed consideration it warrants.[1] To this end, I have presented in this volume a full-length analysis of the origins and evolution of the commitment and the attendant unfolding of a reinvigorated relationship with the exiled Nationalist government. Spanning the half decade from the declaration in January 1950 by President Harry S. Truman of a policy of military nonintervention toward Taiwan to the aftermath of the 1954–55 offshore islands crisis, my study attempts to explain how and why top American decision makers came to reembrace the vanquished Nationalist regime and to transform Taiwan into a pro-American citadel. I have examined the broad sweep of American decision making in its institutional, domestic, and international setting and placed this ongoing process in context with Washington's evolving relationship with Chiang Kai-shek's displaced government.

My study draws on research in private papers and government documents in the United States, Britain, and Canada. With some exceptions, most notably material on covert activities, essential official American records are now open to scholars. The papers of the Republic of China's ambassador to the United States, Dr. V. K. Wellington Koo, at Columbia University, along with Koo's exceptionally detailed memoir, provide particularly valuable information and insight relating to Nationalist attitudes and behavior. I make no claim, however, to have written a full or authoritative account of the Nationalist side of the Washington-Taipei relationship, for which historians must await the opening of indispensable archival sources on Taiwan. To interpret Chinese Communist policies, I have integrated into my analysis the findings of western Asian specialists and Chinese historians, whose scholarship in recent years has benefited from the greater availability of official Chinese documentation for this period.*

My central theme is that the U.S. commitment to Taiwan emerged piecemeal in the context of crises triggered by the outbreak of the Korean War, the Chinese military intrusion in the peninsular conflict, and the 1954–55 encounter with China over the offshore islands. Contrary to the assertions of some historians, I view the North Korean strike across the 38th parallel in the summer of 1950 as a major cause, not merely as the occasion for the interposition of the Seventh Fleet in the Taiwan Strait. The Truman administration, following the reversal of its announced noninterventionist policy toward Taiwan, nonetheless for a time kept an arm's-length relationship with the Nationalist government. It was the crisis precipitated by China's surprise entry onto the Korean battlefield that ultimately drove the administration into a

---

*Throughout this study, I have capitalized "Nationalist" and "Communist" when referring to the Chinese.

fixed defensive posture toward the Kuomintang island bastion and a revitalized political relationship with Chiang Kai-shek and his cohorts. This commitment to Taiwan came to be fused with a hard-line "policy of pressure" (to use historian Gordon H. Chang's apt description) toward China, formalized in NSC 48/5 in May 1951, that aimed at splitting this new Communist giant from its Soviet ally through the reorientation, fragmentation, or replacement of its revolutionary leaders. From this same commitment also sprang an informal quasi commitment to the Nationalist-held coastal islands that contributed significantly to the nearly nine-month face-off with China that erupted in September 1954. Taking issue with "Eisenhower revisionists" such as Stephen Ambrose and Robert Divine, I find more to criticize than to praise in the Eisenhower administration's handling of this nerve-racking episode. Further, I qualify or challenge conclusions reached by a number of other scholars regarding the administration's calculations during the emergency.

The offshore islands crisis further extended and solidified the commitment to Taiwan by spawning the 1954 mutual security pact with the Nationalist government, the famed Formosa Resolution, and a secret defensive commitment (later withdrawn) to the KMT coastal possessions of Quemoy and Matsu. But the crisis strained, as well as strengthened, the bond between Washington and Taipei and motivated Secretary of State John Foster Dulles to pursue a de facto two-China policy that required a modification of the policy of pressure against the Communist mainland. In the aftermath of the crisis, the Eisenhower administration nevertheless made no attempt to seek reconciliation with Mao's China and continued a close, if uneasy, relationship with Chiang's remnant regime.

As the commitment took root and grew between 1950 and 1955, it derived its principal nourishment from American official perceptions of national security interests related to Taiwan, both military-strategic and politico-psychological. In giving definition to the commitment, the direction of the White House and State Department was most decisive, with the Pentagon playing an important but lesser part. Decision making was affected intermittently and secondarily by domestic considerations and by pressures from concerned friendly nations, foremost among them Great Britain, an intimate ally especially interested in how Washington conducted itself toward a divided China. The Nationalist government, despite its absolute dependency on Washington's support, was far from a submissive cold war surrogate and showed itself capable of affecting both the conception and application of American policies.

As the commitment to Taiwan took form, decision makers were assertive and sometimes aggressive, but at the same time cautious, in the support they extended to the Nationalists in military and political matters. At no time did they place a seal of approval on Chiang's avowed strategy of military reconquest of the mainland, and they sought through various means to restrain the headstrong Nationalist president from any provocative military adventures that might thrust the United States into a blowup with China. This was in keeping with an overall commitment to the Nationalist government that, despite growing more expansive and durable after its initiation, remained in notable respects carefully circumscribed.

A Note on Romanization

For the sake of consistency with the source materials for this period, I have used the traditional method of Romanization. Exceptions occur where the usual Romanization of a well-known name of an individual or place at the time deviated from the traditional system: for example, Chiang Kai-shek rather than Chiang Chieh-shih, Peking rather than Peip'ing or Peiching. Also in keeping with contemporary usage, I have identified some Chinese individuals by their English names: for instance, Wellington Koo rather than Ku We-chun and George Yeh rather than Yeh Kung-ch'ao.

The preparation of this book has put me in debt to many individuals and institutions whose assistance and support I wish now to thankfully acknowledge. The volume would not have reached publication without the cooperation and guidance of the staffs of the archives and libraries cited in the list of manuscript collections. Because these individuals are too numerous to mention, I can only take refuge in a blanket expression of gratitude. In writing the book, I have also benefited enormously from the labors of a legion of other scholars whose works appear in the bibliography.

The University of Toronto and the Social Sciences and Humanities Research Council of Canada generously awarded me research grants to carry forward my project. The Department of History, University of Toronto, kindly provided additional funds for two research assistants, James Kiras and Marven Krug, whose energetic digging for material at the library lightened my own burden.

I wish to give recognition to the late Dean Rusk and to a former Foreign Service officer, who wishes to remain anonymous, for sharing their recollections with me. My thanks as well to *Presidential Studies Quarterly* for allowing me to include portions of my article "Eisenhower, Congress, and the 1954–55 Offshore Islands Crisis" in Chapter 9 and to Stanford University Press for permission to use an adapted version of the map of the Offshore Islands and the Taiwan Strait.

A special word of appreciation is owed to my colleague William Berman, who, in addition to giving the entire manuscript his rigorous scrutiny and suggesting helpful changes, bolstered my faith in its merit. I also greatly profited from the valuable commentaries of the two readers for the University of North Carolina Press. Naturally any errors of commission or omission are entirely my own.

To no person am I more indebted than my wife, Nancy, who helped to sustain me through a long period of research and writing with her patience, understanding, and encouragement and who with good grace always found time in her own busy life to read the various drafts of this work with a sharp eye to stylistic improvement. To her I affectionately dedicate this book.

CAT	Civil Air Transport
CCP	Chinese Communist Party
CIA	Central Intelligence Agency
CIC	Commerce International China
CINCPAC	Commander in Chief, Pacific
ECA	Economic Cooperation Administration
EDC	European Defense Community
FOA	Foreign Operations Administration
FY	Fiscal Year
JCS	Joint Chiefs of Staff
JSSC	Joint Strategic Survey Committee
KMT	Kuomintang
MAAG	Military Advisory Assistance Group
MDAP	Mutual Defense Assistance Program
MSA	Mutual Security Agency
NATO	North Atlantic Treaty Organization
NSC	National Security Council
PLA	People's Liberation Army
PPS	Policy Planning Staff
PRC	People's Republic of China
ROC	Republic of China

SCAP   Supreme Commander for the Allied Powers in Japan

SEATO   South East Asia Treaty Organization

UN   United Nations

VFW   Veterans of Foreign Wars

The China Coast and Taiwan

In a brief four-paragraph statement presented to reporters on 5 January 1950, President Harry Truman announced that the United States would not provide military aid or assistance to safeguard Taiwan. The practical effect of this declaration was to leave the island, the final refuge of the Nationalist regime recently expelled from the mainland, exposed to an expected Chinese Communist takeover. The president's statement bore on a knotty problem that had privately occupied foreign policy decision makers since early in the previous year: how to keep this strategically important territory from falling into Communist hands without incurring unwanted responsibilities or liabilities. During the course of 1949 decision makers had secretly searched in vain for a satisfactory solution to this problem. Portending the loss of Taiwan, Truman's statement appeared to mark an unsuccessful end to that search. In the spring of 1950, however, the quest resumed again in earnest, and it was still in progress when the Korean War erupted.

A Nonmilitary Policy

The year 1949 was a crucial one for the future of both China and Taiwan. The Chinese Communists vanquished the Nationalists on the mainland, establishing the People's Republic of China (PRC) on 1 October; the deposed government of the Republic of China (ROC) relocated to Taiwan in December, maintaining its claim as the legitimate government of China. Even before being ejected from the continent, Generalissimo Chiang Kai-shek and his loyalists had looked to Taiwan as their last stronghold. The island, which lay approximately 100 miles off China's southeastern coast and was home to approximately six million Taiwanese, had come under Nationalist sway following the Pacific war. During the previous half century Japan had ruled the island as a colony along with the nearby Penghu Islands (Pescadores), having wrested both from China after the Sino-Japanese War in 1895. The Cairo Declaration jointly issued in December 1943 by President Franklin D. Roosevelt, British prime minister Winston Churchill, and Chiang Kai-shek had prescribed the restoration of this territory to the Republic of China after Japan's defeat. In July 1945 the United States, Britain, and the ROC reaffirmed the terms of the Cairo Declaration in the Potsdam Proclamation, which the Soviet Union and France subsequently endorsed. The Nationalist government accepted the Japanese surrender of Taiwan in October 1945 and, in accordance with wartime declarations, assumed control over it.[1]

Under Taiwan's first Nationalist governor, Chen Yi, the island's inhabitants experienced the misrule that had become a byword for Kuomintang (KMT) governance on the continent. The abysmal conduct of the Nationalists was a major cause of a short-lived uprising beginning on 28 February 1947, whose tragic and brutal suppression left the embittered Taiwanese in the firm grip of the KMT. In December 1948 Gen. Chen Cheng, one of Chiang's oldest and most trusted lieutenants, became governor.[2]

Chen Cheng's appointment was a sign that the Generalissimo had chosen Taiwan as a final redoubt for himself and his die-hard followers. As the People's Liberation Army (PLA) advanced victoriously through northeast China in late 1948, Nationalist troops, party and government officials, and accompanying civilians began to stream to the island in large numbers, commencing an exodus that deposited 1.5 million refugees on Taiwan by the fall of 1949. By year's end Chiang himself had escaped the mainland. Despite his official retirement from the presidency in January 1949, he retained de facto control over the government and military establishment.[3]

As the Communists had marched relentlessly southward, Chiang maneuvered to procure more aid and support from an increasingly balky American government to shore up the crumbling Kuomintang position on the mainland. After fleeing to Taiwan, he continued to place his hope in Washington for the salvation of his regime. The longtime Nationalist leader regarded himself as the indispensable instrument of China's destiny, the successor to the anti-Manchu revolutionary patriot and KMT leader Sun Yat-sen, and the guardian of a traditional Chinese way of life now in danger of being entirely overwhelmed by an alien revolutionary ideology. Convinced that his defeat was temporary and that the inevitable outbreak of a third world war between the United States and the Soviet Union would present an opportunity to regain his lost territory, he made the goal of "mainland recovery" the principal raison d'être and rallying cry of his exiled regime. He espoused a strategy of counterattack that envisaged the eventual repossession of the mainland by his armed forces with American assistance. In the short term, he spared no effort to ensure the survival and security of his island base while awaiting his chance to drive the Chinese Communist Party (CCP) usurpers from power. He sought to regain lost American confidence in his government and to secure sufficient aid and support to maintain Nationalist jurisdiction over the island.[4]

American officials in 1949 viewed China and the Nationalist government with very different eyes than had President Roosevelt at the wartime Cairo conference. Roosevelt, in agreeing to turn over Taiwan to the Republic of China, had acted in the expectation that Chiang Kai-shek's Nationalists would continue to exercise authority over China after Japan's surrender. He envisioned a postwar policy founded on close cooperation with a united, stable, and friendly China that would sustain U.S. interests in East Asia. By 1949 the framework of American policymaking toward China had radically changed. When Dean Acheson succeeded Gen. George C. Marshall as secretary of state in January 1949, the dominant reality in American official perceptions of China was the expected triumph of the Chinese Communists over Chiang's corrupt regime and China's transfer to the camp of the Soviet Union. During Marshall's tenure in the State Department, the Truman administration had rejected both an all-out commitment to save the Nationalists from defeat and a complete break with them, settling on a policy of limited economic and military assistance. The disintegration of KMT forces in late 1948 left no doubt in the minds of State Department officials that Chiang's cause was beyond recovery.[5]

As he had with Marshall, President Truman gave Acheson wide latitude in directing the nation's foreign relations. The chief executive, who was contemptuous both of CCP chairman Mao Tse-tung's revolutionaries and Chiang and his minions, participated only erratically in the formulation of China policy. Though Acheson had gained exposure to the problems of China as undersecretary of state from 1945 to 1947, he was an Atlanticist with no abiding interest in that strife-torn nation or special understanding of it. He viewed China as an area of secondary importance, from the perspective of America's global competition with the Soviet Union. He and his subordinates at Foggy Bottom were disdainful of the Generalissimo and his ossified regime.[6]

China policy after Acheson took charge at the State Department was fluid, provisional, and ridden with conflicting purposes. Anticipating the impending Kuomintang defeat, the department chose not to cut all American links with Chiang but instead to distance the United States from his doomed government, narrow the conduit of aid, and retain freedom of action in China. The American posture toward the Chinese Communists was neither actively accommodationist nor unreservedly hostile. The State Department did little to reach out diplomatically to CCP leaders and basically viewed them with antipathy and distrust. At the same time, it did keep open the options of regulated Sino-American and Sino-Japanese trade and of eventual diplomatic recognition when conditions were right. The department simultaneously pursued a "wedge" strategy whose objective was to loosen the ties between China and the USSR so as to prevent the Communist victory from augmenting Soviet power. The expectation was that Chinese nationalism and anti-imperialism would in time turn against Moscow, particularly because of Soviet inroads in China's northern provinces. In one potential scenario, CCP leaders would follow the deviationist path of Yugoslavia's Marshal Josip Tito. Yet most State Department officials were doubtful that a Sino-Soviet split would materialize in the near term. And they disagreed about how best to foster a rift, whether by means of inducements such as trade and recognition or by coercive tactics to convince CCP leaders that cozying up to the Kremlin did not serve their best interests.[7]

Bureaucratic conflict between the State and Defense Departments complicated the formulation and implementation of China policy. Unlike the State Department, the Pentagon favored a strict hard-line policy toward the CCP and generous assistance to the KMT on Taiwan and to anti-Communist forces on the mainland.[8] Exacerbating these policy differences was the strained personal relationship between the urbane, self-assured Dean Acheson and Louis Johnson, the flamboyant, outspoken, and politically ambitious Washington attorney who became secretary of defense in March 1949. A stalwart pro-Nationalist advocate, as were various underlings in the Defense Department, Johnson exerted influence on behalf of the KMT within the policy-making community and may have conveyed inside (including top secret) information to Nationalist contacts.[9]

The administration conducted its China policy within an increasingly turbulent domestic political environment in 1949. Especially troublesome for the White House and State Department was the China bloc, a small band of influential pro-Nationalist enthusiasts in Congress, mostly Republicans, who were critical of the administration's past and present conduct of China policy and who pushed for more assistance to the Republic of China. Exercising its leverage on Capitol Hill, this bloc did have some limited success in keeping aid flowing to the Nationalists. It carried on its activities in a political milieu fast becoming more charged with partisanship as a result of Republican disappointment following President Truman's unanticipated victory in the 1948 election.[10]

As was the case in Congress, pro-Nationalist zealots among the articulate public were in a minority and wielded only limited influence. The so-called China lobby—a loose collection of Americans and Chinese who championed the cause of the Nationalist government and agitated for U.S. assistance—was still in its infancy; it possessed neither broad public support nor a fearsome reputation. The lobby's thesis that the "loss of China" was the result of neglect and incompetence, if not outright disloyalty, within the State Department under Roosevelt and Truman had yet to gain wide currency.[11] Public attitudes toward China were malleable. Americans were undeniably shaken by the momentous shift in power in the world's most populous country, and only small minorities favored trade with a Communist-controlled China or diplomatic recognition. Still, a plurality of citizens rejected intervention in the civil war and held unfavorable opinions of Chiang Kai-shek.[12]

As the Truman administration plotted its China policy during the denouement of the civil war, it struggled with the tangled problem of Taiwan. Military and civilian decision makers alike were in accord that the island was strategically important. The Joint Chiefs of Staff (JCS) concluded in November 1948 that the seizure of the island by Kremlin-oriented Communists would have "seriously unfavorable" strategic implications for national security: it would give a wartime enemy the capability to dominate the sea lanes between Japan and Malaya and to threaten the Philippines and Ryukyu Islands, would deprive the United States of a base for strategic air operations and control of nearby shipping lanes, and would eliminate the island as a source of food and raw materials for Japan under war conditions.

From his Tokyo headquarters, Gen. Douglas A. MacArthur warned that a Taiwan in unfriendly hands would "invite [the] rupture of our whole defense line in the Far East."[13] As supreme commander for the allied powers in Japan (SCAP), commanding general of the U.S. Army in the Far East, and head of American forces in the Far East Command, this imperious general was a power in his own right. Having spent much of his military career in Asia, he held strong convictions about its overall strategic significance. By late 1948 he was on record as an advocate of a more activist policy in China (which as a navy theater was not under his command) in support of Chiang Kai-shek and his beleaguered Nationalist government. This stance endeared the general, who had presidential ambitions, to pro-Nationalist partisans within the Republican party.[14]

In evaluating Taiwan's strategic value, the JCS and the Far Eastern commander drew on the experiences of the Second World War. Besides being a valuable component in Japan's war economy, the island had been a major base for military operations against China and in Southeast Asia and the southwest Pacific.[15] In addition, as historian John Lewis Gaddis has shown, American military and civilian planners assessed the island's strategic worth in relation to the evolving concept of an American-dominated island defensive perimeter in the western Pacific stretching from the Aleutian Islands to the Philippines.[16]

The paramount American interest in Taiwan lay in the strategic advantage derived from retaining access to the island as a potential wartime base for U.S. military operations while foreclosing its military exploitation by the Soviet Union, particularly in the event of hostilities. From the perspective of the military establishment, whether or not the island remained under friendly control could seriously affect the American security posture throughout the western Pacific. In its November 1948 report, the JCS did not (as one study of Acheson's Asian policies has contended) define the dominant American interest solely in terms of Taiwan's strategic location athwart Japan's sea lanes and its potential resumed role as a major source of food and other resources for its former metropole. Rather, the island was viewed in relation to broader regional security concerns that also included the safety of the Ryukyus and the Philippines. Moreover, what made the prospect of a restored trading relationship between Taiwan and Japan most worth preserving for the JCS was that this would better ensure that the latter would be a boon rather than a burden during wartime. An appraisal of Taiwan's strategic value produced by the Central Intelligence Agency (CIA) on 3 January 1949 echoed the basic conclusions of the JCS report and further argued that the island's economic assets were by themselves not significant enough to warrant "direct US measures" to deny it to Communist control. The CIA analysis, while acknowledging that Taiwan could provide peacetime Japan with a nearer and more dependable source of food than Southeast Asia as well as a market for its manufactures and consumer goods, still regarded the island's military utility as decisive in determining its strategic importance.[17]

Despite placing a high strategic value on Taiwan in their November 1948 assessment, the JCS recommended using only diplomatic and economic means to deny the island to the Communists. In a subsequent report in mid-February 1949, they proposed stationing a few naval vessels there as a show of force, but they still did not deem the island so vital that they were willing to support armed intervention to keep it out of the Communist grip. In rejecting intervention, they cited the disparity between the nation's military strength and its worldwide obligations. The chiefs were acutely conscious of the need to rank strategic interests cautiously at a time when low defense budgets restricted the military resources to fulfill America's global role.[18] In yet another evaluation of Taiwan's strategic importance in April 1949, they ruled out overt military action even if diplomatic and economic steps proved inadequate to prevent a Communist takeover. They did append the caveat that "future circumstances extending to war itself" might cause them to change their minds. In other words, intervention might prove desirable but only in conditions of incipient or actual war.[19]

In early 1949 the State Department secretly set out to detach Taiwan from the mainland by nonmilitary means. Acheson turned aside the JCS proposal to station a few U.S. naval units at Taiwanese ports, protesting that such action would compromise surreptitious efforts to isolate the island from the continent and would raise the "spectre of an American-created irredentist issue just at the time we shall be seeking to exploit the genuinely Soviet-created irredentist issue in Manchuria and Sinkiang."[20] In charting Taiwan policy, one of the secretary of state's foremost concerns was to leave unimpaired the objective of dividing China from the Kremlin. Any overt military initiative aimed at depriving the CCP of Taiwan would mobilize Chinese anti-imperialist sentiment against the United States rather than against the Soviet Union for its encroachment on Chinese territory.

Acheson and his State Department advisers did not envisage propping up an unregenerate KMT government on Taiwan. An unpopular and reactionary administration under the rule of Chiang Kai-shek would be vulnerable to Communist subversion and would be an unfit instrument for the implementation of a major program of economic reconstruction that the department had in mind to stabilize the island. Early in 1949 the National Security Council (NSC) decided to investigate the possibility of increased economic assistance to a separatist and reformist KMT government, leaving open the additional option of clandestine support for a movement for Taiwanese autonomy. In essence, the NSC contemplated a possible two-China solution for the Taiwan problem.[21] Dispatched on a secret errand to Taiwan to determine the feasibility of such an approach, Livingston T. Merchant, counselor in the Nanking embassy, concluded after a three-month mission ending in May 1949 that a Chiang-less and reformist KMT government was not in the cards and that no viable indigenous political force existed.[22]

Persuaded that existing NSC policy was unworkable, State Department officials in the aftermath of the Merchant mission circulated among themselves a number of schemes for more forthright action, including a United Nations (UN) trusteeship (preliminary to a UN-supervised plebiscite to decide the island's future) and American occupation of the island. The proposal for a UN solution received the most considered attention. Such a stratagem, though it had discouraging drawbacks, would enable the United States to support the principle of self-determination and would offer some protection against accusations of great power interventionism and imperialism.[23] The unsettled legal status of Taiwan provided a loophole for a trusteeship, autonomy, or even independence for the island. Neither the United States nor any other power had formally recognized Taiwan's annexation by China. By Washington's lights, the final legal disposition of the island awaited a Japanese peace treaty or other appropriate international action.[24]

In September 1949 the UN solution came up during Anglo-American consultations about China. Ernest Bevin, foreign secretary in the Labour government of Clement Attlee, and his colleagues in the Foreign Office were then considering early recognition of the new government poised to take power on the mainland, hoping among other objectives to encourage Mao Tse-tung to follow in Tito's footsteps. British officials felt little but disgust for Chiang Kai-shek's failed regime, and they were angered by an illegal Nationalist blockade of Communist-controlled ports in north China that locked the sizable British business community in Shanghai in a painful economic squeeze.[25] Although the Foreign Office and the State Department saw eye-to-eye on the goal of separating the CCP from Moscow, they diverged over recognition, trade, and the KMT blockade. The Americans were in no rush to extend recognition, preferred tighter controls on trade than did the British, and acquiesced in the blockade because of the economic pressure it placed on the Communists. As for Taiwan, the British made plain that they had come to terms with eventual Communist occupation of the island and that they were unenthusiastic about a UN solution. London's position, combined with Acheson's own skepticism about a successful referral of the Taiwan question to the world organization, put a damper on further active pursuit of a UN remedy, but the notion of international action to split Taiwan from China remained alive within the State Department.[26]

By October 1949, as the newly proclaimed People's Republic of China took its place on the world scene, the nonmilitary policy had nearly reached a dead end. The State Department had failed to find a way to detach Taiwan from the Communist-controlled mainland either through a reformist KMT government, an indigenous autonomy movement, or a UN maneuver. The CIA forecast that, without U.S. military intervention and occupation, the Nationalist refuge would likely fall by the end of 1950.[27]

Still operating within the parameters of the nonmilitary policy, the National Security Council on 20 October 1949 approved a démarche to Chiang Kai-shek informing him that the United States would not defend the island and further asserting that the future American attitude toward Taiwan (specifically the provision of augmented economic assistance) would hinge on an improved performance and maximum self-help by the Nationalist government. The premise of the démarche was that Taiwan's weakness was the result of misgovernment rather than a lack of money or arms; the Nationalists had transferred more than $100 million in gold, silver, and U.S. currency to the island along with a large stockpile of military material. Some American economic aid and military supplies still reached the island under existing programs. The démarche represented a form of shock treatment to jolt the Generalissimo into a realization that U.S. forces would not come to his rescue and that his regime would have to rejuvenate itself if it expected even to receive expanded economic assistance beyond present modest levels. But no one in the State Department actually believed that he would take the necessary remedial action or that a last-minute overhaul could do more than delay the passing of Taiwan to Communist control.[28]

Following the October démarche, Chiang tried to put a new face on his regime by assigning the post of governor to the American-educated K. C. Wu, a former reformist mayor of postwar Shanghai who had acquired a reputation in the United States as the "La Guardia of China." A genuine liberal, Wu set out to stabilize provincial finances and to reform provincial and local government in order to reduce anti-KMT resentment among Taiwanese.[29] In addition to trying to spruce up his government, Chiang Kai-shek solicited American economic and military assistance through various Nationalist representatives on Taiwan and in Washington.[30]

Late in 1949 the Defense Department began to push for a more assertive approach to keep Taiwan out of Mao's clutches. This pressure reached peak intensity in December at a time when an anxious mood pervaded Washington because of the Communist triumph in China and the recent Soviet explosion of an atomic bomb. Policymakers debated how to make most effective use of $75 million in a "303 fund" earmarked for the "general area of China" under the Mutual Defense Assistance Program (MDAP) approved by Congress in early October. They also neared completion of NSC 48, a comprehensive policy paper for Asia that had been in the works for a number of months.[31] From Tokyo, Gen. MacArthur let it be known that Taiwan ought to be held because of its strategic value. As historian Michael Schaller has documented, the Far Eastern commander also displayed a penchant for independent action toward Chiang's stronghold.[32]

On 23 December the JCS, without removing their stricture against armed intervention, recommended a "modest, well-directed and closely supervised" program of military assistance for Taiwan together with an immediate survey of its defense requirements.[33] The possible availability of "303" funds for Taiwan gave impetus to this proposal. So too did the scheduled formal consideration of NSC 48 by the president and the National Security Council less than a week away. The joint chiefs and defense officials saw the proposal as a means of toughening the terms of this major Asian policy statement.[34]

Making certain that he first had the president in his corner, Acheson easily blocked the JCS proposal at a session with the military chieftains on 29 December. The secretary saw no new convincing military-strategic reason to diverge from the nonmilitary policy. Responding to the argument made by several chiefs that Taiwan was useful in deflecting Chinese Communist expansion in Southeast Asia, he countered that the primary threat in that region was from infiltration and subversion rather than invasion. As for Taiwan itself, he contended that the biggest danger was from internal decay, which was probably irreversible, rather than from an external assault. The military action proposed by the chiefs, in his view, could only postpone a Communist takeover, not prevent it. Such action would, moreover, carry an unacceptably steep political price for the United States: a loss of prestige after visibly trying and then failing to retain the island, an opportunity for Soviet mischief-making in the UN, a tarnished reputation in Asia for backing a discredited government, and the substitution of the United States "for the Soviets as the imperialist menace to China." Despite the present intimate Sino-Soviet relationship, Acheson offered, the United States had to take "the long view not of 6 or 12 months but of 6 or 12 years." The Kremlin's efforts to detach China's northern provinces contained the "seed of inevitable conflict between China and the Soviet Union."[35]

Later that same day, when the National Security Council took final action on NSC 48, Acheson won approval for a reaffirmation of the nonmilitary policy as a part of NSC 48/2. As the finalized version of the Asian policy paper, NSC 48/2 contemplated an ultimate reduction of Soviet power and influence in Asia, but its emphasis was on containment rather than rollback, and it comported on the whole with the State Department's preferred policy agenda for China rather than the Defense Department's more aggressive approach.[36]

The decision to sustain the nonmilitary policy amounted to a virtual abandonment of Taiwan and the Nationalist government. No one expected that Chiang and his loyalists could hold their island haven on their own or that the United States could by diplomatic and economic means alone prevent its eventual absorption into the Communist-controlled mainland. Even the limited military action advocated by the joint chiefs would have, by their own admission, merely delayed the inevitable. Only armed intervention, or a declared defensive guarantee, offered an effective method to protect the island. Yet the JCS still insisted that Taiwan's strategic value did not warrant intervention under present conditions. And the State Department fretted that even additional limited military aid would hinder the goal of dividing China from the Soviet Union, tie the United States once again to Chiang Kai-shek and his bankrupt Kuomintang regime, and invest American prestige in a futile venture to avert Taiwan's predicted appropriation by the Communists.

A "Ringing Pronouncement"

Shortly after Truman's decision against an alteration of the nonmilitary policy, the press got wind of it, igniting a heated political dispute. Republican senator William F. Knowland (California), a prominent figure in the China bloc, promptly proposed a military advisory mission to Taiwan and released a letter from former President Herbert Hoover recommending naval protection for the Nationalist sanctuary and possibly for Hainan Island, located off China's southern coast and then still also under KMT control. Senator Robert Taft, the formidable Ohio Republican conservative, similarly recommended that the U.S. Navy stand watch over Taiwan. Adding to the clamor, MacArthur's headquarters leaked the contents of a confidential State Department information paper that anticipated Taiwan's fall to the Communists and minimized the consequences for the United States of this eventuality. Knowland and Senator H. Alexander Smith, a New Jersey Republican and another heavyweight in the China bloc, immediately demanded the release of the secret document. During the late fall, Smith had conducted a one-man campaign for unilateral American occupation of Taiwan as a possible prelude to establishment of a UN trusteeship.[37]

In part, the rumpus over Taiwan had the earmarks of a right-wing Republican political offensive against the administration; 1950 was an election year, the first since the frustrating GOP political setback two years earlier. In the weeks and months following this outburst, the Republican right wing formed an informal alliance with the China bloc, aggressively exploiting controversy over Taiwan and other aspects of China and Asian policy.[38]

On 3 January Acheson and his advisers convened a "long soul-searching session" to discuss a "ringing pronouncement" to quiet speculation about the government's intentions toward Taiwan.[39] The secretary persuaded Truman to clarify government policy by issuing a short statement drafted by the State Department. Despite opposition from Secretary of Defense Johnson and from his own staff, the president made public the statement two days later, albeit after accepting last-minute revisions favored by JCS chairman Gen. Omar N. Bradley. The policy announcement invoked the traditional U.S. principle of respect for China's territorial integrity and acknowledged the status of Taiwan as Chinese territory. It declared that the United States had "no predatory designs on Formosa or any other Chinese territory" and "no desire to obtain special rights or privileges or to establish military bases on Formosa *at this time* (emphasis added)." To satisfy Bradley, who wanted to retain enough elbowroom to sever Taiwan from the mainland under wartime conditions, the president had consented to insert the qualifying words "at this time" as well as to excise language in the State Department's original version that disavowed any desire to "detach Formosa from China." The statement further averred that the United States would not utilize its "armed forces to interfere in the present situation," involve itself in the Chinese civil war, or "provide military aid or advice to the Chinese forces on Formosa."[40] That same day, in comments to reporters, Acheson flatly stated that "we are not going to get involved militarily in any way on the Island of Formosa."[41]

In practice, the State Department refrained from interpreting the prohibition against military aid so strictly as to require an abrupt or complete cutoff of military material to the Nationalists. The Taipei government still had available to it some $9 million for military supplies remaining in a special fund (originally totalling $125 million) in the 1948 China Aid Act. It could also purchase military material with its own funds in the open market in the United States.[42]

Inspired mainly by domestic contention over Taiwan, the 5 January 1950 statement was also meant for audiences overseas. For Chiang Kai-shek and the Kuomintang, it was a blunt reminder that they could not count on Washington to deliver them from their mainland enemies. For the Chinese Communists, it offered assurance that the United States was winding down its involvement in the civil war and would leave Taiwan unguarded. Such assurance was all the more timely because the Communists had just charged that a secret understanding existed between Washington and Taipei for substantial aid to the island and because Mao Tse-tung and Soviet leader Joseph Stalin were then engaged in critical negotiations in Moscow on a Sino-Soviet alliance and other matters.[43] For the British and other Western allies, as well as for most noncommunist opinion in Asia, the statement would offer welcome evidence of realism in confronting the historic political changeover in China.

Within the administration itself, the announcement represented an attempt by Acheson and the State Department to discourage further challenges to the nonmilitary policy from Johnson and the military establishment. The Pentagon did temporarily refrain from overt efforts to modify the policy. A sulky Johnson was reported to be "keeping quiet and lying low for the time being."[44] The secretary of defense and General Bradley loyally supported the president's decision in secret testimony before the Senate Foreign Relations Committee.[45]

China bloc leaders were predictably irate at the 5 January announcement. In a conference with Senators Knowland and Smith, Acheson vainly tried to put across the reasons for the administration's stance. Setting aside legal technicalities, he insisted that the practical reality was that Taiwan was part of China. For the United States to proclaim its intention to protect the island would, he expounded, contradict the principle of self-determination that it was preaching throughout Asia and expose it to Soviet charges of imperialism at a time when Moscow was itself extending its control over north China. The United States could either fight, if need be, to hold the island or accept the likelihood of its collapse. Since the joint chiefs did not regard the island as vital to national security, it was not worth the risk of war. Regardless, the Nationalist government had enough money to buy whatever military equipment and supplies it needed for defense against an invasion. What was in doubt was its will to fight.[46]

Far from abating, the domestic row over Taiwan intensified after the 5 January pronouncement. Pro-Nationalist zealots and Republican partisans bitterly equated the statement with "appeasement" and refused to accept it as the final word on American policy.[47] Acheson himself took the offensive in Congress and among the public. In a memorable address before the National Press Club on 12 January, he played on favorite themes: the Nationalist government's self-destruction on the mainland, and the need for the United States to accommodate the powerful forces of Asian nationalism and stay out of the way of the coming collision between Chinese nationalism and Soviet imperialism. Unsurprisingly, the secretary omitted mention of Taiwan in identifying a series of essential strategic points in a U.S. island defensive perimeter in the western Pacific.[48]

On 19 January a coalition that included cost-cutting congressmen, isolationists, and China bloc members disturbed by the Truman administration's indifference to Chiang Kai-shek's plight engineered the shocking defeat of a Korean aid bill in the House of Representatives. In order to reverse this setback, the administration agreed to extend the termination date for economic assistance to Taiwan under the China Aid Act from 14 February to the end of June 1950. This concession was not onerous and left the nonmilitary policy uncompromised.[49]

Though noisy, the critics of military disengagement did not represent the dominant viewpoint either inside or outside of Congress. A poll taken in late January showed that 50 percent of a national sample approved of the president's decision not to send military assistance to Chiang Kai-shek while only 20 percent objected. A mid-February assessment of opinion trends on the Taiwan issue prepared within the State Department concluded that "apart from the [pro-Nationalist] minority in Congress and their staunch supporters in the press," the president's decision *has drawn an impressive array of support from editors, columnists, radio commentators, and organizations.*"[50]

The prospects of administration critics improved on 12 February when the national press reported Senator Joseph McCarthy's sensational allegations of communist infiltration in the State Department. The Wisconsin Republican was now launched on the ravaging witch hunt that would carry him to fame and power. Seizing on the innuendoes of extreme pro-KMT activists, he made individuals connected with wartime and postwar policy in Asia, particularly China, his principal targets. McCarthy's spectacular ascent added a sinister new dimension to the emerging alliance of right-wing Republicans and the China bloc.[51]

To shore up bipartisanship and mollify critics of China policy, Acheson in late March removed W. Walton Butterworth, a veteran foreign service officer seen by critics as a symbol of a failed approach in China, from the sensitive position of assistant secretary of state for Far Eastern Affairs, replacing him with the respected and uncontroversial Dean Rusk, who accepted a voluntary demotion from his post as deputy undersecretary of state. Soon afterward, John Foster Dulles, the impeccably bipartisan Republican, consented to an appointment as a consultant in the State Department.[52]

Rusk and Dulles would soon act as sparkplugs for a reconsideration of the nonmilitary policy within the State Department. In the meanwhile, Acheson sped along the process of military disengagement from Chiang's regime. He opposed the sale of medium tanks and jet aircraft to the Nationalists and the provision of any additional military supplies financed by remaining U.S. aid beyond those already in the pipeline.[53] In a late March appearance before the Senate Foreign Relations Committee, in which he was unsparingly critical of Chiang Kai-shek's leadership, he placed the nonmilitary policy in the context of the twin goals of sundering China from the Soviet Union and encouraging centrifugal forces that would hinder consolidation of the CCP's control over its mainland territory. Why should the United States undo these objectives by fighting for an island that was unessential to its own security? Sneering at Chiang's belief in an inevitable third world war that would enable the Nationalists to ride back to the mainland on American coattails, the secretary displayed angry impatience with the "purely provocative" Nationalist air bombardment of mainland cities.[54]

The view of most U.S. intelligence analysts in the early spring of 1950 was that Taiwan would succumb to the Communists in the not too far distant future as a result of invasion and Nationalist internal weaknesses. An intelligence report in late March predicted that a quick defeat would follow an assault expected before year's end, probably between June and December. A group of dissenting armed services analysts held that the report underestimated Nationalist defensive capabilities.[55]

The Communist seizure of Hainan on 16 April together with the Chusan Islands near Shanghai on 10 May appeared to be harbingers of Taiwan's early capture. In actuality, as Chinese documents now reveal, CCP leaders had to postpone a planned military campaign against Taiwan until the summer of

1951, partially because Chiang strengthened the defenses of his home base with 190,000 KMT troops evacuated from Hainan and the Chusans.[56]

In Washington, the outlook for Taiwan seemed bleak. In mid-May the State Department advised all American private citizens to leave the island and secretly prepared for the emergency evacuation of U.S. official personnel. It also interested itself in finding asylum for the Generalissimo.[57] In light of Truman's 5 January statement and the Nationalists' recent military reversals, it now seemed that the long-running Chinese civil war was nearing its decisive conclusion.

The Reappraisal of the Nonmilitary Policy

With time seemingly running out rapidly for a noncommunist Taiwan, American decision makers took another look at the nonmilitary policy. During the two months before the commencement of the Korean War, they considered measures to bolster the island's defenses and to segregate it from the mainland. On the eve of the Korean conflict, the nonmilitary policy remained unchanged, but its continuation had become open to debate.

A bundle of three related factors contributed to the reappraisal of the policy: a changing domestic political environment, a movement toward a more militarized and undifferentiated global activism, and a trend toward greater militancy in Asia along with a further hardening of official attitudes toward the PRC. To start, the domestic brouhaha over China, the rise of McCarthy to prominence on a surge of anticommunist paranoia, and the disintegration of bipartisanship had by the spring of 1950 badly polluted the political atmosphere and had begun to present a danger to the administration's entire management of foreign affairs.[58] Too, a more militarized and indiscriminate cold war perspective was spreading through the national security bureaucracy. In early April Truman was presented with NSC 68, the well-known blueprint for global security calling for significantly higher defense spending. This alarmist document was silent about Taiwan but had direct implications for the nonmilitary policy. Smudging the distinction between vital and secondary strategic interests, it described a world in which a communist gain anywhere represented an equivalent loss for the United States. In taking stock of the power relationship with the Soviet Union, it gave weight to politico-psychological elements such as image and credibility as well as conventional criteria like economic and military strength. In stressing the compatibility and shared goals of communist states and movements, despite national differences, NSC 68 implicitly cast doubt on the emergence of Titoist deviationism in China.[59]

Trends in Asian and China policy similarly affected official attitudes toward

Taiwan. In accordance with NSC 48/2 approved in December 1949, policy-makers sought to construct new positions of strength in the Far East. One area to which they devoted close attention was Southeast Asia, which was seen as a major arena of the cold war and interlocked with U.S. interests in Japan and Western Europe. On 24 April President Truman endorsed NSC 64, which committed the United States to stem communist expansion in Indochina, viewed by top decision makers as the cornerstone of stability in Southeast Asia. On 4 May Truman approved $10 million in aid for the French-backed state of Vietnam. It was axiomatic among policymakers at this time that China was the springboard for revolutionary communism in Asia and a menace to significant U.S. interests in Indochina and throughout Southeast Asia.[60]

The movement to contain communism on China's periphery paralleled a worsening of Sino-American relations and a toughening of U.S. China policy. Following the seizure of U.S. consular property in Peking in January, the State Department withdrew all remaining diplomatic personnel from the People's Republic. Despite an awareness that Mao had consented to hard conditions, the conclusion of the Sino-Soviet alliance in mid-February confirmed the unlikelihood of an early falling out between Peking and Moscow. In several major public addresses, Acheson lashed out at the CCP for its subordination to the Kremlin. The State Department retained some maneuverability with regard to trade, recognition, and the question of Chinese representation in the UN, but it took no positive steps to woo Mao away from Stalin. The wedge strategy was increasingly linked to a stiff line against the People's Republic.[61]

On most aspects of China policy, Washington differed from London, whose own approach to the PRC was more moderate. Whitehall had privately rejoiced at Truman's 5 January statement on Taiwan, which dovetailed with its own readiness to write off the Nationalist regime.[62] Even so, the Foreign Office and State Department diverged on most China-related issues. On the day after the president's announcement, Britain extended diplomatic recognition to the People's Republic. While American officials still kept the door ajar for eventual recognition, they had no desire to soon follow the British lead. In mid-April Dean Rusk and Ambassador-at-large Philip C. Jessup told Canadian diplomats that Washington had no immediate intention to recognize the Peking government and that, if anything, policy was now more firmly against doing so. Jessup maintained that the State Department's primary concern was uncertainty that the Communists could consolidate their control in south China. A prolonged civil war, even the emergence of two governments on the mainland, was a possibility; these circumstances made recognition premature. Rusk added that the Communist treatment of American interests in China along with the situation in Southeast Asia would affect any decision for recognition.[63] Several weeks later Livingston Merchant, the former counselor in Nanking and now deputy assistant secretary of state for Far Eastern Affairs, informed the British Foreign Office that he personally believed that the United States would withhold recognition from the People's Republic even after its expected capture of Taiwan, probably refraining from recognition of any Chinese government for an indefinite period.[64]

In bilateral talks in London in early May, Acheson and Foreign Secretary Bevin were unable to narrow their differences over China or agree on how best to prevent a permanent alignment of Peking with Moscow. Afterward, a disappointed Bevin lamented that the Americans "owing in part to pressure and attacks from the Republicans, have no positive — or indeed any — policy towards China at all." For his part, Acheson would have hardly failed to notice that Britain had reaped no appreciable gains in its relations with Communist China as a result of its accommodationist policy. Bevin had himself admitted uncertainty about the outcome of the course chosen by Britain.[65]

Against this background, a major push for a reconsideration of the nonmilitary policy toward Taiwan began nearly simultaneously in the Pentagon and State Department in late April and early May 1950. In the Defense Department, the impetus for policy revision came from the joint chiefs and from officials in Louis Johnson's office; in the State Department, from Rusk, Dulles, and Paul Nitze, head of the Policy Planning Staff (PPS) and the chief author of NSC 68. Rusk was the key energizer and coordinator among the revisionists in his own department and the principal liaison with Johnson's aides. The new Far Eastern Bureau chief commanded the respect both of Truman and Acheson. Less an Atlanticist than his predecessor, W. Walton Butterworth, and more inclined toward a tougher line in Asia, he was on good terms with Defense Department officials and with Senate Republicans.[66] His advocacy of a new solution for the Taiwan problem arose from a combination of foreign policy, bureaucratic, and domestic political considerations — from the conviction that the United States could not afford a Communist Taiwan and from a desire to reduce contention over the island between the State Department and both the Pentagon and Republican critics.

Only a short time after occupying his new post, Rusk began to nudge Acheson toward a policy reappraisal. In a memorandum on 26 April, he called the secretary's attention to suggestions from the military attachés in Hong Kong and Taipei that the United States take steps to assist the KMT forces so as to gain time to fortify defenses in Southeast Asia, where the Chinese Communists were expected to apply full pressure after they had annexed Taiwan.[67] The next day Kenneth T. Young, a civilian adviser on Far Eastern matters to Maj. Gen. James H. Burns, Johnson's assistant secretary of state for foreign military affairs, approached Rusk's office about a possible review of Taiwan policy.[68] On 2 May, in a memorandum to the secretary of defense, the JCS recommended sending a military survey mission to Taiwan. Invoking NSC 64, the recently approved policy paper for Indochina, the chiefs submitted that the continuation of Nationalist resistance on the island was militarily advantageous in distracting the Chinese Communists from Southeast Asia. They claimed that the Nationalists would exhaust stocks of certain critical military supplies in a few months and already had difficulty in buying what they needed on the commercial market.[69]

In proposing a military survey mission, the JCS were obviously contemplating a modification of the nonmilitary policy. Still, they did not budge from their refusal to sanction armed intervention to defend Taiwan. That refusal was a major impediment for those revisionists in the State and Defense Departments who advocated solutions that looked beyond the provision of additional military aid to more decisive action entailing the use of armed force. As those more adventurous revisionists recognized, any further extension of military aid would constitute merely a stopgap measure that could delay but not block a Communist takeover. Intelligence analysts still maintained that only U.S. military intervention could ensure the long-term survival of a noncommunist Taiwan.[70]

The boldest interventionist schemes emanated from Nitze, Dulles, and Rusk. In early May Nitze concocted a scheme that hitched a possible defensive military commitment to the establishment of a new government under Gen. Sun Li-jen, who several months earlier had become commander in chief of the Nationalist army. The American-educated Sun, who had served effectively as commander of Chinese forces in Burma under Gen. Joseph Stilwell during World War II, was well regarded in Washington for his military competence and progressive views. For a time in early to mid-1949, the general, then the deputy commander of the Nationalist army and head of the Army Training Center on Taiwan, had been the State Department's favored candidate to replace Chen Cheng as governor, but Chiang Kai-shek had checkmated his appointment.[71] Nitze's proposal envisaged a coup d'état led by Sun (but not involving the United States) to oust Chiang and his most prominent loyalists. With a new government in place and with "veiled but vigorous" American guidance, Nitze hypothesized that Taiwan might become a show window for Asia and a platform for clandestine propaganda and subversive activities against Soviet imperialism on the mainland.[72]

Whether this proposal received serious consideration is not known. All the same, it is easy to understand why the PPS director and others in the State Department would relish the removal of Chiang (who had resumed the presidency on 1 March from acting Nationalist president Li Tsung-jen, his defeated political foe) and his stalwarts from power. This would help erase the stigma of defeat and reaction from the island's government, eliminate a major constraint against a U.S. military commitment, facilitate the island's efficient administration and effective defense under American auspices, and enable Washington to utilize the island for a variety of cold war purposes in Asia. The idea of an anti-Chiang coup d'état executed by Sun Li-jen was not new. Acheson and his associates knew that a suspected coup by the general had already been foiled by the Generalissimo at the end of 1949.[73]

Whatever the benefits of a Sun-led coup, the odds were long that the Nationalist army commander could depose the cunning Chiang, a master of the art of political survival and intrigue. After again occupying the presidency, Chiang initiated a purge of the supporters of Li Tsung-jen that resulted in the arrest of numerous high army officers.[74] A U.S. intelligence report in March 1950 dismissed the likelihood of a coup attempt by Sun. Noting that rumors of a possible coup had been in wide circulation on Taiwan in recent months and were known to Chiang's entourage, the report went on to point out that Sun was politically inexperienced and lacked influence with important military and political figures.[75] That same month, Ambassador-at-large Jessup, recently returned from a fact-finding mission to Asia, told State Department colleagues that Sun was "in a pocket" and that his authority did not extend to the air force and navy. In mid-May Robert C. Strong, the U.S. chargé d'affaires in Taipei, observed that "the issue as to whether Sun Li-jen could or would pull a coup d'état doubtless has been dead and buried these several months." In Strong's opinion, the general possessed neither the personality nor qualities of political leadership required to run Taiwan.[76]

Unlike Nitze, John Foster Dulles advanced the idea of military intervention to hold Taiwan without coupling it to Chiang's removal from power. In a memorandum prepared for the PPS director and Rusk (in which they both concurred), the State Department consultant proposed that the United States "neutralize" Taiwan, not permitting its annexation by the Chinese Communists or its use as a Nationalist base for military operations against the mainland. Dulles, who had for some time been uncomfortable with the prospect of letting Taiwan go under, presented Nitze and Rusk with an arresting politico-psychological rationale for armed intervention which mutated the island into an emblem of American resolve.[77] Declaring that the United States was in a "new and critical period in its world position" in which the balance of power had shifted to the Soviet Union and that the appearance of retreat at this time would result in a "disastrous" worldwide deterioration of American influence, he contended that the nation could improve its international fortunes "if at some doubtful point we quickly take a dramatic and strong stand that shows our confidence and resolution." Taiwan was just such a place, Dulles insisted. Regardless of the complications and risks, the United States had to plant its foot there for the sake of global stability and its own prestige.[78]

This memorandum struck such a resonant chord in Rusk that he forwarded it to Acheson under his own name.[79] From late May onward, the salvation of Taiwan increasingly occupied the assistant secretary's attention and energy. On 25 May he met at the Pentagon with Major General Burns and Gen. Lyman Lemnitzer, director of the Office of Military Assistance. The three were in accord that every step should be taken within existing policy to make military material available to the Nationalists and that stepped-up covert action to support resistance on Taiwan was in order, despite its "limited possibilities."[80] To give the Nationalists a psychological lift and offset the cessation of military aid, Rusk requested that the Economic Cooperation Administration jack up its expenditures on Taiwan over the next few months, when weather conditions in the Taiwan Strait favored an invasion.[81]

Realizing that only a military commitment could secure the endangered island, Rusk spent long hours preparing for Acheson's consideration a comprehensive report on all facets of the Taiwan problem that put forward a daring plan of action. Altered conditions since the 5 January statement, the report asserted, required a new approach. The Soviet Union had forged an alliance with China while persisting in its "dismemberment designs" on that country. The two communist partners had recognized Ho Chi Minh's government in Vietnam and had shown an "increasing aggressiveness toward other countries of Southeast Asia." Among noncommunist Asian nations the fence sitters were waiting to see who would "'win' in the struggle in the Pacific." Meanwhile, disillusionment with Communist domination was growing in China. Going beyond the strategic rationale for keeping Taiwan out of Mao's snare, the report argued the desirability of flashing a positive signal of American resolution and determination throughout Asia but particularly in Southeast Asia and Japan. In addition, it pointed out that Taiwan could provide a reservoir of anti–Communist Chinese manpower and a base for covert operations against China.

Rusk's proposed plan of action called for the retirement of Chiang Kai-shek, who was to be induced (the assistant secretary did not say how) to turn over the military and political administration of the island to Gen. Sun Li-jen and K. C. Wu, the provincial governor. The United States would invite Britain and the Soviet Union to join in finding a peaceful solution to the Taiwan question by some reasonable procedure. In the meantime, the Seventh Fleet would prevent hostilities from and against the island. These moves would proceed in conjunction with new American initiatives regarding recognition and the issue of Chinese representation in the UN.[82]

On 30 May Rusk and a small group of upper-level State Department officials reviewed Taiwan policy at length. The conferees agreed that Rusk should discuss with Acheson a plan whereby Chiang would be asked (probably by Dulles during an upcoming trip to Japan) to accept a UN trusteeship. While the trusteeship was pending, American naval forces would insulate Taiwan.[83] The obvious purpose of the plan was to have the UN provide a cloak of legitimacy for U.S. intervention and for the denial of the island to the Communists.

Regrettably, no record exists of how the secretary of state reacted to this proposal, which Rusk almost certainly discussed with him the next day. Yet it is incontestable that, by the first week of June, Acheson was himself giving new thought to how to avoid a Communist expropriation of Taiwan. To British ambassador Sir Oliver Franks, a trusted confidant, he revealed that he and his staff were searching for a way, short of military intervention, to accomplish this objective. Franks reported to the Foreign Office that the secretary feared that a successful invasion would boost the communist cause in Southeast Asia, set in motion a "ripple of unrest," and disperse Chiang's "bad boys" to overseas Chinese communities, where they would become a nuisance. Although Acheson proposed no solution, it was evident to the ambassador that the hands-off attitude of January was no longer quite so firm.[84]

Despite his evident anxiety about the consequences of Communist annexation of Taiwan, the secretary of state was clearly at this point not looking to military action to save the island. Indeed, Rusk himself backed away somewhat from intervention in a memorandum to his superior on 9 June. Detailing a bipartisan policy toward China and Taiwan, he suggested that a UN commission study the Taiwan question with a view to coming up with a recommended solution for the Security Council. In the interim, the council would call on the Communists and Nationalists to cease hostilities between Taiwan and the mainland. The United States would assist Taiwan only to the extent permitted by current policy. Only if the Soviet Union vetoed the creation of the commission, or if Communist forces either tried to frustrate the UN initiative or attacked neighboring states, would the United States consider military measures.[85]

There were other indications that revisionists were having a hard time selling intervention. In mid-June Dulles told a group of pro-Nationalist Republican senators that Truman and Acheson remained adamant on Taiwan.[86] To Nationalist ambassador Wellington Koo, he complained that he found it difficult, in advocating military aid for Taiwan, to counter objections within the State Department that the Nationalists would offer no serious resistance to an invasion and that any additional military supplies would eventually end up in the Chinese Communist arsenal. In blunt language, Dulles enjoined the Nationalists to demonstrate a will to resist so as to move the American public to demand a change in the administration's policy. Koo was far from encouraged that Washington would renew military aid to his government.[87]

Two veteran China specialists in the Office of Chinese Affairs, Philip Sprouse and O. Edmund Clubb, saw drawbacks and obstacles to armed action. Clubb, who would replace Sprouse as director of the office in the next month, warned Rusk that intervention would have harmful consequences: the assumption of a military commitment "uncertain in scope and indefinite in term," a weakening of the American moral position because of the reversal of the president's 5 January statement, and a negative reaction in China and elsewhere in Asia. Clubb questioned the feasibility of a UN trusteeship under U.S. supervision. Acknowledging that a reconsideration of the Taiwan problem was warranted, he pointedly added that "whether the answers will be any different remains to be seen."[88] Sprouse had similar doubts about intervention. A policy review paper (apparently intended for Rusk) that he coauthored with his subordinate W. W. Stuart was generally more skeptical than supportive of the case for this alternative.[89]

Within the military establishment, the advocates of armed action had to contend with the opposition of the JCS. In a stark appraisal of the military consequences of the fall of Taiwan sent to the chiefs on 29 May, MacArthur skirted the edge of interventionism. Joint Chiefs of Staff chairman Bradley found the message so disturbing that he asked to have it brought to the president's personal attention.[90] Nevertheless, when Major General Burns from Johnson's office broached the possibility of intervention with the joint chiefs early in June, they rejected the notion. The chiefs wished only to give additional military supplies to the Nationalists. Burns also encountered resistance to intervention at the State Department. He informed a group of Defense Department officials and military service representatives on 14 June that the State Department was considering action along three lines: "(a) U.S. measures to deny Formosa to the Communists within the existing framework of NSC policy; (b) probabilities of placing the matter in the UN Security Council; and (c) supplementing political and Defense representation to Formosa, including higher ranking representatives." The next day Burns supported direct military action in a conversation with Rusk and Nitze, but they were willing to go no further than to send a flag or general officer to the Nationalist haven in an advisory role and to put the Taiwan question before the UN. Acheson backed his two deputies.[91]

In mid-June, therefore, while less secure than two months earlier, the nonmilitary policy still remained in place. No consensus for intervention had materialized either in the Pentagon or the State Department. The JCS had neither altered their basic assessment of Taiwan's strategic value nor lessened their opposition to the use of military power. They wanted only to send a survey mission to the island in order to reopen the tap for military aid. Acheson was contemplating new measures to save Taiwan yet was patently disinclined to overturn existing NSC policy. He seems to have been leaning toward possible international action through the UN.

The official record reveals little about the secretary's rationale for rejecting intervention at this time. He had a varied palette of reasons from which to choose, however. The JCS had consistently refused to countenance armed action under peacetime conditions. Both domestically and internationally, it would have been extremely awkward, without sufficient cause, to justify a turnaround from the nonmilitary policy enunciated so emphatically in January. Despite the increased volatility of China policy in domestic politics, only a minority of Congress or the citizenry wanted more done to support the Nationalists.[92] Acheson would have assuredly taken into account the probable negative response to U.S. intervention from Britain and other Western allies as well as most noncommunist Asian opinion. He would have reflected seriously on his oft-expressed view that the nationalistic backlash in China to such a move would assist the Communists (and by extension the Soviets) to tighten their control and would impede the long-range goal of removing China from the Kremlin's ambit. Not least of all, he would have been reluctant to make the United States the protector of a Taiwan dominated by Chiang Kai-shek and his adepts.

Apropos of this last point, scholar Bruce Cumings has argued that Acheson was awaiting a coup (likely carried out with U.S. encouragement and/or assistance) to topple Chiang before making a decisive move toward intervention.[93] As already argued, removing Chiang against his will was a daunting undertaking and, even with him out of the way, Acheson would have had other weighty motives to shy away from intervention. Still, it is undeniable that intervention would have been easier with the Generalissimo out of power. Because essential documentation remains closed to researchers, one can only speculate about possible American complicity in an actual attempt to overthrow him at this time. In early June Rusk did receive a secret, handdelivered message from Sun Li-jen in which he volunteered to lead a coup. The Nationalist commander was unclear as to whether he wanted American assistance or merely acquiescence. After burning the message (Rusk feared a leak would endanger Sun's life), the assistant secretary shared its contents with Acheson, who promised to take up the matter with the president. Truman apparently made no decision prior to the outbreak of the Korean War.[94]

Complicating any such decision was the president's awareness that Chiang might voluntarily relinquish his authority over Taiwan if the United States did not abandon the island. On 16 June Truman spoke with Karl W. V. Nix, an Ohio businessman and family acquaintance who had recently had a private interview with the Nationalist leader. According to Nix's later recollection, Chiang had acknowledged his "past mistakes" and stated that "if the President would send someone to Taiwan who would not insult him, he would do anything the President asked." Nix presumably passed along this intriguing message. He may also have delivered a secret letter, which the chief executive later revealed he received from Chiang, in which he offered to step aside if this would better the situation on Taiwan.[95]

Whatever Truman and other government officials had in mind about Chiang's future, preparations to unseat him were evidently underway on Taiwan itself before the Korean War intervened. In later years Rusk denied American involvement in any coup discussions on the island.[96]

However events were unfolding on Taiwan, developments in Tokyo most certainly had a bearing on any eleventh-hour action by the Truman administration to rescue the Nationalist refuge. In late June two separate delegations from Washington, one headed by Dulles and the other by Johnson and Bradley, arrived in Tokyo to confer with General MacArthur about a Japanese peace treaty. Grabbing the opportunity to try to salvage his failing cause, Chiang Kai-shek sent several unofficial emissaries to the scene.[97] Adopting the same posture of apparent self-abnegation he had with the White House, he conveyed a secret, personal invitation to MacArthur to assume command over Taiwan.[98]

The SCAP chief, who for months had been pursuing his own private foreign policy toward the island and who yearned to assume responsibility for its defense, tried again to knock the underpinnings from under the nonmilitary policy.[99] In a forceful memorandum composed especially for his visitors from Washington, the general advanced three major reasons for a more assertive approach — strategic (Taiwan was an "integral part" of the U.S. offshore island defense system), moral (the people of Taiwan deserved an "opportunity to develop their own political future"), and politico-psychological ("a line must be drawn beyond which Communist expansion will be stopped"). A Taiwan under Communist domination would represent a "disaster of utmost importance to the United States," he concluded forebodingly.[100]

Despite this warning, MacArthur still declined to propose direct U.S. military action; instead, he merely endorsed the JCS recommendation of 4 May for a military survey. Johnson, Bradley, and Dulles all found the general's brief persuasive. The defense secretary and JCS chairman flew back to Washington prepared to take up the cudgels for the survey mission.[101]

On receiving MacArthur's memorandum (which Dulles forwarded to the State Department), Acheson huddled with his advisers, except for Rusk, who was out of town. The meeting took place only days before the start of the Korean War. Livingston Merchant, Rusk's deputy assistant, afterwards reported to his superior that the discussion about Taiwan had been "general and inconclusive." Merchant told others in attendance that before determining whether to permit MacArthur to go ahead with the survey, a "prior decision" was necessary "as to what if any change in our present policy we were prepared to make," because the United States would be committed once the general set foot on Taiwan. He added that consultation with the British and probably the French and Philippine governments would be necessary before taking any action. Former Policy Planning Staff director George F. Kennan, also present, laid down two essential conditions for action: Chiang's removal from power, and an advance commitment from the JCS "to go the whole hog if required."[102]

On the eve of the Korean War, therefore, the direction that U.S. policy toward Taiwan would take lacked clear definition. The Pentagon was about to go on the offensive to obtain approval of a military fact-finding mission, while the State Department was undecided about how to respond to this initiative. Merchant and Kennan rightly saw that the logic of a military survey mission pointed toward a full-fledged military commitment. As a result of revisionist exertions over the previous two months, the nonmilitary policy was less securely established within the State Department. By no means, however, had Acheson made any decision to jettison it, and, as in the past, Truman would follow the lead of his esteemed secretary of state. Obviously again actively in search of an acceptable method to prevent the Chinese Communist flag from flying over Taiwan, Acheson was still unready to leap into a military commitment to avoid this unpalatable eventuality. The only new measures to save the island that he is known to have favored at this time were noncoercive. On 23 June he told reporters that the policy set forth in January remained unaltered.[103] Whether he would have backed intervention in the absence of a crisis in Korea is unknowable, yet this seems unlikely.[104] What is indisputable is that a satisfactory solution to the Taiwan problem still eluded policymakers on the eve of that momentous occurrence.

The shocking news of North Korea's surprise attack across the 38th parallel that reached Washington on 24 June 1950 abruptly ended indecision about Taiwan within the Truman administration. Three days later the president announced that he had ordered the Seventh Fleet to intervene in the waters between Taiwan and the mainland to prevent offensive operations against and from the island. Although this military intrusion did not signify a long-term commitment either to defend Taiwan or to buttress the Nationalist government politically, it did dramatically alter the complexion of American policy toward Taiwan, and it brought forth an array of demanding new problems abroad and at home.

Decision for Intervention

Contrary to what some historians have written, the Korean crisis was a major cause for the intervention in the Taiwan Strait and more than just the occasion for it.[1] Despite wavering support for the nonmilitary policy within the State and Defense Departments prior to the crisis, no irresistible undertow pulled government officials toward armed intervention. Although many of the motives were clearly present for such a move, the crisis was itself a significant determining factor in precipitating it. The jolting developments in Korea presented policymakers with a disturbing new set of circumstances that initiated decisive action and gave a powerful momentum to the case for intervention. Certainly the rapidity and unanimity with which officials embraced military action would have been impossible without the Korean crisis.

President Truman conferred with his top civilian and military advisers for the first time during the emergency at Blair House on the evening of 25 June. By then, Secretary of State Acheson already had in mind an immediate plan of action that included the interposition of the Seventh Fleet in the strait. This recommendation for neutralization of the strait — the idea that John Foster Dulles and Dean Rusk had first put forward the previous month — emerged from the deliberations of State, Defense, and intelligence officials who had been working on the crisis. Acheson's endorsement was critical because of the weight his views carried with the president.[2]

Defense Secretary Louis Johnson and JCS chairman Omar Bradley, who had deplaned in Washington the previous day from their Asian trip, arrived at the Blair House conference unaware of Acheson's intention and primed to make a determined pitch for authorizing MacArthur to send a military survey team to Taiwan. As Truman and other officials waited for dinner to begin, the impetuous Johnson seized the floor and asked Bradley to read aloud the memorandum on Taiwan given to them by MacArthur in Tokyo.[3] Sensing that this was an "opening gun in a diversionary argument that Johnson wanted to start with me," Acheson was relieved when Truman deftly postponed discussion of the Asian situation until after dinner.[4] Later, the president turned the floor over to his secretary of state, who during his presentation introduced the neutralization recommendation. Both Bradley and Adm. Forrest B. Sherman, chief of naval operations, endorsed it unhesitatingly, thus uniting the diplomatic and military establishments behind intervention. The president reserved his decision until the next day, but he did order units of the Seventh Fleet to Japan, closer to Korea and Taiwan.[5]

The focus of a second meeting at the Blair House the following evening was a militarized program of action proposed by Acheson. In addition to the interposition by the Seventh Fleet, this program called for the employment of U.S. air and naval forces in Korea south of the 38th parallel and for beefed-up military aid to the Philippines and Indochina. Truman swiftly approved each of these measures. His decisions, among his most fateful as president, asserted American power in Asia and inserted U.S. military might in two areas, South Korea and Taiwan, tacitly excluded from the defensive perimeter Acheson delineated in his National Press Club speech.[6]

Military and strategic considerations were paramount in the decision for intervention in the strait. The strategic importance of Taiwan had never been in question during the reign of the nonmilitary policy. During the spring policy reappraisal, the joint chiefs and various civilian revisionists had also underscored the need to preserve anti-Communist resistance on Taiwan in order to divert the Chinese from Southeast Asia. The Korean crisis enhanced the island's military and strategic significance. Convinced that Moscow had masterminded the North Korean strike, decision makers worried in the early days of the crisis that the invasion might only be a probe or a diversion for a communist offensive elsewhere and that events might escalate into a general war. The JCS had always allowed for military action to hold Taiwan in case of incipient or actual war. Emergency plans for war with the Soviet Union specifically provided that the United States would deny Moscow the use of Taiwan as an offensive base. What is more, it would have made little sense to commit American military power to the defense of South Korea but not to Taiwan, which was strategically more valuable. Once U.S. air and naval forces were bound for Korea, it also became urgent to protect the southern flank of the military operation and to prevent hostilities from spreading beyond the peninsula. Decision makers looked upon China as a spearhead of the Soviet advance in Asia, just as they did North Korea. They assumed that the Chinese had connived in the North Korean assault.[7]

Although U.S. prestige and credibility were not visibly involved in the fate of Taiwan as they were in South Korea, these intangibles entered into the neutralization decision. Dulles, Rusk, and MacArthur had all urged taking a stand on Taiwan in order to counter the impression of American retreat in Asia. While in Tokyo, Dulles had warned Washington that the fall of the island would inflict a serious psychological blow on Japan, creating doubts there about American determination to halt the spread of communism in the Far Pacific.[8] The Korean crisis energized an antiappeasement mood in Washington and gave impetus to an unflinching assertion of U.S. strength and resolve. In these circumstances, it would have been contradictory to oppose open aggression in Korea while turning a blind eye to the likelihood of a similar onslaught against Taiwan. This would have sent the wrong message to friends and foes in Asia and beyond.

The domestic political consequences of inaction in Taiwan would similarly have been unpalatable to the administration. The strident denunciations of the administration's China policies by Republican critics and pro-Nationalist elements, combined with the anticommunist hysteria exacerbated by Senator Joseph McCarthy, had put the White House and State Department on the defensive. The readiness of Truman and Acheson to sanction intervention in Korea arose partly from a recognition that the administration could not afford to lose another Asian country to communism or put another political weapon in the hands of its Republican opponents.[9] If this was now true for Korea, which had not been a pole of political controversy, it was even more so for Taiwan. Truman biographer Robert J. Donovan is correct that the president and secretary of state would have been hard-pressed to justify to Republican critics a commitment of U.S. air and naval forces to South Korea while leaving Taiwan unprotected. A new Taiwan policy was necessary for political unity as the nation moved toward a major military involvement in Korea.[10]

One of the casualties of the new policy was Acheson's previous view that intervention in Taiwan would subvert the long-range goal of bumping China from the Kremlin's orbit. Immediate national security requirements overrode the secretary's reluctance to provoke Chinese nationalism. In any event, he believed that for the near term China would remain a surrogate of the Soviet Union.

In deciding to seal off Taiwan by military means, Truman and Acheson did not intend to take Chiang Kai-shek again under the American wing. The salvation of the Generalissimo and the Kuomintang was a by-product of the intervention, not one of its purposes. In extending American military protection to Taiwan, the president and his secretary of state had no plans to reestablish a close political relationship with the Nationalist government or to throw open American coffers to it. The contempt the two men felt for Chiang was unabated. At the first Blair House meeting, Acheson remarked that the United States "should not tie up with the Generalissimo."[11] Truman, after he approved the interposition the next evening, snapped that he would not give a "nickel" to the Nationalists, who had invested previous aid in American real estate. The president even mused that Taiwan might revert to Japan and come under MacArthur's control — an interesting thought given the later clashes over Taiwan policy between the feisty chief executive and the headstrong Far Eastern commander. A skeptical Acheson cautioned that the unpredictable Chiang might resist such a plan and "throw the whole ball game." Truman still thought that this plan was "the next step."[12] In practice, the notion of substituting MacArthur for Chiang received no further consideration within the administration nor did a coup by Sun Li-jen. Some officials still nurtured hopes of Chiang's voluntary departure, but for all practical purposes the administration for the present resigned itself to his dominion over Taiwan.[13]

In a public statement on 27 June setting forth the measures approved at the second Blair House meeting, Truman announced that he had ordered the Seventh Fleet to stop "any attack on Formosa" and that as a "corollary," he was requesting the Nationalist government to "cease all air and sea operations against the mainland." The Seventh Fleet had orders "to see that this is done." Depicting this action as an ineluctable military response to a new and grave situation created by communist aggression in Korea, he stated that the "occupation of Formosa by Communist forces would be a direct threat to the security of the Pacific area and to the United States forces performing their lawful and necessary functions in that area." Looking ahead, he maintained that the "determination of the future status of Formosa must await the restoration of security in the Pacific, a peace settlement with Japan, or consideration by the United Nations."[14]

The statement contained no reference to the 5 January pronouncement, which it in effect overturned. In ordering the Seventh Fleet to prevent attacks from as well as against Taiwan, the president gave the impression that the intervention was evenhanded. In reality, its main purpose was to bar the anticipated Communist invasion of the island. By restraining military operations launched from either side of the Taiwan Strait, the administration could deny any blatant favoritism toward the Nationalists or aggressive plans against the mainland. Then too, policymakers recognized that a one-sided restriction that applied only to the Communists would leave the Nationalists free to instigate an enemy attack that the United States would then have to repulse.[15] In short, if Washington was to deter the Chinese without actually having to resort to force, it was also necessary to contain Chiang's Nationalists, whose interest lay in a military confrontation between the United States and the CCP.

The 27 June statement set no timetable for the recession of the orders to the Seventh Fleet. In affirming that a determination of Taiwan's status would have to await "the restoration of security in the Pacific" and appropriate international action, the president indicated that the United States did not propose to dictate the island's political future. Behind his support for an international solution to the Taiwan question lay the tacit premise that the island's legal status was undetermined. In effect, the president had pulled away from the position taken by him and Acheson in January that Taiwan was for all intents and purposes Chinese territory. Only on the premise that the island's legal status was unsettled could Washington claim that its intervention did not constitute interference in Chinese internal affairs and was intended only to freeze the political status quo until a suitable international agreement had peacefully decided the island's future. The contention that Taiwan's status was in a legal limbo was henceforth embedded in American policy, thus putting Washington at odds with both Taipei and Peking, which were united in asserting that the island was rightfully Chinese.[16]

The Korean crisis enabled Truman to do an about-face on the Taiwan issue without having to answer annoying questions about his departure from the policy staked out in January. Overshadowed by the Korean intervention, the Taiwan interdiction received limited but generally favorable attention from press and radio commentators. On Capitol Hill, Democrats and Republicans alike commended it, and China bloc members were elated.[17]

Truman's orders to the Seventh Fleet contributed to the fleeting bipartisan consensus on Asian policy that followed his bold decisions in late June.

International Repercussions

In the international sphere, the interposition had the opposite of a calming effect. The 27 June announcement predictably incurred the wrath of CCP leaders, but it also stirred considerable uneasiness and foreboding among leading members of the UN coalition, which supported the collective military operation in Korea. As American decision makers coped with the military and diplomatic exigencies of a collapsing South Korea, they had to contend with the impact of the interposition on their chief Asian adversary and on their own coalition partners.

Chinese Communist Party leaders were quick to express their outrage at the American military move in the Taiwan Strait. Chou En-lai, the PRC's premier and foreign minister, condemned it as "armed aggression" against Chinese territory and as a "gross violation" of the UN Charter. In an address to the State Council, Mao Tse-tung stressed the deceitfulness of Truman's 5 January statement, declaring that the United States had now exposed its "true imperialist face" and that China would not be cowed by its aggressive actions in Taiwan, Korea, and elsewhere in Asia. Early in July CCP authorities initiated a major propaganda campaign across the country featuring the slogan "Resist American Invasion of Taiwan and Korea." The campaign emphasized Taiwan more than Korea.[18]

Despite their vehement rhetoric, the Chinese abstained from a military challenge to the interdiction. Except for an abbreviated campaign around Quemoy, the largest (about fifty square miles) of the string of over thirty small KMT-controlled islands just off the southeastern China coast, the PLA forces opposite Taiwan shifted to a defensive mode. The CCP's Central Military Commission postponed the military campaign against Taiwan planned for 1951 without setting a new timetable. In early September, with a possible Chinese intervention in Korea in mind, this same body transferred a large number of troops designated for the Taiwan campaign to northern China.[19]

Not knowing Peking's plans for Taiwan, Washington had to rely mainly on the threat of military counteraction by the Seventh Fleet to deter an invasion. Although this threat was no bluff, the United States was unable to maintain a substantial military presence in the Taiwan Strait to back it up. The Seventh Fleet was understrength during the summer of 1950 and most of its vessels were needed near Korea. Not until early August did the navy assign a small special task force operating from Keelung at the northern end of Taiwan to regularly patrol the waters between the island and the mainland.[20]

American air photo reconnaissance flights also commenced at this time along the stretch of the China coast from which an invasion might start.[21] Vice Adm. Arthur B. Struble, the commander of the Seventh Fleet, did not consider a major deployment of vessels necessary except in an emergency. He was confident, as he later claimed, that the naval patrol plus air reconnaissance and other intelligence would afford sufficient warning of an impending invasion for him to move his fleet from Korea to break it up, leaving the Nationalists to mop up disorganized remnants that might reach Taiwan.[22]

In the absence of a major military presence in the strait, Washington utilized other methods to convey the seriousness of its purpose to the Chinese. On 29 June the JCS included ten nuclear-configured B-29s in a Strategic Air Command task force about to leave for Guam. This move, which was almost immediately revealed in the press, was apparently designed to warn off the Chinese in Korea and the strait.[23] In late July the chiefs ordered a temporary withdrawal of the Seventh Fleet from the Korean theater for a sweep through the strait.[24] The State Department made sure that the Chinese understood the consequences of an assault on Taiwan. In the likely expectation that the warning would be passed along to Peking, the department informed the Indian government in mid-August that the United States, though anxious to avoid a clash, would retaliate against China's transportation and industrial facilities if the Communists should act as a "cat's paw" for Moscow by attacking the island.[25]

Throughout that summer it remained uncertain whether the Chinese would exercise restraint. Within a short time after the 27 June announcement, Washington received warnings from New Delhi, London, and Taipei that the Communists might soon strike.[26] A CIA memorandum concluded in mid-July that the Communists still had the capability to mount an invasion and that an early attack was probable. The memorandum speculated that the Kremlin, having permitted North Korean military involvement with the United States, might give the green light to the Chinese as well.[27] Within the CIA, State Department, and the military establishment there were concerns that the Chinese might succeed in landing enough troops on Taiwan to demoralize the opposing Nationalist forces and destabilize the KMT government.[28] Until the end of August, intelligence reports held that an assault was a real possibility.[29] By the latter part of September, however, the movement of Chinese troops from the area opposite Taiwan to north China, together with the onset of the monsoon season (which would last until the following April, causing uncertain, sometimes treacherous, weather conditions in the strait), supported the conclusion that the Communists had at least temporarily postponed an invasion.[30]

As decision makers grappled with the problem of deterrence in the strait, they also wrestled with diplomatic difficulties that the unilateral U.S. military action provoked within the UN coalition. Unlike the Korean intervention, the Taiwan interposition lacked the legitimacy conferred by a UN mandate or the support of a bloc of allies and other friendly noncommunist nations. On the contrary, it left the United States diplomatically isolated and was a source of disagreement and strain with key members of the UN coalition. These members had misgivings about Washington's decision to pit itself against Peking in a clash of wills over the last refuge of the discredited Nationalist regime, and they were apprehensive about the impact of this decision on the war in Korea. The 27 June announcement had established a connection between the Taiwan action and the sending of U.S. forces to the peninsula. The appointment of General MacArthur as commander in chief of UN forces in Korea reinforced this Korea-Taiwan nexus because in his existing capacity as Far Eastern commander he also acquired control of the Seventh Fleet after the start of the war. Putting MacArthur in charge of both the Korean operation and the defense of Taiwan blurred the line between the UN-sanctioned enterprise and the unilateral American stance.[31]

Even as the Korean coalition was taking shape in late June, the Indian government let Washington know that it demurred to the measures directed at Taiwan and Indochina in the 27 June statement. Prime Minister Pandit Jawaharlal Nehru and Sir Girja Bajpai, head of the Indian Ministry of External Relations, regretted that the president had intermixed the problem of resistance to aggression in Korea with assistance to reactionary, imperialistic, or colonial elements in Asia.[32] The Taiwan interposition distressed the Canadian government as well. From the outset of the war, one of Ottawa's chief objectives was to limit the conflict militarily; a corollary was to restrain U.S. policy toward Taiwan and to attentuate the Korea-Taiwan connection.[33] Canadian officials wanted to foreclose any Canadian or UN involvement in sheltering Taiwan. They looked askance at Truman's policy toward the island because it threatened to enlarge rather than localize the Korean conflict, represented an undesirable projection of American domestic politics onto the international scene, and lessened the chances of solving the Taiwan question.[34]

Although Britain shared Ottawa's disquiet with the interposition, its attitude was more mixed. The British Chiefs of Staff, as well as pointing out that the interdiction would put a stop to wanton Nationalist air and sea attacks against the China mainland, welcomed the action as evidence of Washington's determination to halt armed communist expansion in Asia and as a deterrent against an attempted Chinese seizure of Hong Kong.[35] Minister of State Kenneth Younger apprised the cabinet that Britain did not consider Taiwan formally part of China and that the interdiction would bring to an end the illegal Nationalist blockade and mining of Chinese ports.[36] On the opposite side of the ledger, officials in London were loathe to enmesh Britain in the defense of Taiwan and worried that a collision between the United States and China over the island could fracture the Korean coalition and have other untoward consequences.[37]

In a brief statement in the House of Commons on 10 July, a Foreign Office spokesman distanced the British government from any commitment to assist in the protection of Taiwan.[38] About this same time, Foreign Secretary Ernest Bevin suggested to Acheson that Washington "play down" the Korea-Taiwan connection in its public statements in order to prevent a breach in the solidarity of the Korean operation. On the other hand, the British, who were then testing the waters in Moscow for a peaceful solution of the Korean conflict, anticipated that this connection would surface in their discussions with Kremlin authorities. Bevin solicited Acheson's views on a hypothetical Soviet agreement to assist in the restoration of the status quo ante in Korea in return for American withdrawal from the Taiwan Strait and Chinese Communist representation in the UN.[39] The secretary of state unequivocally rejected any quid pro quo of this sort.[40] New Delhi was then also engaged in a peace initiative, which for a time confusingly overlapped with London's. Acheson turned thumbs down on a peace plan that Nehru had in mind whose initial step was to admit Communist China to the UN. He suspected that one of the aims of India's informal mediation was to remove the Nationalist regime from Taiwan.[41] The British and Indian initiatives, which both came to naught, touched a sensitive nerve in the State Department, where there was unyielding opposition to any deal that would put the Chinese Communists in the UN or involve (as the U.S. ambassador in London, Lewis Douglas, couched it) a "real estate swap of South Korea for Formosa."[42]

Disclaiming any intention to submit to "Soviet blackmail" on Korea, Bevin did not conceal from Acheson his anxiety about the Taiwan interposition. He expressed disquiet over the implications of the American action for the vulnerable British positions in Hong Kong and British Malaya, as well as for the Attlee government's policy of keeping an exit open for China eventually to leave the Soviet camp. He worried that Sino-American hostilities resulting from an invasion would extend beyond the immediate area of Taiwan and would enable Moscow to attempt to "divide Asia from the West on an Asian problem." The restive foreign secretary suggested to his Washington colleague a "public clarification" regarding Taiwan.[43]

Truman included just such a clarification in a special presidential message on Korea sent to Congress on 19 July. Stating that he wanted to eliminate "doubt in any quarter" about American intentions toward Taiwan, he disavowed any "territorial ambitions" or any craving for "special position or privilege" on Washington's part. The purpose of the neutralization was to insulate Taiwan from hostilities elsewhere in Asia "without prejudice to political questions affecting the island." The United States, he averred, looked forward to a settlement of all such questions by the peaceful means prescribed by the UN Charter.[44]

Truman's explication of American objectives had several aims. One was to reassure Britain and other restless members of the UN coalition that the neutralization had no acquisitive or aggressive intent but was only an interim military measure designed both to prevent Taiwan from becoming still another locus of violent conflict in Asia and to permit a peaceful resolution of the question of the island's future disposition. By depicting itself as a disinterested policeman without selfish or belligerent motives, the United States could hope to reduce its diplomatic isolation and appeal to UN and world opinion. Another purpose of the clarification was to respond to Peking's indictment of the intervention and perhaps offer some incentive for military restraint on its part. Acheson asked New Delhi to transmit the president's statement to Peking and to continue its efforts to persuade the Chinese to forbear from an attack against Taiwan or intervention in Korea.[45]

As had the 27 June announcement, the 19 July statement concealed the American strategic interest in keeping Taiwan out of Chinese Communist hands. Yet strategic considerations very much influenced the outlook of policymakers in Washington. Advising the State Department that Taiwan's loss to the Communists would be "seriously detrimental" to national security, the joint chiefs strongly recommended that the United States plan to maintain the present policy of protecting the island, irrespective of the Korean situation and at least until the determination of its status in accordance with the 27 June announcement.[46]

In the months prior to the Chinese intervention in Korea, the administration would persist in its endeavors to uphold U.S. security interests on Taiwan while solidifying its international position with respect to neutralization and the island's future status.

An Arm's-Length Relationship

Truman's orders to the Seventh Fleet ensured the deliverance of Chiang Kai-shek and his Nationalist government but did not result in a binding military and political association between Washington and Taipei. A basic premise of the interim policy toward Taiwan that coalesced in the aftermath of the intervention was that the United States ought to avoid constricting its freedom of action by "indefinite commitments to the Chi[nese] auth[orities] on Formosa as to our future policy."[47] To serve its near term objectives, Washington was prepared to maintain an arm's-length relationship, but no more, with Chiang Kai-shek's regime. To reembrace the regime would encumber the implementation of a long-range policy toward Taiwan best suited to American interests. More immediately, too close an identification with the Nationalists would destroy the credibility of America's self-proclaimed role as a disinterested policeman in the Taiwan Strait, increase tension with anxious members of the UN coalition, give more grist to Chinese and Soviet propaganda mills, and perhaps even spur a Chinese invasion. In the wake of the interposition, the administration attempted to structure its relationship with the Nationalists in order to skirt these pitfalls. Similarly, it sought to interpret and apply the neutralization order in a manner that minimized diplomatic liabilities and military hazards.

Despite the relief and satisfaction that swept Taiwan following the president's announcement, ambivalence tinged the reaction in high official circles. In formally communicating to Washington his government's acceptance of the ban on offensive military operations against the mainland, Nationalist foreign minister George Yeh pointedly asserted the legitimacy of the ROC's claim to Taiwan and indirectly affirmed that his government's goal was to restore its authority throughout China.[48] In agreeing to abide by the neutralization decree, the Nationalists did not cease to proclaim their determination eventually to recapture their lost territory. The Korean conflict whetted the anticipation of Chiang Kai-shek and his followers that a third world war would create the opportunity to execute their strategy of counterattack with American assistance.[49]

As if to underscore its unwillingness to live contentedly behind an American protective shield, the Nationalist government offered to send 33,000 of its best troops to Korea.[50] Initially tempted by this offer, Truman in the end rejected it on the unanimous advice of Acheson, Johnson, and the JCS. The troops being tendered were of uncertain quality and inadequately equipped, and the joint chiefs felt they were better employed defending Taiwan. Acheson worried that acceptance of the offer would divide the UN coalition and might incite the Chinese Communists to set upon Korea or Taiwan, or both.[51] In truth, though perhaps compatible with the literal terms of the neutralization, the introduction of KMT troops in Korea would have violated its spirit and contradicted the objective of insulating Taiwan from the Korean conflict. Their employment would likewise have made it more difficult to maintain an arm's-length relationship with the Nationalists.

Once Taipei had fallen into line with the neutralization decree, Washington had to define its exact geographic scope and the precise limits for Nationalist military activities vis-à-vis the Chinese Communists. The first task proved less difficult than the second. Washington restricted its military guardianship only to Taiwan and the Penghus, excluding the KMT-held off-shore islands, which the JCS and MacArthur agreed ought to remain outside the Seventh Fleet's protective mission.[52] The State Department privately informed Taipei that the United States would not safeguard these coastal possessions but that neither would it stand in the way of Nationalist defensive operations on or from them.[53] When Quemoy, the most heavily defended of the islands, seemed in danger of invasion in July, Washington offered no military assistance. A report reached the State Department at the time that the Nationalists were even considering abandonment of Quemoy—an event that, if it had come to pass, would have removed the principal focal point of the later Sino-American crisis over the KMT forward positions.[54]

In determining what kinds of Nationalist military activity were out of bounds under the neutralization, decision makers drew a distinction between "defensive" and "offensive" actions. They accordingly gave a favorable nod to air and naval reconnaissance of the mainland and raised no objection to the "visit and search" of Chinese Communist vessels on the high seas. The State and Defense Departments deadlocked, however, over whether to allow the Nationalists to visit and search foreign vessels in international waters; this bureaucratic stalemate left the Nationalists free to continue this practice, which they did.[55]

Diplomatic and military officials also parted company over the preemptive bombing of mainland targets. This issue came to a head in mid-July as a result of a Nationalist request to bomb mainland airfields and troop concentrations in order to disrupt preparations for an expected assault against either Quemoy or Taiwan itself.[56] The president and the State Department considered preemptive bombing inconsistent with neutralization, and both MacArthur and the Nationalists were so informed in no uncertain terms.[57] Amidst heightened invasion fears later in the month, the JCS (with MacArthur in concurrence) proposed giving the Nationalists permission to take "defensive measures," including preemptive bombing, against an amphibious buildup that seemingly menaced Taiwan.[58] Acheson remained unalterably opposed to any preventive air bombardment. Questioning whether such a step was necessary (he had no reliable intelligence of an imminent attack on Taiwan) or would be effective, he contended that it would ignite hostilities between the mainland and Taiwan, would increase the odds of a Chinese incursion in Korea and Indochina, and could even precipitate a direct clash between China and the United States. More than this, it would isolate the United States in the United Nations, perhaps cause some coalition partners to pull their forces from Korea, and make the United States vulnerable to Soviet and Chinese Communist accusations of aggression.[59] Standing behind his secretary of state, Truman saw to it that MacArthur understood that only the president could authorize preventive military action against the mainland.[60]

While the debate over preemptive bombing still boiled in Washington, the SCAP chief landed in Taiwan with a dozen staff officers for a two-day visitation (31 July–1 August) that set off a commotion at home and abroad and caused consternation in Washington. The troubled reaction of President Truman and the State Department to the general's behavior while on the island was understandable in light of the unsettled situation in the strait and the delicate state of Taiwan policy at this time.

MacArthur had gone to Taiwan with the authorization of the joint chiefs in order to make a firsthand assessment of Nationalist military capabilities. On the recommendation of the joint chiefs, the president had recently approved the resumption of military assistance to Taiwan. That decision met with no objection from Acheson, who recognized that Chiang's forces would require additional, albeit limited, aid so that they could effectively back up the Seventh Fleet.[61]

MacArthur's conduct during and immediately after his stay on Taiwan raised the hackles of Truman, Acheson, and other decision makers. The general kept Washington completely in the dark about his talks with Chiang and his military commanders while they were in progress.[62] A mistaken report from the Taipei embassy that he had ordered three F-80 jet fighter squadrons to the island caused the JCS to send him a stiff message that any such order involved political complications and required top-level approval in Washington. Though the general had actually not issued such an order, he did suggest to the Pentagon that U.S. aircraft ought to be dispatched to the island if the Communists invaded it. In a follow-up directive, the joint chiefs instructed him not to base any fighter squadrons on Taiwan or to make any unauthorized commitment to the Nationalists to do so in case of an attack. The intent of neutralization, the chiefs insisted, was to defend the island without deploying U.S. forces on it.[63]

Administration officials were also distressed that the Chiang-MacArthur parleys gave an erroneous impression of a revitalized affiliation with the Generalissimo and his government. The Nationalist president later shrewdly fostered this impression in effusive public comments.[64] The Chiang-MacArthur conversations inspired speculation in the American and international press that the general had acted independently of Washington and had engaged in political talks. To quiet speculation and ensure that his commander fully grasped the administration's policy toward Taiwan, Truman sent Ambassador W. Averell Harriman, one of his most valued subordinates, to Tokyo for a personal consultation in the company of Army Chief of Staff Gen. Matthew B. Ridgway.[65]

Chiang was a "liability," Harriman told MacArthur when they met. The Nationalist leader's desire to use Taiwan as a stepping stone to the mainland conflicted with the administration's own objective to deny the island to the Communists; he could not be permitted to start a war that could suck in the United States. Any wrong move by the United States with respect to Taiwan or mainland China could split the UN coalition and give the Soviets an opening. The presidential envoy suggested that perhaps the best solution for Taiwan was an independent government established through the UN.

In his own remarks, MacArthur dismissed Chiang's mainland ambitions as unrealizable. Yet he also manifested an obsessive enmity toward the Chinese Communists and a disgruntlement with Washington's brusque handling of the Generalissimo. Afterward, Harriman informed the State Department that the general had "accepted the President's position and will act accordingly, but without full conviction."[66] Despite this ambivalent report, Truman publicly declared that he and the general saw eye-to-eye. MacArthur, in a stridently defensive press release, indignantly denied that his Taiwan visit had been in any way improper and voiced veiled criticism of his civilian superiors in Washington.[67]

Shortly after the commander's departure from the island, a new chargé d'affaires and senior military attaché took up residence in the Taipei embassy. Relations had been badly strained for some time between Nationalist officials and the embassy staff headed by Robert Strong; the former were aware of the staff's unflattering reports to Washington about conditions on Taiwan.[68] Strong's replacement was Karl Rankin, a seasoned Foreign Service officer with more than two decades of service in Europe, including stints in Eastern Europe and the Soviet Union, but only a year of Asian experience as consul general in Hong Kong.[69] Rankin's short time in Asia convinced him that the danger posed by the Soviet Union and its Chinese satellite to the countries along China's flank required a tough and comprehensive American response. Once ensconced in the Nationalist capital, he lost no time in trying to dispel the KMT leadership's ingrained suspicion of the American embassy and to prod Washington toward a more forthright and enlarged commitment. He advised the State Department that greater tact, understanding, and consultation were required in dealing with Chiang and other Nationalist authorities. Though recognizing many of the shortcomings of the KMT regime, he did not share Strong's disdain for it, and he was confident of its capacity for gradual self-improvement.[70]

Rankin arrived in Taiwan just as a Far East Command Survey Group, led by Gen. Alonzo P. Fox, MacArthur's deputy chief of staff, was conducting a three-week survey of the Nationalist military to determine their needs. The report of the "Fox Survey" mission concluded that Chiang's army was an important backup to the Seventh Fleet, capable of repulsing Communist landings given sufficient aid and proper military advice. The report, which recommended a $271 million military aid package, threaded its way slowly through the military bureaucracy and only reached the State Department for consideration in early November, shortly after the Chinese first intervened in Korea.[71]

During these months, State Department planners sought to keep a tight rein on renewed military assistance. They did not want the United States to enter into a close-knit relationship with the Nationalist regime, nor appear to contradict the spirit of neutralization, repeat past experiences with KMT profligacy and ineffectualness, or encourage Chiang's revanchist aspirations. Also, the Nationalists were thought to possess much of the material they required for defensive purposes.[72] Prior to late November, Chiang's forces received only a single shipment of ammunition valued at $9.7 million.[73] The State Department similarly looked askance at any sudden or substantial increase in the volume of economic assistance to Taiwan.[74] The department's chariness with respect to increased military and economic aid was another indicator of Washington's cool and careful attitude toward Taipei after the June interposition.

Constructing a UN Strategy

For the first month or so after the intervention, the State Department had dealt with its diplomatic repercussions in an ad hoc fashion. In August the department began to piece together the elements of a coordinated diplomatic strategy to manage the interconnected problems of Taiwan's future disposition, the disputed China seat in the UN, and a charge of aggression lodged against the United States in the world organization by Communist China.

Despite the president's 19 July clarifying statement, the United States continued to play a lone hand in the Taiwan Strait. Its self-appointed role as a disinterested policeman still lacked international legitimacy, and its intervention remained a bone of contention within the UN coalition. The MacArthur-Chiang talks quickened anxiety among coalition partners about the potentially dangerous consequences of neutralization. Canadian external affairs minister Lester B. Pearson, aghast at hearing of the general's visit to Taiwan, immediately registered a vigorous verbal complaint with Acheson and followed with a letter detailing the adverse results of an armed clash between the United States and China over the Nationalist redoubt.[75]

In mid-August the State Department sounded out the Foreign Office in London about placing long-term political problems related to Taiwan "on ice" and developing a common line on the provisional necessity of a military stoppage between the island and the mainland.[76] The department wanted to gain British and other foreign approval for neutralization and the postponement of any permanent decisions about Taiwan's future. Foreign Office officials did see merit in internationalizing support for a military standstill in the Taiwan Strait. They reasoned that the American interposition, whether justified or not, was a fait accompli but that as a strictly unilateral enterprise it regrettably carried the implication of interference in the Chinese civil war and of sponsorship for Chiang's regime. International sanction for provisional neutralization could mitigate some of the liabilities of the intervention by reducing friction between the United States and its coalition partners and by creating another deterrent to a Chinese invasion. Obtaining such a sanction, however, made it impractical "to put the Formosan problem into political as well as military cold storage." Instead, the Foreign Office wanted to take steps toward a permanent solution for Taiwan that took into account China's eventual rights.[77]

The State Department wanted to enlist Britain in a common approach not just to the Taiwan problem but to the thorny question of Chinese representation in the UN. The United States had shown apparent flexibility on this question prior to the Korean War, publicly declaring that it would accept the decision of a majority of the Security Council and would not regard its own negative vote as a veto. Adopting a position of "neutrality," Washington professed that it would refrain from putting pressure on other UN members to bar the Chinese Communists from membership; in practice, it sometimes departed from this self-imposed inhibition.[78] The issue of the disputed China seat caused a widening gap between Washington and London before the war. In mid-June the Attlee government, which had previously announced that Britain would abstain on the question in the UN until a majority existed for Chinese Communist representation, opted for a new policy of voting to replace the Nationalists with the Communists even in the absence of a majority, only to hold back on implementation of this policy because of American opposition. Although the outbreak of hostilities in Korea gave the British government further reason for pause, it remained determined to award Peking its rightful place in the world organization at the Nationalists' expense. In contrast, the United States was now resolved to use all its influence to prevent consideration of the representation question on its merits as long as the war lasted.[79]

The State Department saw palpable benefits in the postponement of any decision on the representation issue for the duration of the war. This would avert a full-dress debate in the UN, pitting the United States against Britain and other friendly nations that favored Communist China's admission, and would ensure that the Communists remained outside of the world body for the near future while the Nationalists retained the China seat. The favorable vote of the Nationalist delegate on the Security Council had provided the margin of victory for the critical 27 June resolution sanctioning armed assistance to South Korea. In light of that vote, a continuing Nationalist presence on the council seemed necessary to guarantee a dependable majority on Korean matters. On top of all this, the White House and State Department had to bear in mind the preponderant domestic opinion against Chinese Communist membership.[80] Though diplomatic and domestic interests required that the United States keep the Nationalists inside the UN and shut the Communists out, the State Department refrained from any long-range commitment to Taipei regarding either the China seat or continued recognition of the Republic of China as the government of China.[81]

On 3 August Acheson received Truman's approval to seek an arrangement with Britain to transfer the representation question from the Security Council to the General Assembly. The secretary's plan was to have the latter body first determine what criteria ought to be considered to resolve the general issue of contested seats and then at some later date apply these criteria to the disputed China seat. The effect of the plan would have been to delay any decision on Chinese representation and to make the General Assembly (where the United States could count on a secure majority), rather than the Security Council, the final arbiter of the seating question. By molding the criteria adopted by the assembly in the right way, as Acheson informed the president, the United States could put the PRC in a weak position.[82]

A third problem for which the State Department had to devise a course of action in the UN arose when, on 24 August, Chou En-lai formally called upon the Security Council to condemn the U.S. action in the Taiwan Strait as a violation of the Charter and insisted on a complete American withdrawal from Taiwan and other Chinese territory.[83] The next day, in a public letter to Secretary-General Trygve Lie, UN ambassador Warren Austin denied Chou's accusations and suggested that the world organization investigate the charge of aggression. Four days later the United States, as proof that it had nothing to hide, joined a majority of the Security Council in voting to place on the agenda a Soviet item containing the Chinese charge.[84]

As August drew to a close, the United States entered into preliminary discussions with Britain and France in anticipation of the opening of the regular session of the General Assembly on 19 September as well as meetings of the Big Three foreign ministers and of the NATO Council also scheduled around that date. These discussions presented an opportunity for the State Department to work towards cooperative action on the problems of Taiwan, the Chinese seat, and the PRC's charge of aggression.

Just days before the talks began, alarm bells sounded in Washington when Truman learned that MacArthur had sent the commander in chief of the Veterans of Foreign Wars (VFW) a message on Taiwan for the organization's upcoming convention. The heart of the message was an emphatic assessment of the strategic value of Taiwan and a justification of American guardianship of the island from the standpoint of U.S. security requirements in the western Pacific.[85] It is unnecessary to repeat here the oft-told story of the enraged reaction of the president, Acheson, and other key civilian and military advisers (the notable exception being Defense Secretary Johnson) to the message and of Truman's order to MacArthur to withdraw it, despite its already having been released to the press.[86]

In no small measure, the outrage enkindled by the message was due to its feared impact on the sensitive Taiwan situation. The statement came to the president's attention only short weeks after the disturbance over MacArthur's Taiwan trip, just a day after Austin had reiterated the government's public rationale for the interposition, and on the eve of important talks with Britain and France about Taiwan and related matters. An unsigned State Department memorandum (possibly prepared by Acheson) detailed at length the probable consequences if MacArthur did not retract the message. To start, this would sharpen misgivings within the UN coalition about the general's overlapping responsibilities in Korea and Taiwan and detract from the unity of the coalition. In addition, it would play into the hands of Soviet propaganda, antagonize Asian and particularly Indian opinion, complicate the handling of the Taiwan issue in the UN, and shove the United States into an expanded commitment to the Kuomintang. Beyond all that, by invoking strategic interests to justify the defense of Taiwan and by stressing the island's proven value as a military base, the message contravened the administration's public explanation for the interposition. The expected effect on Peking's calculations was particularly worrisome. An unretracted message would "tip off" the Communists "that our long-range purpose is to deny Formosa to them," and confront them with "the fact that they can never expect to get it except by military seizure." The Communists might also erroneously surmise that the United States wanted the island as an offensive base against the mainland.[87]

By insisting that Taiwan was strategically too valuable to allow an enemy possession, MacArthur had shed unwanted light on a fundamental premise of the Truman administration's own thinking. It was the public revelation of the general's strategic evaluation that disturbed Truman and his aides, not the assessment itself. The message contained classified information (it borrowed heavily from the commander's 14 June memorandum to the JCS) and cast doubt on the self-professed role of the United States as the disinterested policeman acting out of temporary military exigency in response to the Korean conflict. In trying to sail safely through the international crosscurrents that swirled around the Taiwan issue, the administration could afford no compromise of its public position.

The president moved swiftly to keep the government's declared policy toward Taiwan on track. On 31 August he told reporters that a permanent settlement for Taiwan would have to await a Japanese peace treaty and that the Seventh Fleet would no longer have to remain in the Taiwan Strait "if the Korean thing is settled," since the fleet was there as "a flank protection on our part for the United Nations forces."[88] Acheson and Rusk believed that these remarks were beneficial and that they would place the United States in the "proper position."[89]

The president's comments braced the administration's public rationale for the interposition. His willingness to put a more specific time limit on the mission of the Seventh Fleet clearly indicates that a long-term defensive commitment to Taiwan was not yet entrenched in American policy, despite an evident desire within the State Department and JCS to keep the island safe from the Chinese. Although the joint chiefs were already looking toward a more durable defensive commitment, Truman and the State Department still saw neutralization as a provisional arrangement. It may be that the president and his diplomatic advisers anticipated that by the time the Korean operations had ended (U.S. officials were at this time contemplating a northward drive by UN forces across the 38th parallel) the United Nations would have mandated a military stoppage in the Taiwan Strait that would make the Chinese think twice about an invasion, even if the president had withdrawn the fleet. Using the UN to deny Taiwan to the Chinese had been a recurring theme in State Department discussions since 1949. If the Chinese were to defy the UN under these circumstances, the chief executive could once again insert the fleet if necessary.

Because MacArthur was a Republican favorite, his VFW message inevitably had political overtones. His devotees in the GOP rose to his defense and used the forced retraction to hammer the administration. By late summer the brief surge of bipartisanship after the start of the Korean War had ebbed. McCarthy and his accomplices rode a gathering wave of anticommunist hysteria, and recriminations about Democratic failures in Asia were fast becoming standard fare among Republicans. The approaching midterm elections gave partisanship an even more barbed edge.[90]

A State Department analysis of national opinion completed in September showed a good deal of uncertainty and division about a satisfactory policy for Taiwan. The two strongest strains in the public outlook were a reluctance to see the Communists control the island and a hesitancy to act without the support of at least some UN partners. Republican critics on Capitol Hill, together with a powerful minority of the press, played up the strategic necessity to hold on to Taiwan.[91]

The fallout from the VFW ruckus had not yet settled when American, British, and French officials began talks in Washington and New York touching on the three China-related matters on which the State Department wanted to knit a unified approach. In New York, where the UN delegations of the three allies took up the seating dispute, American representatives put forward a proposal based on the scheme approved by Truman early in August whereby the General Assembly would assume the main responsibility for resolving the issue. The New York talks failed to produce complete agreement on this proposal, and the three allied delegations left a final decision to the upcoming tripartite foreign ministers meeting.[92]

The Washington conversations served as the forum to thresh out the Taiwan question and the Chinese charge of aggression. To deal with the latter, American officials recommended that the Security Council appoint a commission to conduct an on-the-spot investigation and to consult all interested parties, including the Communists. The commission device would preclude a protracted debate on Taiwan in the Security Council in which the People's Republic might demand to participate. The British and French would go no further than to concur that the Security Council should investigate the charge of aggression.[93]

The commission device also figured in the State Department's approach to the Taiwan question. A departmental position paper proposed that the General Assembly create a commission to study and make recommendations on the question, simultaneously calling on all parties to refrain from violent disturbance of the status quo during this deliberative process. State Department planners saw significant advantages in such an arrangement. For one thing, it would defer a potentially divisive debate in the assembly and reduce pressure and propaganda from the PRC and USSR. Also, by enjoining all parties to respect the status quo, it would legitimize a military standstill and therefore, implicitly if not by explicit declaration, the American interposition. State Department officials expected that the proposed arrangement would widen international acceptance of the unilateral intervention and help stave off a Communist attack. If an assault did occur in violation of the assembly's injunction, the United States would be in a stronger international position to respond.[94]

The State Department's proposal would also buy time to work out a suitable resolution of the Taiwan question. The position paper allowed for five hypothetical recommendations by a UN commission: 1) incorporation within mainland China; 2) restoration to Japan; 3) independence; 4) a UN trusteeship; 5) a UN plebiscite to determine which of the above the Taiwanese wanted. Revealingly, none of these alternatives took into account the claims of the Nationalist government to the island. Although the paper was silent about American preferences among the stated alternatives, the first two were clearly unacceptable. The department did not plan to turn over Taiwan to a hostile China or to a defeated enemy. Ideally, Acheson and other State Department officials envisioned an autonomous or independent Taiwan under the domination neither of the PRC nor ROC — in short, a two-China solution.[95]

Like the Americans, the British found attractive the pairing of a UN commission and a military standstill. In bilateral talks with Philip Jessup, Acheson's trusted deputy, and several other ranking State Department representatives, British ambassador Sir Oliver Franks laid on the table a proposal similar in outline to the State Department's approach. The British proposal, however, contained a provision that the General Assembly from the outset would accept the principle that Taiwan should revert in "due course" to China, which for London naturally meant the PRC. The British believed that the Cairo Declaration had to be the lodestone for a Taiwan solution. Franks was unreceptive when Jessup raised the possibility of a plebiscite leading to independence. The British wanted a proposal that recognized the "Chineseness" of Taiwan and that would command the broadest support within the Commonwealth and among Asian nations. Their proposed UN commission would only decide when, and under what conditions, Taiwan would revert to China. Franks reassured Jessup that such a decision would have to take into consideration Peking's behavior in international affairs. No more than the Americans were the British prepared to hand over the island to an aggressive China. To meet the British halfway, State Department officials suggested that the guidelines for the UN commission take note of the competing Chinese claims to Taiwan as well as the wishes of the island's residents; this proposal failed to resolve differences between the two sides. In trilateral discussions that followed, French representatives agreed only that the General Assembly was the best place to handle the Taiwan question.[96]

In devising a diplomatic strategy on this snarled issue, the State Department met resistance from the Joint Chiefs of Staff. Confronted with the reluctance of the military chieftains to have a UN commission even consider the transfer of Taiwan to mainland China, the department countered that it was unfeasible to exclude this alternative.[97] As the diplomats realized, no arrangement that foreclosed this option stood a chance of gaining the approval of Britain or other key nations in the General Assembly, such as India. The department paid scant attention to the Nationalist government in pursuing its plans for a resolution of the Taiwan question through a UN mechanism. Only after the Washington talks did Rusk brief Nationalist ambassador

Koo in general terms about American intentions. In the following weeks, the Nationalists debated how best to frustrate the establishment of the proposed UN commission. From Taipei's vantage point, any suggestion that the United Nations should determine Taiwan's future status was acutely disturbing.[98]

The Nationalists and their American supporters suffered a setback on 12 September when Truman fired Louis Johnson from his Pentagon post, summoning Gen. George Marshall from retirement to replace him. Johnson's ouster removed Acheson's chief rival and a dedicated Nationalist sympathizer from the government. Marshall's appointment incensed the China bloc, which blamed him for the "loss of China." Official commentators on Taiwan put on a brave face at the news of his selection; informal reaction, as gauged by the U.S. embassy, was less sanguine.[99]

On the day of Johnson's removal, Acheson began talks in New York with Bevin and French foreign minister Robert Schuman. During these tripartite exchanges, the secretary of state obtained partial agreement on a unified approach in the UN on the interlinked trio of China-related matters. The representation issue proved the most prickly. Whereas Bevin advocated the seating of the Chinese Communists, Acheson was adamantly opposed, while Schuman maintained an ambivalent middle ground. The three finally agreed that their governments would vote as they wished when the General Assembly convened. Even though Acheson would have preferred that the assembly refrain from any vote on the merits of the issue, he could confidently anticipate that the UN body would refuse to admit the Communists, since only sixteen of its fifty-nine members recognized the PRC. If the vote was negative as expected, Bevin and Schuman were amenable to the creation of a commission to examine the criteria for settlement of cases of disputed representation. On the subject of how to dispose of the Chinese charge of aggression, the two European allies were noncommittal; they neither rejected nor accepted the American plan for a UN fact-finding commission. On the Taiwan question, all three statesmen unanimously endorsed action in the General Assembly in the form of a commission and a military standstill.[100]

Acheson was therefore successful in securing at least a partial consensus on a coordinated UN strategy. This strategy, if successfully concluded, held out the promise that the United States could carve out positions in the world organization that would serve its own interests and objectives, gain broad international acceptance, and win general favor at home.

Collapse of the UN Strategy

The General Assembly convened on 19 September against the backdrop of a stunning reversal in the tide of battle in Korea as a result of the successful Inchon operation by MacArthur's forces only days earlier. For the Truman administration, the UN counteroffensive presented a chance to carry out plans for a rollback of communist rule in the divided peninsula. As MacArthur's men marched northward toward the Yalu River, the State Department pursued its three-fold strategy in the UN.

One component of this strategy fell into place at the first meeting of the General Assembly. The assembly, after defeating by large majorities Soviet and Indian resolutions to oust the Nationalists in favor of the Chinese Communists, approved the establishment of a special committee to study the seating dispute in the light of a uniform procedure to settle such cases.[101] Acheson, in New York at the head of the American delegation, happily reported to Truman that developments in the assembly had been "most successful." As the secretary knew, the president was especially sensitive about the political implications of the representation issue.[102]

Later in the session, the assembly included on its agenda an American item on the Taiwan question, referring it to the First Committee, which had responsibility for political and security matters. This prepared the path for the planned introduction of a proposal to internationalize the question under the aegis of the assembly.[103]

Much less satisfactory from the American viewpoint was the Security Council's handling of the Chinese charge of aggression. On 29 September the council voted by a 7–3 margin to invite a PRC representative to attend its meetings dealing with the charge. The vote was a major victory in the PRC's campaign to take part in UN deliberations. The United States, which voted against the invitation, failed to elicit support for a fact-finding commission. The one consolation for Washington was that the Security Council did not invite the PRC representative to attend meetings until after 15 November; this meant that he would make his appearance only after the midterm elections eight days earlier.[104]

The November balloting preoccupied Truman as he winged his way to Wake Island for a conference with MacArthur. It is hard to dispute scholars who view his celebrated meeting on 15 October with the hero of Inchon mainly as a public relations exercise to refurbish his own and his party's political images.[105] Except for a brief private conversation between the president and general about the VFW blowup, the participants in the conference entirely sidestepped the topic of Taiwan. Both for political and diplomatic reasons, Truman wanted his mid-Pacific rendezvous to go smoothly. Cautioned beforehand by Acheson that an unsettling episode could affect critical relations with Communist China and the State Department's UN strategy for Taiwan, the president assured him that he need not "have any worries on this account."[106]

Even as the Wake Island meeting was in progress, the State Department was gearing up for the implementation of its plan to internationalize the Taiwan question. American and British officials labored to draft an agreed resolution for presentation in the First Committee. Unsurprisingly, the PRC did not look kindly on the anticipated involvement of the UN in the Taiwan question. Chou En-lai, in a telegram to the president of the General Assembly on 17 October, denied the assembly's right to consider the American item and alleged interference in Chinese internal affairs.[107] Near the end of the month, the members of the UN coalition absorbed the chilling news that Chinese units were fighting in North Korea. Although these soldiers had vanished from the battlefield by 7 November, uncertainty and apprehension gripped the coalition.[108]

In this gloomy setting, the British and Americans on 11 November finished their work on the agreed resolution. The final draft provided for a commission to study and make recommendations for the future of Taiwan after conferring with "all governments, authorities and parties concerned." Until the assembly considered and acted upon the results of the commission's labors, there were to be no attacks from or against the island or attempts to change its status by force. The resolution alluded to the Cairo Declaration and noted that "two parties" claimed the island.[109]

Combining a UN commission and a military standstill, the agreed resolution squared with the administration's stated intention to rely on international action to decide Taiwan's future status but also implicitly legitimized the U.S. interposition. During the drafting process, American representatives refrained from insistence on any preferred long-range solution for Taiwan. The resolution left open the possibility that the commission might conclude that the island belonged to the PRC. To satisfy the British and other Commonwealth members, American officials had to make significant concessions on phrasing and content.[110] Even so, some Commonwealth representatives had misgivings about entangling the UN in the Taiwan question and suspected that the Americans wanted the resolution mainly as a cover for their defense of Taiwan.[111]

On 15 November, just as the resolution was due for introduction in the First Committee, the ground began to crumble from underneath it. John Foster Dulles, who had taken on the assignment of shepherding it through the committee, faced an unexpected rebellion within the American delegation to the General Assembly. The delegation, which included a number of Republican and Democratic notables, almost unanimously opposed the resolution as worded because it seemed slanted toward the Chinese Communists.[112] The disapproval expressed by the political appointees on the delegation was especially significant as a barometer of negative domestic reaction to a UN strategy that chanced the transfer of Taiwan to the Communists. The limited Chinese intervention in Korea had hardened opinion against Peking. The political climate had also worsened during the recent midterm elections. The communism-in-government theme, often paired with indictments of a misbegotten Democratic Far Eastern policy, was prominent in GOP campaign rhetoric. At the time, Republican gains in Congress were widely credited to Senator McCarthy and his followers.[113]

Later, a chastened Dulles reported to Acheson that a resolution that would meet the requirements of the delegation as well as the British and a majority of the assembly was beyond reach.[114] On 24 November Acheson further learned that the JCS objected to the resolution in its existing form because it would neutralize Taiwan militarily just as the situation in the Far East was taking a disturbing turn. As a result of the brief Chinese incursion, the chiefs were reconsidering the ban on Nationalist offensive operations against the mainland.[115] Already badly weakened, the cornerstone of the UN strategy gave way only days later as a result of the massive Chinese intervention against MacArthur's advancing forces.

The Chinese intervention was a tragic consequence not just of the American rollback policy in Korea but also, among other causes, of the Taiwan interposition. Mao Tse-tung and other proponents of intervention within the CCP leadership viewed American actions in Korea in the context of perceived menacing developments elsewhere on China's borders. Present-day scholarship on the origins of the intervention shows that a major reason why Mao chose to fight in the peninsula was his belief that the United States intended to crush the Chinese Revolution, using Korea, Taiwan, and Vietnam as staging areas for an offensive against China's territory. Taiwan and Korea were inextricably meshed in the minds of Mao and his comrades. The interjection of the Seventh Fleet in the Taiwan Strait, besides necessitating indefinite postponement of plans for an invasion of Chiang's asylum, confirmed their fears that the United States posed a danger to the security and survival of the PRC. The aggressive and duplicitous Americans, so CCP leaders believed, had decided to reinvolve themselves in the unfinished civil war on the side of the KMT. MacArthur's actions and statements with respect to Taiwan reinforced this perception.[116]

Chinese leaders were right to look behind Washington's announced motives for its intervention. The overriding reason for the American action had been to deny Taiwan to them, and this, indeed, remained a fixed if unpublicized goal of U.S. diplomacy in the months that followed. But the Chinese were mistaken in concluding that Washington had realigned itself with Chiang Kai-shek and that it wanted Taiwan as a base for the overthrow of their revolutionary government (clandestine disruption and harassment were a different matter, however). The fact was that Washington had no desire to become Chiang's patron once again, let alone help him actualize his back-to-the-mainland ambitions. In the best of worlds, the White House and State Department would have preferred a Taiwan under the thumb of neither Chiang nor Mao.

Top American civilian decision makers were alive to Chinese sensitivities about the interposition and concerned about a military counteraction either against Taiwan or in Korea or Southeast Asia. This was evident in their arm's-length relationship with the Nationalists, their cautious application of the neutralization decree, and their efforts to sustain the image of the United States as an impartial policeman. Yet decision makers failed to comprehend how deeply the intervention intensified Chinese fears of an aggressive United States set on strangling the "New China" in its cradle. Their vision was blurred by ignorance, ideological animus, and the false assumption that Peking was subservient to Moscow, all of which also contributed to their miscalculation of the Chinese reaction to rollback in Korea. In the end, therefore, both Chinese and American misperceptions related to Taiwan contributed to an expansion of the Korean conflict that neither side wanted, that poisoned Sino-American relations for more than two decades, and that pushed the United States back into the embrace of Chiang Kai-shek.

The Chinese plunge across the Yalu River in November 1950 confronted decision makers in Washington with a grim new crisis that wrought pivotal changes in American policy toward Taiwan. In a setting of international and domestic emergency, and of fierce hostility to the PRC within and outside the government, decision makers initiated a long-term defensive commitment to Taiwan and an entangling political relationship with the Nationalist government.

Taiwan and an Expanded War

American officials reacted to the all-out Chinese offensive with shock, fear, and bitter anger. Their overoptimistic evaluations of Chinese restraint now discredited and their hopes for early victory dashed, they faced a formidable new foe who in their judgment had contemptuously challenged American power and UN authority. They could find no extenuating circumstances for what they looked upon as a blatant act of aggression by a compliant Soviet proxy. They admitted no causal connection between the American incursion in the Taiwan Strait and the Chinese intervention in Korea.[1]

For Chiang Kai-shek and his adepts, the massive Communist assault was a boon. Both a prolongation of the Korean conflict and a combustible confrontation between the United States and Peking would better serve their purposes than the successful conclusion of General MacArthur's "end-the-war offensive." Nationalist interests were not advanced by a stabilized situation in East Asia that would freeze the status quo and foreclose the reestablishment of Kuomintang rule on the mainland.[2] As American diplomatic personnel on Taiwan reported, the Nationalist leadership was convinced that Washington's new antagonistic attitude toward Communist China presaged substantial military aid, an abandonment of the prohibition against offensive military operations, and assistance for the reconquest of the mainland. Official circles were abuzz with talk and planning for mainland recovery. The Nationalists believed that a world war ending in the defeat of the Chinese Communists would solve their problems and that the war had already in fact begun.[3]

Taipei did not importune Washington to create a second front on the mainland, but it did renew its offer of 33,000 soldiers for service in Korea.[4] Just about the same time, MacArthur recommended acceptance of the KMT troop contribution that he and the joint chiefs had declined the previous summer. The UN commander estimated that the troops could reach Korea within two weeks, providing him with trained reinforcements unavailable elsewhere on short notice. No longer was it possible, he observed, to reject the troops on the grounds that they were needed to defend Taiwan, which was now relatively free from danger of attack, or that their presence in Korea would give the Chinese Communists a pretext for intervention in the peninsular war.[5]

The joint chiefs were at this time hard-pressed to give MacArthur the fresh troops he badly needed to replenish his depleted units. Just the same, both civilian and military leaders in Washington reacted skeptically to the general's recommendation. Despite the Communist intervention, they still saw much more to be lost than gained from the presence of Nationalist troops on the Korean battlefield. In a reply sent to MacArthur by the JCS (which Acheson and Defense Secretary George Marshall had a hand in drafting and Truman endorsed), the chiefs cautioned that the employment of KMT soldiers might extend the hostilities to Taiwan and other areas, disrupt the unity of the UN coalition, and compromise American leadership on Far Eastern issues in the United Nations.[6] Undaunted, MacArthur would reiterate his recommendation a month later, with no more success.

Unlike the Nationalists, American decision makers did not accept the inevitability of a global conflict. Within days of the November onslaught by the Chinese, the Truman administration revised its war aims from the forceful unification of Korea to the restoration of the prewar status quo. Korea was considered a strategic backwater and the Soviet Union, not its Chinese ally, the real enemy. Concerned with saving American lives, shoring up Western European defenses, and safeguarding an exposed Japan, top American leaders shrank back from a general war with China that might draw in the Soviet Union and spiral uncontrollably into World War III.[7]

Despite this decision to forsake rollback and the aversion to a showdown with Peking or Moscow, the administration did seriously study and debate retaliatory measures against China short of general war during the bleak early winter of 1950–51, a time when the fate of the U.S.-UN enterprise in Korea appeared to hang in the balance. The controversial figure of Douglas MacArthur loomed large in this debate. Disdainful of a timid limited war strategy, the UN commander at the end of December proposed a U.S. naval blockade of the Chinese coast, air and naval bombardment of mainland industrial and strategic targets, the use of Nationalist troops in Korea, and the lifting of the restriction on Nationalist offensive operations against China, with the possibility of a counterinvasion by Chiang's forces.[8]

The debate within the government over an expanded war took place in a vortex of domestic and international pressures. Chinese entry into the war inflamed popular passions in the United States against Mao's regime, exacerbated partisan strife over foreign affairs, and intensified the Red Scare. Paradoxically, the disheartening turnabout in Korea produced both disillusionment with the war and a readiness on the part of a militant segment of public opinion to hit back at China itself. Within the GOP, MacArthur's aggressive strategy became the accepted party line.[9] Dreading the consequences of this strategy, America's Western allies led by Britain exhorted the administration to curb the general, confine the hostilities, and strive to the utmost to obtain a swift cease-fire.[10]

In the end, civilian and defense officials in Washington reached a consensus in favor of a limited war rather than overt retaliatory action against China. This consensus had obvious implications for policy toward Taiwan and relations with the Nationalists. Especially pertinent was the decision not to hurl KMT troops into battle on the mainland. Since this particular decision preserved the neutralization policy and deprived the Nationalists of a chance to reestablish a foothold on their lost territory, it warrants closer examination.

As a result of the Chinese intervention, military authorities recommended lifting the ban on Nationalist offensive operations against the mainland and utilizing KMT troops across the strait. It will be recalled that on 20 November 1950, after the brief initial Chinese incursion, the joint chiefs indicated that a reconsideration of the neutralization policy was necessary. On 2 January 1951, only days after MacArthur proposed his retaliatory strategy, the chiefs informed Marshall that merely denying Taiwan to the Communists would not satisfy American military and strategic requirements. The United States had to "retain complete freedom of action" to permit its own or Nationalist forces to use the island for offensive operations.[11] Ten days later, in a proposed contingency plan for extended war in Korea and China, the military chieftains called for the elimination of the prohibition against Nationalist offensive operations and for logistic support for such undertakings. The chiefs were aware that Gen. Matthew B. Ridgway, the new commander of the U.S. Eighth Army in Korea, had seconded MacArthur's idea of a Nationalist diversionary attack on south China as had (with caveats) army representatives on the Joint Strategic Plans Committee attached to the JCS.[12]

On 17 January the National Security Council convened to discuss NSC 101/1, an NSC staff paper specifying countermeasures against China that incorporated the views of the JCS, the State and Defense Departments, and other elements of the policymaking apparatus. The document revealed a lack of agreement on the JCS proposal to permit and lend logistical assistance to Kuomintang mainland operations.[13] An alternate paper prepared by the State Department went part way toward the JCS position by suggesting the preparation of plans for Nationalist offensive action with American material support. But the department was in no hurry to flash a green light for a Nationalist advance across the strait. Its paper also underscored the need to contain the Korean conflict and avoid a general war, support the UN, and preserve solidarity with the Western allies.[14] Taking charge at the NSC meeting, Acheson rejected NSC 101/1 as inadequate. The use of Nationalist troops against the mainland, he asserted, lacked demonstrable military effectiveness and "bristled with political difficulties." He reminded his listeners that it was necessary to maintain a proper balance between European and Asian interests and to keep the British on side. Acheson carried the field; both Marshall and Truman agreed with him that the NSC paper needed revision.[15]

Although NSC 101/1 was never reworked or resubmitted as intended, over the next few weeks both the joint chiefs and the State Department continued to examine the issue of a Nationalist offensive role on the mainland. A JCS report concluded that Nationalist forces, despite their present dubious combat readiness, could execute limited operations under certain conditions but only with American aid and guidance and only if the Soviet Union did not intervene. Claiming that considerable disillusionment with the Communists existed in China, the document predicted that the arrival of Nationalist troops would "inspire hope" among millions of Chinese and stimulate guerrilla activity.[16]

State Department officials, too, believed that a substantial number of Chinese yearned for the overthrow of the Communist regime. Unlike the JCS, they were unconvinced that this sentiment translated into mass support for the return of Chiang Kai-shek.[17] They questioned whether it was worth diverting scarce supplies and equipment to mainland operations for which the

Nationalists were unprepared and which stood little chance of success. Once on their home ground, Acheson scoffed, no one knew whether Chiang's soldiers would fight or simply say, "Thanks, boys, we are going to see our families."[18]

In a climactic State Department–JCS meeting on 6 February, military representatives pulled back from their advocacy of a second front spearheaded by KMT troops. This meeting sealed the consensus between the military and the diplomats against overt expansion of the war under existing circumstances. By this point the military emergency in Korea had eased, and while MacArthur still pressed for escalation, his voice no longer commanded its former authority among the JCS.[19]

The consensus against an expanded war by no means ended discussions of a Nationalist counterattack within the national security bureaucracy. For now, however, the neutralization policy remained unaltered. In a significant development, the State Department also now operated on the premise that the mission of the Seventh Fleet would continue indefinitely, barring a major change in the Asian arena.[20] Though in future months Truman administration officials would give further consideration to a revision of the Seventh Fleet's mission that would permit Nationalist operations against the mainland, never did they contemplate a complete withdrawal of the fleet that would leave Taiwan exposed to a Chinese invasion. No further thought was given to President Truman's 31 August observation that the Seventh Fleet need not remain in the Taiwan Strait after the windup of the Korean operation. The provisional defensive commitment to Taiwan had congealed into long-term commitment.

A War for Korea and Taiwan

The early winter of 1950–51 was a period of crucial diplomatic as well as military decisions for the Truman administration in Korea. Not only did the administration elect to confine the war to the peninsula and to discontinue the attempt to roll back the North Korean communist regime, it also persisted in rejecting any conditions or concessions for a cease-fire and peace settlement. As in the military realm, the administration's course of action in the diplomatic sphere had direct implications for its policy toward Taiwan. In insisting on a no-strings-attached approach to negotiations, the administration placed itself at loggerheads with the Chinese Communists, who demanded that their claims to Taiwan and to the UN China seat figure in any cease-fire arrangement. Chairman Mao Tse-tung, flushed by early sensational military victories, was unprepared to settle for a return to the status quo ante in Korea and was bent on imposing a humiliating military and diplomatic defeat on the United States.[21] For their part, American leaders were indisposed to "reward aggression" by conceding their enemy's conditions for a cease-fire. Britain and other Commonwealth nations, together with various other UN partners, were all generally more flexible than the United States and more understanding of China's motives for intervention, and they tried to construct cease-fire proposals that would entice these two antagonists to the peace table.[22] But because Washington and Peking assumed irreconcilable positions, finding an acceptable formula for a cease-fire and peace talks proved impossible. Of the diplomatic issues barring the path to peace negotiations, none was a bigger stumbling block than Taiwan.

Chinese Communist Party authorities made an American pledge to withdraw from Taiwan a sine qua non for a cease-fire. Interweaving their intervention in Korea with the stymied campaign to "liberate" the Nationalist island retreat, they made the U.S. interposition in the Taiwan Strait conspicuous in Chinese public and private diplomacy. In a historic speech before the Security Council on 28 November, Gen. Wu Hsiu-chuan became the first representative from the People's Republic of China to address the world organization. Wu headed a delegation from the PRC invited to sit with the council during discussions of Taiwan and Korea. Most of Wu's impassioned two-hour address consisted of a scathing attack on duplicitous American statements and actions with respect to Taiwan.[23]

Wu and his colleagues remained in New York for more than three weeks during which time they engaged in private talks about a cease-fire with Secretary-General Trygve Lie and Sir Benegal Rau, India's representative at the UN. The Chinese set down three preconditions for a cease-fire: 1) evacuation of UN troops from Korea; 2) withdrawal of the Seventh Fleet from Taiwan; and 3) seating the PRC in the UN. Rau came away from his first two talks with the Chinese representatives convinced that they placed great, perhaps even paramount, emphasis on the Taiwan question.[24] On 11 December Chou En-lai insisted to the Indian ambassador in Peking, K. M. Panikkar, that before talks about the future of Korea could begin the United States had to affirm the Cairo and Potsdam Declarations and accept in principle the withdrawal of the Seventh Fleet. Though Taiwan might seem important to the United States, the foreign minister emphasized, it was vital to China.[25]

The Chinese intervention stiffened American opposition, first evidenced during the abortive British and Indian peace initiatives in July 1950, to any concessions involving a UN seat or a withdrawal of the Seventh Fleet in order to stop the fighting in Korea. Dealt a stunning military and psychological blow by the Chinese, threatened for a time by a possible rout of UN forces, and buffeted by powerful domestic tensions, American leaders regarded as anathema any bargains with Peking that smacked of capitulation to black-mail by an aggressor.

British prime minister Clement Attlee and his companions experienced firsthand this uncompromising attitude during consultations in Washington with Truman and his aides in early December. Attlee and his entourage hoped to reach an agreement to localize the war, to seek a cease-fire and start negotiations on a Korean settlement, and to move toward a resolution of the Taiwan and UN representation issues.[26] Truman and his advisers were pessimistic about successful negotiations with the Chinese and were dead set against any preconditions or advance concessions. Unlike the British, they considered China little more than a satellite of the Soviet Union, and they were unconvinced that a more adaptable policy would serve to detach Peking from Moscow.[27]

The British failed to persuade the Americans that discussions with the Chinese about a cease-fire and Korean settlement would have to extend beyond Korea proper to such issues as Taiwan and a UN seat. The Americans refused to budge from their opposition to Chinese Communist membership in the world organization, which as Truman bluntly reminded the British was "political dynamite in the United States."[28] It was Taiwan that occasioned the keenest debate, however. Led by Acheson, the American participants made it unmistakably clear that the United States would not permit the Communists to gain control of Taiwan, whether by force or negotiations. Backed by Marshall and the JCS, Acheson stressed that denying the island to the Communists was of vital political and military importance, since its loss would have damaging consequences in Japan and the Philippines and would open a dangerous gap in the island defense system in the western Pacific. Keeping this defensive barrier safe was all the more essential if UN forces had to abandon Korea. "Formosa is too dangerous a thing for them [the Chinese Communists] to have to play with," the secretary warned. "We must hold the islands."[29]

As a compromise, Prime Minister Attlee proposed that the United States continue its protection for Taiwan while withdrawing its support from Chiang Kai-shek in order to permit a UN commission to administer the island until Peking learned to "behave." This scheme appealed to Truman, whose repugnance for Chiang was as intense as ever, but left Acheson and Marshall unimpressed. Acheson felt that Chiang's rule was an inescapable reality and an undeniable factor in keeping Taiwan out of Communist hands. Marshall saw no replacement for the Generalissimo who had his stature.[30]

These exchanges erased any doubt in the minds of the British that the United States regarded its defense of Taiwan, irrespective of Chiang's dominance, as essential to its national security as long as the Chinese Communists were a menace. The British themselves, sharing the American opposition to Chinese expansion, conceded that the island ought to remain separate from the mainland for the foreseeable future. The conversations also drove home the American insistence that commitments on such issues as the UN seat and Taiwan in advance of cease-fire talks were out of the question. The Americans did allow that negotiations on Far Eastern issues might follow a cease-fire.[31]

A joint communiqué issued at the end of the Truman-Attlee talks was silent about Anglo-American differences over Taiwan and made no mention of U.S. strategic interests in the island. Noting that Peking and Taipei equally insisted on the validity of the Cairo Declaration and had expressed reluctance to have the issue resolved by the UN, the statement declared that the Taiwan question "should be settled by peaceful means and in such a way as to safeguard the interests of the people of Formosa and the maintenance of peace and security in the Pacific, and that consideration of this question by the UN will contribute to this end."[32] Despite this bow to UN consideration, the communiqué was clearly weighted against any solution that would transfer Taiwan to Communist China.

Following the Truman-Attlee talks, the Taiwan issue continued to bedevil efforts by Britain and other friendly nations to bridge the chasm separating the United States and China over a cease-fire. The Korean crisis was at the top of the agenda at a conference of Commonwealth prime ministers in London beginning early in January 1951. By this point the southward advance of Chinese troops had carried them across the 38th parallel and the United States wanted to forge ahead in the General Assembly with a resolution condemning Chinese aggression in the peninsula. Britain, India, and other nations were afraid that such a resolution would put negotiations beyond reach and pave the way for retaliatory action against China. At the United Nations a Cease-fire Group, commissioned earlier by the General Assembly to explore the terms for a cessation of hostilities, attempted to draft a viable peace proposal.[33]

Attlee told his Commonwealth associates in London that to devise any peace plan that did not deal with Taiwan would be unrealistic, since this issue perhaps touched the Chinese "most nearly." India's Nehru, too, was certain that Peking would refuse to consider any Korean settlement independently of the Taiwan question. Prior to the London conference, the Indian prime minister had lamented to Attlee that "the main obstacle to peace talks with China has been Formosa."[34] While the Commonwealth meetings were in train, the British put out feelers to the Americans about the acceptability of a cease-fire proposal that included provisions both for a UN solution to the

Taiwan question based on the Cairo Declaration as well as for Chinese Communist entry into the UN. Washington was uninterested.[35]

Despite this setback, Britain and other Commonwealth nations were instrumental in the preparation of a statement of "five principles" for a cease-fire and peace settlement that was drafted by the UN Cease-fire Group and adopted by the General Assembly on 13 January with American agreement. The last and most crucial of these principles offered the PRC the prospect, following a cease-fire, of participation in a UN-sanctioned conference to seek a settlement of Far Eastern issues, including Taiwan and the disputed Chinese seat, such an accord to be arrived at in conformity with the principles of the UN Charter and "existing international obligations" (in the case of Taiwan, this meant the Cairo Declaration).[36]

Because this cease-fire bid appeared to give away too much to the Communists, Acheson found it hard to swallow. Facing what he later called a "murderous" choice, he decided to recommend its acceptance to Truman in order to preserve U.S. leadership in the United Nations, in spite of the negative reaction expected from South Korea and from Congress and the press. He counted on Peking to reject the UN offer so that the United States could then push ahead with the passage of an aggressor resolution.[37] The secretary paid little heed to the opinions of the Nationalists, who were deeply angered by Washington's weak-kneed acceptance of the Cease-fire Group proposal.[38]

Chou En-lai's reply to the UN proposition, made public on 17 January, was as intransigent as Acheson had hoped and anticipated. Stating that China would not countenance a cease-fire before negotiations, the premier outlined an alternative proposal that gave no real ground on China's demands for a UN seat and American withdrawal from Taiwan.[39]

For Washington, the time had passed for any additional gestures of accommodation to the Chinese. The government's approval of the five-principle proposal infuriated the China bloc and its conservative Republican allies.[40] On 1 February the United States, overcoming the objections and resistance of some of its UN partners, successfully pushed through the General Assembly a resolution censuring Communist China for aggression.[41]

The passage of the aggressor resolution ended serious discussions of a cease-fire until the summer, by which time the Chinese no longer had the upper hand militarily in Korea. As long as total victory remained within grasp, the CCP leadership appeared unwilling to consider any settlement inconsistent with China's declared aims. The Truman administration, for its part, was unprepared to satisfy these demands. The Taiwan issue significantly influenced the positions taken by both sides toward a cease-fire. Though efforts to stop the fighting did not founder only or even primarily because of this issue, it was incontestably a major reason for their failure and so directly contributed to the continuation of the peninsular conflict. In this sense, the war in Korea had also become a war over Taiwan.

Taiwan and the Secret War against China

The period after the Chinese swarmed across the Yalu witnessed if not the beginning, then certainly a rapid acceleration of American covert operations against China. While deciding against an overt expanded war, the Truman administration did embark on a secret limited war under the aegis of the Central Intelligence Agency. The conduct of this clandestine war enlarged the American presence on Taiwan and thrust the United States into a closer relationship with the Nationalists.

A major part of the secret war was assistance to anti-Communist guerrillas on the continent. The United States had already moved toward such backing before the Chinese intervention. Shortly after the start of hostilities in Korea, the JCS recommended that the CIA exploit guerrilla activity in China in order to restrict Peking's ability to reinforce North Korean forces. The State Department swiftly approved such operations.[42] At this time the CIA had already begun to funnel financial aid to Civil Air Transport (CAT), the American-owned private airline based on Taiwan that had previously served as a paramilitary adjunct of the Nationalist government. The CAT soon became the CIA's own secret air force in Asia.[43]

Not a great deal appears actually to have been done to aid guerrilla groups until after the Chinese intervention. Writing from the Taipei embassy in December 1950, Karl Rankin expressed satisfaction that "a good deal of preparatory work has been done during the past year" to support mainland anti-Communist forces, but he exhorted that now was the time "to go into action on an effective scale and to show results." He observed that "there are no evidences of activity here [on Taiwan] on our part other than for a certain amount of clandestine intelligence work, punctuated with the occasional swish of a cloak and gleam of a dagger." His impression was that the Nationalists themselves extended only minimal encouragement and support to anti-Communist guerrillas, restricted almost entirely to those with access to the KMT-held offshore islands.[44]

Rankin's ardor for covert assistance to anti-Communist resistance on the mainland was shared in Washington. The same deliberations that resulted in a consensus against an overt expanded war produced another in favor of clandestine support for anti-Communist guerrillas. A unanimous recommendation for such support appeared in NSC 101/1, the NSC staff paper that incorporated the views of the foreign affairs bureaucracy on countermeasures against China. In early April 1951 the JCS approved collaboration with other agencies to aid guerrilla movements.[45]

More than the immediate exigencies of the Korean conflict motivated decision makers to foment instability in China. Their determination to promote anti-CCP resistance mirrored a greater harshness in the overall American official attitude toward the People's Republic. One of the objectives for U.S. China policy prescribed in a State Department paper presented to the National Security Council in January 1951 was "to break the Kremlin control over China or to support the replacement of any government in China which is under the control of and in alliance with Moscow."[46] The United States, in other words, would aim either to reorient the Soviet-dominated regime in Peking away from the Kremlin or to replace it. The desire to sever China from the Soviet Union was, of course, present in State Department thinking before the Korean War; so too was a reluctance to accept the durability of the CCP's control over the mainland or at least all parts of it. Never before, however, had the department so forthrightly enunciated its support for a rollback of CCP authority as long as Mao and his companions were aligned with Moscow. The next month Dean Rusk told a Canadian diplomat that the State Department wanted to "get China unhooked from Russia" and wished the Peking government to fall. Confiding that highly secret intelligence indicated upheaval within the Communist regime, the assistant secretary stated that the United States would not take any overt action to topple the government but would try to "confuse and impede" it.[47]

During the winter and early spring of 1950–51, military and civilian analysts within the government closely scrutinized available information on guerrilla activities in China. Discounting exaggerated Nationalist claims of upwards of 2 million men united under KMT leadership, analysts varied considerably in their own estimates of the number of guerrillas, their figures ranging from 300,000 to 1 million. In agreement that most resistance groups operated independently, without either direction or support from Taiwan, they found no evidence of a guerrilla "movement" in the sense of coordinated activity. Consisting largely of former KMT soldiers, bandits, and disgruntled peasants, the guerrillas lacked overall leadership, adequate supplies and funding, and ideological focus. They could harass the Communist regime but posed no danger to its survival.[48]

The disorganized character of guerrilla resistance did not deter the CIA from initiating a major program of support. Led by its dynamic director, Gen. Walter Bedell Smith, the agency was awash in funds thanks to the Korean War. East Asia was the most promising growth area for clandestine activities.[49] Central Intelligence Agency personnel began to stream into

Taiwan in the early spring of 1951, operating under the cover of Western Enterprises, Inc., a private military procurement agent for the Nationalist government. In May Rankin ruefully noted that Madame Chiang Kai-shek, who had quickly learned how much money Western Enterprises had available, had already entertained its agents at her home, where he himself had not yet stepped foot.[50] The presence of both Western Enterprises and Civil Air Transport on Taiwan transformed Chiang's redoubt into an essential base for the secret war against China. The CIA establishment grew to more than 600 persons, providing training and logistical support for guerrillas, overflight capabilities, propaganda facilities, and other services. The agency applied a two-track approach to assistance for anti-Communist forces, supporting both pro-Nationalist elements and "third force" groups unaligned with the KMT.[51]

Many of the details of the clandestine war against China remain hidden in the shadow of secrecy; the paper trail that the historian can follow is slender. Among the anti-Chinese operations were raiding expeditions against coastal areas by KMT guerrillas and marines based on the offshore islands. One such raid in July 1952 reportedly involved 12,000 men.[52] The best documented and most notorious episode in the covert war revolved around the activities of KMT army remnants who had fled from Yunnan province in the final days of the civil war, taking refuge in the remote mountainous region of northern Burma. The CIA enlisted these ragged troops, led by Gen. Li Mi, the last Nationalist governor of Yunnan and the former commander of the KMT 97th Division, in a project for the invasion of Yunnan. This undertaking, code-named Operation Paper, involved CAT, Western Enterprises, and Overseas Southeast Asia Supply Company, a sister CIA cover firm in Bangkok. Li Mi's CIA-equipped forces eventually rose to 12,000 men with the addition of local brigands together with reinforcements airlifted by CAT from Taiwan. On three different occasions, in May and July 1951 and August 1952, these forces struck into Yunnan, only to be driven back in each instance. As will be seen in Chapter 6, Operation Paper was not only an abject military failure but had vexing diplomatic consequences for the United States.[53]

The payoff from the secret war against China appears to have been modest at best. The CIA discovered only 175,000 guerrillas, almost none under Chiang Kai-shek's direction. Determined to root out subversive elements and fearing that Nationalist forces, perhaps with U.S. help, might initiate a counterattack against the mainland and join hands with resistance groups, Peking intensified its counterrevolutionary efforts during the Korean War.[54] Nationalist foreign minister George Yeh confessed to Senator William Knowland in late 1952 that Communist suppression had taken a heavy toll on mainland resistance contingents and that the scattered survivors could not hold any extensive area on their own.[55] Just the same, American officials valued hit-and-run attacks and harassing guerrilla operations because they kept the Communists off balance and tied down as many as 200,000 troops.[56]

Chiang's Nationalists were arguably the biggest beneficiaries of the secret war against China. The covert war deepened the American stake on Taiwan and created more extensive ties with the Nationalist government. It resulted in an informal relaxation of the ban on Nationalist offensive activities, creating a double standard in the application of the neutralization policy. The surreptitious fight against China failed to bring Chiang any nearer to recapturing the mainland; it did draw him into a more intimate association with Washington.

Large-Scale Aid for Taiwan

The Chinese intrusion in Korea opened the vault in Washington for substantial economic and military aid to the Nationalists. Taiwan received an injection of more than $40 million in supplementary economic aid for fiscal year (FY) 1951, and its allocation for fiscal year 1952 amounted to more than $80 million.[57] Military spending similarly soared upward. In February 1951 the president authorized an additional $50 million for the immediate needs of the Nationalist army. In March the State Department consented to a recommendation from the Pentagon for a $237.7 million allotment to Taiwan for the upcoming fiscal year, somewhat more than 40 percent of the entire Mutual Defense Assistance Program (MDAP) appropriation for the Far East. Despite its preference for a more modest level of expenditure, Foggy Bottom followed the lead of the Pentagon.[58]

With the Nationalist armed forces slated once more to become major aid recipients, Washington proceeded to set conditions for its assistance. Decision makers did not want American largesse used for unauthorized offensive operations or as a gravy train for grasping Nationalist officials. In a secret exchange of notes concluded in early February, Taipei agreed to use the forthcoming military aid only for internal security and the defense of Taiwan and to accept U.S. personnel to administer and oversee it.[59]

On 19 April the Defense Department disclosed to the public that the United States would measurably increase military spending for Taiwan and dispatch a Military Advisory Assistance Group (MAAG) there.[60] The announcement came on the same day that General MacArthur, whom Truman had dismissed from his commands nine days earlier, delivered a tearful farewell speech to Congress. Whether or not its timing was deliberate, the announcement did put the administration in a stronger position to rebut MacArthur's imputations of defeatism in Asia. On 1 May the first contingent of MAAG personnel arrived in Taipei.

The period from the early winter of 1950 to the early spring of 1951 had been critical in the coalescence of the commitment to Taiwan. Rejecting an expanded war strategy, Washington declined to lend assistance to a Nationalist counterinvasion of mainland China. Repudiating Chinese terms for a cease-fire, it refused to trade the China seat in the UN and a military withdrawal from the Taiwan Strait for a Korean armistice. The Chinese intervention pitched the United States into a close and enduring association with Taiwan. Washington now undertook a long-term defensive commitment to the island and recognized the necessity and desirability of a more supportive relationship with the Nationalist government. The collaboration with the Nationalists in the secret war against China, the resumption of large-scale economic and military assistance, and the assignment of a Military Advisory Assistance Group to Taiwan signalled the metamorphosis of Chiang Kai-shek's regime into an American client.

4

Although the winter and early spring of 1950–51 was a watershed in the development of an enduring military and political commitment to Taiwan, this expanded commitment emerged without any comprehensive review of Asian policy, or much explanation to the public, or a concerted diplomatic approach in the international arena. But in the spring and early summer of 1951, the Truman administration acted to remedy these deficiencies. On 17 May the president approved NSC 48/5, which would serve as the basic statement of U.S. policy in Asia for the remainder of his term. Even as the National Security Council was preparing this document, the administration braced itself against the cascade of censure caused by Truman's shocking dismissal of MacArthur. That domestic frenzy over the general's firing prompted the administration to publicize its views on East Asian policy and to challenge its extremist critics. By the time the clamor had subsided, the administration had defined major elements of its broadened commitment to Taiwan more fully and candidly. In a counterattack against its pro-Nationalist detractors, it also began an investigation of the China lobby.

In the international sphere, the administration strove to support the Nationalist government's self-professed position as the legitimate government of China, at least insofar as this was feasible, and to keep a free hand regarding the disposition of Taiwan. The administration successfully pursued its diplomatic objectives at the United Nations and during the complex process that led to the signing and ratification of the Japanese peace treaty and to the conclusion of a separate peace between Japan and Nationalist China.

The MacArthur Crisis and NSC 48/5

The stunning announcement on 11 April 1951 that the White House had sacked MacArthur ignited a firestorm of public outrage and Republican vilification that for a time threatened to discredit irretrievably Truman's presidency. Within Western allied nations, in contrast, overwhelming approval and relief greeted the news of the freewheeling general's removal.[1] On Taiwan, the spirits of Nationalist leaders plummeted to their lowest ebb since January 1950.[2]

Taiwan loomed large in the final rupture between Truman and MacArthur. The general's unauthorized announcement on 24 March of a Korean peace plan, amounting to an ultimatum to China, sabotaged a planned cease-fire initiative by Washington and seemed calculated to force a showdown with the enemy. MacArthur defied Washington's authority in the apparent belief that he was foiling a plot within the UN and the administration to purchase peace at the expense of the Nationalist government's control over Taiwan and of its seat in the world body. The publication soon afterward of his inflammatory letter to House minority leader Joseph Martin, giving a stamp of approval to the Massachusetts Republican's call for an American-backed second front on the Chinese mainland using Chiang's forces, sealed MacArthur's fate. Thwarted by administration opposition to his expanded war strategy, he invited martyrdom in the apparent expectation that he could then better carry his own views to Congress and the public.[3]

By coincidence, on the same day on which Truman recalled the Far East commander, the Seventh Fleet began a photo reconnaissance operation and a naval sweep through the Taiwan Strait. At the insistence of the State Department, the navy agreed to refrain from an overt show of force and to exclude Hong Kong and Hainan Island from the sweep. The department wished to avoid agitating the British, who might perceive the naval demonstration as a MacArthurite provocation.[4] Secretary Acheson also quashed plans devised by MacArthur's headquarters (about which the Foreign Office had alerted the department) that would have included dummy landing operations in the naval and air maneuvers off the China coast. This little known incident may have contributed to the decision to relieve the general of his commands.[5]

Amid the furor over the recall, the president on 17 May approved NSC 48/5, a new top-level statement of Asian policy. Setting its sights on the reduction of Soviet power and influence in this area of the world, the document affirmed as primary American objectives China's detachment from its close alliance with Moscow and its transformation into an independent, nonaggressive nation. Relying on a hard-line approach to accomplish these goals, NSC 48/5 called for a punishing war of attrition in Korea, unilateral trade restrictions and UN political and economic sanctions against Peking as well as its exclusion from the UN, and support for anti-Communist resistance in China. The American aim would be to weaken or sever the Sino-Soviet alliance by the removal or fragmentation of the Peking regime or by a change in its character and external policies. The policy paper dictated that the United States should seek to foster non-Communist leadership in China and to motivate the Chinese people to reorient or replace the existing government. In a word, NSC 48/5 sought not merely the containment of Communist China but its realignment or rollback.

The document contained the first exposition of basic U.S. policy toward Taiwan since December 1949, when NSC 48/2 had ratified the policy of military disengagement. Taking as its starting point the integral connection between Taiwan and the security of the island defense line in the Far Pacific, NSC 48/5 ordained that the United States "deny Formosa to any Chinese regime aligned with or dominated by the USSR and expedite the strengthening of the defensive capabilities of Formosa." To these ends, it confirmed the decisions taken in the aftermath of the Chinese intervention to provide Taiwan with long-term military protection in tandem with major economic and military assistance. Acheson eliminated phraseology in an earlier draft that he felt would "commit us to all-out and limitless assistance to Chiang Kai-shek." He also cautioned that the United States should not obligate itself to keep Taiwan indefinitely apart from the mainland. The final version of the policy paper left open the possibility that Taiwan might some day rejoin a peaceable China.[6]

Even while acknowledging the present weakness of Chiang's armed forces, NSC 48/5 described them as a "potential asset" in a major Far Eastern war, and it stipulated that Pentagon plans for a broadened war with China were to include the "participation defensively or offensively" of Nationalist troops. Despite these adumbrations of a Nationalist military role beyond the defense of Taiwan, the paper did not subscribe to the KMT's goal of mainland reconquest. While looking toward the eventual establishment of an amicable Chinese government, NSC 48/5 submitted that the Chinese themselves would have to determine its makeup. The document, which was decidedly ambivalent about Nationalist prospects on the continent, indicated that Chiang's government would need to make political changes to increase its drawing power across the Taiwan Strait. In authorizing assistance to anti-Communist resistance elements in China, the paper did not earmark aid for pro-KMT dissenters alone. It envisaged the possible emergence of a "third force" around which resistance elements could rally and within which the Nationalists might eventually find a role. For all this, NSC 48/5 recognized an interest in enhancing the reputation and influence of the Nationalist government in China. It implicitly intermeshed overall U.S. support for the Nationalists with a policy of pressure against the Communist regime.[7]

On 18 May, just a day after the president's approval of NSC 48/5, Assistant Secretary Dean Rusk caused an uproar with an address before the China Institute of New York City. In a celebrated passage, he anathematized the Peking regime as "a colonial Russian government — a Slavic Manchukuo on a larger scale." Asserting that the Nationalist government "more authentically" represented the sentiments of most of China's people, he stated that the United States would continue to give Taipei "important aid and assistance." Adding that such help was alone insufficient to determine China's future, he declared that it was up to all Chinese to pool their efforts to liberate their country.[8]

Coming only a few weeks after the announcement of a major military assistance program for Taiwan and in the middle of the clamor over MacArthur's dismissal, Rusk's famed "Slavic Manchukuo" speech captured newspaper headlines and touched off a spasm of speculation and controversy. Commentators in the press and on Capitol Hill disagreed about the meaning and merit of the Far Eastern Bureau chief's words. Some accepted the State Department's explanation that the speech represented only a restatement, in perhaps overly forceful language, of current China policy. Most observers concluded that it marked a shift toward closer association with Chiang Kai-shek and the KMT. Pro-Nationalist partisans grudgingly welcomed the speech as a belated endorsement of their own views, whereas critics condemned it as a kowtow to the MacArthurites and as an obstacle to a Korean cease-fire.[9] The British Foreign Office, which agreed with the faultfinders, registered its misgivings with the State Department. An apologetic Acheson replied that Rusk had not intended to announce any change in China policy; having delivered the speech without first showing it to his colleagues or to the secretary himself, he had failed to gauge the likely reaction to his utterances.[10]

Rusk himself evinced surprise at the reaction to the speech in a strained conversation with British ambassador Franks. Heavy Chinese casualties in Korea, the assistant secretary explained, made the moment seem right to beam a message to China via the Voice of America with the aim of inducing Chinese leaders to demonstrate by word or action that they were not thralls of the Soviet Union. The speech had said nothing new, but it might put an end to the "unjustified hopes" of the "*Washington Post* school" that the administration was waiting for the right opportunity to pull away from or undercut Chiang Kai-shek as well as the "unjustified fears" of Republicans that this was actually what it planned.[11]

Rusk plainly had both Chinese and American audiences in mind when writing the address. Employing the "scolding" technique favored by State Department China expert John Paton Davies, he wanted to shame the Chinese into asserting their nationalism.[12] He admitted in his memoirs that the "Slavic Manchukuo" label was "more taunt than statement of fact, a response to Peking's [own] rhetorical campaign" against the United States.[13] Be that as it may, the label did reflect the conviction of government officials that China was subordinate to the Soviet Union. The assistant secretary's comments to Franks indicate that an additional purpose of his remarks was to remove questions about the administration's support for the Nationalists in the minds of anti-Chiang liberals and pro-Chiang conservatives alike. Years later, he recalled that his principal intended audience was indeed American domestic opinion.[14] It is a reasonable surmise that he particularly wanted to reinforce the administration's vulnerable flank on China policy against the furious assault by the Republican right under the banners of MacArthur and McCarthy.

The reaction to Rusk's 18 May speech suggested that the administration had not yet adequately conveyed to the citizenry and Congress the nature of its enlarged commitment to Taiwan. In their public statements about Taiwan following the Chinese intervention in Korea, government officials had kept quiet about any major departure from the objectives proclaimed after the June interposition and they still shied away from an admission of the important American strategic interest in Taiwan. In spite of the announcement of large-scale military aid for the Nationalists in the spring of 1951, officials had not sufficiently recast declaratory policy toward Taiwan to reduce public confusion and contention.

The MacArthur hearings that began on 3 May 1951 presented an incentive and opportunity for the administration to explicate its current policy as well as to rebut the claims and accusations of Republican critics. The investigation of MacArthur's removal and of the military situation in the Far East by a joint Senate committee of the Foreign Relations and Armed Services Committees became a forum for a highly politicized debate on the administration's war strategy and Asian policy.[15]

Taiwan figured prominently in the prolonged inquiry. Among the issues the joint committee examined were the use of Nationalist troops in Korea and China, the strategic value of Taiwan, U.S. policy toward the island before and after the outbreak of the Korean War, and the administration's current and future intentions toward the KMT asylum. Administration witnesses generally fared well in their testimony, despite sometimes sharp interrogation. Effectively disputing MacArthur's war strategy, Secretary of Defense Marshall and the joint chiefs questioned the utility of employing Nationalist troops, most of whom were inadequately trained and equipped, either in Korea or elsewhere outside Taiwan. In secret testimony excised from the public transcript, they were even more deflating in their evaluation of Chiang's forces in their present condition. Even so, they refused to foreclose the future use of these troops in either Korea or mainland China.[16]

The hearings gave MacArthur and the defense establishment a chance to air their assessments of Taiwan's strategic significance. The deposed general exaggeratedly depicted the island as the keystone of the nation's defenses in Asia, declaring that "we practically lose the Pacific Ocean if we give up or lose Formosa." Marshall and the joint chiefs denied that the island's loss would be so disastrous; yet they maintained, as did MacArthur, that a Taiwan in unfriendly hands could have perilous consequences and that American security interests demanded that no hostile power gain control of it.[17] Their testimony made evident that differences over the strategic value of Chiang's refuge had not accounted for MacArthur's removal and that the Seventh Fleet's protection of the island rested on long-term security considerations rather than merely temporary military requirements connected with United Nations operations in Korea. For the first time since the Taiwan interposition, Pentagon representatives publicly delineated the strategic necessity for the defense of the island.

Most of the burden for explaining the administration's policy toward Taiwan, past and present, fell on Acheson. Despite gruelling questioning by conservative Republicans who wanted to demonstrate that the State Department had written off the island and its Nationalist masters before the war in Korea, the secretary stood his ground. He insisted that prevailing conditions and limited military resources had necessitated that the government use only nonmilitary means to preserve Taiwan, although civilian and military planners were in agreement that the island was strategically valuable.[18] His description of pre-Korea policy was selective and self-serving, crafted to put him and his subordinates in the best possible light and to downplay past differences with the Defense Department. He left unmentioned the State Department's disenchantment with Chiang, its concern for British and Asian opinion, and its preoccupation with not driving China irretrievably into the arms of the Soviet Union. In later testimony, former Secretary of Defense Louis Johnson did not contradict the essentials of Acheson's account, though he did lay more emphasis on State-Defense rivalry and on anti-KMT sentiment among the diplomats.[19]

In expounding current policy, Acheson offered categorical assurance that the United States would refuse to allow the island to fall into the grasp of an adversary either by force or negotiation. To prevent a forceful takeover, the United States would continue its military protectorship and its defensive aid to the Nationalist government. The secretary reiterated that Washington would abstain from concessions involving the disposition of Taiwan or a UN seat for Communist China in order to secure a Korean cease-fire. While keeping open a UN solution for the island, he precluded a trusteeship imposed against the wishes of the Nationalists. He also retreated somewhat from the position that the United States would not regard its negative vote in the Security Council against Chinese representation as a veto.[20]

By the time Secretary Acheson concluded his testimony both the committee and the public were losing interest in the hearings. The inquiry lapsed into a roundelay of familiar Republican denunciations of a failed China policy under the leadership of two Democratic presidents. The din over General MacArthur's recall abated, leaving the administration bruised but undefeated, while MacArthur himself gradually faded from the scene.[21] Nonetheless, there were still voices in the press, Congress, and the public who called for a decisive victory in Korea by means of an enlarged war. A Gallup poll in April 1951 indicated that 54 percent of interviewees favored bombing Manchuria, a blockade of Chinese ports, and assistance to the Nationalists to strike at the mainland.[22]

If the MacArthur hearings failed to silence the debate over a retaliatory strategy, they did establish common ground between the administration and conservative Republicans on certain basic aspects of Taiwan policy. In what amounted to a minority report, eight Republican senators on the joint congressional committee placed their imprimatur on the administration's avowed intention to retain Taiwan in friendly hands, provide aid to the Nationalist government, and oppose Chinese Communist membership in the UN. The senators gloatingly recorded that testimony before the committee had definitively documented Taiwan's strategic importance and had clarified "for once and all" U.S. policy toward the island.[23] In aligning its declared policy more closely with its operational policy, the administration had achieved some degree of political cover against the fulminations of pro-Nationalist partisans, while intervening with greater determination itself in the Chinese civil war.

Stalking the China Lobby

In a surprise announcement at the MacArthur hearings on 8 June, Acheson revealed that the president had directed federal agencies to assemble information on the China lobby with a view either to possible prosecution of individuals for illegal activities or to an investigation of the lobby by Congress. The day before, Wayne Morse, the maverick liberal Republican senator from Oregon, had injected the subject of the lobby into the hearings with a recitation of a litany of allegations about its shady activities.[24]

For more than two years previously, stories about the China lobby had appeared in newspapers and magazines, accompanied in some instances by calls for an investigation.[25] The unexpected introduction of the issue in the MacArthur hearings kicked off a new round of press speculation and debate. Nationalist representatives angrily denied the existence of any lobby under their government's direction or instigation. Individuals reputed to belong to the lobby such as Arthur Kohlberg, head of the American China Policy Association, and Frederick C. McKee, chairman of the Committee to Defend America by Aiding Anti-Communist China, disavowed any formal connection with Chiang's government. "The real 'China Lobby,'" sneered Kohlberg, "is the pro-Communist lobby within the State Department."[26]

Though the public squall over the China lobby soon blew over, the White House quietly carried on its own probe. Far from being disinterested, the purpose of this operation was to launch a political vendetta against Senator Joseph McCarthy and his cohorts. The cacophony over MacArthur's dismissal sharpened the politics of anticommunism and vaulted McCarthy to new heights of reckless arrogance. The Wisconsin senator was in the vanguard of a no-holds-barred offensive against the administration from Republican conservatives, a few Democratic renegades, and a host of allies in the public arena. And it was the State Department that bore the brunt of this "attack of the primitives." Foreign Service officers, once stationed in China and now blamed for its loss, were prime targets.[27] In one episode early in March 1951, department officials suspected that the Nationalist embassy had fed material from police records on Taipei about some of these "China hands" to ultraconservative columnist and radio broadcaster Fulton Lewis, Jr. Rusk informed Rankin that the Nationalists had to keep out of domestic politics.[28]

In late March George M. Elsey and several other members of Truman's staff discussed a congressional investigation of the China lobby with representatives from the State Department and the staff of the Democratic National Committee. The White House aides concluded that an investigation "would be beneficial in a number of ways, that it would be highly embarrassing to a sizeable group of Republicans in and out of Congress, and that it would reveal interesting information on the financial backers of Senator McCarthy, Senator Knowland, and a number of others."[29] Apparently at the bidding of the White House, the State Department commissioned its legal adviser, Adrian S. Fisher, to collect material on the lobby within the department and to recommend a plan of action. In early June Fisher sent the White House a brief memorandum that a disappointed Elsey dismissed as "watery." The impetus for further investigation seems to have come from Truman himself; he was reportedly ready to investigate the lobby "from hell to breakfast." A less zealous Acheson hesitated to start an inquiry without knowing where it would end.[30] The existence of a nefarious China lobby subsidized by American aid money diverted by profiteering Nationalist officials was, and long remained, an article of faith with Truman.[31]

So it was that the president authorized an interagency committee, consisting of representatives from the Departments of State, Justice, and Agriculture and from the Bureau of Internal Revenue and the Federal Reserve Board, to conduct an investigation of the lobby.[32] The resources devoted to the entire project were an indication of just how far Truman and his aides were ready to go to discredit extremist foes who had harnessed the politics of disloyalty and the myth of the betrayal of China as political weapons against the administration.

In October 1951, after four months of digging, the investigation ended inconclusively. A White House summary report confessed that "we do not know a great deal more than we did at the outset." The probe had unearthed little concrete information about the detailed operation of the lobby. Despite clear indications that "a substantial amount of money, largely from unascertained sources" had been expended for a pro-Nationalist publicity and propaganda campaign and that a "very close connection" existed between this campaign and certain politicians and public figures, no legal proof existed of money changing hands between "Chinese Nationalist sympathizers and American political personalities." Though there was reliable evidence of "large-scale corruption and profiteering" by some Nationalist officials during and immediately after the Second World War, this was not a new revelation, and any connection between these ill-gotten gains and the pro-Nationalist campaign remained conjectural.[33]

In April 1952 two lengthy articles critical of the China lobby appeared in *The Reporter*, once more thrusting this contested topic back into the news. While researching this journalistic exposé, the investigative team from the liberal magazine had been in contact with White House staff members who oversaw the Truman administration's own inquiry.[34] Blending penetrating reportage with innuendo and thinly substantiated allegation, the articles constituted the most extensive and sensational study of the lobby to appear in print to that time.[35] A furious Nationalist embassy accused the magazine of malicious misrepresentation.[36] Pro-Nationalist partisans branded the articles as a smear and as a desperate attempt to cover up the Truman administration's blunders in Asia. In the midst of this burst of notoriety, a handful of liberal columnists and newspapers joined Senator Wayne Morse in asking Congress to look into the lobby.[37] Their appeals met with no response on Capitol Hill.

In the end, neither the White House nor liberal critics were able to track down, let alone slay, the shadowy entity that the term "China lobby" evoked. To the extent that such a lobby existed, it was so loosely organized and disparate that it was difficult to pin down. Then too, however much the White House and liberal critics might deplore the lobby's malign influence, most of its activities were aboveboard and legitimate. Unequivocal proof of suspected irregular or unlawful practices among some elements was hard to ferret out. Furthermore, in the fiercely anticommunist milieu of the day, the lobby's message found wide support. Critics laid themselves bare to harsh censure and red-baiting from pro-Nationalist extremists.[38] Any expectation the White House once had that it could turn the issue of the China lobby against its Republican enemies proved unfounded. Instead, the issue became yet another battleground in the domestic conflict over internal security and Asian policy.

On the Diplomatic Offensive

In spite of the failure of the China lobby gambit, by the end of the MacArthur hearings the administration had fortified its domestic position on Taiwan policy. Leaving no doubt of its commitment to the safety of the island and to substantial defensive assistance for its Nationalist rulers, it had reaffirmed that the United States would continue to recognize Nationalist China and would strenuously resist any move to expel its representatives from the United Nations and replace them with those of the aggressor regime in Peking. Notwithstanding that pressures for an expanded war persisted, that past China policy remained a whipping boy for the administration's foes, and that the ravages of McCarthyism worsened, the administration had set forth the basics of a policy toward Taiwan that was acceptable to most Republicans and to the vast majority of American opinion. Apart from the issue of an expanded war, current policy toward Taiwan was no longer much of a political football or a catalyst for domestic agitation. The administration had forged a consensus on at least the minimum requirements of the American relationship with Chiang's government.

In the diplomatic realm, the administration's main objectives were to uphold the international position of the Nationalists vis-à-vis their mainland rivals, to the extent that this was practical, and to retain freedom of action in dealing with the disposition of Taiwan. The administration wished to accomplish these goals while minimizing friction with friends and allies with differing views in these matters. The State Department, after the collapse of its UN strategy in November 1950, was left without a diplomatic package to legitimize American armed interposition in the Taiwan Strait and to put off to the future any international decisions on the issues of Taiwan's future status and the disputed China seat in the UN. Although neutralization remained without any international sanction, the Chinese intervention in Korea eliminated it as a point of contention within the UN coalition. By the spring of 1951 Britain and other coalition partners, tacitly if not openly, had accepted the necessity of the U.S. military presence in the strait for the duration of the Korean conflict. Similarly, with British cooperation, the administration was able to pigeonhole the issues of Taiwan's future status and the China seat as well as arrive at an arrangement to proceed toward a multilateral peace treaty with Japan without involving the rival Chinese governments.

The MacArthur crisis coincided with a breach in the Attlee government caused by the resignation on 22 April of Aneurin Bevan, the fiery minister of labor. The chief spokesman for left-wing Labourites, Bevan took exception to the government's excessive deference to Washington's leadership in foreign affairs, and he made no secret of his distaste for America's shortsighted and dangerous policies in Asia. His resignation over a budget issue strengthened the hand of Labour moderates, who felt that Britain should not permit disagreement over China policy to weaken its ties with the United States or to strain the Western alliance, all the more so because Washington was already under heavy domestic fire over its policy and because Peking had proven so recalcitrant in Korea and in its relations with London. By the first months of 1951 Anglo-Chinese relations had markedly worsened and British official attitudes toward the People's Republic, while still more pragmatic than the American, were less pliable than before the Korean War and Chinese intervention. Early in May Herbert Morrison, Ernest Bevin's successor in the Foreign Office, initiated a series of noteworthy concessions to Washington on Chinese issues.[39]

At the urging of Secretary Acheson, Morrison consented to a proposal for a "moratorium" on the question of Chinese representation in the United Nations. Under this procedural arrangement, the world organization would for a specified period postpone any substantive deliberations or votes on the question.[40] The moratorium agreement marked a significant retreat by Britain, which since September 1950 had voted to accept the credentials of the Chinese Communists whenever the representation question arose in UN bodies and agencies. The United States, in contrast, had sought to postpone consideration of the question until after the war in Korea had ended. By consenting to the moratorium, the Labour government contrived not just to appease the State Department and put a stop to unconcealed Anglo-American dissension at the UN over the China seat but to cut loose from an unproductive policy that had failed to ameliorate relations with Peking.[41] Adopted by the Conservative government after its return to power in the fall, the moratorium had the practical effect of preserving Nationalist China's place in the UN and excluding the PRC. As a result of the Chinese intervention in Korea, there was strong support in the world body for this procedure.[42] The moratorium became the instrument by which the Truman administration and its successors until 1961 implemented a diplomacy of postponement to maintain the status quo on the China seat.

As well as concurring in the moratorium, Britain agreed to shelve the question of Taiwan's future disposition. Declaring in the House of Commons on 11 May that it would be "premature" to discuss the future of the island while military operations continued in Korea, Morrison maintained that a resolution of this question in accordance with the Cairo Declaration would have to await a "genuine and satisfactory Far Eastern settlement, the first step toward which must be a settlement in Korea." He also submitted that the Japanese peace treaty was not the place to attempt a permanent solution of this involved question.[43] The immediate reason for Morrison's statement was to counter allegations by MacArthur before the joint congressional committee that Britain was ready to cede Taiwan to China.[44] Its broader purpose was achieve a modus vivendi with Washington on Taiwan's disposition without compromising London's position that the island should ultimately go to the PRC. But the statement made plain that Britain was in no hurry to take up the Taiwan issue or to hand the island over to Peking. Britain thereby tacitly acquiesced in de facto Nationalist control of the island and in the American neutralization. In remarks before the Canadian House of Commons at this same time, External Affairs Minister Lester Pearson similarly disallowed any international discussion of Taiwan's disposition until after the Korean War, and he explicitly endorsed the neutralization.[45]

Morrison's statement had a particular bearing on Anglo-American consultations then in progress on a Japanese peace treaty; differences over Taiwan and China had intruded themselves in these discussions, threatening to impede early conclusion of a settlement. The rapid completion of a generous peace with Japan that would lock the defeated Asian enemy within the American orbit and win the consent of the Senate was then a top priority for Washington. Beginning in September 1950, John Foster Dulles, the chief American negotiator, had conducted bilateral talks with the wartime Pacific allies and with the occupation government of Japanese prime minister Yoshida Shigeru. These talks had culminated in an American draft treaty presented to Britain for consideration in late March 1951.[46] Much to Dulles's dismay, London wanted the treaty to require Japan to cede Taiwan to "China," which by Britain's own lights could only mean Peking, and it also wished to invite Communist China to participate in the treaty negotiations.[47]

The State Department rejected out of hand the British stance. By engaging in bilateral talks (which included Nationalist China) in preparation of the American draft treaty, the department had hitherto bypassed the intractable problem of the two Chinas. Now, not only had the British raised the problem, they had done so at a time when the American commitment to the KMT government had hardened and anti-Chinese sentiment in the United States was at a fever pitch because of the bloodletting in Korea.[48] Responding to the British position, the State Department refrained from insistence on the participation of the Taipei government in the final negotiation of the treaty, but it was adamant against the involvement of the PRC. And it most definitely did not want to use the treaty to solve the contentious issue of the disposition of Taiwan.[49]

Unlike the British proposal that the treaty cede Taiwan to "China," the American draft kept the island's status in a legal limbo by simply stipulating that Japan renounce its rights, titles, and claims.[50] This provision carried no risk of legitimizing either Peking's or Taipei's claims to Taiwan and allowed the United States to continue to maintain that the island's legal status was undecided. In a conversation with Sir Oliver Franks, Dulles observed that the United States preferred to retain some "international concern" over the island's disposition. A practiced international lawyer, he realized that Washington's assertions that its neutralization did not interfere in internal Chinese affairs was credible only if the legal status of Taiwan remained unsettled. Revealing his attraction to an eventual two-China solution, Dulles alluded to future international action that might establish a largely autonomous, neutral Taiwan with continuing access to trade with Japan.[51] If the State Department did not want to turn Taiwan over to the Communists, neither did it wish to limit future policy flexibility by assigning sovereignty to the Nationalists.[52]

At the time of Morrison's conciliatory 11 May statement, American and British experts had made headway in composing the text of a joint draft treaty, but they left unresolved the issues of the disposition of Taiwan and Chinese participation in the peace settlement.[53] While the foreign secretary's statement in the Commons suggested that Britain was prepared to be flexible on the first issue, it was silent about the second. Journeying to London in early June, Dulles plunged into a final conference with British diplomats on the treaty draft. He and Morrison concurred that the treaty should merely record Japan's renunciation of sovereignty over Taiwan.[54] On the issue of Chinese participation, the well-known Dulles-Morrison agreement broke the deadlock between the Americans and British by providing that neither Chinese government would be invited to sign the multilateral treaty and that Japan would decide for itself "its future attitude toward China . . . in the exercise of the sovereign and independent status contemplated by the treaty."[55] In effect, Japan could enter into a separate bilateral peace treaty with either Taipei or Peking on substantially the same terms as the multilateral treaty after that compact had come into force. British officials themselves wanted an independent Japan to establish relations with Mao's China rather than Chiang Kai-shek's shriveled regime, among other reasons because they believed that restoration of Japan's traditional commerce with the mainland would best serve the island nation's long-term economic needs and lessen Japanese competition with British markets in Southeast Asia.[56]

The British cabinet did not embrace the Dulles-Morrison agreement with open arms because of doubts among some members that it offered adequate protection against a Japanese decision to make peace with Nationalist China.[57] In point of fact, as a result of secret assurances received from Prime Minister Yoshida prior to the London talks, Dulles had reason to feel confident that Japan would do just what these British skeptics feared.[58] In any event, the Dulles-Morrison agreement removed a major impediment to the successful conclusion in July 1951 of an Anglo-American draft treaty, which paved the way in turn for the consummation of a multilateral treaty.[59]

By the summer of 1951 the Truman administration's policy toward Taiwan was in decidedly better shape in the international sphere than it had been at the time of the Chinese intervention in Korea. With the Chinese fighting the UN in the peninsular conflict, the neutralization of the Taiwan Strait was no longer a sore point with close allies. The Anglo-American moratorium agreement now guaranteed that the representation issue, for a time at least, would remain quiescent in the world organization. In talks with John Foster Dulles, British officials went along with the American desire to leave Taiwan's disposition undecided in the Japanese peace settlement and to exclude the People's Republic from the negotiation of this instrument. At the same time, the Dulles-Morrison agreement left an opening for Japan to conclude a separate bilateral peace with Nationalist China. In the months following this agreement, Dulles exerted every effort to make certain that Japan marched through that entryway.

A Separate Peace for Nationalist China

The signing of the Japanese peace treaty at the San Francisco conference on 8 September, followed later that same day by the sealing of a security pact between Japan and the United States, were undisguised triumphs for American diplomacy and for Dulles, the chief architect of these accords. Just the same, this victory would remain incomplete until the Senate had consented to the peace settlement. The task of guiding the treaty through the upper chamber also fell to the adept Dulles, who had consulted closely with key senators during the negotiations and enwrapped the document in a protective cocoon of bipartisanship. The one issue that could dissolve the solid political and popular support for the settlement was China. Fifty-six senators went on record after San Francisco disapproving ties between Japan and Communist China. To avoid rough handling of his cherished treaty during the ratification process, Dulles knew that he would have to nail down the certainty that Japan would make peace with Nationalist China. The accomplishment of that objective required adroit, sometimes stealthy, maneuvering among Tokyo, Taipei, and London, each with its own favored design for Sino-Japanese relations.[60]

Prior to San Francisco, Yoshida gave Dulles a written promise that Japan would not negotiate a bilateral treaty with CCP-ruled China.[61] His own preference, however, would have been to pursue diplomatic contacts with the Communist government rather than with Chiang's routed regime; that fledgling government, regardless of its political ideology, was now the master of the Chinese mainland, a natural market and source of raw materials for Japan. The premier's personal views on China policy were more in tune, as were those of most Japanese, with the pragmatism of the British outlook than the rigidity of the American. Yet he necessarily subordinated these views to the paramount objective of ending his country's prolonged occupation and aligning an independent Japan with the preponderant economic and military power of the United States. He nonetheless tried to preserve at least the option of future relations with the mainland.[62]

A Japan isolated from the mainland and tethered to the Kuomintang was not a prospect that the British government relished either. In the months after San Francisco, the British tried to tilt Tokyo toward the PRC. They insisted that Washington abide by the Dulles-Morrison agreement and let a sovereign Japan decide its "future attitude towards China."[63]

The form, content, and timing of a bilateral treaty with Japan were matters of utmost concern to the Nationalist government, which smarted over its exclusion from the Japanese peace treaty and the failure of that instrument to confirm its legal title to Taiwan. After Dulles had initiated bilateral consultations on a Japanese treaty the previous fall, Taipei had determined that its weakened international position required the closest possible cooperation with Washington to achieve its own treaty objectives. Sharing the American preference for a liberal, nonvindictive peace, it wanted not just to have its sovereignty over Taiwan definitively acknowledged, but to participate in the settlement with Japan on an equal, nondiscriminatory basis, as it believed befitted Nationalist China's status as the legal government of China and one of the major victorious allies.[64]

The absence of a provision in the peace treaty for Taiwan's cession had rankled Nationalist leaders; the exclusion of the Republic of China from the peace conference enraged them. Chiang Kai-shek blasted the Anglo-American decision to withhold an invitation to his government to participate in the treaty, and a wave of indignation swept over Taiwan.[65] Dulles, after returning from the London talks, met with Ambassador Wellington Koo six times in a span of three weeks in an effort to assuage the Nationalists and lay the groundwork for a separate peace between Tokyo and Taipei. Dulles got along well with the veteran diplomat, whom he had known since the 1918 Paris Peace Conference, and he had taken pains to keep him abreast of his discussions with Britain and other nations. He now informed Koo of the substance of his agreement with Morrison and the secret understanding with the Yoshida government. By the end of the Dulles-Koo exchanges, the Nationalists had resigned themselves to their humiliating exclusion from the prospective peace conference. In order to salvage as much pride and prestige as possible, they made it their goal to minimize the impression of discrimination in having to negotiate and sign a separate peace treaty with Japan. For this reason, they objected to having to wait to conclude their bilateral treaty until after the multilateral treaty had come into effect, when occupied Japan would have already regained its sovereignty. Stretching the meaning of the Dulles-Morrison agreement, Dulles conceded that the Nationalists could enter into a pact that could come into force "about the same time" as the multilateral treaty, so that "in fact [Nationalist] China would be on an equal footing with other Powers vis-à-vis Japan."[66]

Dulles also instructed Koo that Taipei could not expect to conclude an unrestricted bilateral treaty inasmuch as its claim to authority over all of China's territory was a "fiction" and Japan would refuse to accept such a claim. A scope of application formula was necessary, he contended, so that both signatories understood that the document pertained only to territory under actual Nationalist control.[67]

Behind Dulles's insistence on such a device were two other unspoken considerations. The first was his belief that it would be permissible under the Dulles-Morrison agreement for Japan and Nationalist China to sign a *limited* bilateral peace treaty *before* the Japanese peace treaty came into effect. Such a treaty, delimited by a scope of application formula, would not, in his opinion, eliminate future Japanese relations with mainland China. He had hinted at such a limited treaty in a conversation with Morrison after the San Francisco conference. When the foreign secretary had expressed the hope that "nothing would be done to crystallize the Japanese position toward China" until after the multilateral treaty came into force, Dulles had replied that Japan would naturally incline toward at least recognition of the Nationalist government and would want to put trade, diplomatic, and consular relations with Taiwan on a peacetime basis. This would not necessarily imply Japan's acceptance of the Nationalist government's claim to speak for all of China. While Morrison thought a "de facto" arrangement between Tokyo and Taipei was acceptable before the multilateral treaty came into effect, any Japanese recognition before then of the Nationalist government as the legitimate and effective voice for all of China was out of bounds. It seems that Dulles liberally interpreted a "de facto" arrangement to include a bilateral treaty limited to territory over which the Nationalists had actual control.

A second probable motive for Dulles's emphasis on a scope of application formula was to preserve the option of a two-China solution somewhere down the road. By consenting to such a formula, the Nationalist government would tacitly admit that it did not possess effective authority over all of China's territory. By the same token, it would also underscore Taiwan's separateness from the mainland. As has been seen, Dulles had in mind the future possibility of a neutral, autonomous Taiwan.[68]

Not wanting to dilute its claim to represent all of China, Taipei shrank from acceptance of a scope of application formula. Nearly four months passed before it settled on phraseology which appeared to satisfy State Department requirements.[69] The department shrewdly linked agreement on an acceptable formula to the exercise of American influence to bring about a Sino-Japanese treaty before the multilateral treaty came into force.[70] After the San Francisco ceremonies came and went without any progress toward bilateral negotiations, Taipei finally succumbed to American arm-twisting. Nationalist officials were apparently fearful that without American sponsorship a bilateral treaty might elude them. They insisted that only prodding from Washington could overcome Japan's own inclination, because of British influence and the lure of trade with the mainland, to postpone such a treaty indefinitely.[71]

In late October and early November several vague and contradictory statements by Yoshida prior to the Japanese Diet's ratification of the peace settlement intensified Nationalist anxiety about his government's intentions.[72] The prime minister's equivocation also caused nervousness in Washington because the Senate was scheduled to consider the treaty early in the new year. A disturbed Dulles admitted to Koo that perhaps the premier had experienced a change of mind about a bilateral treaty with Taipei.[73] In December the American diplomat traveled to Tokyo to extract from Yoshida a written assurance that Japan would sign a bilateral accord with the Nationalists. Impressing on him that the Japanese peace treaty would not clear the final hurdle in the Senate if Japan's China policy diverged from that of the United States, Dulles obtained the prime minister's agreement to send him a ghosted letter (written mostly by Dulles himself) for publication before or during the debate in the upper chamber.[74]

In its final form, the famed Yoshida letter stated that Japan was ready to enter into a treaty normalizing relations with Nationalist China "in conformity with the principles set out in the multilateral Treaty of Peace." The terms of this bilateral treaty would be "applicable to all territories which are now, or which may hereafter be, under the control of the National Government of the Republic of China."[75] This particular provision constituted a delicately balanced scope of application formula; it required Japan to recognize Taipei's authority only over the limited territory actually in its possession while leaving the future extent of that control open-ended so as to accommodate Taipei's insistence that it would one day regain the mainland.

As a political stratagem, the Yoshida letter was a masterstroke. It committed Japan to normalize relations with the Nationalist government but did not foreclose trade and other ties with the mainland; it all but extended a formal invitation to Taipei to enter into a bilateral treaty, allowing the Nationalists to save face by not appearing to be supplicants in seeking negotiations with their defeated enemy; and it provided the needed guarantees to expedite unencumbered ratification of the Japanese peace treaty. A likely additional benefit in Dulles's eyes was that the scope of application provision was legally consistent with a future two-China solution for Taiwan.

Dulles could scarcely have failed to grasp that the British would construe the letter as a violation of at least the spirit if not the actual terms of the Dulles-Morrison agreement, which precluded any decision by Japan about a separate peace with either China until after the formal restoration of its sovereignty. While in Tokyo, Dulles read to Sir Maberly E. Dening, the head of the British mission, a memorandum presented earlier to Yoshida that in effect urged Japan to negotiate a limited treaty with Nationalist China. Because such a treaty did not prejudice Japan's future relations with mainland China, Dulles professed that it would not contravene his agreement with Morrison. The skeptical British ambassador thought otherwise. Anthony Eden, Morrison's successor in the new Conservative government of Winston Churchill, quickly confirmed Dening's assessment and so informed the State Department.[76] Whereas Dulles saw a loophole in the agreement permitting a limited bilateral treaty circumscribed by a scope of application formula, British officials were unmistakably of a different opinion.

Conferring with Koo back in Washington, Dulles's dwindling patience with London was manifest. Without divulging the existence of the Yoshida letter to the ambassador, he expressed confidence that Japan intended to sign a bilateral treaty with Taipei. If British resistance persisted, he declared, "then the United States should, and he believed would, disregard the British opposition."[77]

The arrival of Churchill and Eden in Washington on 5 January 1952 for a round of talks presented an occasion to address Japan's relations with the KMT government and other aspects of China policy. The return to power of the Conservatives brought no departure from the Labour government's basic approach in East Asia but did result in a more cooperative spirit in coping with Washington's harsh China policy. Although Eden was more reserved toward the United States than the septuagenarian Churchill, whose ardent solicitude for the Anglo-American "special relationship" was well known, both leaders attached too much importance to friendship with their transatlantic ally to jeopardize it because of China.[78]

In recalling the Truman-Churchill talks, Acheson later noted that the two sides came closer together on all East Asian issues save one — Japan's relations with a divided China.[79] Gratefully acknowledging the burden of leadership the United States carried in the Far East, the prime minister pledged that Britain would do its utmost to follow and assist. He characterized his own nation's relations with China as "essentially a fiction" because the latter had declined to establish diplomatic relations, and he waxed enthusiastic about the American guardianship of Taiwan, asserting that it would be "shameful" to leave the island's population to the "tender mercy of the Communists." He and Eden agreed with Acheson that the emergence of "Titoism" in China was too remote a prospect on which to base current policy.[80] In a speech before Congress, Churchill gave prominence to common aims in the Far East, backing Washington's policy in Korea and Southeast Asia and applauding its protection of Taiwan.[81]

The issue of Japan's relations with the two Chinas was left to Acheson, Dulles, and Eden. Without specifically discussing the text of the Yoshida letter, Dulles mentioned a "direct communication" he had received from the Japanese prime minister, stating his nation's intentions toward a treaty with Nationalist China, that would be made public during the Senate's consideration of the multilateral treaty. Despite this intriguing revelation, Eden did not press for additional specifics.[82]

Released to the public on 16 January, the Yoshida letter removed the last potential obstacle to the ratification of the Japanese treaty. But it stimulated subdued resentment against the United States in Japan for forcing Yoshida to bend to a pro-KMT policy and raised a political tempest in Britain. Morrison charged a violation of the spirit of his agreement with Dulles, and although

Eden's public comments were more circumspect, he too was personally convinced that the American diplomat had not played fairly. The affair left a residue of distrust of Dulles in the Foreign Office.[83]

Nationalist foreign minister George Yeh officially learned of the letter on the day of its publication. After clarifying several points with the State Department, he promptly indicated his government's readiness to commence negotiations with Japan for early conclusion of a peace treaty.[84] The talks between Nationalist China and Japan, which began in Taipei on 17 February, made only halting progress; at times the Japanese delegation appeared to be deliberately stalling. The Senate's ratification of the multilateral treaty on 20 March removed an incentive for Japanese flexibility.[85] The American mission in Tokyo reported that little sentiment existed in the country for a treaty with the Nationalist government and that Yoshida had to proceed gingerly.[86] In fact, the prime minister may have wanted to conclude a treaty that merely normalized economic and trade relations with Taiwan rather than a full-fledged peace accord.[87]

The negotiators finally reached agreement on a bilateral peace pact after nearly ten weeks of hard bargaining and some timely prompting by Washington. One of the last issues they settled was the phrasing of the scope of application formula, which they agreed would follow the language of the Yoshida letter. The signing of the treaty took place on 28 April, just seven-and-a-half hours before Japan officially became a sovereign nation.[88] The Nationalists hastily pushed forward the preparations for the signing ceremony so as to ensure the two parties affixed their signatures before Japan regained its formal independence. For the Nationalist leadership, the treaty was less than an unalloyed victory. A common assessment among informed opinion on Taiwan, according to the British consul on the island, was that it was the "best obtainable in the existing situation."[89]

The separate peace between Taipei and Tokyo was a measure of how strong yet limited the American commitment to Nationalist China was in the international arena. Despite maintaining that the Republic of China remained the legitimate government of China, Dulles and the State Department were unprepared to throw a spanner into the negotiation of the critical Japanese peace settlement by insisting on the ROC's right to participate. The morale and prestige of the Nationalist government were secondary, in this instance, to the restoration of an independent Japan incorporated within the American security system. So as to avoid a contretemps with other signatories and retain freedom of action for both the present and the future, Dulles and his colleagues also disappointed the Nationalists by excluding a provision in the settlement formally ceding Taiwan to them. Once the Japanese peace treaty was in hand, Dulles made a separate peace between Japan and Nationalist China a priority. Such a bilateral instrument, besides being necessary to prevent the China issue from impeding the ratification of the multilateral treaty, would soothe Taipei's hurt feelings and boost its prestige as well as hobble Japan's pursuit of an independent China policy. To obtain this peace pact before the multilateral treaty came into force, Dulles pressured and manipulated both Tokyo and London, not permitting either to stand in Washington's way. He and the State Department squeezed the Nationalists, who relied on Washington's sponsorship of the bilateral treaty they desired, into accepting the necessity of a scope of application formula acknowledging China's divided sovereignty. In the final analysis, it was Washington's preferred vision of Sino-Japanese relations which prevailed, not that of Tokyo, London, or Taipei.

By the early spring of 1952 the contours of the U.S. commitment to Taiwan were more sharply defined at home and abroad than a year earlier. At home, the Truman administration had articulated major elements of that commitment during the MacArthur crisis and had achieved a broad measure of popular and political agreement on at least the minimum requirements of American policy toward Taiwan while parrying MacArthurite recommendations for an expanded war involving Nationalist troops. The administration's public statements, while necessarily omitting top-secret elements contained in NSC 48/5, did narrow the previous gap between operational and declaratory policy. Abroad, the administration had shored up the international position of the Nationalist government by devising the moratorium procedure with Britain to keep the representation issue dormant in the UN and by ensuring that Japan made peace with the Nationalists after the latter's unavoidable exclusion from the multilateral treaty. At the same time, however, it kept a free hand regarding Taiwan's status by means of the provision in the multilateral treaty that ceded the island to neither of the two Chinas and, more indirectly, through the scope of application formula contained in the peace accord between Tokyo and Taipei. In defining its commitment domestically and internationally, the administration had carefully set boundaries on it.

As a consequence of its expanded commitment to Taiwan following the Chinese intervention in Korea, the United States entered into a less strained and more supportive association with the Nationalist government than the previous arm's-length relationship. Though by no means free from disagreement and stress (as evidenced during the negotiation of the Japanese peace treaty and the Japan-ROC treaty), this new association did bring Washington and Taipei appreciably closer together by the end of the Truman administration.

The Changing Face of Taiwan

The arrival in Taiwan in early May 1951 of the first personnel from the U.S. Military Advisory Assistance Group released a surge of hope on the island not seen since the intervention of the Seventh Fleet nearly a year earlier. Viewed as a harbinger of generous military aid, the MAAG was also a welcome emblem of a more helpful and reliable connection with Washington.[1] At the same time, a watchful wariness tinged the reactions of Nationalist officials to an enlarged American presence on the island. An undercurrent of mistrust, even outright anti-Americanism, was reportedly present at the senior levels of the government and armed forces.[2]

It fell primarily to the American mission on the island to build mutual confidence and to ensure that the Nationalists put U.S. aid to efficient and constructive use in support of Washington's objectives. The head of the mission, the pro-Nationalist Karl Rankin, preferred the velvet glove to the iron fist in performing this assignment. After his posting to Taiwan to replace the more critical Robert Strong, the chargé d'affaires worked hard to dispel the cloud of controversy that had darkened the embassy before his arrival. Under his direction, the prestige and authority of the mission climbed among Nationalist leaders. Though Washington declined to elevate him to the rank of ambassador, which he craved, his opinion carried weight in the corridors of power in the State Department and on Capitol Hill.[3] He ably hosted a procession of American dignitaries, politicians, journalists, and government officials, who descended on the island after the spring of 1951.[4] Rankin was confident that American aid and advice, paired with Nationalist cooperation and self-help, could transform Taiwan economically, militarily, and politically. He predicted to Dean Rusk in November 1951 that over a span of four to six years the island could become economically self-supporting, a military asset, and a "rallying point for freedom-loving Chinese everywhere."[5] On a visit to Washington that fall, he presented a moderately upbeat progress report to Truman. The president, after remarking that he had not previously heard so optimistic a view, grumbled that he had never forgiven Chiang for failing to defeat the Communists when he still had the upper hand on the mainland. Had the Generalissimo, he asked, gotten rid of the incompetent and corrupt elements in his administration? Rankin assured him that corruption was no longer a serious problem and that the government's conduct had improved markedly.[6]

By the conclusion of his term of office, Truman had less reason to express surprise at a positive assessment of the situation on Taiwan. By then, he and other decision makers, heartened by reports of tangible progress on the island, had fashioned a more favorable impression of the capabilities of Chiang's Nationalists. Compared to its condition at the time of the U.S. interposition in June 1950, Taiwan appeared in better shape, both economically and militarily. Although forward movement toward political liberalization was negligible, the jobbery and maladministration for which the Kuomintang had been notorious was much less in evidence.

Progress was greatest in economic matters. Before the Second World War, the Taiwanese had enjoyed the highest standard of living in East Asia, outside Japan. During the war and immediate postwar years, the island had experienced a precipitous economic decline. The process of reconstruction and recovery was not far advanced at the time of the U.S. intervention. An alarming gap in Taiwan's international balance of payments had nearly consumed foreign exchange reserves. Inflation was rampant, and the currency was in danger of collapse.[7] One of the few positive economic developments at this time was a land reform program begun in 1949 in cooperation with the Joint Commission on Rural Reconstruction, a body of Chinese and American rural experts established under the China Aid Act of 1948. Over a five year period this program significantly reduced farm tenancy.[8]

As has been seen, Washington did not authorize a big boost in economic aid for Taiwan until after the Chinese intervention in Korea. As plans for large-scale economic assistance jelled in the first half of 1951, officials in the State Department and Economic Cooperation Administration (ECA) drew up guidelines to promote American objectives without saddling Washington with unwanted responsibilities and costs; these officials were determined not to give the Nationalists either free rein or a blank check. The principal goal of the aid program was to foster financial stability and a productive, balanced economic system. American dollars were definitely not to provide a "short term springboard" for a return to the mainland. The Nationalists would have to understand that "maximum self-help" would be required and that Washington would not foot the bill for the "reckless diversion" of Taiwan's own resources to unjustified military spending.[9]

In conjunction with the Defense Department, the State Department and ECA prepared an aide-mémoire presented to the Nationalist government in mid-July 1951 that clearly conveyed the message of self-help and fiscal restraint. The aide-mémoire requested that Taipei devise for Washington's consideration an effective procedure to supervise and control budgeting and spending by all levels of government for military and civilian purposes. The request stopped just short of actually making economic and military assistance conditional on such an agreed procedure.[10] Washington's intrusiveness upset Chiang, divided his cabinet, and angered the military establishment, which was unaccustomed to budget strictures or civilian oversight and oriented its own planning toward an eventual counterattack against the mainland.[11] In the final analysis, however, the Nationalist government had no choice but to satisfy the requirements spelled out in the aide-mémoire.[12]

By the end of 1952 the economic picture had noticeably brightened. Prices had generally stabilized, government budgets were approximately in line with revenues, and production in most areas reached the highest levels since the war. Less burdened with short-term problems, the Nationalist government drafted a four-year plan for a self-sustaining economy, which American observers in Taipei and Washington took as an encouraging sign that it sincerely intended to plan and work toward an eventual cessation of economic aid.[13]

In military as well as economic matters, there was visible improvement. The Nationalist armed forces benefited from U.S. military aid and from advice and instruction supplied by the MAAG under its chief, Maj. Gen. William C. Chase. The size of the MAAG, which stood at about 250 just after its arrival, mushroomed to 744 by the end of 1952.[14] Chase, a career army officer, was a self-acknowledged "MacArthur man," who had participated in the liberation of the Philippines and after the war had commanded the First Cavalry Division in Japan. MacArthur had, before his dismissal, personally tapped him to head the MAAG sent to Taiwan.[15]

When he first set foot on the island, Chase found a depressing military situation. The navy and air force were small, run-down, and operating with old vessels and planes. The marine corps was ill equipped and possessed few landing craft. The army was "understrength, underequipped, poorly trained, and overofficered." Many soldiers had little more than "grass sandals, palm leaf hats, very brief shorts, and old [World War I] Springfield rifles."[16]

The principal task facing Chase and his team was to reorganize, reequip, and train the armed forces so that they could effectively assist in the defense of Taiwan. Chase, however, interpreted this mission in "dynamic terms" to include possible "counterlandings" on the mainland in the event of a Chinese attack.[17] The entire Nationalist military establishment numbered over 600,000 men, but not all of it received direct U.S. aid. One of the MAAG's main objectives was the creation of a streamlined army of twenty-one divisions totalling somewhat over 240,000 troops.[18] The MAAG also made military modernization on the American model a priority, establishing military training schools, starting a National War College, and introducing American-style strategic concepts, tactics, and instruction methods throughout the armed forces.[19]

This impulse toward reorganization and reform sometimes encountered stiff resistance from the Nationalist leadership. A case in point was the system of political commissars. Based on Soviet practice, this setup placed a political officer beside every combat officer at nearly all levels of military command. The commissars, who engaged in political training and acted as watchdogs and informers, engendered fears, suspicions, and timidity within the armed forces.[20] Amounting to a parallel system of command, they were under the authority of the Political Department of the Ministry of National Defense headed by Chiang Ching-kuo, the Generalissimo's eldest son and widely regarded as his heir apparent. A powerful figure with an intimidating reputation, Chiang Ching-kuo directed not just the political commissars but most of the secret police. Chase privately deplored his anti-Americanism and sinister authoritarianism, and he considered the commissar system "vicious." Yet his strong objections to the worst features of the system produced only minor concessions.[21]

In trying to fulfill his mission, Chase also ran into problems with Washington. His biggest complaint, which Rankin echoed, was that the pace at which military supplies and equipment arrived in Taiwan was too slow. This naturally piqued the Nationalists as well, especially because the actual flow of material fell well short of the dollar amounts authorized by Congress. Of approximately $300 million in military aid legislated by Congress for FY 1951 and 1952, only a scant $25 million had reached the island by February 1952.[22] Even though the pace of deliveries did speed up in the latter months of 1952, 70 percent of the programmed material for FY 1951 and 1952 had still not arrived by December.[23]

In his memoirs, Chase ascribed the sluggish flow of deliveries to the Truman administration's animus toward Chiang Kai-shek.[24] There is no evidence in the documentary record to support such a conclusion. Neither was Washington cleverly using the carrot of military assistance to hasten desired changes in the island's civilian and military administration. The truth was that Taiwan was in less urgent need of supplies and equipment than other areas such as Korea, Indochina, and Western Europe. Because of its lower position in the pecking order for deliveries and the heavy demand elsewhere for scarce supplies and equipment, Taiwan had to wait longer for what it needed. The island was not in any immediate danger, and its ultimate safety depended on U.S. naval and air power, not on the Nationalist armed forces, whose defensive role was considered secondary and supplementary.[25]

Despite shortages of material, the efficiency of the armed forces improved steadily as did their morale.[26] Along with the upturn in the economy, the headway made in military preparedness provided reassuring confirmation in Washington that the new relationship with the Nationalists was paying dividends.

Washington was considerably less energetic in pushing for political reform than for economic or military improvement. The policy paper NSC 48/5 stipulated that the U.S. should "encourage political changes in the Nationalist regime which would increase its prestige and influence" in China.[27] But American officials refrained from conspicuous or heavy-handed interference in Taiwan's internal affairs, which would arouse ill-feeling and opposition, complicate the achievement of more immediate and salient goals, and give the impression abroad that Taiwan was little more than an American colony.[28] As will be seen, some high officials in the CIA and the State Department were drawn to the notion of wholesale political reform during the winter of 1951–52; however, the idea did not develop beyond the talking stage. Policymakers never took firm, concerted action in support of political liberalization, preferring to nudge rather than shove the Nationalists in this direction, as was often the American practice in relations with friendly authoritarian governments.

Karl Rankin was definitely not keen on arm-twisting as a method to liberalize Chiang Kai-shek's regime, believing that the Nationalists were slowly relaxing their authoritarianism on their own initiative. He scoffed at the view that Chiang was a "ruthless dictator, surrounded by a coterie of corrupt generals and politicians, with no notion of good government and whose sole ambition is to ride back to power on the Mainland on the wave of a third world war fought largely by Americans." The pliable chargé d'affaires did concede that the Generalissimo and his cohorts needed occasional reminders that a demonstration of democracy on Taiwan was important if they were to regain the mainland; yet it would not do for Washington to overlook the island's special internal security requirements or to press for democracy at the expense of more crucial objectives.[29]

Despite gestures toward democracy and the rule of law, Taiwan was demonstrably a one-party police state run by the Kuomintang and dominated by Chiang Kai-shek and his entourage. Although the KMT included Western-educated progressives, who were unhappy with the Generalissimo's military-police establishment, authoritarian elements held sway. This was manifested during local elections for mayors and magistrates held in 1950–51. The KMT's meddling and manipulation in these elections increased after its candidates made a poor showing in initial ballotings, which were relatively free.[30] Regardless of its political complexion, informed observers no longer scorned the Nationalist government as moribund and decrepit. Nationalist officeholders seemed determined to profit from the mistakes made on the mainland and to shed the government's poor reputation and odor of failure.[31] In October 1952 John M. Allison became the first upper-level State Department official to visit Taiwan since before the Korean War; a career Foreign Service officer and Japanese specialist, Allison had at the beginning of the year replaced Dean Rusk (who left the State Department to become president of the Rockefeller Foundation) as head of the Bureau of Far Eastern Affairs. He found that the Nationalist regime, while not entirely free of its old faults, had made considerable gains in some areas.[32]

The changing face of Taiwan did not go unnoticed among policymakers in Washington. By May 1952 Ambassador Koo, an attentive observer of the official mood, had already detected a far more sympathetic and congenial attitude among top decision makers than two years earlier.[33] That fall, during courtesy visits by Foreign Minister Yeh to the White House and State Department, both Truman and Acheson commented on the promising reports they had gotten from Taiwan. The secretary approvingly noted that American press opinion had become more favorable, in some cases even laudatory.[34]

The upbeat news from Taiwan did give American leaders justifiable cause for satisfaction. Economically and militarily, the island was undeniably in better condition. Even if Chiang's authoritarian rule remained fundamentally unaltered, the KMT had begun to exhibit a capacity for honest and competent administration, and it was showing signs of putting American aid and advice to productive use. A corollary of these developments was a closer relationship between Washington and Taipei.

Sanctuary, Springboard, or Strategic Asset?

The progress that earned the plaudits of Truman and Acheson occurred while Taiwan remained safely behind a shield of American military might. The policy of neutralization, whose declared purpose was to insulate the Taiwan Strait from a conflict of arms between the Nationalists and their mainland foes, continued as the official basis for the mission of the Seventh Fleet. Immersed in the war in Korea, the Chinese showed no interest in seizing Taiwan. Washington still applied the neutralization policy asymmetrically to the advantage of the Nationalists but continued to abstain from any commitment to defend the KMT-controlled offshore islands. For the first time, however, decision makers actively encouraged and assisted the Nationalists to retain these coastal possessions. Despite the desire of the Nationalists to use their protected sanctuary on Taiwan as a springboard for a return to the mainland with American help, decision makers did not sanction the KMT's strategy of counterattack. Between the fall of 1951 and the end of 1952, ranking officials in Washington did nonetheless debate various offensive roles for Nationalist troops outside Taiwan, including military action on the mainland. Furthermore, in spite of differences among them over the actual deployment of these troops, a broad agreement solidified that Chiang's armed forces constituted a potential strategic asset in the high-stakes contest with the Chinese, which then raged from Korea to Southeast Asia.

Discussions about an offensive military role for the Nationalists took place in the absence of any danger to Taiwan itself. Intelligence analysts held that the Chinese, already heavily engaged on the battlefield in Korea, would not hazard an all-out attack that they and their Soviet mentors recognized would almost certainly fail. Except for a buildup of airpower, China's capability to launch an invasion or even a limited surprise attack did not improve substantially from April of 1951 to the spring of the following year. Chinese military preparations and propaganda gave no indication of planning for an early strike.[35] This being the case, the navy maintained only a sea patrol and air surveillance in the strait.[36]

In late July 1952 a two-carrier task force did conduct a sweep along the China coast. A spokesman for Adm. Arthur Radford, commander of the Pacific Fleet, announced that the purpose of the maneuver, during which about 100 U.S. planes flew "just outside" the three-mile limit, was "to give the Communists something to think about."[37] While this show of force did remind the Chinese of what awaited them if they attempted to breach the strait, it was carried out primarily with the diplomatic and military standoff in Korea in mind. With the truce talks at Panmunjom at a deadlock and the fighting at a stalemate, Washington looked for new ways to exert military pressure on the enemy.[38]

In giving the "Communists something to think about," the naval sweep reflected the combativeness toward China that informed the views of Admiral Radford, who in March assumed responsibility for the Taiwan-Philippine area from Gen. Matthew Ridgway, the Far Eastern commander. Radford acquired direct command of the Seventh Fleet in the waters around Taiwan as well as of Taiwan MAAG, whose chief now reported to Washington through him.[39] Not one to shrink from a decisive confrontation with the Chinese, Radford had found merit in some of MacArthur's proposals for an expanded war. Staunchly pro-Nationalist, he esteemed Chiang Kai-shek as "one of the great men of our times," and he personally believed that the United States should aid him in his quest to recapture the mainland. Even if restricted to Taiwan, he believed that Chiang's forces performed a valuable function by pinning down large numbers of Communist troops along the China coast that might otherwise be diverted to Korea or elsewhere.[40]

Despite the ostensibly evenhanded character of the neutralization policy, the United States in practice continued to wink at or connive in KMT harassing activities. The Nationalists carried out raids along the China coast and in other ways participated in the covert war against the mainland. With Washington's tacit approval, they conducted "visit and search" operations against foreign-flag merchant vessels, most of them British, destined for Communist ports, sometimes seizing cargoes and ships. It was believed that the Communists owned and operated most of the intercepted ships, despite their foreign registry. In their impact on China's total seaborne trade, these Nationalist naval actions were no more than a nuisance, while at the same time they intensified Sino-American animosity and aggravated Anglo-American relations.[41]

Since its inception, the neutralization policy had excluded the KMT-held islands off the China coast. Ruling out any assistance by U.S. forces, Washington had essentially left it to the Nationalists to defend them if they so wished. The only stricture imposed on the Nationalists was that the islands not serve as points of departure for offensive operations by combat troops garrisoned on Taiwan (many of them being trained and equipped by the United States). The CIA had, however, helped to develop the islands as guerrilla and intelligence gathering bases.[42]

In April 1952 the question of American policy toward the offshore islands arose unexpectedly when Rankin cabled Washington that Gen. Chou Chih-jou Chow, chief of the Nationalist General Staff, believed that these outposts were in greater jeopardy than at any time since mid-1950. Without proposing a reversal of current policy, Rankin stressed the value of the islands for the defense of Taiwan, for the interdiction of seaborne commerce, and for intelligence collection and the support of mainland resistance. Their capture would, he contended, represent another advance for the Communists and would damage the psychological and practical interests of both the Nationalists and the United States.[43] The chargé's message anticipated similar assessments during the later crisis over the islands in 1954–55.

Washington's reply to this cable contained a reformulated policy toward the offshore islands that the State Department and Pentagon had agreed upon. While reiterating past guidelines, including the injunction against the use of American forces to defend the islands, the message included the first positive indication that Washington wanted the Nationalists to fight for these outlying positions. The communication authorized MAAG to offer encouragement and advice to the Nationalists with this objective in mind and to permit them to divert limited quantities of U.S. military material to the protection of the islands. Rankin conveyed this information to Chiang in strict confidence.[44]

The reformulated policy marked the beginning of a shift toward a quasi commitment to the KMT forward bases. Without departing from the no-defense policy (whose existence remained concealed), the United States now took a direct interest and part in keeping them in the possession of the Nationalists, thereby assuming a stake in their retention and a measure of responsibility for their safety. The quasi commitment, which evolved from this initial step, would make it much more difficult for Washington to remain indifferent to their occupation by the Chinese Communists, as decision makers would discover during the 1954–55 crisis.

For Chiang and his followers, the offshore islands were their nearest remaining territorial links to the mainland to which they yearned to return in triumph. The swift recovery by force of arms of the lost Nationalist domain on the continent was the unceasing refrain of the Generalissimo and his inner circle. Keeping this goal alive was necessary, they believed, to sustain the morale of the civilian and military refugees who had joined them in exile. Yet the reconquest of the mainland was no mere propaganda ploy. Chiang missed few opportunities to sell the idea to his American visitors.[45] Assuring them that a counteroffensive would neither require American combat troops nor precipitate Soviet intervention, he claimed that the coastal provinces of Fukien, Kwangtung, and Chekiang were militarily vulnerable and that their inhabitants would overwhelmingly welcome the restoration of his government.[46] For all their bravado, Chiang and others in the Nationalist hierarchy did not deceive themselves that their forces were presently capable of a counteroffensive or could, even when better prepared, undertake a successful landing on the continent without U.S. air, naval, and logistical assistance. They pinned their hopes for such assistance on the outbreak of a general war or the adoption by Washington of a more bellicose policy toward Peking as a result of new Chinese aggression or a collapse of the Korean truce negotiations.[47]

Given such hopes, Chiang's remedies for the Korean stalemate were predictable. Dismissing the truce talks as a Communist tactical device, he predicted their inevitable failure. Favoring an expanded war, he advocated a naval blockade of China, the bombing of targets in Manchuria and possibly south and central China, and an American-assisted deployment of Nationalist troops on the mainland.[48] The Generalissimo lacked any direct leverage over U.S. policy in Korea, however.[49]

Though the Truman administration declined to endorse Chiang's scheme for mainland recovery or to deviate from its limited war strategy in Korea, planners and decision makers did privately canvass methods to tighten the military vise on Peking, some of them involving Nationalist troops.[50] The competition with China (and its Soviet patron) throughout the Far Pacific preyed on the minds of officials, stimulating a consideration of more muscular approaches. Besides Korea, the theater of conflict that most exercised the administration was Southeast Asia, a vital region imperiled by communist-led insurrections behind which appeared to loom the menacing specter of China. In Indochina, the United States had formed an uneasy partnership with a beleaguered France in its conflict with Ho Chi Minh's Vietminh. Administration officials regarded this war as critical as the one in Korea and found it just as frustratingly intractable. The possibility of an open Chinese invasion in Indochina or in neighboring countries excited fears in Washington and was a topic of discussion with Paris, London, and other concerned capitals.[51]

Domestically, the military and diplomatic gridlock in Korea magnified the war's unpopularity together with dissatisfaction with the administration's limited war strategy. Public opinion surveys in the spring and summer of 1952 showed majority sentiment to end the conflict through more military coercion.[52] Expecting to parlay dissatisfaction with a "no win" policy into votes in the November presidential election, representatives of the Taft wing of the GOP continued to champion a MacArthur-style military victory. Early in the year Senator Taft himself, pursuing the Republican nomination, whipped up a flurry of controversy when he reportedly backed a Nationalist invasion of the mainland.[53] The neutralization policy predictably drew the fire of Republicans who were attracted to a more venturesome war strategy. With characteristic recklessness, Joseph McCarthy vilified Truman's decision to use the Seventh Fleet to protect the mainland from a Nationalist invasion as "one of the most treasonable orders in history." [54] Chosen over Taft as the Republican standard-bearer, Gen. Dwight D. Eisenhower did not take up his defeated rival's cry for an expanded war, but during his fall campaign, he did astutely capitalize on the country's war weariness and desire for an early resolution, while remaining vague about his own future action, other than to pledge that he would go to Korea if elected. [55]

In this worrisome international and domestic setting, American officials considered whether and how to use the military resources on Taiwan other than for defense of the island. Chiang's army, despite its inadequacies, was one of the largest anticommunist assemblages in Asia, and it constituted a potentially valuable reserve of manpower. Ever since the Chinese intervention in Korea, the JCS had kept open the option of an offensive role for Nationalist troops. In a November 1951 memorandum opining that "neutralization" was no longer a suitable description of U.S. policy toward Taiwan, the chiefs asserted the necessity not just to maintain the island in pro-American hands but to develop the capability of the Nationalist armed forces for use in the event of an expanded war in the Far East. [56]

The Central Intelligence Agency pushed even more vigorously for an offensive mission for Nationalist forces. On 11 December 1951 CIA director Walter Bedell Smith wrote to Secretary of Defense Robert Lovett (who had replaced George Marshall in September) suggesting the covert and overt use of Nationalist military units outside Taiwan. Although this letter is classified, it is possible to reconstruct its essential content from other sources. Observing that Chiang's forces represented a "waning asset" that would have to be built up and utilized "within the immediate future, if we are to get any benefit from them," Bedell Smith suggested the rotation of Nationalist units to Korea and their use in "temporary thrusts onto the mainland." He also proposed the training and equipping of units for offensive operations, the expansion of Taiwan-based covert programs, and support for the eventual return of the Nationalists to the mainland. This last step would be feasible only if Chiang's regime carried out a thoroughgoing political housecleaning to demonstrate its fitness to govern China. [57]

In referring to Chiang's troops as a "waning asset," the CIA head was pointing to the fact that they were an aging force whose numbers would shrink as time passed. The average age of the Nationalist military, which was made up predominantly of mainlanders, was about twenty-seven. Despite a need for youthful replacements, KMT authorities were reluctant to conscript large numbers of Taiwanese whose loyalty and willingness to serve on the mainland were suspect and whose labor and skills were difficult to spare from the island's economy.[58] Without replenishment, attrition would take its relentless toll of Chiang's forces as they grew older.

Some upper-level figures in the State Department saw advantages in involving the Nationalists in a more aggressive strategy toward China. Among them was John Foster Dulles, who predicted to Koo in late December 1951 that the long-term survival of Nationalist China was at risk without help from the United States to extend its authority beyond Taiwan. "If she [Nationalist China] was confined to Formosa," Dulles explained, "both her manpower and her resources would diminish as time went on. The half million troops there would become old and the whole Government would rot and die." Not only that, but Japan needed a well-disposed government on the mainland with which to continue its traditional trading relationship. The United States therefore had to pursue a "positive policy vis-à-vis Communist China and help to bring about a situation whereby the Peiping regime could be replaced by a friendly Government through reestablishment of Nationalist China on the mainland." Lamenting that the administration's present defensive policy, useful as a short-term expedient, left the initiative to the enemy in the long run, Dulles concluded that a tougher approach was required. He told Koo that he had prepared a memorandum for Truman advocating just such a course and that he was conferring that same day with representatives from the Pentagon, the CIA, and the NSC to convince them of its soundness.[59]

Whether Dulles actually wrote such a memorandum or participated in such a conference the available record does not reveal. His espousal of an aggressive policy toward China was not new, however. In the emotional heat of the Chinese intervention a year earlier, he had similarly recommended a more combative line, including the use of Taiwan as a covert and possibly open base for hostile activities by the Nationalists against the mainland.[60] Alongside a protective and separatist strain in Dulles's attitude toward Taiwan, which inclined him to inoculate the island from a Communist takeover and to make provision for some form of two-China arrangement, there existed a militant strain that disposed him to treat the island as an offensive platform from which the Nationalists could distract, harass, and undermine the Communist regime. In his remarks to Koo, one can likewise detect an underlying dissatisfaction with the administration's overly defensive and reactive anticommunist policies that was then also rife in the Republican right wing. After leaving the State Department in early 1952, Dulles got back into the swing of GOP politics and openly reproached the administration in this vein.[61]

The memoirs of John Allison confirm that in the early months of 1952 various civilian and military elements were weighing the use of Nationalist troops on the mainland. Allison succeeded Rusk in January and was in close contact with Dulles, whom he had assisted with the Japanese peace treaty. On 3 January 1952, less than a week after Dulles's meeting with Koo, Allison submitted a lengthy memorandum to Acheson commenting on some proposals then under consideration, including one (presumably Bedell Smith's) that recommended that the United States adopt a more aggressive approach to the use of KMT forces and guerrillas on the mainland if the Nationalist government politically reformed itself. Approving this tack, Allison stressed the benefits for Japan of having an amicable mainland government with which it could associate politically and economically, as well as the need to keep the Chinese Communists occupied within their own borders so as to distract them from Southeast Asia. He speculated that the British might even take a more kindly view of a U.S. policy toward China that foresaw the eventual recovery of the mainland by a genuinely rehabilitated Nationalist government. To expedite reform, he contemplated the possibility of convincing Chiang, when the time was right, to relinquish control to younger and more liberal elements.[62]

A day later, meeting privately with Congressman Walter Judd to sound him out about this new approach, Allison declared that the United States had to end its "policy of indecision" toward Communist China and steer a more positive course. If it was assumed that the Communist regime was in China to stay, the United States should concentrate on detaching it from the Soviet Union; if not, it should back the Nationalists — with strict supervision, yet with a "determination to win." A viable "third force" did not exist, in his opinion. If the government should choose a new offensive strategy, it would need the support of Judd, Knowland, and other Republicans in Congress to assure a truly bipartisan policy. Not unexpectedly, the assistant secretary's candid overture struck a responsive chord in the Minnesota lawmaker.[63]

It must have seemed to Allison that the new course he had sketched held the promise of placating the China bloc and of placing the State Department's entire East Asian policy on a more secure political footing. The department was under siege from Republican detractors for its failed Asian ventures and for having harbored officials who were "soft" on communism or disloyal. By early 1952 anticommunist crusaders had already claimed as victims a number of individuals identified with past China policy, and they were in pursuit of others.[64] Allison's remarkable proposition to Judd was revealing of the pressure felt within the department from the Republican right and of an emphatic pro-Nationalist orientation now present among some key officials at Foggy Bottom.

In a memorandum on 4 March 1952, the JCS appeared to line up, at least part way, with Bedell Smith's recommendations. Leery of a major expansion of covert operations involving Taiwan, the chiefs opposed the recruitment and training of Nationalist troops for such purposes. They found merit, however, in their use for overt offensive operations, and they proposed that two divisions receive training and equipment for such missions, if funding and other commitments allowed. Cautioning against pressing too hard for reforms in the administration of the island, they did second the desirability of programs enabling the Nationalists to contribute to containment in Asia and "thus to lead to the possible eventual liberation of Communist China by the Chinese people under Chinese Nationalist leadership supported by other free nations of the world." They were in full accord that Taiwan had to be "strengthened as an anti-Communist base militarily, economically, politically, and psychologically."

Underscoring the military-strategic value of the island, the JCS maintained that a noncommunist Taiwan was "of major importance to United States security interests, and is of vital importance to the long-term United States position in the Far East." Taking this assessment as their premise, they laid out five essential guidelines for policy toward Taiwan: first, deny the island to any Chinese government aligned with or dominated by the USSR; second, take unilateral action, if required, to guarantee that the island remained available as a base for U.S. military operations; third, continue the mission of the Seventh Fleet "relative to the protection of Formosa" until the Nationalists could defend themselves; fourth, support a pro-American regime on the island; fifth, develop the Nationalist government's "military potential."[65]

Later that month, the Pentagon called upon the National Security Council to undertake a top-level review of the policy toward Taiwan formalized in NSC 48/5.[66] On 2 April, when the NSC convened to discuss the five JCS guidelines (designated as NSC 128), it was evident that the State Department frowned on a departure from existing policy. Questioning the purpose of NSC 128, Acheson asked whether the guidelines were intended to confirm or to alter the "clear and affirmative" policy in NSC 48/5. Several of the guidelines, he observed, raised difficulties that would require careful study.[67]

Afterward, the National Security Council shunted NSC 128 to a committee of representatives from the State and Defense Departments and the CIA. When these officials gathered on 9 April 1951, the JCS interpreted NSC 128 in a way that averted a showdown with the State Department. The chiefs acknowledged that their guidelines were compatible with existing policy, except for the third, which redefined the mission of the Seventh Fleet to permit Nationalist strikes against the mainland. Even this particular guideline, they explained, did not propose an immediate change in policy but merely consideration of such a step as a future option. In short, rather than discard the neutralization policy, the chiefs were content to have a question mark placed next to it for now. This recommendation proved acceptable to the State Department. The result was a rewording of the third guideline so that it preserved neutralization but with the proviso that the Seventh Fleet's current mission remain "under continuous review in the light of the world situation and the situation in the Far East." This proviso foreshadowed the deneutralization of Taiwan at the outset of the Eisenhower administration. For the remainder of the Truman administration, however, the existing mission of the Seventh Fleet to prevent attacks from both sides of the Taiwan Strait remained unchanged.[68]

The most impassioned appeal at the State-Defense-CIA meeting for a more forceful pro-Nationalist policy came from Allen Dulles, the CIA's deputy director. Describing Taiwan as a "waning asset" (as had his superior the previous December), Dulles predicted that the situation on the island would deteriorate over time if the Nationalists lost hope of regaining the mainland. Morale would suffer, defections from the armed forces might occur, and even a revolution was not inconceivable. For this reason, the CIA wanted a review of current policy so as to generate initiatives to ensure that Taiwan remained an "asset." Policy Planning Staff director Paul Nitze was opposed to any premature moves, yet he did foresee future contingencies in which the United States might want to employ Nationalist troops offensively. Both he and Allison, who was also present, referred specifically to problems in Southeast Asia.[69]

The ultimate result of this pivotal meeting on 9 April was to foreclose any significant deviation from the Taiwan policy enshrined in NSC 48/5.[70] The joint chiefs, when push came to shove, had declined to throw their weight behind the CIA's bold recommendations. The State Department's reaction to the JCS guidelines indicated a distinct lack of enthusiasm for a shift to a more aggressive China policy involving Nationalist troop landings on the mainland.

Despite the rejection of this course of action, the idea that Nationalist forces might serve a useful purpose outside of Taiwan had wide currency within the military and elsewhere within government. The NSC 48/5 policy statement already envisaged a possible offensive role for KMT troops in certain circumstances. Although the existing military assistance program for Taiwan was primarily defensive, calling for a "well-trained but austerely equipped army of 21 Divisions, a small modern air force and a navy capable of little more than coastal patrol," it did authorize furnishing enough equipment to "permit the offensive employment of at least limited numbers of these forces." The scale of military aid to Taiwan exceeded the level necessary to arm and train the Nationalists simply for defensive purposes.[71]

On 1 May 1952 the Joint Strategic Plans Committee recommended that the commander in chief, Pacific (CINCPAC), devise plans for two Nationalist offensive contingents of different sizes, a two-division force of approximately 25,000 and a ten-division force of about 150,000. The JCS subsequently directed CINCPAC to determine what operational and logistical support would be needed to assist a force of either size to perform missions in Korea, Southeast Asia, or China.[72] During this same period the National Security Council conducted a review of policy in Southeast Asia. On 25 June the president approved NSC 124/2, a blueprint for a stronger policy in that troubled region, which included recommendations for covert and overt counteractions against the Chinese if they should openly intervene there. In such a contingency, the document sanctioned the use of "anti-communist Chinese forces, including Chinese Nationalist forces, in military operations in Southeast Asia, Korea, or China proper."[73] One option contemplated in such circumstances was the Nationalist seizure of Hainan Island, but Chiang Kai-shek was uneager to commit his troops to such an enterprise, preferring a foothold on the mainland.[74]

Of the possible destinations for Nationalist forces considered in Washington during the summer and fall of 1952, Korea received the most attention. Though Chiang did not renew the offer of troops turned down by Washington in 1950, he did cagily intimate that he was still open to a deal if the United States properly equipped the units he might volunteer to send.[75] The push to transport Nationalist troops to Korea came from Gen. Mark W. Clark, who in mid-May replaced General Ridgway as head of the Far East Command. Bridling under the restraints of the limited war strategy, Clark believed that battlefield victory required a major escalation. Looking for ways to apply more military muscle against the enemy in the peninsula, he cast an eye on the reservoir of manpower on Taiwan.[76]

Barely two weeks after he assumed the Far East Command, Clark put in a request for two Nationalist divisions.[77] Viewing this request favorably, the JCS incorporated it into a formal proposal, but they made any decision to send the two divisions conditional on the consent of Chiang and the UN allies as well as on the availability of funding and equipment.[78] The proposal came before the NSC on 6 August 1952 at a time when the Korean conflict was at a diplomatic and military impasse, numerous Republicans clamored for decisive action, and the public's patience was stretched thin. Siding with the JCS, CIA director Bedell Smith assured the NSC that the removal of two divisions from Taiwan would not measurably weaken the island's defenses. Truman, unwilling to commit himself, authorized further study of the JCS recommendation and the development of a "firm plan" for his consideration.[79]

The postponement of a decision allowed opposition to build to the JCS proposal within the Pentagon and the State Department. Disagreeing with his JCS colleagues, Gen. J. Lawton Collins, the army chief of staff, preferred a fresh infusion of Korean troops over the employment of Nationalist forces. Defense Secretary Robert Lovett came to share this viewpoint.[80] State Department representatives remonstrated that the UN allies and most Asian nations would oppose the insertion of Nationalist troops into the conflict and that using them would wipe out any chance of an armistice. Acheson especially worried about negative reaction within the UN coalition.[81]

The proposal, besides having this formidable lineup against it, failed to find favor with Truman. At a session with top civilian and military advisers in late September, he declared that the greatest value of Chiang's soldiers lay not in Korea but as a threat to the China coast.[82] Though the president made no formal decision before his term expired, the JCS recommendation lost momentum.

In debating whether to send KMT troops to Korea, officials also discussed the use of Chiang's forces elsewhere in the region. The State Department posed no objection to possibly readying two Nationalist divisions on a contingency basis for combat in Indochina or on Chinese Communist territory.[83] A high-level policy council in the Defense Department looked forward to arriving at a conclusive agreement within the government on a plan to train and equip KMT divisions for employment outside of Taiwan.[84] But such an agreement did not materialize in the last months of the Truman administration. Still, the concept of a strategic reserve — the idea that KMT forces might serve a useful offensive role as U.S. military requirements dictated — was now firmly lodged within the government. This widespread and heightened recognition of the potential offensive utility of the Nationalist military reinforced the U.S. military-strategic interest in Taiwan and placed an additional premium on a reliable cooperative relationship with the Nationalist government.

By the end of the Truman administration, American policy toward Taiwan was strikingly different than three years earlier. In his 5 January 1950 statement announcing a policy of military noninvolvement, the president had implied that the island and its Nationalist rulers were ultimately expendable. By the eve of the Democratic chief executive's departure from office, the Nationalist government had become a de facto ally. The Korean emergency in June 1950 had prompted a reversal of the nonmilitary policy, but it was the crisis caused by the Chinese intervention in Korea that propelled Washington into an enduring military and political commitment to Taiwan.

By the close of 1952 an assortment of national security interests, both military-strategic and politico-psychological, undergirded this commitment. A mainstay was the view that the island's loss to an enemy would seriously weaken the American defensive posture in the Far Pacific. In addition, the Nationalist regime was seen as a helpmate in the protection of Taiwan, as an instrument in the clandestine harassment and subversion of China, and as a possible supplier of manpower for combat outside KMT-held territory. With the Chinese fighting in Korea and appearing to endanger Southeast Asia, the presence of a sizable Nationalist force on the island was regarded as a useful potential threat against the south and southeast China coast. American officials also thought that the Nationalist government, despite past failures and present imperfections, could serve (in the words of a September 1952 summary of U.S. policy toward Taiwan prepared in the State Department) as "an essential weapon in the continuing political struggle with the Communist world, especially the Chinese segment of it."[85] On top of all this, the military and political commitment to Taiwan dovetailed with a policy of pressure toward China, formalized in NSC 48/5 in May 1951, that set American sights on splitting China from the Soviet Union through the reorientation, fragmentation, or replacement of the Communist regime.

Despite the expanded commitment to Taiwan that coalesced after the end of 1950, there were distinct limits to the support extended by Washington to the Nationalist government in military and political matters. During the winter of 1950–51, and again during the course of 1952, Washington refrained from any deployment of Nationalist troops against the mainland or in Korea, despite the extensive consideration that officials gave to these courses of action. Not only that, Washington consistently refused to embrace the KMT goal of mainland reconquest. Though the prospect of an eventual reinstatement of Nationalist rule on the mainland with American assistance tantalized some civilian and military decision makers in late 1951 and early 1952, most top officials remained resistant to this idea. The neutralization policy, even if more tentative by the end of 1952, still remained in place. Despite a reformulated policy toward the offshore islands in April 1952 tying the United States more closely to their fate, Washington still excluded them from the defensive mission of the Seventh Fleet.

In political matters, too, the American commitment was bounded. Even as it reinvigorated its relations with the Nationalist government, Washington also extended covert support to "third force" Chinese elements on the mainland and elsewhere. And while backing the Nationalist government in the international arena, it did not insist on that government's participation in the Japanese peace treaty or propose that the treaty recognize its claim to Taiwan. One of John Foster Dulles's probable motives in requiring a scope of application provision in the Japan-ROC peace accord was to preserve the future option of an autonomous Taiwan.

As a result of its enlarged commitment to Taiwan, the United States had entered into a patron-client relationship with the Nationalist government that each side found mutually expedient and advantageous. For Washington, maintenance of the relationship was essential because American national security interests necessitated a secure, capable, and responsive government on the island. For Taipei, the relationship was vital to guarantee its suzerainty over the territory it controlled, to maintain the flow of economic and military aid, to prevent its position in the international community from being usurped by the Communists, and to sustain the hope of regaining the mainland. By the end of 1952 there was a more penetrative American presence on Taiwan, and U.S. officials had come to view both the Nationalist government and conditions on the island more positively. Washington's relationship with Taipei had grown discernibly more cooperative and civil. Nevertheless, as events had shown in 1951–52, an underlying current of distrust persisted in Washington and was also present in Taipei. The interests and objectives of the two sides overlapped but also diverged in key respects, most fundamentally over the forcible restoration of Nationalist authority on the mainland. So in taking the Nationalists under the American wing again, the Truman administration built a nest in which to not only protect and succor but also closely monitor its fledgling protégé.

If Republican campaign rhetoric was taken as a reliable guide, the ascent of Dwight Eisenhower to the presidency after two decades of Democratic occupancy heralded new departures in foreign affairs. Exploiting discontent over the nation's diplomatic deficiencies and failures, the GOP in the 1952 electoral contest proffered a more robust cold war strategy as an alternative to Truman-Acheson containment and harnessed the issues of China and particularly Korea to their own partisan purposes.[1] Despite an improved relationship with Washington, Chiang Kai-shek and his subordinates would not have shed any tears at the departure from office of Truman and Acheson, especially when they could look forward to a more rewarding association with a friendlier Republican administration and a seemingly more compatible foreign policy agenda. Eisenhower's selection of John Foster Dulles, widely identified as a Nationalist well-wisher, to head the State Department was auspicious. So was the fact that the Republicans had captured both houses of Congress and that prominent figures in the China bloc now commanded key leadership positions on Capitol Hill.

Even before the inauguration, Chiang signalled his expectation that the incoming administration would jettison the misguided practices of its predecessor in shaping overall Asian policy and relations with his government. In a message transmitted orally by Foreign Minister Yeh to Eisenhower and Dulles early in January 1953, the Nationalist leader asked to be consulted on

East Asian matters, stressing the need for a coordinated global anticommunist policy that placed Europe and Asia on an equal plane. He submitted that Taiwan would require more military aid, including jet aircraft and destroyers, if the new administration should adopt a more spirited approach in Asia. Eisenhower, though promising to confer with Chiang about Far Eastern issues and particularly about China, was noncommittal about additional military assistance but did indicate that he had in mind a more positive Asian policy to which Nationalist China would be expected to contribute.[2]

Afterward, Dulles huddled privately with Yeh and gave him a preview of Eisenhower's announcement the next month modifying the existing orders to the Seventh Fleet so as to allow the Nationalists to undertake offensive operations against the mainland — the famous "unleashing" of Chiang Kai-shek, as the popular press invention would characterize deneutralization. Asked by Dulles whether it would be possible to "manage" the Generalissimo, the Nationalist diplomat confessed that he himself had "a hell of a job" trying to do so.[3]

Dulles would soon enough experience for himself the difficulty of "managing" the wily and stubborn Nationalist ruler. True enough, the new administration did deneutralize the Taiwan Strait and in other ways sought to ingratiate itself with Chiang and his American devotees. Yet it was no more willing to give the Generalissimo a free rein or to subordinate American interests and goals to those of the Nationalists than had been the Truman administration. Traveling an established path, it did not fundamentally alter the commitment to Taiwan or recast the relationship with Chiang's government.

A New Dispensation?

To maximize its international visibility and domestic impact, President Eisenhower chose his State of the Union address on 2 February to publicize his decision to lift the barrier against Nationalist offensive operations across the Taiwan Strait. Explaining that it was illogical for American naval power to "shield Communist China" when the Chinese refused to stop fighting in Korea in spite of UN armistice proposals, he denied that his action implied any aggressive intentions by the United States.[4]

Eisenhower's sensational announcement was the first of a string of moves by the neophyte administration in its early months to reinforce the impression of a fresh approach toward Chiang's stronghold and the entire Far Pacific. Later in February Rankin had conferred on him the rank of ambassador, partly to demonstrate confidence in the Nationalist government and to upgrade its political prestige.[5] Early in March, as another sign of Taipei's new standing in Washington, Eisenhower feted Madame Chiang Kai-shek at a White House dinner.[6] Personnel changes at the State and Defense Departments likewise appeared to augur a break with past policies in Asia. Dulles fired John Carter Vincent and John Paton Davies, despite the lack of evidence that these two Foreign Service officers and China hands, who had become ensnared in the Red Scare, were disloyal or security risks. To fill the politically sensitive post of assistant secretary of state for Far Eastern Affairs, he selected Walter Robertson, a polished Virginia banker and former member of the Foreign Service, who had briefly served in China in 1945–46. Recommended by Walter Judd, Robertson was a staunch backer of Chiang and his Kuomintang government and was utterly contemptuous of the Communists. Reassuring as his appointment may have been to Taipei and pro-Nationalist enthusiasts, he did not enter the coterie of Dulles's most trusted advisers.[7] At the Pentagon, Eisenhower authorized the replacement of the incumbent chiefs of staff, whom Republican notables had stigmatized for excessive loyalty to the Truman administration's policies. This clean sweep of the military chieftains culminated in July in the appointment of Adm. Arthur Radford as the new JCS chairman. Not only did the Pacific commander in chief's views on national defense policy harmonize with Eisenhower's, but his reputation as an "Asia First" admiral ensured his selection a warm reception among Republican right wingers.[8]

Although it appeared at first glance that Eisenhower and Dulles had joined the camp of Chiang's avid rooters, this was far from the case. The two men, who fashioned an intimate partnership in the making of foreign policy, were both confirmed Atlanticists; they believed that Europe, not Asia, was the premier battleground of the cold war. Though critical of Democratic errors in the Far East, they shied away from the overly exuberant remedies of the Asia-firsters. Limited in their Asian experience, they possessed only a generalized knowledge of China, in which was intermixed an assortment of unflattering stereotypes about Chinese and Asians. Privately, they were far from dewy-eyed admirers of the leadership of Chiang Kai-shek. In their unsentimental view, he was not a valiant anticommunist paladin, temporarily exiled on Taiwan, but a flawed yet necessary ally, whose island fortress would remain his permanent home, short of a major upheaval on the continent.[9]

Eisenhower and Dulles's support for Chiang and his KMT government would be expedient and instrumental, just as it had been for Truman and Acheson, and would remain tied to the military-strategic and political-psychological value of an anticommunist Taiwan. While publicly championing Chiang's government, the two leaders never endorsed its plans for mainland reconquest. What is more, despite frequently hostile public rhetoric toward Communist China, they would sometimes reveal a surprising degree of pragmatism and flexibility in their private discussions and calculations. But their enmity toward the CCP regime ran deep and, combined with the need to sustain a cooperative relationship with Taipei, set narrow limits on their readiness to deviate from a hard-line policy against Peking. As well, they were not prone to exceed the limits of public tolerance of the People's Republic or to ruffle Chiang's partisans unnecessarily.

The president and secretary of state recognized that they could ignore the domestic political dimension of their diplomacy, particularly regarding China, only at their own peril. Popular abhorrence of Communist China, sharpened by the bloodshed in Korea, was unremitting at this time.[10] Within its own party ranks, the administration had to cope with the Old Guard, which, despite entering into a fragile entente with the more moderate factions in the GOP after Eisenhower bested Taft for the nomination, remained a hotbed of neoisolationist, Asia-first sentiment. Several scuffles early in the administration between the White House and members of the right wing, albeit unrelated to China, confirmed the potential for an intraparty schism over foreign affairs. Until his fatal illness forced him to relinquish his post as Senate majority leader in June, Robert Taft labored to construct a partnership with the White House and to minimize right-wing obstruction. His successor, William Knowland, lacked the Ohio senator's stature and political adroitness and quickly earned Eisenhower's private scorn, not the least because of his knee-jerk support for Chiang Kai-shek.[11]

Because of recent history and his own past record, Dulles was determined not to have his right flank turned on foreign policy. His onetime close association with Alger Hiss, his service in the Truman administration, his high profile role as a spokesman for Thomas Dewey and the internationalist wing of the Republican party—all offered cause for right-wingers to distrust him, in spite of his partisan blasts against containment during the campaign year. The secretary had no desire to share the fate of his Democratic predecessor, whom the Republican right had pilloried. After taking office, he gave Joseph McCarthy and his fellow anticommunist zealots leeway to carry on a purge within the State Department. As the administration's chief ideologist, he also presented a stern anticommunist visage to the country and to the world at large. Scrupulously attentive to the political and public relations facets of his job, he constantly kept an ear cocked for thunder on the right.[12]

While mindful of the right wing, Dulles, no less than Eisenhower, wished to avert the bruising partisanship experienced by the Truman administration in its latter years. The two men aspired to restore bipartisanship in foreign affairs.[13] To do so, they would have to depoliticize China policy, a task that the previous administration had begun but that still remained unfinished. During the next three years, they would in large measure complete this process by appeasing, co-opting, and blunting the right wing and by establishing an amicable working relationship with Democratic leaders on Capitol Hill.

The influence of domestic politics was manifest in Eisenhower's deneutralization announcement. As Dulles admitted in a candid moment with an aide, domestic considerations were paramount in the decision to modify the mission of the Seventh Fleet.[14] Freeing the Nationalists to take military action against the mainland would delight the right wing and betoken the administration's readiness to fulfill campaign pledges to pursue a more vibrant Asian policy and to act boldly to end the drawn-out war in Korea. Dulles had favored deneutralization since at least mid-March of the previous year, and he probably obtained Eisenhower's approval for this change during the president-elect's return trip from Korea, when the two conferred on board the cruiser *Helena* en route from Guam to Hawaii.[15]

The deneutralization announcement reaped more than enough public approbation to gratify both men. Press and radio commentary was overwhelmingly positive. Republican spokesmen hailed the new policy and most Democrats went along with it, though some with misgivings.[16]

Domestic objectives apart, the deneutralization announcement did have psychological utility with respect to the somber situation in Asia. The announcement was an initial feint in a war of nerves to convince the Chinese Communists to accept a peace settlement in Korea.[17] Eisenhower later claimed that it conveyed the unspoken message that American patience with the deadlocked armistice talks was wearing thin and that the Chinese could not count on the continuation of past restraints on military action.[18] In justifying deneutralization to several allied leaders, Dulles brought Indochina, as well as Korea, into the picture. He told Canadian statesman Lester Pearson, for instance, that the move was meant to create a threat to China's geographical center so as to deter an invasion of Indochina and possibly prevail upon Peking to redeploy some of its forces from North China and Korea to the south China coast.[19] The possibility of a Korean armistice reinforced fears in Washington of increased Chinese aggressiveness, perhaps even intervention, in Indochina, where the French were struggling merely to hold their own against the Chinese-supplied Vietminh. In April 1953 a new sense of crisis developed in American official circles when the Vietminh successfully invaded Laos, hitherto outside the main arena of the war.[20]

Eisenhower's announcement drew a predictably scornful condemnation from Peking.[21] Yet Chinese documents now indicate that CCP leaders, far from brushing off the revision of the Seventh Fleet's orders as a mere propagandistic scarecrow, were on the alert against a possible Nationalist attack.[22] Washington refrained, however, from giving the impression that plans were afoot to hurl Chiang's soldiers against the mainland. Joint Chiefs of Staff chairman Bradley publicly questioned the ability of the Nationalists to attack the mainland in the immediate future. The general, who had not been consulted in advance about the new policy, privately described it as "eyewash."[23] While this dismissive remark contained a large kernel of truth, it overlooked the fact that he and his fellow chiefs had been pointing toward just such a modification since the Chinese intervention in Korea.

Wanting to allay worries that the president's announcement might portend a widening of hostilities in East Asia, the State Department had beforehand privately assured selected allied governments that the move would have no immediate military consequences.[24] The actual announcement elicited a mixed reaction among key allied nations.[25] The biggest fuss occurred in Britain, where the altered policy aroused detractors across the political spectrum but most conspicuously within the Labour party and its left wing led by the fiery Aneurin Bevan.[26] Distancing the Conservative government from the American decision, Anthony Eden told the House of Commons that the revised mission of the Seventh Fleet would have "unfortunate political repercussions without compensating military advantages"; yet he also tried to calm fears of bellicose designs on Washington's part.[27]

Lest Chiang Kai-shek misconstrue the essentially symbolic significance of deneutralization, the State Department impressed on him that Washington was not inviting a request for additional assistance and that the revised policy would leave unaltered the existing missions on Taiwan of the MAAG and the Mutual Security Agency (MSA), the successor of the Economic Cooperation Administration.[28] Catching Washington's drift, Chiang went out of his way not to appear too much the firebrand. In a brief and restrained official statement, he praised the president's announcement as "not only judicious but militarily and morally sound." The Nationalist foreign ministry instructed its representatives abroad to forbear from any suggestion that a mainland assault was imminent.[29]

As the aftershocks from Eisenhower's dramatic pronouncement rippled across the international scene, the president and his advisers pondered how best to hasten the end of the war in Korea. The JCS and Gen. Mark Clark were still on record in support of the employment of two KMT divisions. During his prepresidential trip to the war-torn peninsula, Eisenhower learned that using these divisions was militarily desirable but politically complicated.[30] Dulles knew that opinion within the State Department was against a diversion of Nationalist troops to Korea.[31]

Chiang himself seemed to be of two minds about volunteering his forces. Early in the new year Yeh told Dulles that his government did not favor dispatching its troops to Korea.[32] However, when Mark Clark paid a visit to

Taiwan in April, Chiang offered to send two or three of his best divisions if Washington so requested.[33]

In the final analysis, the conflicting signals from Taipei were irrelevant because Washington's military plans to terminate the war made no provision for the use of Nationalist troops, whether on the peninsula or the Chinese mainland. By early April 1953 the NSC Planning Board had devised NSC 147, "Analysis of Possible Courses of Action in Korea," which outlined two main strategies to end the fighting, one preserving existing restrictions on military operations across the Yalu River and the other removing them and extending the hostilities to China. Nationalist forces did not figure in either of these strategies. Neither were KMT troops assigned any role in the final version of NSC 147, sanctioning a stepped-up war in Korea and a wider conflict against China, to which Eisenhower gave the nod at a pivotal NSC meeting on 20 May.[34] This significant policy document demonstrated conclusively that deneutralization was an empty threat.

A New "Leash" on Chiang

Another development ensuring that deneutralization would remain little more than a political gesture and a scare tactic was the imposition of new restrictions on Nationalist offensive military activities. When Eisenhower had first proclaimed the altered assignment of the Seventh Fleet, the assumption in Washington was that Chiang's forces were incapable of major freelance operations against the mainland. Lacking the wherewithal to inflict substantial damage on the Communists, the Generalissimo was in no position to exploit new offensive opportunities across the Taiwan Strait. In an unforeseen twist, a scheduled delivery of jet bombers to Taiwan called into question this assumption, setting in train urgent discussions to devise a new method to curb unwanted Nationalist offensive operations.

The shipment of military material and hardware to Taiwan, already having sped up in the latter half of 1952, further accelerated in the early months of the Eisenhower administration. In the pipeline for delivery by the end of June were forty-five F-84 jet fighter-bombers, whose combat range extended to inland targets in China. In late March the JCS alerted the State Department that the conjunction of deneutralization with the imminent arrival of the F-84s would give Chiang both the freedom and the means to conduct offensive air raids against the mainland. A bomber strike could trigger Chinese Communist retaliation and require an American counteraction, as a result of which the United States could find itself in a brawl with China in which the Soviet Union might join.[35] Recognizing the frightening implications of giving the Nationalists unrestricted possession of the bombers, Secretary

Dulles immediately swung into action. At his prompting, the NSC held up shipments of the aircraft until the Nationalist government had committed itself "not [to] engage in offensive operations considered by the United States to be inimical to the best interests of the United States."[36] The clear purpose of this move was to use the F-84s as an incentive to convince Chiang to clamp on a new pair of American-made shackles.

On 23 April the Nationalist government officially agreed to confer with Washington about "any offensive military operations against [the] mainland of China which would radically alter [the] pattern or tempo of operations hitherto undertaken." This restrictive understanding allowed the Nationalists to carry on their mainland raids but not to further expand their offensive military activities without prior consultation with Washington. In a separate understanding, Taipei promised advance consultation about any offensive operations involving U.S.-supplied jet aircraft. Satisfied with these undertakings, Washington released the F-84s for delivery.[37] These agreements, for all practical purposes giving the United States a veto over any undesirable offensive forays against the mainland, represented a virtual reinstatement of neutralization in a different guise.

In a parallel development, Washington issued a new directive to CINCPAC on 6 April that enlarged the U.S. military presence on Taiwan and improved coordination with Nationalist military authorities while simultaneously increasing oversight of their planning and activities. The directive, prepared by the State Department and JCS, had the personal approval of Eisenhower and Dulles.[38] As a follow-up to this directive, Radford required that the Nationalists submit to him through MAAG all plans for mainland offensive activities, including those originating in the offshore islands.[39]

As both the F-84s episode and the directive to CINCPAC clearly revealed, distrust of the Nationalists as well as apprehension that they might snooker the United States into a clash with China were very much present in the new Republican administration. To be sure, in a variety of ways beginning with the deneutralization announcement, the administration had shown a more positive disposition toward Chiang and his acolytes. Yet an undercurrent of wariness contoured its relationship with the Nationalist government, just as during the preceding Democratic administration. It was therefore unsurprising that within four months after Chiang's symbolic "unleashing" he was once again securely tethered.

Taiwan and the Korean Armistice

The Eisenhower administration did not approve new comprehensive policy statements for China and Taiwan until the fall of 1953, but earlier in the year it did adopt interim guidelines. These were contained in NSC 154/1, "United States Tactics Immediately Following an Armistice in Korea," which the president ratified on 7 July in the last weeks of the war. Predicated on the expectation that an aggressive China would still endanger American regional interests after a Korean truce, the document called for unceasing pressure on the CCP regime and reaffirmed the sponsorship of the Nationalist government.[40]

The denouement of the Korean struggle could hardly have delighted Chiang. The war had been his deliverance, and his own interest lay in its extension, not its termination. Even so, diplomatic discretion required that he not openly oppose an armistice. In a series of three personal letters to President Eisenhower before the truce, he did reveal something of his own anxiety about the traps awaiting the United States in any negotiations with the communist bloc. In his final missive, which reached the State Department on 23 June, he made a strong appeal for the immediate conclusion of a mutual security pact between the United States and South Korea.[41]

This letter arrived just as the armistice talks had fallen into disarray as a result of South Korean president Syngman Rhee's unauthorized release of 25,000 North Korean prisoners of war.[42] The timing and content of Chiang's letter (Rhee had demanded a mutual security treaty as a condition for his acceptance of an armistice agreement) seemed calculated to encourage the South Korean president in his intransigence; this, at least, was how the State Department read its meaning. An irate Dulles, who through a combination of tough talk and concessions was then trying to bring Rhee into line, shot off a stern message to the Generalissimo, admonishing him that persistent obstructionism by the South Korean president could lead to a withdrawal of U.S.-UN forces from the peninsula and that from this would follow a "reconsideration of US-Formosa policy with [a] result not now predictable."[43]

The purport of Secretary Dulles's warning was not lost on Taipei, which protested that the purpose of Chiang's letter had been misunderstood.[44] The incident quickly blew over as Rhee reluctantly acquiesced in truce terms along the lines favored by the United Nations Command. Taipei did not indulge in any public second-guessing of the armistice agreement, despite its own private dissatisfaction with terms that left Korea divided (with disturbing implications for a divided China).[45]

The tenor of Dulles's message, with its dire intimation of a withdrawal of support from the Nationalists, doubtless reflected, in the heat of the moment, the secretary's penchant for rhetorical overkill and perhaps a desire to exert pressure on Rhee through Chiang. Still, Dulles had not hesitated to use blunt language and an implied threat to remind Chiang that the United States would brook no mischievous interference from him. The incident reportedly stung Chiang and still smarted months later.[46]

Unmaterialized Expectations

During the course of 1953 additional evidence presented itself to the Nationalists that the change of the guard at the White House and the State Department had not transformed the basic character of U.S. policy toward Taiwan. Testing the boundaries of its relationship with the new administration, Taipei requested a much larger economic and military assistance program, expressed interest in a bilateral security pact and an American-sponsored Pacific pact, and tried to involve the United States more directly in the defense of the offshore islands. To a greater or lesser degree, the outcome of each of these initiatives left Taipei disappointed.

With the retaking of the mainland their uppermost goal, the Nationalists asked for a big jump in economic and military aid after the Republicans took power. That request fell flat in Washington. The consensus of a gathering of representatives from the State and Defense Departments and the MSA in May 1953, at which Rankin was present, was that the Nationalists could expect no substantial boost in aid for FY 1954. As the participants realized, total foreign aid funding would be tight because of an economy-minded administration and a penny-pinching Congress.[47] Beyond that, officials had no wish to foot the bill for a rapid Nationalist military buildup aimed at the recovery of the mainland. As the new Far Eastern Bureau chief Walter Robertson told the conferees, no one "seriously believed that the National Chinese army could retake the China mainland without very substantial assistance, including troops, from the U.S." Since the involvement of American manpower in such a venture was unacceptable in present circumstances, the alternative was to strengthen the Nationalist forces so that they could defend Taiwan and serve as a "strategic reserve" to resist Communist aggression "wherever it might occur, whenever it was feasible to employ the forces, whenever and wherever it was desirable to employ them."[48] The concept of a strategic reserve advanced by Robertson, a carryover from the Truman administration, projected the development only of a limited offensive capability for Nationalist forces and fell short of Chiang's more ambitious designs.

Rankin was disappointed that he had only modest additional funding to offer to the Generalissimo after returning from consultations in Washington. The ambassador was himself disposed to proceed faster and further toward an offensive military buildup. Not unlike the Nationalists themselves, he was convinced that unless mainland China was "in due course" liberated from Communist domination, "the rest of Asia will eventually go down the same drain."[49]

The pace and scope of military assistance to Taiwan, and the related question of the exact role of the Nationalist forces, occupied President Eisenhower and the National Security Council prior to approval of NSC 146/2 on 6 November 1953. This statement of basic policy toward Taiwan (which will be discussed later in the chapter) concretized the strategic reserve concept while leaving in abeyance a final decision about its implementation. Subparagraph 12-a of the document called for the development of an army of about 350,000 with restricted offensive prowess; a small navy that could conduct coastal patrol, antishipping, and commando operations; and an air force for limited air defense, troop support, and interdiction. A force of this size and character, it was believed, could present a deterrent threat to China and constitute a strategic reserve for the entire region.[50] Though such a force could undertake limited combat operations on the mainland or elsewhere, it could do so only with American assistance. Chiang Kai-shek would possess an offensive military capability, but Washington would decide if, when, and where to use it.

One of the attractions of the strategic reserve concept for American officials was its compatibility with the New Look, the national security strategy adopted by the NSC in October 1953 shortly before its approval of NSC 146/2. Prescribing a defense doctrine that blended cost cutting, reduced U.S. conventional forces, and greater dependence on nuclear deterrence, the New Look included among its tenets an increased reliance on indigenous ground forces supported by U.S. air and naval power. This tenet fit neatly with the creation of a strategic reserve on Taiwan that would make available a pool of American-trained and -equipped manpower for use as needed in East Asia.[51]

Despite the advantages of such a reserve, the NSC divided over the implementation of subparagraph 12-a. Without quarreling in principle with the strategic reserve approach, the president hesitated to approve a large hike in military appropriations for Taiwan; he preferred to strengthen the Nationalist forces over the long term rather than aim at D-day readiness for a specific date. Withholding its definitive consent, the NSC flagged subparagraph 12-a for future review.[52]

Early in 1953 the Nationalist government sounded out Washington about the negotiation of a mutual security pact. Taipei hankered to solemnize the American defensive commitment to Taiwan, which since June 1950 had been unilateral and unformalized in any binding agreement. It did not escape Taipei's notice that other anticommunist nations in the Far Pacific, such as the Philippines, Australia and New Zealand, and Japan, were already coupled with their American protector through defense treaties and that South Korea was pressing for similar treatment.

Ambassador Koo first broached the idea of a mutual defense treaty in a conversation with Dulles in mid-March 1953. Admitting that a formal pact would make little difference from a military standpoint, he played up its psychological benefits in buttressing the international stature of his government, providing certain assurance of its survival, and uplifting the spirits of anticommunist Chinese on Taiwan and elsewhere. Dulles did not warm to Koo's suggestion, saying that he foresaw difficulty in defining the scope of such a treaty. Would the accord extend to the Nationalist-occupied offshore islands or, for that matter, to the mainland territory that the Nationalist government claimed but did not control? A pact that incorporated the offshore islands and the mainland could entangle the United States in unwanted obligations.[53]

Concluding that a bilateral treaty was not in the cards for now, Taipei instead recycled a proposal for a Pacific pact that predated the Korean War. In 1949 Chiang and Syngman Rhee had failed to excite Washington's enthusiasm for an anticommunist alliance of Asian nations joined and supported by the United States, in effect a Pacific version of the North Atlantic Treaty Organization (NATO).[54] Taipei now decided that the moment was ripe for a revival of this concept. Chiang took up a proposal for a multilateral pact with Rankin in July, only to be told that the impetus would have to come from Asian nations and that the United States would not take the lead. In the following months Taipei jockeyed to create a groundswell for a pact. Nationalist hopes shot up in early September 1953 when Senator Knowland publicly proposed an Asian collective security system during a visit to Taiwan. Late in November Rhee traveled to Taipei to consult with Chiang about a Pacific alliance. The two of them looked to the newly elected president of the Philippines and American favorite, Ramon Magsaysay, to lead a movement for it. When Magsaysay refused to step out in front, the Rhee-Chiang venture came to an abrupt halt, and Taipei put the idea of a Pacific pact back on the shelf.[55]

Through all this, Taipei had been unable to corral Washington into taking the initiative. Truth to tell, American officials considered such a pact unfeasible as long as disagreements, grievances, and tension persisted among potential participants within the region. Furthermore, they considered Nationalist China's inclusion impracticable because of objections from other Pacific nations.[56]

By the time Taipei had given up on a Pacific defense coalition, it had already resuscitated its proposal for a bilateral treaty. The signing of the mutual defense pact between the United States and South Korea in October 1953 catalyzed the Nationalist government into action. Foreign Minister Yeh took advantage of a five-day sojourn on Taiwan by Vice President Richard Nixon in early November to sell the Nationalist treaty proposal.[57] On 19 December he gave Rankin a copy of a draft defense accord based on similar American treaties with Korea, Australia and New Zealand, and the Philippines.[58] Despite their yearning to enter into negotiations for a formal military union with their American defenders, the Nationalists would be kept waiting at the altar still longer because of Washington's chariness. Another year would pass before they would consummate the alliance they craved.

One of the obstacles to the early conclusion of a bilateral security treaty would be, as Dulles had adumbrated, Washington's unwillingness to obligate itself to safeguard the offshore islands. The decision to deneutralize the Taiwan Strait did not affect the existing no-defense policy toward the islands. To keep the Communists in the dark about American intentions, the policy remained secret and was made known only to a select number of Nationalist officials.[59] Unbeknownst to Washington, the previous summer Mao Tse-tung had approved a plan for the seizure of certain KMT-held islands just off Fukien and Chekiang provinces. That plan was expanded in the spring of 1953 to include the subjugation of Quemoy, located just two miles from the harbor of Amoy, the main port on the Fukien coast.[60]

As a result of an upswing in Chinese military activities in the offshore islands in the early summer of 1953, high-level American military and civilian officials for the first time addressed the question of whether or not to stick to the no-defense policy, foreshadowing the major debate that would occur over this same issue during the later crisis over the islands. In late June, after the Communists snatched several lesser KMT-controlled islets, Admiral Radford, then in his last weeks as CINCPAC before becoming JCS chairman, recommended a revision of his directives to free him to assist in the defense of those KMT-occupied islands that Washington judged essential to the safekeeping of Taiwan.[61] Unmoved, the Defense Department still insisted that the Nationalists bear sole responsibility for the protection of all the islands.[62] Late in July Adm. Felix B. Stump, who had assumed the command vacated by Radford, renewed his predecessor's petition for authority to shelter certain essential islands.[63]

In the meantime, Chiang made his own demands on Washington. He asked that the United States include the six divisions he kept on the offshore islands within its military aid program (they currently received only limited American material), integrate the islands into the defense of Taiwan, and announce that the Seventh Fleet would step up its surveillance around them because of their relation to the security of the Nationalist island home.[64]

Chiang's request, along with Stump's recommendation, precipitated a significant round of discussions in Washington. Holding that Nationalist retention of the islands was militarily desirable but unessential to the defense of Taiwan, the JCS were unwilling to tamper with the no-defense policy. They saw no need, nor did State Department officials, for the public announcement that Chiang wanted.[65] Such a declaration, as the military chieftains and diplomats were doubtless aware, skirted the margin of a defensive commitment and would compromise the calculated ambiguity of the administration's public posture. Given the negative response to Chiang's request, it was a foregone conclusion that Stump's recommendation for an explicit defensive commitment would likewise fail to gain the consent of the JCS. In a sign of adaptability, the chiefs did instruct the Pacific commander to prepare contingency plans for the employment of U.S. forces to guard the islands in case of a future change of policy.[66]

During the same span in which Washington reaffirmed the no-defense policy, it further involved itself in encouraging and assisting the Nationalists to protect the islands. On the advice of MAAG chief Maj. Gen. William Chase, Chiang reluctantly agreed to dispatch one of his crack divisions to bolster the weak defenses of the Tachen Islands, the northernmost and most vulnerable of his coastal outposts, on which the Communists appeared to have their eye.[67] Washington augmented the Nationalist navy with two destroyers and more than 120 smaller vessels, and it cleared the way for the rotation to the offshore islands of MAAG-trained and -equipped forces from Taiwan.[68] Furthermore, the islands assumed a greater politico-psychological significance among top officials because of a perceived connection (which Chiang did his best to reinforce) to Nationalist morale. Articulating a conviction that would remain a key element in the administration's outlook, Dulles averred that the loss of the islands would "deal a severe political and psychological blow" to Taiwan's government.[69]

So even without a repudiation of the no-defense policy, the multiplying American connections with the islands and a deepening appreciation of the importance of their retention ensured that decision makers could not simply write them off in the event that the Communists tried to occupy them. The quasi commitment that had begun to crystallize the previous year now solidified, indirectly and informally implicating the United States in the guardianship of these exposed specks of territory hugging the China coast. Though linked to the commitment to Taiwan, that quasi commitment possessed its own logic and momentum. As the investment of Nationalist military resources and prestige in the islands increased with Washington's encouragement and aid, the consequences of losing the islands for Chiang and his followers became all the more serious. By the same token, Washington assumed at least an implicit obligation to do all that it could to preserve the Nationalist presence and entwined its own prestige with the fate of the islands and their KMT defenders. All the same, so long as decision makers refused to abandon the no-defense policy, they retained a degree of flexibility. Despite now benefiting from a larger measure of American assistance, Chiang's fighting men still bore the burden of defense alone. A more preferable outcome for the Generalissimo would have been the westward extension of the defensive perimeter to his forward bases, which would have enmeshed American military power at the doorstep of his mainland enemy. At the end of the brief summer squall over the islands in 1953, that objective had drawn nearer but was still beyond his grasp.

KMT Irregulars in Burma

The issue that most strained the Washington-Taipei nexus in 1953 was the removal of Kuomintang irregulars from upper Burma. This issue engaged the Eisenhower administration and Chiang Kai-shek in a test of wills, matching the former's superior leverage against the latter's obduracy and guile. For American leaders, the presence of the KMT guerrillas had become an embarrassing liability that severely damaged relations with Burma and placed Taiwan and, indirectly, the United States on the hot seat in the United Nations. For Chiang, the 12,000 or so soldiers represented a foothold on the Asian continent, the largest active force of anticommunist Chinese outside Nationalist-occupied territory. That its nucleus under the leadership of Gen. Li Mi had recently benefited from the patronage of the CIA must have made Washington's insistence on evacuation all the more puzzling and galling to the Nationalist president.

Operation Paper, the CIA project to sponsor Li Mi's guerrillas, had folded after a third failed attempt in August 1952 to establish an enclave in Yunnan province. The routed irregulars retreated once more to the remote northeastern frontier region of Burma, where they fragmented into ill-disciplined contingents under Li Mi and various "jungle generals." Engaging in banditry and marauding Burmese villages, they also conducted a lucrative illicit trade in opium, mostly through Thailand but also reportedly via Taiwan. Taipei supplied them with a modest amount of aid. In the fall of 1952 the irregulars began to penetrate new areas of Burma and allied themselves with the Karens, an indigenous rebel group. Fighting soon broke out between the irregulars and the Burmese army.[70]

By early 1953 the KMT troops had become Burma's most serious problem and a festering grievance in its relations with the United States. The irregulars endangered the fledgling nation's internal security, diverted its armed forces from their struggle against domestic insurgents, and were an obstacle to tranquil relations with China. Burmese neutralist leaders feared that their presence might give Peking a pretext to assist communist insurrectionists or even to intervene militarily.[71] Unable to defeat or expel the irregulars, the Burmese government looked to the United States for a solution, believing that the troops took their orders from Taipei and that the Nationalist regime was itself little more than an American puppet. Burmese leaders likewise strongly suspected that the soldiers had received clandestine U.S. assistance, despite denials by the State Department (which, except for a chosen few, remained officially ignorant of CIA involvement).[72] To goad the United States into finding a remedy, Rangoon notified Washington on 17 March 1953 that it wished to terminate the American economic aid program for Burma by the end of June. This decision strengthened the conviction of American ambassador William J. Sebald that "the sine qua non of U.S.-Burma friendship was a settlement of the KMT problem."[73]

By the time the Eisenhower administration took office, the wheels had already been set in motion within the State Department, Pentagon, and CIA to gain Chiang Kai-shek's consent to the evacuation of the irregulars to Taiwan.[74] Carrying forward this initiative, the new leadership in Washington sought to obtain the Generalissimo's swift agreement in principle to a repatriation plan.[75] Dulles worried that Burma might take the KMT irregulars issue to the UN or that its government might even be forced into a coalition with its communist opponents. He gave credence to a report from Sebald that the communists might have infiltrated the ranks of Li Mi's troops.[76] To remove any doubts in Taipei about the unity and resoluteness of top American officials, Eisenhower, former CIA chief and now Undersecretary of State Walter Bedell Smith, and the new CIA director Allen Dulles put in a strong word for repatriation with Madame Chiang Kai-shek during her visit to Washington early in the new year.[77] So it was that in the very same period that the Eisenhower administration trumpeted its new deneutralization policy, it essayed to close a sordid chapter in the secret war against China, simultaneously freeing Chiang (at least in theory) to strike at the mainland while pressing him to remove the largest active contingent of KMT loyalists still on the continent. What the Generalissimo made of this curious conjunction would be interesting to know, but there is no doubt that he was not of a mind to see the irregulars ousted from Burma. Asserting that their withdrawal would contravene his liberationist policy and signify a retreat in the anti-Communist struggle, he claimed that his authority over them was circumscribed in any case.[78]

On 12 March the State Department learned that the Generalissimo refused to consent in principle to the evacuation of the irregulars.[79] An angered Dulles instructed Rankin that a refusal to take this essential step might prompt Washington to "take [a] new look [at the] whole Chinese situation to determine whether or not its present policies toward Formosa are sound." The implication was that by flouting American will the Nationalists would adversely affect decisions about aid to Taiwan.[80] Feeling the heat, the Nationalist government backtracked by agreeing to cooperate with the United

States in the removal of Li Mi's forces but only on the understanding that it did not exercise total control over them and could only accomplish what was reasonable or feasible under such circumstances. Despite these caveats, the State Department accepted this undertaking.[81]

Taipei's qualified concession came too late to sidetrack Rangoon's request on 25 March that the General Assembly brand the Nationalist regime an aggressor for its interference in Burma.[82] The Burmese complaint also put Washington on the defensive, both because the United States was the Nationalists' patron and because of widespread suspicions, spread by stories in the American and world press, that its own skirts were not clean in the affair.[83] With timely assistance from the British, the American delegation to the General Assembly engineered the passage of a face-saving resolution on 23 April that merely condemned the activities of "foreign forces" in Burma without naming Taiwan but that did call for the disarmament of these forces and either their internment or withdrawal.[84]

In going along with a diluted resolution sparing Taipei from censure, Burmese leaders knew that Washington had made progress in organizing a mechanism to remove the irregulars. The next month a four-power joint military committee with representatives from Taiwan, Burma, Thailand, and the United States began discussions under UN auspices in Bangkok. The talks, which extended into the fall, bogged down because of the inability of the committee to draft an evacuation plan that Burma, Nationalist China, and Li Mi and other "jungle generals" could all approve.[85] The State Department had indications of conflict within the Nationalist government over withdrawal.[86] Accusing Taipei of only going through the motions of cooperation, the Burmese obtained firm evidence that it was still supplying the troops, despite prior assurances to the contrary.[87] Their patience at an end, the Burmese left the talks in a huff in September, resumed military operations against the irregulars, and again brought the KMT problem to the General Assembly.[88]

In these disappointing and trying conditions, Washington worked hard for quick agreement on an evacuation plan. Eisenhower personally appealed to Chiang to secure the withdrawal of as many men as possible and to disavow those who remained.[89] The Nationalist leader approved the evacuation of only 2,000 troops but did agree to disown those who refused to depart.[90] To Washington's relief, Burma accepted this plan while still insisting that the only satisfactory ultimate solution was total withdrawal.[91]

Despite the subsequent repatriation of about 2,000 soldiers to Taiwan, delays and irregularities in the evacuation, together with the small number of arms surrendered, persuaded Rangoon that the exercise was a sham.[92] The U.S. embassy in Bangkok suspected that the evacuation was a "smokescreen" for a continuation of KMT activities and that Li Mi, in cahoots with elements in the Nationalist government, proposed to retain control of the remaining soldiers in order to maintain opium smuggling operations.[93] Even the empathetic Karl Rankin, who took Chiang at his word that he had only restricted authority over the soldiers and who tried to reconcile the American and Nationalist viewpoints, conceded that the Generalissimo's heart was not in the evacuation.[94]

The completion of the evacuation on 8 December 1953 coincided with the General Assembly's adoption of a second temperate resolution on the KMT issue. The resolution, which again spared the Nationalist government from censure, passed without objection from Burma after Taipei agreed to repatriate several thousand more soldiers.[95] Another 3,700 did relocate to Taiwan, raising the total number who departed from Burma to approximately 6,000.[96]

From Washington's perspective, the twin evacuations represented a satisfying if less than ideal outcome to a sticky predicament requiring it to deal with a balky Asian client, an incensed Asian neutral, and an aroused United Nations. The departure of a sizable contingent of the irregulars ended the dispute with Taiwan, mollified Burma, and defused the KMT issue within the UN. Yet U.S. relations with Rangoon had suffered harm, and the Burmese were left to contend with the large number of irregulars still remaining in their territory, who were a source of trouble for them and of concern to Washington into the 1960s.[97] American relations with Taiwan did not emerge unscathed either. Rankin lamented that nothing since the China White Paper had so poisoned relations with the Nationalists.[98] Be that as it may, Chiang had expertly spun out his resistance, making concessions only under firm pressure and usually at the final hour. Afterward, intelligence collected in Taipei disclosed that the Nationalists had adopted, and for a time followed, a secret plan (Operation "Heaven") for token compliance with the first UN resolution. Apprised of this plan, Ambassador Sebald sadly concluded that the United States had been "thoroughly hoodwinked" by the Nationalists.[99] Only with frustrating slowness and painstaking difficulty did the Eisenhower administration achieve a partial removal of the irregulars. The entire affair provided an instructive lesson for Eisenhower and Dulles in Chiang Kai-shek's manipulative skills and the limits of their influence over him.

The Diplomacy of Postponement Affirmed

Disagreeable as were the tribulations caused by the problem of the KMT irregulars at the UN, a potentially far more disruptive and injurious issue was the seating of Communist China. Since May 1951 the United States, by means of a moratorium on substantive discussions or votes on this issue, had successfully practiced a diplomacy of postponement in the world organization. As the Eisenhower administration groped toward a Korean armistice, the scaffolding constructed by Acheson's State Department to sustain this diplomatic strategy began to buckle as a result of slackening resistance to Peking's admission in London and other foreign capitals. Even as trends in foreign opinion made the diplomacy of postponement more problematic on the international front, its continuation was all the more imperative domestically for the administration because of fierce opposition to Chinese Communist entry on the home front. The administration's quandary was how to avoid being scissored between these two divergent realities.

As long as the Korean War lasted, the noncommunist bloc in the UN followed the American and British lead in extending the moratorium. The prospect of an armistice now opened the possibility that Britain, joined by other Western nations and by Asian neutrals such as India, might attempt to seat the Chinese once the bloodletting had ceased. It was conceivable that the representation issue might find its way on to the agenda of a post-armistice Korean peace conference, despite the American contention that such a conference should deal strictly with Korean problems.[100] The State Department was alert to the dangers awaiting on this issue in the post-armistice period, as was the Taipei government. Not only would the admission of Communist China represent a devastating political and psychological setback for the Nationalists and increase the prestige and influence of Mao's China, it would constitute a major diplomatic defeat for the United States and diminish the confidence of the American public in the United Nations.[101] A July 1953 opinion poll showed that 60 percent of those surveyed disapproved of seating the Chinese Communists in the Security Council even if they agreed to peace terms in Korea.[102]

The GOP right wing was ready to rise up in arms at any indication of softness in U.S. policy toward China and Taiwan. A front-page story in the New York Times in early April that reported that the State Department had under consideration a UN trusteeship for Taiwan leading ultimately to an independent Republic of Formosa drew immediate fire from the Republican right and necessitated a swift denial by the White House.[103] As the truce talks at Panmunjom entered the home stretch, rumors and reports of rising international sentiment for Chinese Communist membership in the UN again spurred the right wing into action. In May and June the White House had to beat back an attempt by Knowland and New Hampshire Republican Styles Bridges, along with other Senate colleagues of a similar persuasion, to attach a rider to an appropriations bill that would have cut off U.S. funds from the UN if Peking became a member.[104] In convincing Knowland and Bridges to drop the rider, Eisenhower promised (as he later related to Dulles) that he would inform the allies that the temper of Congress was such that any effort to push for China's admission would have "the most unfortunate results." He furthermore pledged that "so long as Red China was constituted on its present basis, under its present leaders, and so obviously serving the ends of Soviet Russia," his administration "would *never* be a party to its recognition and its acceptance in the United Nations."[105]

Eisenhower's words seemed practically to guarantee that Washington would continue its diplomatic quarantine so long as China was under CCP domination. In reality, the president and Dulles did not hold such an extreme position. In later public statements, both men were careful not to rule out recognition and admission to the UN if the Communist regime "purged itself" (in Dulles's words) of its aggressive ways and abided by the UN Charter.[106] In other words, their opposition to Chinese Communist membership was conditional rather than absolute and was tied to the behavior of the CCP government rather than to its Marxist-Leninist character. Dulles was at least theoretically open to a two-China solution to the representation question. Looking toward the ten-year review of the UN Charter scheduled for 1955, he privately contemplated an altered representation arrangement that would give India the China seat in the Security Council and install the People's Republic and Taiwan in the General Assembly.[107] As a practical remedy for the representation conundrum, this scheme had many liabilities. The administration could not have advanced it publicly without inviting a nasty domestic fight not to mention the denunciations of Taipei and Peking, both fervidly opposed to the two-China concept. It strained belief that the Soviet Union, ignoring its Chinese ally, would permit a Charter amendment incorporating the two-China arrangement. Feasibility aside, the scheme did have a potential advantage as a time-buying device to justify deferring consideration of the representation issue until at least 1955. Dulles no doubt recognized its short-term tactical utility in sustaining the diplomacy of postponement in private discussions with key UN members.

Essential to the efficacy of that diplomacy was the cooperation of Britain. Eisenhower administration officials, anticipating that in the postarmistice period concerned major allies such as Britain would become increasingly restless with the U.S. hard-line against China, were determined to overcome, rather than bend to, this restiveness.[108] One aspect of postarmistice China policy that occasioned no disagreement between London and Washington was the future disposition of Taiwan. Though the Foreign Office did at this time give some thought to a provisional arrangement for a neutralized Taiwan for a period of five to ten years, nothing came of these ruminations. Content with the status quo on the Nationalist bastion, Prime Minister Churchill regarded it as "a matter of honour with the United States to preserve an asylum on Formosa for those who have fought against the Communization of China."[109]

On the issue of Chinese representation in the UN, Britain tried to preserve its own flexibility while remaining in the good graces of its transatlantic ally. In the period leading up to and following the Panmunjom truce, Churchill's Conservatives had to cope with escalating pressure at home, most notably from the Labour party, for the seating of the People's Republic.[110] Within the Commonwealth, the British government had to take special note of Nehru's contempt for Chiang's reactionary regime and his conviction that Peking's representation in the UN was an indispensable part of any post–Korean War settlement in Asia. Nevertheless, Churchill hesitated to cross swords with Washington over the representation issue. He told the Indian prime minister at a meeting of Commonwealth prime ministers in June 1953 that a suitable interval would have to pass after a Korean armistice before pressing the United States to reconsider its opposition to the seating of the Chinese Communists. He himself was receptive to eventual dual representation for the two Chinas.[111] At bottom, Churchill saw no gain in jeopardizing Anglo-American friendship over Peking's admission to the world organization. Uppermost in his mind at this time was his quest for an East-West summit, for which he needed the cooperation of his skeptical American allies.[112]

In the postarmistice period, London's strategy was to continue the moratorium but only on a short-term basis so as better to stave off domestic criticism and so as to permit a reconsideration if warranted by events in East Asia.[113] As the opening of the Eighth General Assembly approached in September 1953, the State Department and Whitehall set about negotiating the terms for a moratorium extension. American officials wanted to renew the moratorium for the entire eighth session (which could extend the arrangement into 1954) whereas the British plumped for a less rigid formula. The two sides finally settled on an extension through the end of 1953.[114]

The representation issue was one of a cluster of Asian and European problems reviewed at a conference of the Big Three in Bermuda in December. At this meeting, Eisenhower and Dulles attempted to firmly hitch their British and French allies to the American wagon on the seating question and insofar as possible on other aspects of U.S. China policy. In a disquisition on that policy at one session, Dulles justified aid to Chiang as a means of protecting Taiwan, pinning down some 400,000 Communist troops stationed opposite the island to guard against an invasion, and exerting maximum torque on the Sino-Soviet relationship. Observing that the opportunities to split China from the Soviet Union seemed greater after Stalin's death earlier in the year, he served up an apologia for the policy of pressure, which he compared to the less convincing view that "being nice" to Peking would increase strain on its alliance with Moscow. Though Churchill and Eden could not have missed the implied criticism of Britain's more moderate strategy, they refrained from an unproductive debate over how best to drive the Chinese and Soviets apart. Eden merely advised against severing all contacts with Peking.[115] Unsatisfying as he found the Dullesian coercive approach, the foreign secretary was persuaded, as he apprised the British cabinet before Bermuda, that the American attitude toward China was the product of "emotional, political and military pressures" that made it difficult for the United States to follow a "realistic policy."[116]

The outcome of the Bermuda conference was favorable for the diplomacy of postponement. Eisenhower and Dulles were unyielding on the representation issue. French foreign minister Georges Bidault assured the secretary that his government believed that a UN seat for China would have to await the restoration of peace in Indochina. In a private conversation with the president, Churchill vouchsafed that Britain would vote with the United States to keep China out of the UN. "After all," he quipped, "we do prefer the United States over China as an ally."[117] Early in January 1954 London consented to an extension of the moratorium for the remainder of the Eighth General Assembly, in effect prolonging it until the following September.[118]

The Eisenhower administration had little maneuvering room on the representation issue after taking office. Both U.S. foreign policy objectives and domestic opinion dictated that Eisenhower and Dulles mount the ramparts against Chinese Communist membership, just as Truman and Acheson had done before them. Without subscribing to an absolute ban on Peking's admission, the two Republican leaders set standards for its entry that tilted the odds heavily against any reconsideration of American policy in the foreseeable future. Although Dulles's two-China scheme revealed a certain adaptability in his personal views (and in Eisenhower's, since the secretary almost certainly discussed the proposal with the president), the idea fell well short of the mark as a practical solution to the contentious representation problem. Because of the international momentum for Chinese Communist membership created by the Korean armistice, the new GOP administration had to move into high gear to sustain the diplomacy of postponement and to allay anxious public and congressional opinion. That it succeeded on both counts was the result of its own vigorous efforts and the unwillingness of close allies, Britain in particular, to defy its will.

China, Taiwan, and the New Look

The Eisenhower administration had been in office more than nine months before it got around to approving its first comprehensive policy guidelines for China and Taiwan. One reason for the delay was that the National Security Council awaited the completion of the searching examination of national security strategy that culminated in the adoption on 30 October 1953 of NSC 162/2, the top secret statement of the New Look. Shortly thereafter, the NSC ratified NSC 161/1 and NSC 146/2, the first dealing with Communist China and the second with Taiwan and the Nationalist government. All three documents confirmed that the Eisenhower administration's policies toward the two Chinese rivals would for the most part move in the grooves cut by its Democratic predecessor.

Essentially prescribing a more assertive and lower-cost version of Truman-Acheson containment that emphasized atomic firepower, the New Look did not envision a significant redirection of U.S. foreign policy in East Asia. The NSC 162/2 policy guideline conceded that the Chinese Communist regime was unlikely to be shaken loose in the foreseeable future, short of a major war, and it acknowledged the solidity of the Sino-Soviet alliance while allowing that basic differences might in the long run strain or rupture the partnership.[119]

Similar conclusions about the relative stability of both the Chinese Communist government and the Sino-Soviet alliance were present in NSC 166/1, which defined objectives and strategies to pilot decision makers in their policymaking toward Mao's China. Although not sanguine about the short-term prospects for subverting Communist control, this document enunciated as a fundamental objective "a reorientation of the Chinese Communist regime or its ultimate replacement by a regime which would not be hostile to the United States." It rejected as too costly and risky any attempt to overthrow the regime with either American or Chinese Nationalist forces. If liberation by military means was deemed unacceptable, so too was an accommodationist policy using concessions to seduce Peking into improved relations, because this was unlikely to induce better behavior. Rejecting war or appeasement, the statement in effect settled on a continuation of the policy of pressure.[120]

If less optimistic about changes in the status quo in China and framed in different circumstances, NSC 166/1 was still tailored from much the same cloth as NSC 48/5, which it replaced. Both documents directed policymakers to create Achesonian "situations of strength" in East Asia, reduce Chinese Communist power, impair Sino-Soviet relations, and seek the reorientation or replacement of the Communist government (though NSC 48/5 had also contemplated the fragmentation of the CCP leadership). Refusing to accept the permanence of Communist domination over the mainland or of the Sino-Soviet alliance, both policy papers advanced a hard-line, as opposed to a militant liberationist or accommodationist, strategy.

In tandem with their approval of NSC 166/1, Eisenhower and the National Security Council placed their imprimatur on NSC 146/2, the new policy directive for Taiwan and the Nationalist government. Repeating themes also first sounded during the Truman administration, NSC 146/2 did introduce several variations. The statement underlined more emphatically both the strategic significance of Taiwan (describing the island as an "essential element in the U.S. Far East defense position" whose preservation in noncommunist hands was necessary even at the risk of general war) and the political value of the Nationalist government in the ideological contest with Communist China. Reflecting the Eisenhower administration's fascination with psychological warfare, the document proposed that Taiwan become a base for psychological operations against the Communist regime. In contrast to NSC 48/5, NSC 146/2 did not envisage the possible emergence of a "third force" in China that might ultimately merge with the Kuomintang; the new policy prescription permitted "discreet contact" and encouragement, but no commitment of support, for "third force" groups. An accompanying NSC staff paper concluded that the Nationalist government, for all its flaws, represented "the only effective non-communist Chinese political force in being." It was recognized within the policymaking bureaucracy that past efforts in support of "third force" elements had yielded no positive results and had nettled Chiang.[121]

Making plain that the U.S. commitment to the Nationalists implied no obligation to "underwrite" their government or "guarantee" their recovery of the mainland, NSC 146/2 placed the accent on the performance and potential of the Nationalist government on Taiwan itself—on upgrading its military capabilities, making it more efficient and representative, enhancing its international stature and political appeal, and constructing a strong economy. American aid, combined with Nationalist self-help, was expected to make possible the fulfillment of these objectives. The problem, as NSC staff analysts admitted, was how to maintain the supervision and control over the Nationalist government required for effective assistance while preserving "a maximum degree of Chinese independence and self-reliance." In other words, analysts wondered how best to manage the patron-client relationship with the Taiwan government so as to preserve the requisite American influence without either stifling the initiative of the Nationalists or provoking their resistance. They admitted that KMT authorities tolerated supervision and control only as a price for needed aid and that their dependency on the

United States bred resentment along with a particular sensitivity to advice rendered at a high level, especially if disclosed publicly. The nonarticulated corollary of these observations was that American officials were best advised to tread carefully in trying to steer the Nationalists in the right direction.

During its first year in office the Eisenhower administration had fostered the impression of a more supportive relationship with Taiwan. True, the administration's dealings with the Nationalists were generally more cordial and respectful, and certain high civilian and military officials, such as Walter Robertson and Adm. Arthur Radford, were emotionally attuned to the KMT cause. Yet wariness and distrust were far from absent within policymaking circles and certainly not from the perspectives of Eisenhower and Dulles, who were unsentimental and toughminded in their appreciation of the Generalissimo and his refugee regime. As the secretary of state demonstrated on several occasions, he could be sharp and demanding when Taipei frustrated American objectives.

Overall, U.S. policy toward Taiwan did not change substantially during the first year of the new Republican administration. New restrictions on offensive operations had followed Eisenhower's deneutralization announcement. At Washington's insistence, 6,000 KMT irregulars had vacated Burma. Adding to Nationalist disgruntlement, the United States had declined to pour large amounts of new money into a military buildup on Taiwan and had rebuffed a binding treaty commitment to the Nationalist government. While entangling itself more deeply in the offshore islands, Washington had still refused to enclose them within the Taiwan defensive perimeter. On the UN representation issue, both foreign policy and domestic interests had required a continuation of the diplomacy of postponement. Dulles kept his two-China scheme under wraps. Lastly, the adoption of the New Look strategy did not set in train a major reconfiguration of existing policies toward the two contending Chinese regimes.

Above all, a basic tension still existed between the U.S. policy of guarded military support for Chiang's government and the latter's ultimate objective of recovering the mainland with American assistance. In a December 1953 report to the State Department, Ambassador Rankin called attention to the high hopes among Nationalist leaders that had attended the coming to power of the Eisenhower administration. The events of the year had deflated these expectations, as the Nationalists searched in vain for evidence that the administration would endorse an eventual large-scale counteroffensive and in due course proffer the needed help. By year's end this and other disappointments had caused a slump in Nationalist morale and a perceptible cooling of relations with Washington.[122]

7

Although the crises precipitated by events in Korea in June and November 1950 had been crucial in molding Taiwan policy, the worrying situation in Southeast Asia, particularly Indochina, also had a lesser but significant influence. In the winter of 1949 and the spring of 1950 various critics of the nonmilitary policy toward Chiang Kai-shek's refuge had played up the military and psychological connection between Taiwan's safety and the need to counter a perceived Chinese threat in Southeast Asia; this linkage was a factor in the decision to neutralize the Taiwan Strait. As the United States expanded its indirect involvement in the war in Indochina through mounting military assistance to the French, the connection grew stronger between the American military-strategic interest in Taiwan and fears of Chinese intervention in Indochina or elsewhere in Southeast Asia. The diversionary value of the KMT troops on Taiwan increased as did their potential usefulness as a strategic reserve for deployment in Southeast Asia in the event of Chinese military intrusion. Secretary Dulles had in part justified the Eisenhower administration's decision to revise the June 1950 two-way ban against offensive operations between China and the mainland as a means of inhibiting Chinese intervention in the French struggle with the Vietminh.

By early 1954 the American-assisted French military effort in Indochina was nearing its ill-fated climax. At a meeting of the Big Four foreign ministers early in January, Dulles reluctantly acquiesced in a decision to include

Indochina on the agenda of a conference on Korea scheduled for Geneva in which the People's Republic of China would participate. By the time the conference opened in the Swiss city in late April, France's military fortunes had sunk to the point that Eisenhower deliberated whether to employ American armed forces to break the Vietminh stranglehold on the besieged French outpost at Dienbienphu. Choosing not to rush to France's rescue with unilateral military intervention, the president nonetheless agreed with his secretary of state on the urgent necessity to limit Western losses at Geneva (where negotiations on Indochina began on the day after the demise of Dienbienphu on 7 May) and to retain an opening for the United States later to build a barrier against additional communist gains. Resigned to the Vietminh's control of the territory north of the 17th parallel as a result of the negotiations concluded at Geneva in late July, the Eisenhower administration subsequently acted to shore up the noncommunist government in the south and to construct the South East Asia Treaty Organization (SEATO), which was formally inaugurated in Manila the following September.[1]

The unnerving developments at Geneva and in Indochina cast a particularly large shadow over Taiwan during the first eight months of 1954. Either directly or indirectly, they affected the way in which American decision makers perceived and acted upon a variety of issues relating to the island and its Nationalist overseers — specifically, the offensive use and capability of the Nationalist armed forces, the preservation of the Nationalist government's seat in the UN, the negotiation of a mutual security treaty with Taiwan, and the defense of the offshore islands. The impact of events in Geneva and Indochina was also very much in evidence in the late summer as a confrontation with China brewed in the Taiwan Strait.

Disputes over Arms and Men

As they absorbed the bleak news from Indochina during the spring of 1954, Eisenhower and Dulles on several occasions thought out loud about using the Nationalists for "harassing tactics" and "diversionary activities" to slow the Chinese advance in Southeast Asia.[2] What sorts of mischief they had in mind is unknown. One form of harassment that the United States already practiced was the covert program of coastal raids by the Nationalists carried out under the auspices of the CIA's front organization, Western Enterprises. This program had, however, become stagnant by the spring of 1954 because the raids had proven unproductive.[3] To worsen matters, there was friction between Taiwan MAAG and Western Enterprises as well as between the latter and Nationalist authorities, who were unhappy with the dubious character and high-handedness of some CIA personnel.[4] In any event, the days of the notorious Western Enterprises were numbered. By the summer of 1954, acting on a presidential directive, the CIA was in the process of transferring responsibility for anti-Chinese coastal raiding and maritime interdiction to MAAG; that transfer had taken effect by March 1955.[5]

As Eisenhower weighed his military options in Indochina, he flirted with the insertion of Nationalist troops. Contingency plans approved in January 1954 did permit the utilization of Nationalist manpower in Southeast Asia but only if the Chinese first openly intervened.[6] Evidently the idea of deploying Chiang's soldiers in the Indochina conflict even in the absence of prior Chinese intervention tempted the president, but he recognized that this risked countermoves by Peking.[7] Regardless, it was highly doubtful that the French would have looked favorably on the idea, given their reluctance to antagonize the Chinese and their awareness of lingering resentful memories among Indochinese of the rapacious conduct of some KMT generals in the Nationalist zone of occupation in 1945–46.[8]

Added to all this, Chiang showed no inclination to volunteer his troops for Indochina.[9] Cautioning Washington that no amount of American aid to the French could salvage the situation there, he preferred that the United States funnel its assistance to Nationalist China and other wholly independent and reliably anticommunist nations in the western Pacific, whose combined strength could reduce the threat to Southeast Asia. To divert the Chinese Communists from Indochina, he recommended a flanking assault by his forces in south China.[10]

Though casting doubt on the success of the American-assisted French enterprise, Chiang tried to capitalize on the grave situation in Indochina to squeeze more military aid from Washington and to advance his restorationist goal. In December 1953 the Nationalists presented Radford with the so-called "Kai plan," a proposal for a rapid ballooning of their armed forces that they rationalized as a means of preparing for strategic missions such as a diversionary counteroffensive in south China.[11] Pending implementation of the Kai plan, the Nationalists wanted to organize their army more efficiently for offensive action by having MAAG train and equip twenty-four infantry divisions rather than the twenty-one currently covered by the U.S. aid program.[12] The JCS, concluding that the Kai and 24-division plans would result in inflated force levels, rejected them both in September 1954.[13]

By the time they got around to turning down these Nationalist proposals, the joint chiefs had settled for less than even their own optimum projections for Nationalist force levels. Following the National Security Council's decision in November 1953 to defer final action on subparagraph 12-a of NSC 146/2, which had set targets for force levels that Eisenhower found too costly, the chiefs, early in 1954, recommended an even more expensive military buildup, only to have the NSC again withhold its consent. Congress was then paring down the entire military assistance program and other higher priority demands, particularly the conflict in Indochina, had a greater claim on available funds. In July, after further review, the joint chiefs grudgingly endorsed more modest force levels for the Nationalists, in effect resigning themselves to a less than optimum version of a strategic reserve for Taiwan.[14]

As the bureaucratic wheels turned in Washington, still another player entered the debate over Nationalist force levels in the person of Gen. James A. Van Fleet, the retired former commander of the U.S. Eighth Army in Korea. With a mandate from the Pentagon to undertake a survey of American military assistance programs in the Far East and adorned with the prestigious designation of special presidential representative with the personal rank of ambassador, Van Fleet headed a large mission that descended upon Taiwan, Japan, South Korea, and the Philippines in the spring and early summer of 1954. The conclusions of his top secret report, fashioned in the context of the French collapse in Indochina, were critical, alarmist, and provocative. Among his specific recommendations was the development of Nationalist offensive military potential through implementation of a variant of the 24-division plan put forward by Taipei. In the event of another Chinese Communist aggression, he proposed that the Nationalists invade Hainan Island and then the Liaotung Peninsula.[15]

The Van Fleet report, whose tenor Eisenhower apparently found too extreme, got short shrift when it reached the National Security Council in early October 1954.[16] By this time the president and his top advisers were caught up in the offshore islands crisis and were engaged in their own reconsideration of U.S. policy in East Asia. The issue of Nationalist force levels had faded from sight. In any case, the JCS had for all practical purposes resolved the issue when they rejected the Kai and the 24-division plans and had themselves acquiesced in a reduction of the scope and pace of their own optimum program for a strategic reserve. By the end of 1954 the state of the Nationalist armed forces still left much to be desired; Washington deemed them to possess only "limited combat effectiveness."[17]

Geneva and the Diplomacy of Postponement

As the drama of Dienbienphu played to its fateful climax and the negotiations on Indochina unwound at Geneva, the Eisenhower administration once again toiled to undergird the diplomacy of postponement. Like the Korean armistice, the Geneva conference affected the international and domestic dynamics shaping the administration's calculations on the UN representation issue: it threatened to create an international groundswell for

China's admission while it simultaneously increased the vigilance of pro-Nationalist partisans ready to mobilize domestic opinion against any back-sliding by the administration. Especially because 1954 was a congressional election year, the administration could not afford any international setbacks on the politically charged representation issue.

To prevent the Geneva conference from taking up extraneous matters, Dulles made clear at the meeting of Big Four foreign ministers that convened in Berlin in January 1954 that the participants in the upcoming gathering in Switzerland would have to confine themselves strictly to the specific problems of Korea and Indochina. The secretary of state also torpedoed a Soviet proposal for a five-power conference, to include the People's Republic, that would tackle a broad array of Far Eastern questions.[18]

In the aftermath of the Berlin conference, speculation and fears surfaced in the United States that Communist China's presence at Geneva would augment international pressure to recognize Peking and admit it to the UN.[19] In a speech on 29 March before the Overseas Press Club in New York (an address best remembered for his somber appeal for "united action" in Indochina), Dulles declared loyal support for Nationalist China and firm opposition to Communist China's recognition or representation in the UN.[20] Besides soothing domestic opinion, the purpose of this pronouncement was to bolster Taipei's confidence in American steadfastness and to stiffen the spines of Western allies who might want to grant recognition or a seat in the world body to the Peking government.

For the Nationalist regime, the Geneva conference bode nothing but ill. Formally objecting to Communist China's involvement, Taipei disassociated itself from any decisions by the participants affecting its own interests. Too, it was afraid that the conference would enhance Peking's standing in the world community and give impetus to its international recognition.[21]

As Taipei feared, Geneva did give a big lift to the stature of the People's Republic.[22] Although Dulles and other American diplomatic representatives present at the conference did their utmost not to accredit the PRC's legitimacy or respectability, the secretary did hesitatingly approve meetings between mid-level members of the American and Chinese delegations to discuss the release of some seventy-six U.S. citizens held in China and the return to their own homeland of Chinese nationals detained in the United States.[23] Continued after the conference through the American and Chinese consuls in Geneva, these conversations made slight progress but would later provide the diplomatic platform for more significant ambassadorial-level talks following the offshore islands crisis.

The PRC's enhanced international status spelled trouble for the diplomacy of postponement. During a late June visit with Churchill to Washington,

Anthony Eden advised Dulles that considerable sentiment existed in Britain, Europe, and the Commonwealth "to face the problem [of Chinese representation] squarely and get it over. Only if the boil were lanced would the patient's temperature be reduced." The foreign secretary withheld any guarantee that his own government would maintain a united front with Washington. A solemn Dulles warned that the representation issue could have damaging consequences for Anglo-American relations and that Congress would insist on U.S. withdrawal from the world organization if Peking gained admission. Adamant against Chinese Communist membership under present circumstances, Dulles dangled before Eden a plan whereby the scheduled review of the UN Charter in 1955 might eventuate in a two-China arrangement in the General Assembly with India assuming the China seat in the Security Council — the same scheme that the secretary of state had first considered the previous year.[24] By putting off any immediate decision on the representation issue, the plan served a tactical purpose for Dulles, who needed British cooperation to continue the diplomacy of postponement. But the secretary also appears to have seen enough intrinsic merit in the plan later to ask John Dickey, an international lawyer, to look into a Charter amendment incorporating it. Eisenhower raised no objection when Dulles informed him of this request.[25] The two-China representation plan failed to gain any adherents in the Foreign Office, which saw nearly insurmountable barriers to its implementation.[26]

If a degree of flexibility was present in Eisenhower and Dulles's longer range thinking about the representation issue, none existed in their current policy. In fact, that policy stiffened after Senator Knowland started another brush fire on the issue following the Churchill-Eden visit in late June. Amidst reports that events at Geneva had swung UN opinion more favorably toward Communist China's admittance and that Britain now accepted such an outcome as inevitable, the Californian announced that he would resign as party floor leader to campaign for American withdrawal from the world body if Peking gained entry. Taking his cue from Knowland, Nevada Democratic senator Pat McCarran introduced a resolution authorizing an American pullout if the UN opened its doors to the Chinese Communists. Although some Senate Democrats questioned the wisdom of the withdrawal resolution, a solid congressional consensus existed against Peking's admission.[27]

Hastening to stamp out the blaze that Knowland started, Eisenhower and Dulles emphatically restated their opposition to a seat for Communist China while expressing their disapproval of a threatened American withdrawal. So concerned was Dulles with the domestic and international volatility of the representation issue that for the first time he pledged that the United States would, if necessary, cast its veto in the Security Council to keep out the

Communists. In addition, he asserted that the membership question was an "important matter" that under the Charter required a two-thirds majority in the General Assembly.[28] His announcement meant that the United States would not permit a majority of the Security Council or the General Assembly to resolve the representation issue in Peking's favor. The most immediate payoff of the announcement was to strengthen Dulles's hand in convincing Knowland to drop the withdrawal resolution for a less radical proviso that Eisenhower could accept ("He thinks he's Horatius at the Bridge," the president privately fumed at the senator's ill-considered showboating).[29]

For additional assistance in dousing the flames on Capitol Hill, Eisenhower turned to his old wartime comrade at 10 Downing Street. Underscoring the salience of the representation issue for Anglo-American accord, the president successfully appealed to Churchill for an extension of the moratorium.[30] The prime minister was unprepared to risk a breach with the United States over a question to which he attached less than overriding significance. The rigidity of Washington's China policy and the shenanigans of Knowland and his companions grated more on Eden. All the same, the foreign secretary understood the political sensitivity of the issue across the Atlantic, and he was mindful that the Anglo-American alliance was already strained because of differences over Indochina.[31]

With London having chosen to maintain its collaboration in the diplomacy of postponement, the State Department worriedly turned its attention to Paris, where since mid-June a new government had resided led by Prime Minister Pierre Mendès-France, whose supple diplomacy contributed to the accords that finally concluded the Indochina War. Throughout the proceedings at Geneva, French representatives had borne in mind American abhorrence of any bargain that traded a cessation of Chinese assistance to the Vietminh for international recognition of the People's Republic and its admittance to the UN.[32] After the conference, French ambassador Henri Bonnet hastened to assure Dulles that his government contemplated no deviation from its past policies with regard to either recognition or UN membership.[33]

The General Assembly, convening its ninth session in September 1954, approved an extension of the moratorium but, on British insistence, only until the end of the year.[34] Despite the limited term of this renewal, the diplomacy of postponement had once more worked for Washington. Both external and domestic considerations made the continuing effectiveness of that diplomacy essential to the American government. Whatever confidence Eisenhower and Dulles placed in an eventual two-China solution for the epresentation question, they understood quite well that any relaxation of their present unswerving rejection of Chinese Communist membership was incompatible with the twin policies of pressure against Peking and of support for Taipei as well as with domestic political imperatives. Yet, as Dulles admitted to the NSC early in October 1954, it was becoming harder for the United States to block Communist China's admission. "We could probably hold out for a while longer on this position," he predicted, "but certainly not for the indefinite future."[35] The secretary was apprehensive that the clock was running out on the diplomacy of postponement.

Chiang's Elusive Treaty

During the same months in 1954 that the Eisenhower administration manned the barricades against Communist China's entry into the UN, the Nationalist government importuned the State Department for the negotiation of a mutual security pact to solidify its own relationship with the United States and jack up its sagging international status. The same unsettling international developments connected with Geneva, which exacerbated the representation issue, furnished additional incentive and justification for Taipei to pursue the bilateral treaty that it had first solicited a year earlier.

Taipei chose the hiatus between the Berlin and Geneva conferences to once again raise the topic of a security pact, having received no inkling of the State Department's reaction to the draft treaty it had submitted in December 1953. Entreating Washington to sign a treaty before Geneva, or at least announce its intention to do so, Foreign Minister Yeh maintained that the psychological lift this would give the inhabitants of Taiwan would be all the more timely because of widespread opinion among them that the Geneva conference was a preliminary step toward Communist China's admittance to the UN.[36]

In a parallel initiative within the State Department, Walter Robertson went to bat for a treaty. The Far Eastern Bureau chief discerned advantages in formalizing the relationship with the ROC before Geneva. Advising Dulles in late February that a bilateral concord would offset Taipei's misgivings about the conference, he further contended that such an alliance would promote the broad objectives of NSC 146/2, put Nationalist China on the same footing as other anticommunist nations already part of the U.S. alliance system in the Asia-Pacific area, and improve the morale of Taiwan's political leadership and armed forces.[37]

Impressed with these arguments, Dulles was still unconvinced that the hour had arrived to tie the knot with Taiwan. An announcement before Geneva of a proposed defense pact with Nationalist China would offend the British and French, who would construe it as provocative and designed to upset the upcoming negotiations. As well, the secretary anticipated that a treaty with Taiwan might be "harder to sell to the Senate" than the recently ratified pact with South Korea.[38] A canvass of opinion within the State Department revealed a firm consensus outside the Bureau of Far Eastern Affairs against moving ahead with negotiations on a security pact; opposition arose in part from the view that the timing was wrong before Geneva.[39]

In addition to these considerations, the question of how to define the scope of application of a security treaty with the ROC still puzzled Dulles. How would such a pact deal with the offshore islands and with Nationalist China's lost mainland territory? Dulles had yet to find a formula that would not only keep the United States free from any obligation to protect the offshore islands but also conceal American intentions from the Communists. Nor had he come up with phraseology that would avoid military entanglement in the Nationalists' quest for mainland recovery but not connote disapproval of this goal. In some respects, the secretary told Koo in mid-May, the more fluid ad hoc defense arrangement already in place with the Nationalist government had more to recommend it than a formal treaty.[40]

Once the Geneva conference was underway, Dulles continued to steer clear of a treaty. When he hinted at a possible compact with the Nationalists in a conversation with Eden at Geneva in late April, the foreign secretary objected that it would alienate Asian opinion.[41] An announcement during the conference that the United States would enter into such an accord would have rankled both the British and French at a time when relations with them were already frayed by differences over the right course to follow in Indochina and at the bargaining table in Geneva. Following the conference, the creation of what would become the South East Asia Treaty Organization became a top priority for the administration. A move toward a defense treaty with Taiwan could easily disturb the difficult and complicated multilateral bargaining process required to make SEATO a reality.[42]

International considerations apart, Dulles remained uncertain how the Senate would receive a mutual security pact with Nationalist China. Georgia Democratic senator Walter George advised him in mid-June that such a treaty would add nothing to the existing defense relationship with Taipei and would serve no useful purpose.[43] As the ranking Democrat on the Foreign Relations Committee and his party's de facto spokesman on foreign affairs in Congress, George was a commanding figure whose opinion counted a good deal in the State Department and at the White House. Dulles may also have hesitated to raise the issue of a treaty in a congressional election year, when partisan feelings over China had already flared, and at a time when the Senate was heading toward a showdown with McCarthy.[44] In any case, with a few exceptions such as Congressman Walter Judd, notables in the China bloc refrained from putting pressure on the administration for immediate negotiation of a treaty.[45]

Nonetheless, at the end of August, as Dulles prepared to fly to Manila for the final SEATO negotiations, a renewed recommendation from Robertson tipped the balance of opinion within the State Department in favor of sanctifying the relationship with Taiwan. New circumstances since Geneva, the assistant secretary explained to his superior, argued in favor of a defense pact. First, the anticipated formation of SEATO had heightened Taipei's "sense of being discriminated against" and its desire for a bilateral treaty. Such a treaty was also consistent with the long-range U.S. goal to create a collective security arrangement for Northeast Asia—a NEATO to complement SEATO. Second, the Chinese Communists had during the summer begun a fervid propaganda campaign for the "liberation" of Taiwan. By demonstrating American resolve to protect Taiwan even at the risk of war, a treaty would remove much of the sting from this campaign as well as deflate expected international appeals to alter the island's status. Third, Chiang Kai-shek had for the first time personally expressed a willingness — provided that Washington concluded a treaty—to guarantee that he would not commence a major military operation without U.S. approval. Such a pledge would afford an extra measure of control over Nationalist military activities and of protection for the United States against an unwanted armed encounter with Communist China. Adding to these arguments, Robertson submitted that a treaty need not divulge U.S. intentions regarding the nondefense of the offshore islands and would supply a congressional sanction for what until now had been solely a presidential commitment to defend Taiwan and the Penghus.[46]

Robertson's initiative elicited a more positive response from his colleagues than six months earlier. With only a few exceptions, reactions were generally favorable.[47] Dulles himself now recognized the "probability" that it would be necessary "ultimately" to negotiate a treaty. Nonetheless, he wanted to put off a decision on timing because of the "complexities of the off-shore island problem."[48] By late August, signs of trouble had appeared around the coastal islands, and the secretary had not yet found a scope of application formula that satisfied his requirements with regard to these Nationalist possessions.[49]

Though still hesitant to take the final step, Dulles had drawn perceptibly nearer to approval of a treaty before he departed for Manila. The successful conclusion of the SEATO pact during his stay in the Philippine capital eliminated one more reason to hold back; he no longer had to worry that the negotiation of a U.S.-Taiwan treaty would hinder this coveted objective. Moreover, the establishment of SEATO left Chiang Kai-shek's domain an even more conspicuous outsider given the profusion of American defense treaties in the Far Pacific. Wishing to allay the Nationalists' sense of diplomatic isolation, Dulles on his return to Washington made a brief stopover in Taipei, but he sidestepped a renewed request from Chiang for a bilateral security treaty.[50]

In the more than six months from Robertson's initial protreaty gambit to his late August initiative, Dulles had never categorically rejected a mutual defense treaty. His objections related primarily to terms and timing rather than to desirability. Despite persistent Nationalist pleas, he could afford to bide his time because a treaty was not a military necessity and because he was under no compelling domestic pressure to start negotiations. On the other hand, international complications connected with the Geneva conference and the SEATO negotiations, together with uncertainty about the reaction of the Senate, made hasty action imprudent. And Dulles still worried about how a pact would deal with the offshore islands and with mainland territory claimed by the Nationalists but outside their control. Even so, he was leaning toward a treaty by September. The crisis over the offshore islands, which began while he was in the Philippine capital, would furnish the decisive impetus for the negotiation of Chiang's elusive treaty.

Origins of the Offshore Islands Crisis

As a result of the crisis over the KMT-occupied islands that began in September 1954, the Taiwan area for the first time become the scene of a major confrontation between Peking and Washington. The Sino-American contest over these pocket-sized coastal territories originated in conflicting interests and objectives rooted in mutual rivalry, suspicion, and fear and exacerbated by distorted analysis by each side of the other's intentions and actions. The basic ingredients that gave rise to this encounter were in evidence as it began to come to a head during the spring and summer of 1954 in the context of developments at Geneva and in Indochina.

Despite an increase in Chinese air and naval activity around the offshore islands in March, alarm bells failed to go off in Washington.[51] From Taipei, Rankin sounded a lonely note of concern that the Communists could gobble up the islands at will unless the United States interjected its own air and naval forces.[52] Peking did appear to have incentives aplenty to release the islands from Chiang's control. The Nationalists utilized them for intelligence gathering, guerrilla activities, coastal forays, and harassment of local fishing and seaborne trade. The presence of KMT forces on Quemoy (and its smaller sister island, "Little" Quemoy) denied mainland inhabitants the free use of the port of Amoy and its surrounding waters; their occupation of Matsu and its companion islands, about 110 miles northwest of Taiwan, similarly inhibited use of the port of Foochow. A nuisance and an irritation, the KMT-held offshore possessions were also an affront to Chinese sovereignty and prestige. They were, from Peking's perspective, a reminder of the unredeemed territory still under the sway of Chiang's American-sponsored outlaw regime, and their location near the mainland made it easier for that regime to keep the torch of reconquest burning.[53]

Early in 1954 the Chinese intensified their planning and preparations for a military campaign in the islands. By the late summer CCP military and political leaders had selected as their immediate target the Tachen Islands, the weakest spot in the KMT coastal chain of about twenty-five islands. They set aside a more ambitious plan approved in 1953 that called for an assault on Quemoy, the best defended of the Nationalist forward positions. As Chinese forces carried out preliminary probes in the Tachens in the spring and summer, CCP leaders took precautions to avoid inciting U.S. military action.[54]

In mid-May the Chinese capture of several islets in the Tachens suddenly alerted Washington to a looming menace there.[55] Eisenhower and other ranking decision makers were indisposed to countenance a Chinese breakthrough in Chiang's northernmost outposts. News of the French defeat at Dienbienphu on 7 May left the fate of Indochina hanging in the balance. Radford was not alone in believing that "we would not wish the Reds to have any more victories in the Far East."[56] Furthermore, the quasi commitment to the islands was so embedded in official thinking by this time that decision makers could not remain indifferent to a Chinese threat. According to Everett F. Drumwright, the deputy assistant secretary of state for Far Eastern Affairs, there was a recognition throughout the government of the "great importance" of the coastal islands "tactically and psychologically to the defense of Formosa."[57] Eisenhower and Dulles were convinced that serious damage would result to American prestige in Asia from the loss of the militarily more important islands; the president also believed that some of the islands were integral to the defense of Taiwan. Yet both the chief executive and his secretary of state recognized the hazard of an overcommitment of American prestige and military power. Eisenhower therefore backed away from a public declaration that the United States would assist in defending the islands. To warn off the Chinese, he did approve periodic visits by U.S. naval vessels to the Tachens. A naval show of strength in late May went off without incident.[58]

The administration's deliberations in May foreshadowed some of the difficulties encountered when the full-blown crisis over the outlying islands broke out in September. On the one hand, the military value of the major islands, as well as the negative politico-psychological consequences of their surrender for Nationalist morale and U.S. credibility in Asia, meant that the administration could not remain passive in the face of a Communist threat.

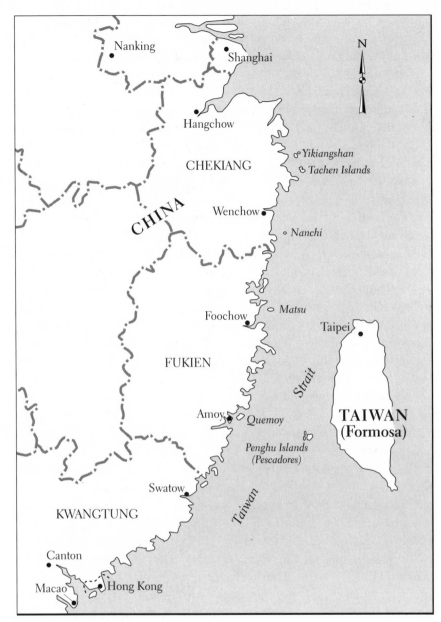

Offshore Islands in the Taiwan Strait

(Adapted from *Friends and Enemies: The United States, China, and the Soviet Union, 1948–1972*, by Gordon H. Chang, with the permission of the publishers, Stanford University Press. © 1990 by the Board of Trustees of the Leland Stanford Junior University.)

On the other hand, Eisenhower and Dulles felt that an extension of the American defensive perimeter to the islands involved an unwarranted investment of the nation's reputation and military resources. So long as the Chinese abstained from an attempt to occupy any of the major islands, the existing no-defense policy, in combination with a public posture of ambiguity, would suffice to preserve the Nationalist presence and American interests. If deterrence through uncertainty failed and the Chinese went on the offensive, the president and his advisers would face a painful choice between the possibility of losing the islands or having to resort to military intervention to save them. Eisenhower did not entirely rule out the latter.[59]

For now, policymakers could avoid any hard choices about intervention or nonintervention. Only sporadic disturbances occurred in the islands during the remainder of the spring and summer. In July Dulles turned aside another Nationalist request for a public statement such as the one proposed the previous year that insinuated the existence of a defensive commitment.[60]

The flaunting of American air and naval power in the Taiwan Strait served a purpose beyond scaring off the Communists. More broadly, it was one way in which the Eisenhower administration tried to telegraph its resolve to Peking and Moscow during and after the Geneva conference. Not wanting either adversary to draw the wrong conclusion from the defeat of the American-backed French military effort in Indochina, the administration essayed to assert American strength and resolution in Asia and convey a readiness to deploy superior U.S. air and naval resources against aggression where and when it so chose. Two seemingly unrelated incidents in June and July were part of this larger design.[61]

The first involved the capture by the Nationalist navy of the Soviet tanker *Tuapse* on 23 June in the South China Sea, between Taiwan and the Philippine island of Luzon. After escorting the vessel (which carried kerosene, useable as jet fuel) to Taiwan, the Nationalists held both it and its crew in custody.[62] Moscow immediately lodged an angry protest at the State Department, charging that only American, not Nationalist naval forces, could have carried out the seizure.[63] Though the State Department denied this accusation, American hands were far from clean because Eisenhower, a week before the capture, had secretly approved a recommendation from Dulles to inform the Nationalists of the location of Soviet tankers en route to Communist China. The administration had never before given Taipei such information (obtained from U.S. air and naval surveillance).[64]

Intended to embarrass the Soviets and remind them of the long reach of U.S. power in the Asia-Pacific area, the capture of the *Tuapse* took an unexpected turn for the administration when Moscow upped the ante by giving air and naval protection to its other transport vessels then in the vicinity of

China. The Soviets, so CIA director Allen Dulles surmised, had reckoned that Washington had ordered the seizure as the first implementation of a policy of intercepting all communist shipping in the area, and they were not about to submit passively.[65] Chiang too had a surprise up his sleeve for Washington. His government refused to release the tanker and its crew, ignoring protestations from Washington that their detention was illegal and incitive. Although it was easy for the Nationalists to conclude that these remonstrations were merely for the record, the fact was that Washington genuinely wanted to close the book on this misbegotten enterprise.[66] The continuing detention of the vessel and its crew became a nagging irritant in relations with Moscow and another source of frustration in dealings with Taipei.

Exactly a month after the *Tuapse* interception, two Chinese aircraft shot down a British commercial airliner near Hainan Island with a loss of thirteen lives, including three Americans. Both the British and American governments condemned this attack, for which Peking later offered an apology and indemnity.[67] The United States immediately sent two aircraft carriers to the scene, ostensibly to protect rescue operations. Within days, a pair of U.S. carrier-based planes had destroyed two Chinese fighters near Hainan. Washington claimed that the U.S. aircraft were in international waters when the Chinese fighters opened fire on them, whereas the New China News Agency charged that the American jets had initiated hostile action while in Chinese air space above Hainan.[68]

Whatever the particulars of the military engagement, high officials in Washington were undeniably delighted that this opportunity had arisen to bloody Peking's nose. In fact, they seem to have ordered the two aircraft carriers to the Hainan area with just such an eventuality in mind.[69] By coincidence, the downing of the British airliner occurred just as the Geneva conference ended. The destruction of the airliner plus the reported attack by Chinese fighters on U.S. aircraft enabled Washington to heap opprobrium on the Chinese for their barbarous behavior, thereby mocking their pretensions to international recognition and respectability just as they were basking in the glow of their accomplishments at the Geneva conference. Public outrage in the United States over the two episodes diverted some attention away from the troubling outcome of the conference.[70]

Like Washington, Peking too was bent on exhibiting its resolve and capability to its adversary. The PRC, immediately after Geneva, began an unprecedented full-throttle propaganda campaign for the "liberation" of Taiwan and other KMT-held territory.[71] Scholarly analyses using available Chinese sources have identified two major nondomestic reasons why CCP leaders decided to turn up the heat in the Taiwan area at this time.[72] One was that they viewed U.S. Taiwan policy as part of a broader pattern of harassment, strategic encirclement, and threat directed against the PRC. They believed that the United States, driven by its imperialistic nature and its animus toward a CCP-led China, wanted to place the PRC in a strategic vise and perhaps in time directly assault the mainland. Misperceiving American intentions, they failed to understand that Washington contemplated neither aggressive action from Taiwan by U.S. forces nor assistance to Chiang for mainland reconquest.

A second reason why Chinese leaders wished to fix attention on Taiwan was their fear that the United States wanted to absorb the island permanently within its sphere. The tightening bond between Washington and Taipei contradicted their own desire to reunify the nation and end the civil war. The longer the U.S.-KMT union went unchallenged, the greater the danger of the institutionalization of the status quo in the Taiwan Strait and of the permanent separation of Taiwan from the mainland.

By late July 1954 the PRC leadership had gotten wind of the possible negotiation of a mutual defense treaty between Washington and Taipei.[73] Such a treaty would, from their vantage, place Taiwan beyond reach for the indefinite future by giving technical legitimacy to the American occupation of the island and by formally incorporating it into the ring of American alliances that enclosed the PRC. What is more, there were disquieting signs that the United States might include Taiwan in a Northeast Asian security arrangement with South Korea and Japan. At a press conference on 3 August 1954, Dulles stated that such a military coupling was under consideration. The Chinese press accused Washington of scheming to create a NEATO to link with the SEATO it was then constructing. Actually, a NEATO was not in the works in Washington (though it was a long-term U.S. policy objective), and the Nationalists themselves considered such an alliance presently unrealizable.[74]

The massive Taiwan liberation propaganda campaign could serve the ends of CCP leaders by bringing the Taiwan question into the international spotlight, reasserting China's claims and grievances, and impeding the conclusion of a U.S. alliance with Chiang. But Mao was convinced that his American imperialist adversaries were too haughty to show restraint unless "driven into a tight corner." Turning to "coercive diplomacy," he believed that carefully calibrated military action could dramatize China's dissatisfaction with the existing state of affairs in the Taiwan area and obstruct the negotiation of a mutual defense treaty. According to some scholars, Mao intended to confine military action for the purpose of political demonstration only to the bombardment of Quemoy (which Peking ordered in late August) and saw the planned campaign in the Tachens as an essentially military operation whose main objective was the acquisition of this KMT-held territory.[75]

Whatever the distinction drawn by Mao and his associates between their military activities in Quemoy and the northern offshore islands, it was understandable that American decision makers would view these hostilities as interrelated parts of a single campaign to drive the Nationalists off their coastal bases.

In Washington, the official frame of mind toward China in the late summer of 1954 was antagonistic, edgy, and prone toward muscle flexing. On 18 August the National Security Council began consideration of NSC 5429, a review of U.S. policy in the Far East prepared by its Planning Board to take into account conditions since Geneva. Asserting that communist successes in Indochina had reduced American prestige and imperiled U.S. security interests throughout that part of the world, the draft policy paper listed four alternative courses of action toward China arranged in ascending order of militancy: alternative A, the least aggressive, called for placing relations on the same footing as with the Soviet Union; alternative B, the existing policy, mandated a reduction of Chinese power by means short of war; alternative C proposed a lessening of that power even at the risk of war but without purposely instigating one; and alternative D, the most truculent, prescribed a combative policy to use force to prevent any further Communist expansion in Asia.[76] Anchored in the premise that China's goal was to communize all of Asia, the document showed no awareness that the animosity and pugnacity of Chinese leaders toward the United States might stem in part from fears of strategic encirclement and possible armed action against their territory.

The members of the National Security Council, both military and civilian, divided over the alternatives presented in NSC 5429. No one endorsed alternatives A or D, the most moderate and most militant options. In a written statement prepared in advance of the meeting, army chief Matthew Ridgway objected to all four alternatives, maintaining that a principal U.S. goal should be to separate China from the Soviet bloc. In contrast, three other JCS members, representing the navy, air force, and marines, went on record in support of the more robust policy described in alternative C (with amendments that clarified and moderated it somewhat).[77] Admiral Radford lined up with the majority of his JCS colleagues at the 18 August session.

Among civilian NSC members, Harold Stassen, the avidly pro-Nationalist director of the Foreign Operations Administration (FOA), was the most belligerent, stating that the United States should "take on" the Communists after their next aggressive move. Preferring a more moderate tack, Secretary Dulles offered several reasons for caution: the danger that the United States might career into a war with Communist China that would invite the disapproval of world opinion; the changing views of the allies toward China; and the evolving complexity of the Sino-Soviet alliance, which the United States could not overlook even if an eventual rupture was still in the future. Dulles recommended continuation of the current policy pending further study of the proposed alternatives.

Like his top foreign affairs adviser, President Eisenhower did not foresee a sundering of the Sino-Soviet partnership in the near term, and he worried that a collision with China would isolate the United States from world opinion. Still, alternative C had a strong pull on him. Bowing to Dulles's concerns, he agreed to postpone further discussion of NSC 5429 until the secretary presented a report to the NSC in a month's time. Yet he also stipulated that alternative C (with the JCS amendments) should be the basis for those deliberations. Looking ahead, he anticipated that the NSC would very likely end up with essentially this alternative. Without having made a final decision, the president had nonetheless pointed U.S. China policy in a more risk-taking direction.

Before the close of this meeting, the NSC also took up the question of whether to extend an American defensive commitment to the offshore islands. Radford proposed a change in the no-defense policy, declaring that the United States had to hold the islands because of their military value and because it "simply could not afford to lose any more ground in the Far East." Eisenhower, too, was loathe to let the Communists have the islands. Describing them as "vital outposts for the defense of Formosa," he commented that "we should go as far as possible to defend them without inflaming world opinion against us." Without coming to any conclusion about Radford's recommendation, the NSC commissioned the Defense Department to prepare a report on U.S. policy toward the islands. This request left a revision of the no-defense policy on the table for further discussion. In the meantime, it was apparent that leading decision makers were in no mood to retreat before a Communist provocation.[78]

As the temperature rose in the Taiwan Strait as a result of the PRC's liberation campaign, the administration sent warning signals to Peking. On 17 August Eisenhower told reporters that "any invasion of Formosa would have to run over the 7th Fleet."[79] Two days later, four U.S. destroyers paid a visit to the Tachens.[80] Asked by newsmen on 24 August whether the United States was obligated to safeguard the KMT-held islands, Dulles avoided a clear-cut answer, but he did stress the close connection between some of the islands and the security of Taiwan, adding that any decision about American protection would be primarily military.[81] These remarks caused a nervous shiver in London, where the Foreign Office was keeping a worried watch over the strait, and prompted Eden to urge the Americans to keep the thermostat down and give full weight to political, as well as military considerations, in determining whether to defend the islands.[82]

As the British foreign secretary appealed for restraint, Dulles brooded over the effect on American credibility of a Communist success in the islands. Finding any further loss of prestige in the Far East after Indochina unpalatable, he was willing, so he told a number of intimate advisers, to "take a strong line militarily [in the offshore islands] which might involve de facto belligerency for a certain period." At the same time, he wanted the United States to preserve a "*flexible* position" which involved no commitment to the "long-range, permanent defense of these islands." Their defense had to be "determined in the light of the then applicable political and military considerations for the area." Dulles's words show the emphasis he placed on politico-psychological reasons for keeping the islands out of the hands of the Chinese and how closely, in his own mind, the quasi commitment to their defense had edged to a full commitment. While shying away from a long-term obligation binding the United States irretrievably to their protection, he seemed prepared to chance a military scuffle with the Chinese to keep them safe.[83]

So as Dulles enplaned for Manila in early September, the tableau for confrontation was set in the Taiwan Strait. Increased militancy and risk-taking were evident both in Peking and Washington. Following Geneva, the PRC had initiated the Taiwan liberation campaign and prepared to undertake a limited political and military offensive in the offshore islands. In Washington, the disturbing developments at Geneva and in Indochina contributed to a further hardening of official attitudes toward China and to a determination to shore up U.S. credibility and strategic interests. Making unmistakably clear that the United States would defend Taiwan, policymakers also communicated their strong interest in the security of the outlying islands. Though the secret no-defense policy did remain in place, JCS chief Radford had set in motion an initiative to overturn it. In any event, the quasi commitment was so firmly implanted in official perceptions that decision makers would not shrink from a Communist challenge in the islands when it came.

On 3 September 1954 Chinese coastal artillery near the port of Amoy opened fire across the two-mile harbor separating the mainland from Quemoy. The bombardment marked the start of a harrowing nearly nine-month encounter with China and one of the most trying foreign confrontations of the Eisenhower presidency. Before the 1954–55 offshore islands crisis was over, it would plunge U.S.-Chinese relations to their lowest point since Korea, tighten as well as wrench the bond between Washington and Taipei, and severely stress United States relations with close allies.[1] The possibility of a war between the United States and China over seemingly insignificant specks of land off the China coast strained the nerves of the American public and of fearful foreign onlookers. The crisis saw President Eisenhower obtain unprecedented discretionary authority from Congress for military action, brandish the nuclear cudgel against China, extend and then withdraw a defensive commitment to Quemoy and Matsu, and make an extraordinary secret offer to Chiang Kai-shek to coax him into a withdrawal from his island outposts. On the diplomatic side, Secretary Dulles pursued a convoluted course to resolve the crisis, peacefully if possible, but above all on terms that optimized American interests and goals.

Throughout the protracted span of the taut contest with China, Eisenhower and Dulles dominated the administration's decision making. The crisis went through four discernible phases during which the two leaders and their principal advisers debated and implemented different strategies to cope with evolving perceptions of Chinese intentions and to accomplish American objectives. An excruciating dilemma would vex policymakers throughout the crisis: how to avert the unpalatable military and especially the politico-psychological consequences of a Communist takeover of Quemoy or other important Nationalist-held coastal islands but at the same time avoid U.S. armed intervention under circumstances that would result in an unwanted war with China, to be fought without the benefit of supportive allies or sympathetic national and international opinion.

During the first phase of the crisis, from early September 1954 to mid-January 1955, Eisenhower and Dulles followed a generally circumspect strategy, sticking to the secret no-defense policy while maintaining a public posture of ambiguity to deter the Chinese. Meanwhile, Dulles endeavored to weave a diplomatic web to stabilize the Taiwan area both in the short and longer term. Four months after the beginning of the crisis, this web still remained incomplete and fragile.

The Crisis Begins

Although it had been evident for some months that trouble was stirring in the offshore islands, the shelling of Quemoy caught Washington by surprise. Eisenhower was ensconced at the summer White House in Denver, and Dulles had just alighted in Manila for the SEATO negotiations. Neither was present when the National Security Council, with Vice President Nixon in the chair, convened in the capital on 9 September to confer about the unsettling new development in the Taiwan Strait. Three days later, following Dulles's return from Asia, the president and the NSC assembled at Lowry Air Force Base near Denver to decide on a course of action.

Coming during the shrill "Liberate Taiwan" propaganda campaign and in seeming defiance of American efforts to warn off the Chinese in the coastal islands, the bombardment of Quemoy engendered a sense of crisis among high-level policymakers, who were already inclined toward a test of wills with China. Heightened by the downing on 4 September of a U.S. navy patrol plane in the Sea of Japan by two Soviet aircraft, the crisis animated a lively dispute over whether or not to jettison the no-defense policy. For the first time, decision makers had to confront head-on the grave implications of the quasi commitment to the defense of the islands.

To assist decision makers, intelligence analysts worked overtime to decipher Chinese intentions and to assess the threat to Quemoy and other coastal islands. They agreed that the Chinese could overwhelm any of the islands in a matter of days, except for Quemoy, whose capture would require a time-consuming and costly assault. They did not doubt that the Chinese aspired at some time to appropriate the islands, and while unable to predict when the PLA would actually storm the KMT-occupied outposts, they did identify an assortment of motives for an early move against them. On balance, however, intelligence experts anticipated that the Chinese would follow a strategy of measured risk by abstaining from an all-out attack as long as they were uncertain of the U.S. reaction. Analysts detected no buildup for an invasion of Quemoy and saw no present danger to Taiwan itself. The CIA speculated that the Chinese might have timed their artillery barrages to affect the Manila conference. Later in the month Allen Dulles reported that the shelling of Quemoy might only be a feint, with the Tachen Islands the actual objective.[2]

Chinese documentary evidence bears out the CIA chief's suspicion that the PLA's target was the Tachens rather than Quemoy or Matsu. The bombardment of Quemoy, besides serving a political purpose by drawing international attention to the PRC's vehement opposition to the status quo in the Taiwan area and to the rumored negotiation of a mutual security pact between Washington and Taipei, appears to have been a diversionary move in the planned campaign against the northernmost Nationalist islands.[3]

Before the Chinese had even begun to rain shells down on Quemoy, a militant majority of the JCS led by Admiral Radford had set about to reverse the no-defense policy. In a memorandum dated 2 September prepared in connection with the NSC's mid-August request for a Pentagon review of that policy, these JCS hawks urged the necessity of a selective defensive guarantee for ten of the islands then under Nationalist control. The proposed selective guarantee would remain secret, so as not to create a risk-free opportunity for the Communists to grab those islands left unshielded. The JCS hawks stressed the politico-psychological, rather than the strictly military, consequences of the forfeiture of the major islands. Although valuable as bases, early warning sites, and potential obstacles to an invasion, none of the islands was essential to the defense of Taiwan and the Penghus. From a military standpoint, the worst consequence of their capture would be the loss of some 64,000 American-trained and -equipped troops garrisoned on them, more than 40,000 on Quemoy alone. When the JCS hawks turned to politico-psychological considerations, they pulled out all the stops, predicting that Communist seizure of the key islands would seriously impair the morale and international stature of the Nationalists, lessen American prestige worldwide and particularly in the Far East, and enervate the leadership and strategic position of the United States throughout the Far Pacific.[4]

This recommendation for a revamping of the no-defense policy split the National Security Council when it met for the first time in Washington.

Taking up the banner for a selective defensive guarantee, Radford contended that the United States had invested "100%" of its prestige in the retention of the islands by having encouraged and assisted the Nationalists to keep them. He was confident that U.S. air and naval units could protect the islands, provided that American commanders had authority to strike at mainland military installations.[5]

In advocating a defensive commitment, Radford did not speak for the entire defense establishment nor even for all the joint chiefs. In a familiar dissenting role, Gen. Matthew Ridgway had taken issue with the conclusions of his more martial colleagues. A selective guarantee, the independent-minded army chief of staff insisted, would require a large American force to back it, including ground troops, and would eventually draw the United States into a general war with China. The intrinsic military importance of the islands was clearly incommensurate with such a sizable and perilous commitment. As for the nonmilitary consequences of the loss of the islands, Ridgway left that to civilian authorities to evaluate.[6] Also squaring off against the JCS hawks was Secretary of Defense Charles Wilson, no admirer of Chiang Kai-shek. For the blunt and outspoken Pentagon chief, a defensive commitment to any of the Generalissimo's forward positions spelled war with China. Wilson would continue to speak out against a protective guarantee in later debates. The fact that he did not enjoy Eisenhower's confidence and was not one of the heavyweights on the NSC limited his influence, however.[7]

Undersecretary of State Walter Bedell Smith, who was in charge of the State Department while Dulles was away, was more tentative in his views than either the JCS hawks or Wilson. He did oppose any defensive commitment without a reasonable certainty that it was possible to hold Quemoy against the Chinese.[8]

In the absence of the president and the secretary of state, the NSC arrived at no decisions at its Washington meeting. On that same day Dulles was in Taipei for his post-Manila rendezvous with Chiang. Although he skirted the topic of the offshore islands in his talk with the Nationalist president, he was at this point leaning toward a defensive commitment, at least with regard to Quemoy, even if the result was (as he had cabled Washington from Manila) a "committal of US force and prestige [that] might lead to constantly expanding US operations against [the] mainland." While not wanting to repeat the French mistake at Dienbienphu by making a symbol of a military strongpoint that the enemy would then expend immense casualties to overcome, he advised that if it was possible to retain Quemoy with U.S. assistance, "then much of the Communist prestige stemming from Dien Bien Phu will have been cancelled out."[9] Attractive as a Dienbienphu-in-reverse might have been to Dulles, Eisenhower was more afraid of a replay of the French debacle, doubting that Quemoy could hold out indefinitely if the Chinese were prepared to accept heavy losses.[10]

On 12 September the president gathered in Denver with the entire National Security Council, his secretary of state included, for a full-dress review of the tense situation. By this time the bombardment of Quemoy had claimed the nervous attention of newspaper editorialists and other opinion leaders; no consensus existed among them about what to do.[11] Disagreement persisted among the president's military and civilian advisers as well. The joint chiefs, having looked more closely at Quemoy's relevance to the protection of Taiwan and at its defensibility if the United States intervened, had again divided, with Ridgway once more the lone maverick. Denying that Quemoy was "substantially related" to Taiwan's defense, the army chief asserted that placing the island under an American protective umbrella would require a major redeployment of U.S. forces in the region and chance an all-out military conflict with China, if not a world war. The JCS hawks, contending that not just Quemoy but Matsu and the Tachens were "substantially related" to the protection of Taiwan, held that direct American military involvement could ensure Quemoy's safety so long as U.S. commanders had the authority to hit mainland targets, using atomic weapons if necessary.[12]

Among the civilians on the NSC, only FOA director Harold Stassen sided with the JCS hawks, but the youthful former Republican governor of Minnesota was not in the front rank of policymakers.[13] Defense Secretary Wilson was again the most vociferous critic of a defensive commitment. Yet even he did not advocate any alternatives, such as a reduction or removal of Nationalist forces, which would have contradicted the existing quasi commitment.[14]

Indeed, the quasi commitment defined the parameters for the entire debate within the NSC. No one second-guessed past policies that had encouraged and aided the Kuomintang to entrench itself on the islands and that had associated American prestige with their protection. A strong feeling existed within the NSC that, whatever their military value, the islands had assumed so much symbolic import for both the Nationalists and the United States that their loss would constitute a considerable politico-psychological defeat.

This was assuredly President Eisenhower's conviction, as his remarks at the Denver meeting underscored. Even though the assessments of the joint chiefs now seem to have persuaded him that the offshore islands were not "vital outposts for the defense of Formosa" (as he had described them less than a month earlier), the president was positive that the seizure of a major island such as Quemoy would deal a harsh blow to Nationalist morale and American prestige and that the United States could not remain indifferent to such an outcome. Despite this, he refused to overturn the no-defense policy, drawing the line against the selective guarantee recommended by the JCS hawks. Accepting the worst-case scenario of Ridgway and Wilson that a collision over the islands would land the United States in a war with China and having in mind the Korean experience and New Look strategy of nuclear retaliation, he declared that in a fight with the Chinese over the islands he would not spare mainland military installations or use only conventional weapons. But he shrank from the dire prospect of no-holds-barred hostilities with China touched off by a scrap over the islands. Bent on striking a balance between the nation's limited military resources and the demands of a global anticommunist strategy, he cautioned against "making too many promises to hold areas around the world and then having to stay there to defend them." If there was to be a general war, he preferred to "go to the head of the snake," the Soviet Union, not China.

Looking beyond military and strategic considerations, Eisenhower hesitated to enter into a war over the coastal islands without congressional authorization. "Whatever we do must be done in a Constitutional manner," he insisted, expressing his own conservative view of the president's war powers and his determination not to repeat Truman's mistake in Korea by bypassing Congress. On top of this, he was dubious that the administration could "put the proposition of going to war over with the American people at this time" or count on the ready support of Britain or other Western allies.[15]

Thus, in rejecting the recommendation of the JCS hawks, the president took into account an assortment of military and nonmilitary factors: the likelihood of a wider conflict with China, the primacy of the global contest with the Soviet Union, the lack of sufficient military resources to keep pace with an unchecked proliferation of strategic commitments, constitutional restraints, and the need for public and allied support. These same factors would throughout the crisis impress on him the dangers of overcommitment in the offshore islands.

Eisenhower was unquestionably in agreement when Dulles told the NSC at its Denver meeting that the United States faced a "horrible dilemma" in the offshore islands. The politico-psychological consequences of weakness in the face of the Communist threat, the secretary lamented, were no more acceptable than a war with China, possibly involving atomic weapons, which most of world opinion and many Americans would condemn. Dulles's view had moderated since his first messages from Manila, at least in part because he wanted to keep in step with the president. As during his entire tenure as secretary of state so during the offshore islands crisis, he never forgot that his relationship with Eisenhower was his indispensable source of authority and power.

As a means of avoiding impalement on either horn of the "horrible dilemma," Dulles proposed to the NSC a plan to freeze the status quo in the offshore islands through a resolution of the UN Security Council. He reasoned that the United States stood to benefit from such a resolution whether or not the Chinese and the Soviets accepted it. If they did so, the islands would be out of immediate danger and still remain under Nationalist control; if not, the United States, by having first resorted to a peaceful remedy, would be in a much stronger moral position before national and international opinion to justify intervention to save the islands.[16] Eisenhower readily gave Dulles the go-ahead to explore with the British and the Nationalists his plans for an internationally sanctioned cease-fire. His decision restrained the JCS hawks and meant that the administration would continue secretly to withhold a defensive commitment while publicly keeping the Communists guessing about American intentions.

A secondary benefit of the UN cease-fire plan, at least in Dulles's mind, was that it might enable the United States to skewer the Soviet Union on the Taiwan issue. In plotting his UN stratagem, the secretary had reckoned that it would put the Soviets in a difficult fix: if they went along with a Security Council injunction barring China from using force in the offshore islands, they would impair relations with their ally; if, on the other hand, they opposed or vetoed such a measure, they would lessen the credibility of the "peace offensive" that they had begun after Stalin's death to relax international tensions and to propagate a more benign image in world affairs. Either way, the Kremlin would be the loser and the Sino-Soviet alliance would suffer.[17]

American officials spotted signs that Soviet leaders were careful in their backing of the Chinese on the Taiwan issue. A statement by Communist Party first secretary Nikita Khrushchev in a speech in Peking on 30 September that the Soviet people supported the "noble cause" of Taiwan liberation did not especially disturb Kremlin watchers in Washington.[18] Allen Dulles assured the NSC that Khrushchev was "rather a brash fellow" whose "rather extreme statement" should be taken "with a grain of salt."[19] Tellingly, the Soviet leader had pledged no specific action by the USSR. U.S. ambassador Charles E. Bohlen reported from Moscow that the Soviet government appeared to be playing down the Taiwan issue so as to avoid the impression of a commitment to the Chinese.[20]

Shortly after the Denver meeting on 12 September, the word went out to Taipei that the Nationalists would have to continue to protect the offshore islands on their own.[21] While expediting the allocation and shipment of military material to Chiang's armed forces, Washington tried to curb KMT military activities that would incite the Communists.[22] The Pacific commander in chief maintained close supervision of Nationalist defensive air strikes against mainland targets.[23] After Communist artillery barrages against Quemoy abated, the Nationalists stopped their own shelling of the mainland at American behest.[24] As an additional precaution, Eisenhower ordered the suspension of assistance both for mainland raids (they had been in abeyance anyway) and for interdiction of communist shipping.[25]

Domestic and international circumstances during the fall and early winter months of 1954 contributed to the Eisenhower administration's cautious crisis management. Although Eisenhower and Dulles were undoubtedly aware that they would put themselves in the crosshairs of pro-Nationalist partisans, in and outside of Congress, if they should simply cut loose from the islands, these pro-Chiang zealots exerted less influence on the two leaders than some scholars have claimed.[26] Correctly reading the national mood during the Denver deliberations, what most concerned the two of them was that U.S. intervention would split the country and the Congress. The uncertainty and division about intervention that surfaced among articulate opinion at the outset of the crisis persisted in the following weeks. Among the general public, there was disagreement even about how far the United States should go to defend Taiwan itself.[27]

The midterm elections presented still another incentive for the administration to act circumspectly in the Taiwan Strait, because the return of a Republican majority to Congress pivoted on their outcome. Even after the results of the November balloting gave the Democrats control of the legislative branch, the administration had reason to avoid precipitous actions in the strait, because this might unduly strain its cooperation with the opposition party in foreign affairs. The Democratic win also further distanced the administration from the Republican right wing, whose dissatisfaction with Eisenhower had been mounting throughout 1954 and whose power within the GOP the president had sought to reduce. The Senate's censure of Joseph McCarthy in early December 1954 struck a hard blow against the Old Guard, much to Eisenhower's private satisfaction.[28] The declining influence of the right wing (home to many members of the China bloc) gave the administration more leeway to pursue a careful strategy in the offshore islands.

If Eisenhower and Dulles did not compartmentalize domestic and foreign affairs, neither did they view events in the China-Taiwan area in isolation from developments elsewhere on the global scene. In particular, as they showed at Denver, they worried about the impact on the Western allies of a decision to defend Quemoy and other coastal islands. The NATO alliance was then in a disturbed state because of the French Assembly's rejection of the European Defense Community (EDC), which occurred only days before the shelling of Quemoy commenced and threw into confusion plans for German rearmament. Happily for Washington, these plans went forward under a different arrangement at the end of October as a result of the signing of the Paris accords recognizing West Germany as a sovereign state and accepting it into NATO. The negotiation of the accords was a personal triumph for Anthony Eden, to whom Dulles was appropriately grateful.[29] As Eisenhower and Dulles grappled with the conundrum of the offshore islands, they kept in sight the need to prevent additional stress on the Western alliance (NATO members still had to ratify the Paris accords) and to nurture a harmonious relationship with Eden, who they knew would disapprove of American intervention to protect any of the islands.

Another factor that sustained the administration's cautious strategy during the fall and early winter was that Chinese actions in the islands did not threaten an immediate emergency. At Denver, Dulles anticipated that the situation would not turn critical for some time because of Chinese uncertainty about American intentions and because of unfavorable weather and sea conditions in the Taiwan Strait during the monsoon season, which would last until the following spring.[30] After mid- to late September, no further serious outbreak of fighting occurred in any of the coastal islands until early November, when Chinese naval, air, and artillery bombardment for a short time pounded the Tachens. During the fall and early winter, U.S. intelligence was unable to detect preparations for a large-scale attack against any of the KMT forward positions.[31]

Between London and Taipei

The absence of an imminent emergency gave Dulles much needed breathing space in which to move forward his UN venture. In order to give flight to that project, he turned for help to London and Taipei. From the British, he sought cooperation in planning and implementing a UN cease-fire initiative; from the Nationalists, he wanted at least acquiescence in such an undertaking. In the weeks after Denver, he immersed himself in an arduous process of discussion and negotiation with both parties, one an intimate ally and the other a valued client, each wanting to pull him in a different direction. Satisfying both London and Taipei taxed the practiced diplomatic skills of even the artful Dulles. By early November he had obtained only conditional British approval of a plan for a UN initiative, and he had barely managed to allay Nationalist rage over a proposed cease-fire, despite having offered Taipei a mutual security treaty as a balm.

Before approaching the Nationalists, Dulles wanted to ensure that the British endorsed his UN plan. On 17 September, during a stopover in London to talk to Eden, he proposed a cease-fire initiative in the Security Council in order to at least provisionally neutralize the offshore islands. Concealing the still extant secret no-defense policy, he warned that the United States "stood on the great divide between peace and war" over the "crucial issue" of what to do about the islands. He theorized that the UN initiative might start a "process of far-reaching negotiations" that could perhaps lead to a broader Far Eastern settlement and to a resolution of Anglo-American differences in that part of the globe.[32]

Even without the tantalizing appeal of a wider settlement extending beyond the offshore islands, Eden had abundant reason to encourage Dulles in his search for a peaceful solution. The UN initiative gave Britain a chance to play its familiar moderating and restraining role in American policymaking in East Asia. The British chiefs of staff believed that Quemoy was neither essential to the safety of Taiwan nor defendable against an invasion.[33] Churchill's cabinet was eager to find a path out of the crisis that avoided a blowup between the United States and China, which otherwise might imperil regional and possibly world peace and jar Anglo-American relations.[34] Conservative government leaders recognized only too well that British opinion, and most certainly the Labour opposition, would not support Washington in a showdown over seemingly trivial bits of land off the China coast. Ever since the Geneva conference, Sino-British relations had been on the upswing, and in September the Chinese and British governments inaugurated diplomatic relations.[35]

Despite his understandable keenness to seek a peaceful exit from the crisis, Eden was initially noncommittal when Dulles broached the cease-fire initiative, realizing that it could easily fall victim to Chinese noncooperation and a Soviet veto. As an alternative, he suggested direct negotiations between the United States and China. That idea left Dulles cold; domestic opposition, he protested, made it impractical. Other reasons also accounted for this summary rejection. The secretary of state had an instinctive distaste for direct talks with the Chinese and knew that conversations with them about the offshore islands would rile the Nationalists. As well, he regarded the offshore islands issue as nonnegotiable in present conditions.

Upon reflection, Eden persuaded himself that the only satisfactory course was to lend Britain's support to the UN initiative, doing everything possible to facilitate its acceptance in Peking and Moscow. For this reason, he obtained Dulles's agreement that the Security Council should invite the Chinese Communists to participate in its discussions of a military standstill. He and Dulles agreed that New Zealand should introduce the cease-fire resolution.[36] The Commonwealth island nation then held one of the rotating seats on the Council and was well suited to front the UN initiative because of its Pacific location and its bonds with both Britain and the U.S.

In early October the United States, Britain, and New Zealand held secret tripartite discussions in Washington to draft a cease-fire resolution and to hammer out an agreed minute defining the ground rules for their collaboration. It quickly became apparent that the British wanted a broader scope for the initiative than the Americans. This disagreement stemmed in part from the British belief that Dulles himself saw the resolution as a way of facilitating a wider settlement of China-related issues — a conclusion which the American diplomat's suggestive remarks along this line to Eden and others had fostered.[37]

Whatever impression he had given about his own expectations, Dulles resisted British efforts to enlarge the scope of the initiative beyond the narrow objective of dousing the flames around the offshore islands. As far as larger goals were concerned, the most he now offered was an increased likelihood of a peaceful adjustment of problems in the Taiwan area if the initiative should prove productive — a far cry from the more expansive vista that had enticed Eden.[38] Not only was Dulles unwilling to employ the initiative to kick start a process leading to a Chinese-American démarche, he did not believe (as did his British counterpart) that its usefulness hinged on Chinese Communist acceptance of a proposed cease-fire; he rightly expected that the People's Republic would reject the UN's jurisdiction over the offshore islands. He hoped that the mere introduction of a cease-fire resolution in the world body might itself serve as deterrent: CCP leaders, though they would likely repudiate such a resolution, might be loathe to flaunt the UN and world opinion by actually attacking the islands.[39] At the conclusion of their tripartite deliberations, the United States, Britain, and New Zealand settled upon wording for the agreed minute and the cease-fire resolution (which called on Peking and Taipei to terminate hostilities and recommended peaceful methods to prevent the recurrence of fighting) that restricted the scope of the UN action as Dulles wished. In keeping with Eden's desire to smooth the pathway for acceptance of the resolution by Peking and Moscow, the minute did stipulate advance notification of the two communist governments prior to the resolution's introduction.[40]

Scheduled for implementation in mid-October, the UN initiative, now code-named "Oracle," ran afoul of Chiang Kai-shek only a few days before reaching its takeoff point. The Generalissimo learned of the planned introduction of the cease-fire resolution from Walter Robertson, who flew to Taipei specifically to break the news to him and to overcome his expected strong opposition.[41] As a sweetener to help him swallow this bitter pill, Robertson brought an offer to negotiate a mutual defense treaty.

The unstable situation in the strait, coupled with the need to win Chiang over to the UN initiative, had convinced Dulles, who had been tilting toward a defense pact since late summer, that the moment was now opportune to grant the Generalissimo the alliance that he had long craved. Both Ambassador Rankin and Robertson recommended a pact to offset the harmful effect on Nationalist morale of the UN action. The assistant secretary also depicted a treaty as the best way to make it "absolutely clear" to the Chinese Communists that the United States would defend Taiwan.[42] Dulles subsequently obtained Eisenhower's consent to negotiate a treaty, provided that Chiang went along with the UN initiative and that the compact was defensive in nature, allowing "only operations which we jointly agreed on as in the common interest."[43] The treaty would, in other words, keep a rein on Chiang but would preserve the option of offensive operations with mutual consent. The need to retain tactical flexibility, allow for unforeseen circumstances, and indulge Nationalist aspirations for mainland recovery made an absolute ban on offensive activities impractical. Even so, now that the wars in Korea and Indochina were over, Dulles doubted that it was any longer necessary to maintain Taiwan as a threat to China's flank or as a base for harassment.[44]

Despite Robertson's proffer of a mutual security pact, Chiang took umbrage at the UN initiative (which the State Department envoy concealed had been hatched in Washington), protesting that it would have a "destructive effect" on morale throughout Taiwan and among pro-KMT Chinese everywhere and would "play into Communist hands." A cease-fire and neutralization of the offshore islands, he predicted, would lead to a similar solution for Taiwan, then to a UN trusteeship and Chinese Communist membership in the UN, and finally to Communist occupation of his stronghold. Reminded by the assistant secretary that he could not count on the United States to protect the offshore islands, Chiang avowed that his troops had orders to fight to the last man, with or without the intervention of the Seventh Fleet. Dismissing the argument that the UN action would improve his chances of keeping possession of the islands, the Nationalist president agreed only to conditionally reserve his government's position in the Security Council on such action until Moscow and Peking had made known their reactions.[45]

A Diplomatic Seesaw

In an ironic twist, the decision to offer Chiang a mutual defense treaty to surmount his resistance to Oracle induced Eden to have second thoughts about proceeding with the UN venture. Intended to grease the wheels for Oracle in Taipei, the treaty offer caused an abrupt slamming of the brakes in London. Whereas Chiang and his advisers viewed the treaty as a prerequisite for their reluctant acquiescence in the UN initiative, Eden and his associates saw it as a possibly insuperable obstacle to the initiative's success. Oracle would remain at a dead stop until Dulles and his subordinates found a way out of this quandary.

From the British perspective, the unexpected revelation that Washington planned an alliance with Taiwan altered the character of the UN exercise. Eden and others felt that, to avoid later charges of bad faith, it would be necessary to inform the Chinese and Soviets about the treaty before the introduction of the cease-fire resolution, further reducing the odds against their acceptance of the latter. Without knowing more about the terms and objectives of the treaty, the British refused to proceed with Oracle.[46]

Hastening to appease the British, Dulles once again dangled before them the prospect of progress toward a wider adjustment of China-related issues, this time adding the lure of a two-China solution for Taiwan. Stressing that the treaty would ensure that the KMT haven would not be a "privileged sanctuary"—in other words, the United States would not make safe the island while permitting the Nationalists to use it for offensive operations against the mainland—he hypothesized that such a pact with Chiang's government, in tandem with the cease-fire resolution, could result in the pacification of the Taiwan Strait.[47] As the British were quick to comprehend, the secretary of state's assurance that the United States would confine Chiang's Nationalists to Taiwan (unless the Communist regime collapsed or major uprisings shook the mainland) contained the germ of a two-China arrangement. Elaborating on his thinking to Eden in Paris on 20 October, Dulles posited that the combination of a restrictive defense treaty with a cease-fire resolution leading to a solution for the offshore islands offered an opportunity to separate Taiwan from the mainland. In turn, this could lead to an early relaxation of the China embargo and, over time, to the acceptance of two Chinas, both of which might conceivably have seats in the General Assembly. He added, however, that he placed little faith in the practicality of dual representation in the assembly. This admission indicated that the two-China scheme to resolve the seating dispute in the UN had lost most of whatever appeal it once had for him.[48]

If Chiang Kai-shek had gotten wind of what Dulles was telling the British, charges of double-dealing and betrayal would have rocked the U.S.-Taiwan relationship. Beneath the secretary's private and public professions of loyalty and steadfastness to the Nationalist government, there did lay another layer of pragmatism and expediency and an attraction to an eventual two-China solution. Dulles had for some time harbored thoughts about eventual autonomy or independence for Taiwan. As has been seen, he had shown a penchant for a two-China arrangement during his service in the State Department in the Truman administration and again, after becoming secretary of state, in his contemplation of a two-China scheme for dual Communist and Nationalist membership in the General Assembly. Most recently, in a memorandum he prepared before the Denver meeting, in which he marshalled his arguments for his UN plan of action, he predicted that a "probable *ultimate* outcome of UN intervention, if [the] Soviet Union permitted, would be the independence of Formosa and the Pescadores."[49]

Whatever Dulles's attraction to a formalized two-China solution as a long-range goal, he did not intend to try to make it a reality in the near term nor to seek reconciliation with a hostile Chinese Communist government. What he aimed at in present conditions was a de facto two-China arrangement in which Taiwan would remain apart from the mainland while the Communists and Nationalists would keep in check their mutually aggressive designs. He saw a restrictive defense pact with the Nationalist government as a way both to guarantee Taiwan's separation from the mainland and to curb Nationalist offensive operations against Communist-held territory. As for the UN cease-fire resolution, even if the Communists repudiated and the Nationalists merely tolerated it, it would at least uphold the principle of neutralization for the offshore islands. Despite hints to the British of a larger settlement of China-related issues, he was also not about to abandon the policy of pressure against the Communists, initiate a process of normalization with them (unless, against all odds, they suddenly conformed to Washington's standards of appropriate international behavior), or undermine or cause a rift with Chiang's Nationalists. American national security interests and domestic opinion set limits on his willingness and ability to break the mold of existing China policy.

After further consultation with Washington, the British decided to postpone a decision on Oracle until after they had seen the terms of the U.S. announcement of the impending treaty negotiations. Because the announcement was to precede the submission of the cease-fire resolution to the Security Council, they wanted to make certain that it projected the kind of restrictive defensive treaty that Dulles claimed to have in mind. He had averred that the treaty, besides placing controls on Nationalist offensive operations, would not protect the offshore islands.[50] Nevertheless, British officials were deeply ambivalent about the treaty and about Oracle. Viewed optimistically, they felt that a combination of a restrictive defensive treaty with a cease-fire resolution leading to a Nationalist retreat from the offshore islands could stabilize the Taiwan Strait. Once it was clear that Washington considered Chiang's government only a local regime, it might then be possible for the Americans, in time, to move toward recognition of Mao's China and acceptance of its entry into the UN. On the pessimistic side, the British suspected that the treaty would fail to shackle Chiang, and they feared that the Chinese would turn their backs on the UN initiative.[51]

Despite their ambivalence, British officials saw little alternative but to keep Oracle alive while hoping that a satisfactory treaty formula would emerge from Washington. They understood that, at a minimum, Oracle was a useful instrument to monitor and moderate U.S. policymaking. Wider China-related issues aside, the immediate objectives they kept before them were the cessation of fighting over the offshore islands, the avoidance of any commitment by Washington to their defense, their eventual relinquishment by the Nationalists, and reliable assurance that Taiwan would not be a "privileged sanctuary."[52] In short, the British wanted a clear and firm line drawn between Taiwan and the mainland, creating a situation from which the settlement of other China-related issues could later follow. This meant not just tying down the Nationalists to Taiwan but getting them off the offshore islands.

Dulles himself unquestionably wanted to pen in the Nationalists on Taiwan, though he was less eager that they vacate the offshore islands. In speaking with British officials, he did allow for the possibility that, if a restrictive defensive treaty and a cease-fire resolution were in force, the Nationalists, seeing less value in the islands as outposts, might reduce or even entirely remove their garrisons.[53] Still, his immediate and uppermost goal was to keep the major islands under Nationalist control without having to engage American forces in their defense. For military and particularly politico-psychological reasons, he regarded their retention by the Nationalists under present circumstances as an urgent priority.

As London held in suspension a decision on Oracle, Dulles had to deal with surging Nationalist discontent with the proposed cease-fire resolution. Recoiling from the two-China implications of the resolution, Foreign Minister Yeh (who was in the United States for the session of the General Assembly) along with Koo and T. F. Tsiang, the Nationalist representative to the UN, denounced the neutralization of the offshore islands as tantamount to a request that the Nationalists forsake their cherished goal of mainland recovery.[54]

As Dulles moved to create a de facto two-China arrangement through the resolution and a restrictive defense treaty, he had to contend with the Nationalist government's obsession with mainland recovery and with the strategy of counterattack it had espoused since its exile to Taiwan. To expect Chiang and his followers to resign themselves to permanent exile was, he realized, impracticable. Mainland recovery was too vital to the Nationalist government's claim to legitimacy as the true representative of the Chinese people and to the morale of the military personnel and civilians who had fled from the mainland. What Dulles wanted was that the Nationalists retain their goal of mainland reacquisition but give up their strategy of counterattack. Reporting on his post-Manila conference with Chiang at the Denver meeting, he had observed that the Nationalist leader was "beginning to get tired and had aged considerably" and that his statements about reconquest lacked their previous conviction, leading Dulles to wonder whether the Generalissimo himself believed his own words. Eisenhower commented that Chiang's only hope lay in being summoned back to the mainland following a general uprising on the mainland, like Napoleon from Elba. Dulles saw no evidence that such an insurrection would occur.[55] Neither the president nor secretary of state was under any illusion that Chiang could make good on his aggressive liberationist rhetoric.

During the course of the offshore islands crisis, Dulles would attempt to prod the Nationalists to accept a more realistic strategy of mainland recovery. In a conversation with Yeh in late October, he advised that the Nationalists patiently bide their time until the Communist regime disintegrated. Because despotisms were inherently unstable and prone to sudden collapse, he postulated that such an opening would inevitably arise, though exactly when was unpredictable.[56] What Dulles proposed in effect was a strategy of opportunism rather than counterattack. In the following months, he would strike the same theme in further discussions with Yeh and with Chiang himself.

As Nationalist displeasure with the UN initiative intensified, State Department representatives laid the groundwork for the negotiation of the mutual defense treaty by consulting congressional leaders. Both Senate majority leader Knowland and Georgia senator Walter George, the ranking Democrat on the Foreign Relations Committee, gave their blessings to a defense pact.[57]

On 28 October Dulles described his plans for a treaty and the UN initiative to the National Security Council. Absent from his presentation were the intimations of a wider settlement for the China-Taiwan area that he had dropped into the ears of the British. Advocating the continuation of most existing policies toward China, he proposed the negotiation of a security pact for Taiwan that would exclude the offshore islands and bar Nationalist use of their island home as a "privileged sanctuary." As in Korea and Germany so too in the China-Taiwan area, he reasoned, the United States would oppose national unification through military means; this would not preclude Nationalist offensive operations, by joint agreement, in the event of large-scale uprisings on the mainland or a crumbling of the Communist regime. Addressing one of Eisenhower's major concerns, Dulles emphasized that a treaty would provide incontrovertible constitutional authority for the president's employment of U.S. armed forces to defend Taiwan and the Penghus.

Because the conflicts in Korea and Indochina were now over, the presidential orders to the Seventh Fleet were no longer as constitutionally secure a basis for intervention as they once had been.[58]

Before passing final judgment on Dulles's twin proposals, the president had to contend with the recalcitrance of the joint chiefs of staff, who had gone on record that the existing unilateral defensive commitment to Taiwan was preferable to a mutual security pact.[59] At a combined State-JCS conference held the day after the NSC met, Admiral Radford submitted a report of the Joint Strategic Survey Committee (JSSC) asserting that the treaty and UN initiative would together "terminate the role of the Chi[nese] Nat[ionalist]s as a counter-revolutionary force."[60] In a memorandum of his own, Radford expressed a readiness to recommend a treaty, since the Nationalists wanted one, but he withheld his approval from the UN initiative unless the Nationalists gave it their wholehearted consent. The admiral detected a dangerous relaxation of policy toward Communist China in the views presented by Dulles the previous day. He reiterated his belief that, without U.S. protection, the offshore islands would fall to the Communists.[61]

Clearly, Dulles's proposed course of action did not sit well with the JCS hawks. They preferred a commitment to defend the offshore islands to a chancy scheme to neutralize them, and they failed to see a compelling military reason for a security pact with the Nationalist government. Wanting a more muscular China policy, a treaty that excluded the offshore islands and that fenced in Chiang's military forces had nothing to offer them.

Having given the JCS a hearing, Eisenhower held to his favorable opinion of Dulles's proposals when the NSC conferred again on 2 November. The president was content to have his secretary of state tread cautiously through the diplomatic thicket represented by the mutual security pact and UN initiative. An airing of the offshore islands issue at this meeting revealed that the lineup of opinion among the president's military and civilian advisers remained unchanged since September. Eisenhower himself was still convinced that domestic and world opinion would look dimly upon a war with China over the offshore islands—a view echoed by Dulles, with the telling caveat that if U.S. intervention should come to appear more justifiable, the no-defense policy might change. The president also opined that a general war with China meant war with the Soviet Union too, since the "Soviet empire would quickly fall to pieces" if Moscow refused to lend support to its ally. To preserve a posture of ambiguity in the offshore islands, Dulles stated it would be possible to "fuzz up" the language in the defense treaty so as to keep the Communists in doubt about the U.S. reaction to an attack. Taking stock of where matters stood with respect to the Chinese Communist threat in the strait, the secretary could offer no "comprehensive and clearcut solution"; the only recourse, he counseled, was to remain flexible and to "probe and explore the situation."[62]

"A Difficult Negotiation"

Even as Dulles spoke, the Chinese were themselves conducting a military probe off the Chekiang coast. On 1 November the PLA initiated air, naval, and artillery attacks on the Tachen Islands, soon following with the capture of one of the smaller isles.[63] Uncertain of what the renewed military activity portended, decision makers in Washington acted with restraint, denying the Nationalists permission for immediate retaliatory bombing against mainland air bases in the Tachens area and instructing Admiral Stump, the Pacific commander in chief, to permit them to launch retaliatory strikes only if Communist air attacks continued and only under precise guidelines. Also, the Seventh Fleet was under orders not to engage Chinese forces or assault mainland targets, except in self-defense or to repel an attack against Taiwan.[64]

Although the fighting in the Tachens soon subsided, it underlined for policymakers the potential for a major convulsion in the offshore islands. Dulles wanted to get a cease-fire resolution before the Security Council as quickly as possible. Because the implementation of Oracle had become linked both in London and Taipei to the mutual security treaty, he pushed for the rapid conclusion of the pact. The treaty talks, which began in secret on 2 November, spanned nine sessions held over a two-week period. Except for the first and last sessions, Dulles did not personally participate, assigning Assistant Secretary Robertson and Walter P. McConaughy, the director of the Office of Chinese Affairs, to conduct the negotiations with the Nationalist team of Yeh and Koo.[65]

On 23 November Dulles and Yeh initialed an agreed text of a treaty along with an exchange of notes. In what the secretary described to Eisenhower as "a difficult negotiation," each side had made concessions yet preserved its essential requirements.[66] In deference to Nationalist sensitivities about their sovereignty and status, the texts of the treaty and collateral notes imparted an impression of mutuality and reciprocity that belied the obvious inequality of the partnership. All the same, the Nationalists had fulfilled a major goal by formally binding themselves to the United States in a mutual security pact that would enhance the prestige and legitimacy of the KMT government, legally cement the American defensive commitment to Taiwan and the Penghus, and put Nationalist China on a par with other U.S. allies in Asia.

Though the Nationalists wanted Washington to underwrite the safety of the offshore islands, the defensive commitment enshrined in the treaty did not extend beyond Taiwan and the Penghus. So as to cloak American intentions about the islands from the Communists and leave an opening for U.S. intervention, the treaty contained vague and indeterminate language that "fuzzed up" its scope of application. Article VI specified that, in addition to Taiwan and the Penghus, the treaty would be "applicable to such other territories as may be determined by mutual consent." In addition, Article VII gave the United States the right by mutual consent to deploy its armed forces "*in and about* [emphasis added] Taiwan and the Pescadores" for the purposes of their defense.[67] In a word, the treaty did not obligate the United States to protect the offshore islands while leaving it free to do so. The treaty's terms were thus consistent with the secret no-defense policy and with the posture of ambiguity.

Contrary to the view of Dulles's biographer Townsend Hoopes, it is unlikely that Eisenhower could have used the treaty as leverage to compel a total or substantial withdrawal of KMT troops from the islands, except perhaps from the more vulnerable and less valuable Tachens.[68] Not even a security pact with his American protector could have compensated Chiang for the symbolic defeat and loss of face involved in a complete or partial evacuation of major islands such as Quemoy and Matsu. Be that as it may, Eisenhower hesitated to put the screws on Chiang to withdraw. The "Generalissimo could quit us cold and renounce Formosa itself if pushed too far," he told the NSC.[69] Key decision makers believed that a Nationalist pullout from the islands would endanger Taiwan itself. The president anticipated that if the Nationalists departed from the islands, the Communists would then make Taiwan their next target.[70] The subject of a withdrawal from the islands never came up during the treaty negotiations. Washington's preference remained that the Nationalists resist the capture of the islands, not retreat from them.

As it was, Washington did extract compensation for the treaty in the form of restrictive provisions in the exchange of notes. The notes were the instrument by which the United States formalized its control over Nationalist offensive operations. From the start of the talks, both parties had agreed that the treaty would be purely defensive and that the U.S. would require a binding understanding that the Nationalists would not initiate offensive actions without its consent. Such an understanding was a logical extension and amplification of oversight and restrictions to which the Nationalists had already acceded in the past. Chiang had personally assured Washington beforehand that he would agree to refrain from major operations without its approval if a treaty came to fruition. Besides no doubt anticipating that Washington would insist on a quid pro quo of this kind, he would also have recognized that his actual latitude to carry on offensive operations was already tightly circumscribed by existing agreements with the United States, the limitations of his own armed forces, the military superiority of his adversary, and his reliance on American goodwill and aid. He openly acknowledged that his successful return to the mainland would require U.S. logistical and material assistance. In practice, therefore, whatever freedom he now possessed to conduct major offensive military operations across the Taiwan Strait was more symbolic than real.

Still, the understanding that Washington obtained did impinge on Nationalist pride and sovereignty and on the paramount goal of mainland recovery. For this reason, the Nationalists objected to the inclusion of this restrictive provision, along with another (discussed below) relating to KMT troop transfers from Taiwan and the Penghus, in a protocol to the treaty. Wanting to minimize the connection between these two restrictions and the security pact itself, the Nationalists preferred to incorporate them within a less formal exchange of notes.[71] To avert the embarrassment the stipulations could cause on Taiwan, they also requested that the notes remain secret, but the Americans insisted that open disclosure was indispensable for Senate ratification of the treaty.[72] Too, Dulles needed to publicize them so that interested foreign capitals, particularly London, Peking, and Moscow, as well as the international community at large, would know that the United States had a veto over Nationalist military adventures.

The scope of the restrictive provisions occasioned the stiffest bargaining between the American and Nationalist negotiating teams. Differing with their American counterparts, the Nationalists wanted to exclude maritime interceptions of communist bloc vessels trading with the mainland from the understanding about offensive operations, arguing that these search and seizure activities had been ongoing since 1949 and fell in the category of self-defense. Dulles himself conceded this point to the Nationalists, who in turn agreed to continue the existing practice of consultation with American representatives prior to ship interceptions.[73] He also personally intervened to resolve an impasse arising from Nationalist displeasure with a restrictive provision limiting their right to remove forces from Taiwan and the Penghus, a stipulation whose obvious purpose was to permit the United States to prevent Chiang from overconcentrating his troops on the offshore islands. The two sides finally accepted language included in the exchange of notes that prohibited the removal, without joint agreement, of American-trained and -equipped Nationalist forces from Taiwan and the Penghus "to a degree which would substantially diminish the defensibility of such territories."[74]

Despite their weaker position, the Nationalists could justifiedly feel satisfied with the overall outcome of the negotiations. They had benefited from Dulles's eagerness to soften their resistance to the UN initiative and to expedite the negotiations so as to move ahead with Oracle in consort with the British. After the initialing of the treaty text and exchange of notes, the Nationalists did moderate their stand on the cease-fire resolution without, however, giving it their approval. The successful negotiation of the mutual defense pact purchased for Washington only a qualified and provisional acquiescence in the UN initiative.[75]

The very day that he initialed these documents, Dulles showed them to British ambassador Sir Roger Makins along with a draft announcement describing the purpose and character of the treaty.[76] British officials had decided beforehand that they would proceed with Oracle only if the announcement made clear that Taiwan would not be a "privileged sanctuary" and that the United States was free of obligation to defend the offshore islands. A statement fulfilling these two conditions, so they hoped, would perhaps dampen Chinese anger over the treaty and give Oracle more of the appearance of a genuine attempt to find a solution rather than a cold war propaganda exercise or mechanism to keep the coastal islands in the possession of the Nationalists.[77]

The actual announcement, which maintained the posture of ambiguity and left unmentioned the exchange of notes, confirmed British suspicions that the Americans would attempt to "fluff the issues."[78] After Dulles declined either to alter the announcement or to amend the treaty and exchange of notes, the British informed Washington that they wanted to hold Oracle in abeyance for now.[79] Lacking an alternative to Oracle and still anxious to restrain Washington, they kept the initiative at a full stop without actually derailing it. Dulles agreed that a delay was in order until after the public release of the treaty text and exchange of notes.[80]

Both London and Washington had another persuasive reason to postpone Oracle. The climate for its implementation had grown considerably more turbulent as a result of an announcement by Peking radio on 23 November that eleven U.S. airmen and two civilians had been sentenced to prison terms ranging from four years to life on espionage charges. The airmen were the pilot and crew of a B-29 downed over Chinese territory in January 1953 while on a leaflet-dropping mission under the UN Command in Korea. The two civilians, publicly identified by Washington as employees of the Department of the Army, were in reality CIA operatives captured while on a mission in northeastern China in November 1952.[81] The Chinese announcement caused a furor in the United States and excited an angry response in other Western nations. The State Department immediately lodged a strong protest in Peking through the British legation.[82] The sentences meted out to the Americans ratcheted up the tension between the United States and the PRC, driving them further apart. The Chinese action injected a highly emotional dispute into what was already a strained situation and introduced a new complication to the international diplomacy of the offshore islands issue.

In Washington, both outside and inside the government there were some individuals who wanted to retaliate forcefully against the Chinese. Amid unanimous condemnation of Peking, Knowland called for a naval blockade to force the release of the prisoners.[83] The JCS recommended the seizure and detention of Chinese Communist vessels until Peking freed the captives.[84] Although an ad hoc group of representatives from the State Department, Pentagon, and the CIA concluded that a congressionally authorized partial naval blockade was a feasible option, the State Department's legal adviser cautioned that such military action was an act of war and would contradict UN obligations.[85] A special intelligence estimate gave little ground for confidence that any blockade would bring about an early release of the prisoners.[86]

In spite of public anger and the pugnacity of Knowland and some of the national security bureaucracy, Eisenhower rejected retaliation. Dismissing a blockade as a bellicose act with potentially serious consequences, he privately railed at the California Republican for his irresponsible suggestion. "Can't he see that this move by the Chinese," the president grumbled to his press secretary, "is part of the general Communist plot to divide us from our western allies and try to defeat ratification of the Paris agreements?"[87] Just as his Europe-first perspective had tempered his response to the offshore islands problem, so now it mitigated his reaction to Peking's sentencing of the captive Americans.

While denouncing the Chinese outrage, Eisenhower and Dulles publicly appealed for patience. Showing no enthusiasm for a blockade at a press conference, the president suggested that the UN should take a responsibility in the matter, since the eleven airmen (he tacitly excluded the two CIA operatives from his remarks) were prisoners of war held illegally in contravention of the Korean armistice.[88] His suggestion met with overwhelming approbation in the press and Congress.[89] American and British representatives at the United Nations subsequently drafted a resolution condemning the imprisonment of the eleven airmen and requesting the Secretary-General to seek their release and that of other detained UN personnel. Following the General Assembly's approval of the resolution on 10 December, Secretary-General Dag Hammarskjöld arranged for a meeting with Chou En-lai in Peking.[90]

The administration's judiciousness, together with fast footwork by the UN, quieted hotheads such as Knowland. In the meanwhile, Peking was up in arms as a result of the signing of the mutual security treaty on 2 December, one day after Dulles announced its negotiation. In a stern official statement deploring the treaty as "a grave warlike provocation" against the PRC, Chou

En-lai solemnly restated his government's intention to free Taiwan from the "Chiang Kai-shek gang of traitors" and the "armed occupation" of the United States.[91]

The signing of the U.S.-ROC mutual defense treaty garnered mostly favorable commentary in the American press and on Capitol Hill.[92] Eight days after the signing ceremony, the formal exchange of notes between Dulles and Yeh took place without publicity. Bowing to Nationalist sensitivities, Dulles withheld their publication until the Senate's consideration of the treaty drew nearer.[93]

Pleased that public reaction to the alliance had "gone off smoothly," Dulles once again tried to get Oracle underway, only to find that Eden still had cold feet.[94] The controversy over the captured airmen and the fierce reaction from Peking to the compact between Chiang and the Americans had, in the foreign secretary's judgment, reduced even further the slim chance of Chinese concurrence in the UN initiative.[95] Meeting with Eden in Paris on 17 December, Dulles agreed with him that conditions were unpropitious for Oracle and that it should remain in reserve for the time being.[96]

Thus, three months after Dulles had first proposed UN action to Eden, Oracle remained immobilized, mainly because of British skepticism and recalcitrance. Eden pinned most of his cautious hopes for Oracle on Chinese cooperation, without which he feared the initiative would simply become a cold war ploy and propaganda weapon. His apprehension was well-founded. Dulles did not count heavily on Chinese collaboration; the primary value of a cease-fire resolution for him was as a disincentive for a Chinese Communist attack and as a moral prop in the event of U.S. intervention. Despite Oracle's repeated postponement, he could take comfort that it might still serve his purposes if the situation in the offshore islands should worsen.

The mutual security treaty, though in gestation within the State Department for some months, owed the timing of its birth to Oracle, serving as a tacit trade-off for Nationalist acquiescence in the UN initiative. More than that, Dulles saw the pact and the exchange of notes as devices to stabilize the Taiwan area. As a start toward this goal, he believed that Taiwan must remain safe against forcible absorption by the mainland and that the mainland should no longer remain under the threat of Nationalist military harassment or (however improbable) military reconquest. By both guaranteeing the security of Taiwan and restricting Nationalist offensive military actions, the treaty and accompanying notes contained the potential for a de facto two-China arrangement. Then too, by formalizing the defensive commitment to Taiwan while camouflaging intentions toward the coastal islands, the treaty might, so Dulles supposed, deter Peking from an attempt to gobble up any KMT-held territory. What is more, the exchange of notes, once publicized, might alleviate Peking's fears that the United States would carry Chiang back to the mainland on its shoulders. In combination with the UN initiative, the treaty and notes appeared, therefore, to offer some promise that diplomacy alone could pacify the Taiwan Strait.

A Revised Policy of Pressure

The stabilization of the Taiwan area through mutual restraints of military action on the part of both the Nationalists and Communists was central to Dulles's pursuit of a de facto two-China arrangement. As in other divided nations such as Korea and Germany, the secretary thought the U.S. could advocate stabilization while it continued to recognize, assist, and defend one of the opposing governments and maintained an antagonistic stance toward the other. Though his quest for a de facto two-China arrangement did not require any move toward reconciliation with Communist China, it did necessitate some modification of existing policies toward both it and Taiwan.

During the final months of 1954, a fractious interagency debate occurred over the final form of NSC 5429/2, the statement of U.S. policy toward the Far East that Eisenhower provisionally approved in August. Because of Dulles's disquiet with that document, which had incorporated the high-risk, militarized approach favored by the JCS, the president had left the door open for further review in the fall. The ensuing debate culminated in the approval in late December of NSC 5429/5, which eliminated the most belligerent features of NSC 5429/2. Stating that the United States should defend its vital Far Eastern interests "if necessary at the risk but without being provocative of war," the new policy paper still provided a license for brinksmanship but lopped off the earlier statement's hair-trigger specifications for military action.[97]

Most but not all of the components of the policy of pressure remained undisturbed by NSC 5429/5. Among the basic objectives listed in the document were the disruption of the Sino-Soviet alliance and either the "reduction of Chinese Communist power and prestige" or the attainment "by reorientation" of a mainland government whose aims were not in conflict with vital American interests. Conceding that the CCP had established effective control over the mainland, the paper offered meager promise of its early collapse. All the same, on the premise that totalitarian states were inherently unstable and susceptible to internal crises and unexpected breakdowns, the document did not accept the irreversible durability of Communist rule. This viewpoint was particularly congenial to Eisenhower and Dulles, for whom the intrinsic weakness of police states was an article of faith. Even so, in a noteworthy departure from both NSC 48/5 and NSC 166/1, the two earlier statements of U.S. Far Eastern and China policies adopted by the Truman and Eisenhower administrations, respectively, NSC 5429/5 did not inscribe the replacement of the Chinese Communist regime as a formal stated goal. This change marked the last gasp of the rollback element in American China policy and a final coming to terms with the inability of the United States to foster a reversal of the results of the Communist revolution. As such, the change represented an adaptation to the reality of two Chinas for the indefinite future. In a seeming gesture toward accommodation with Communist China, the document even kept open the option of a negotiated settlement either of a general character or of specific issues. On the recommendation of a doubtful Dulles, the NSC later amended this provision to remove the implication that negotiated agreements were readily achievable. This amendment demonstrated how little confidence Dulles and the rest of the NSC actually placed in parleys with Peking.[98]

Still yet another important policy modification surfaced in NSC 5429/5. In a revision of past practice, it mandated that the United States "refrain from assisting or encouraging offensive actions against Communist China, and restrain the Chinese Nationalists from such actions, except in response to Chinese Communist provocation judged adequate in each case by the President." Amounting to virtual prohibition against Nationalist offensive action against their Communist adversary except for retaliatory purposes and with American approval, this provision was in some respects an outgrowth of the guarded commitment to Taiwan in place since 1950 and of previous less strict restrictions on military ventures by Chiang's forces. Yet never before had the NSC approved such a sweeping injunction against Nationalist offensive activities. Even when Truman's neutralization decree was still in force, the NSC had sanctioned covert sorties against the mainland. Except for intelligence gathering excursions, NSC 5429/5 curtailed all such raids, which had proven ineffectual in any case. The injunction did not apply to Nationalist interceptions of communist bloc vessels trading with the mainland, which Taipei viewed as defensive in nature and which Dulles had already exempted from the restrictive understanding on offensive action in the exchange of notes.[99] Like that understanding, the inhibition contained in NSC 5429/5 mirrored Dulles's view that the pacification of the Taiwan area required stringent restraints on Nationalist offensive activities and that it was no longer necessary or useful to sustain Chiang's forces as a potential counterrevolutionary threat. The inhibition in effect buried the 1953 deneutralization order (which had only a symbolic life in any case) and incarnated the objective of stabilizing the Taiwan area behind which hovered the unstated goal of a de facto two-China arrangement.

As a companion to NSC 5429/5, Eisenhower in mid-January 1955 approved

NSC 5503, delineating U.S. policy toward Taiwan and the Nationalist government. Consistent with NSC 5429/5, NSC 5503, too, put a clamp on Nationalist offensive actions. Otherwise, the paper reaffirmed familiar aims: the preservation of the security of Taiwan and the Penghus; improvement of the KMT armed forces; the evolution of a more efficient and representative Nationalist government capable of attracting growing support on the mainland and serving as "the focal point of the free Chinese alternative to Communism"; the growth of a stronger and more self-reliant Taiwan economy; and the continued acceptance by the UN and the most of the world community of the Nationalist government as the sole government of China. The NSC 5503 guideline whisked through the National Security Council without objection from any quarter. The JCS hawks abstained from an attempt to reopen the issue of the offshore islands. Upholding the course of action agreed upon at Denver, the paper confirmed the no-defense policy (except if Taiwan itself came under attack) and prescribed UN action to preserve the status quo in the islands.[100]

Absent from NSC 5503 was an assessment of what the future might hold in store for the Nationalist government. For such an appraisal, decision makers could turn to a national intelligence estimate produced shortly after the offshore islands crisis began. Projecting probable developments on Taiwan through mid-1956, this document forecast that the Nationalist leadership would be unable to create any new and dynamic political program, that the international stature of the KMT government would continue to decline, that serious weaknesses would still beset Taiwan's improving economy, and that despite an appreciable upgrading of the Nationalist armed forces, their capabilities would still pale beside those of the Chinese Communists. Viewing the Nationalist government as an "anomaly" whose survival would continue to depend on the United States, the report predicted that, if adverse trends persisted, a "greatly weakened Republic of China" would "in time probably be reduced either to an aspirant for control of China, largely discarded by the world, or to a modest republic of the island of Taiwan."[101]

Given its feverish reading of the Chinese Communist challenge in the Taiwan Strait and the objectives it defined for itself, the Eisenhower administration pursued a relatively prudent strategy in the initial phase of the offshore islands crisis. Rejecting the selective defensive guarantee proposed by the JCS hawks, the administration relied heavily on the posture of ambiguity to deter the Chinese. Taking precautions to prevent deliberate or unintentional provocations by the Nationalists, it similarly issued orders to the U.S. naval command in the Pacific to exercise restraint in the Taiwan area. All the while, Dulles tried to set the stage for the introduction of a cease-fire resolution in the Security Council. To do so, he needed to overcome the resistance of the British and the Nationalists. A shrewd operator, he wooed the former with the prospect of a mutually agreeable adjustment of China-related issues, while courting the latter with the negotiation of the mutual defense treaty. The secretary of state saw the cease-fire resolution as a deterrent, but also as a moral cover, if the United States should need to intervene in the coastal islands. Paired with the restrictive provisions in the exchange of notes that accompanied the mutual defense pact, the resolution served his goal of stabilizing the Taiwan area and locking in place a de facto two-China arrangement. The change in basic policy objectives toward China and the codification of restrictions on Nationalist offensive operations in NSC 5429/5 were likewise consistent with this goal. In early January 1955, after five months of start-and-stop diplomacy, this endpoint was still not within reach. Though Dulles had encoiled the Nationalists in restrictions against offensive operations, barriers still remained to the introduction of the cease-fire resolution. Meantime, despite the relative quiet in the offshore islands, the Chinese had kept up their Taiwan liberation propaganda campaign and their military probes. Early in the new year, when they readied themselves to invade the Tachens, the crisis in the offshore islands took a new turn, and Dulles had to scramble to devise another plan of action.

On 10 January 1955 Chinese Communist bombers conducted a large raid on Tachen Island, the heaviest attack against any of the offshore outposts since the shelling of Quemoy in September. Following this air strike and the capture eight days later of Yikiangshan, an islet just north of the Tachens, the crisis in the Taiwan Strait entered its second phase. Coinciding with an impasse over the imprisoned fliers, the Tachens operation now convinced Dulles that the course set in September was inadequate to stem a Chinese advance whose goal he believed was Taiwan itself. He designed a new strategy that he, the president, and other administration officials expanded and refined during an eventful five-day span that culminated on 24 January with a special presidential message to Congress on Formosa.

As war fears escalated at home and abroad, Eisenhower and Dulles put their new strategy into action. Domestically, the period after the Formosa message witnessed the creation of a jittery popular and congressional consensus in support of the chief executive. Internationally, it saw a multiplication of efforts to resolve the crisis through diplomacy — all to no avail. Meanwhile, the president and secretary of state had to cope with pointed disagreements with the Nationalists and with Britain and other close allies. Those "damned little offshore islands," an exasperated Eisenhower moaned in mid-February. "Sometimes I wish they'd sink." [1]

A New Strategy

The pounding inflicted on Tachen Island by the Chinese air force occurred just as UN secretary-general Dag Hammarskjöld concluded his mission to Peking to secure the release of the imprisoned American airmen. Hammarskjöld regarded his assignment as a chance not just to plead his case for the innocence of the airmen but to expand the role of his UN office and to contribute to a reduction of tension between the Chinese and Americans. The schooled Swedish diplomat was on record as favoring the PRC's participation in the UN.[2] Though cordially received by Chou En-lai, he achieved no breakthrough on the prisoner issue. Nevertheless, he was "moderately optimistic" at the end of his five-day stay in Peking because Chou had not linked the release of the prisoners to any other matter and had given the impression that they might gain their freedom at a later date as an act of leniency so long as the United States refrained from pressure and saber rattling. Hammarskjöld brought back photographs and other documentary material about the prisoners together with an invitation from Chou for their families to visit them.[3]

After the secretary-general's lack of success became public knowledge, Eisenhower still kept open the passageway for a settlement of the issue through the UN and cautioned his fellow citizens that "impetuous words or deeds" might endanger the lives of the prisoners.[4] The president's moderation did not extend to approval of family visits. Here he followed the lead of Dulles, who treated Chou's offer as a propaganda trick and saw the Hammarskjöld mission as a flat failure. To the disappointment of the secretary-general, who felt that the visitations might eventuate in an early release of the prisoners, Dulles refused to have the State Department issue passports valid for travel to Communist China to the invited kin.[5]

By the time the secretary of state had informed the families of his decision on 26 January, the offshore islands crisis had heated to the point that he could blame the mounting belligerency of the Communists for the travel prohibition.[6] The imprisoned airmen issue faded into the background as the potential for war over the islands absorbed Congress and concerned citizens. The issue had nonetheless struck a raw nerve within the administration and the country. Dulles, viewing the Chinese as haughty and intractable, suspected that they regarded the prisoners as hostages to ensure American acquiescence in their designs on the islands, and he brooded that they might interpret U.S. self-discipline on the prisoner issue as weakness.[7] His reading of the issue and of the Hammarskjöld mission contributed to his growing belief that a show of resolve was necessary in the Taiwan Strait.

When the Chinese offensive showed no sign of ending after the 10 January aerial bombardment of Tachen, Dulles rethought the strategy first crafted in September. On 18 January 10,000 PLA troops in the People's Republic's first major coordinated air-amphibious-land operation successfully stormed Yikiangshan, inflicting heavy casualties on its 1,086 KMT defenders. The administration's posture of ambiguity had given Mao reason to move forward cautiously with the planned Tachens campaign but not to cancel it.[8]

Though Yikiangshan had negligible military significance, its capture stimulated renewed pleas from the Nationalists for more direct American military support.[9] Coming on the heels of the aerial blitz against Tachen, the offensive against Yikiangshan, together with Nationalist pressure for strong-willed American action, persuaded Dulles that he needed to devise a new and bolder strategy in the strait. He was certain that the Chinese intended to overrun the Tachens along with the rest of the offshore islands and eventually to try to make good on their pledge to "liberate" Taiwan. Since a posture of ambiguity now seemed insufficient to keep the Communists at bay and since the Nationalists were unable by themselves to hold the islands against a determined attack, the United States, in his view, now needed a more venturesome plan of action.

But, Dulles asked himself, what kind of action? A defensive guarantee for all the islands would overcommit American military resources and unnecessarily encompass islands that were of lesser military importance and not readily defendable from Taiwan. From the standpoint of military value and defensibility, the secretary believed that only Quemoy, and perhaps Matsu, warranted a defensive commitment.* The Tachens had only a marginal relevance to the security of Taiwan, and their distance (200 miles) from the KMT redoubt made them especially difficult and costly for the Nationalists to protect. An American air-naval screen for them would require the continual presence of two aircraft carriers on a rotating basis, an unwarranted deployment of naval power required elsewhere in the Asia-Pacific region. By contrast, Quemoy was within easy range of air and naval bases on Taiwan and had considerably more usefulness in guarding against an invasion across the strait.

Dulles now envisaged a fresh strategy with three elements, one old and two new: the old was the implementation of Oracle; the new consisted of an American-assisted evacuation of all the offshore islands except Quemoy in

---

* In the common usage of the day, the Quemoy and Matsu island groupings were often conflated into the singular "Quemoy" and "Matsu." This will be the usage followed here, unless the context indicates otherwise.

combination with a publicly declared defensive commitment to the latter. President Eisenhower and Admiral Radford subscribed to this plan of action at a luncheon meeting with the secretary on 19 January. The three men concurred that the defensive guarantee would last until the UN had arranged an effective cease-fire. The new strategy acquired still another element at this meeting when the president decided to seek a congressional grant of authority sufficiently broad to permit U.S. military action against the mainland in the defense of Quemoy. Consultations with Yeh, British ambassador Makins, and the congressional leadership were to begin immediately.[10]

The next five days were hectic and pressure packed. As consultations proceeded with the Nationalists, the British, and key legislators, top decision makers finalized a modified version of the new strategy and set the stage for its execution. This entire process sped forward under the lash of Eisenhower and Dulles's insistence on rapid action, since the Chinese could make a grab at the Tachens at any time. Unbeknownst to Washington, CCP leaders chose to postpone an invasion of these islands planned very soon after the capture of Yikiangshan.[11]

Following the 19 January luncheon meeting, Dulles conferred individually with Makins and Yeh about the proposed plan of action. While awaiting responses from London and Taipei, the president and secretary of state set out "to educate Congress as to the requirements of the present situation."[12] They knew that unreserved bipartisan support would be necessary to obtain a swift and overwhelming mandate from the legislative branch. (No doubt they recalled that the previous spring, during the death throes of Dienbienphu, congressional leaders had balked at unilateral U.S. intervention to salvage the failing French military effort in Indochina. Dulles had at that time prepared a blanket congressional resolution authorizing the president to use armed force in Southeast Asia but had never unveiled it to legislators.)[13] The next day the president met with House Speaker Sam Rayburn and House minority leader Joseph Martin, who both told him that he already possessed ample authority to protect vital national interests. Still, Rayburn assured him that the lower chamber would quickly pass a joint resolution granting him the authority he desired to take military action in the Taiwan area.[14] Whether Eisenhower revealed to the two congressmen his decision to defend Quemoy is unknown. At a gathering with other legislative leaders, Dulles (and Radford, who was also present) did strongly imply that the United States intended at least temporarily to protect some of the offshore islands. The secretary urged prompt approval not just of the grant of authority requested by the president but of the defense treaty with Taiwan. He theorized that one reason why the Chinese were making a move against the Tachens was to frighten the United States so that the pact would remain unratified; its quick endorsement by the Senate might therefore cause them to back off in the offshore islands. He observed that even when the treaty came into force the president needed and wanted a congressional sanction empowering him to do whatever was necessary to defend Taiwan and the Penghus.[15] Speedy approval of the alliance with the Republic of China became yet another element in the administration's new strategy.

Later that same day Dulles detailed this strategy to the National Security Council. Alluding to the domestic scene, he remarked that abandonment of the offshore islands might well spark a revolt in Congress, at which point Eisenhower chimed in that "there was hardly a word which the people of this country feared more than the term 'Munich.'"[16] These comments undeniably show that the two men were apprehensive about a domestic backlash against appeasement of the Chinese in the islands. Even so, national security interests were paramount in their rejection of a do-nothing policy. Furthermore, what most disturbed them in measuring the domestic impact of their actions was a potential schism in political and popular opinion in the event of military intervention. This was a powerful motive in their decision to ask Congress for a wide grant of authority to employ American military force in the Taiwan area.

The proposed change in strategy drew fire from some members of the NSC. A trio of skeptics, consisting of Defense Secretary Wilson, Robert Cutler, the presidential special assistant for National Security Affairs, and Secretary of Treasury George M. Humphrey, warned that a defensive commitment to Quemoy (and possibly Matsu, Dulles had added) could result in war with China. Of the three, Humphrey possessed the most influence with the president, with whom he had a warm personal rapport.[17] Despite the strenuous objections of these dissenters, Eisenhower stood firmly behind the new approach. The administration, in his view, faced a test of its New Look policy, which was predicated on a combination of U.S. air and naval might and reliable indigenous manpower. He failed to see how the United States could undercut the morale of Chiang's armed forces by casting off the offshore islands and then expect these same soldiers to fight for Taiwan.

At Denver four months earlier, the fear of war had moved Eisenhower and Dulles to sustain the no-defense policy. Now they had concluded that a more daring strategy, one that incorporated the protection of Quemoy and possibly Matsu, carried a lesser risk than being swept along in what the president called a "dangerous drift." Reckoning that China did not want to "get tough with us in a big way," Dulles estimated that there was "less than a 50–50 chance" that the new course of action would lead to war. What the Chinese aimed at, he suspected, was an erosion of the American position in the area rather than a military showdown.[18]

Unarguably the most perilous feature of the new strategy, the commitment to assist the Nationalists to shield Quemoy (and Matsu) constituted an act of brinksmanship—an implementation of NSC 5429/5's injunction to uphold vital Far Eastern interests "if necessary at the risk but without being provocative of war." The vital interests at stake in this instance were not Quemoy and Matsu themselves, whose retention was considered militarily unessential even if desirable, but rather the maintenance of Nationalist morale and American credibility that seemingly hinged on their safekeeping. As well, the readiness of Eisenhower and Dulles to chance a shoot out with China over the islands arose from a hardened conviction that the real final objective of their Asian adversary was Taiwan itself, a necessary strongpoint in the nation's security network in the Far Pacific. "If we wait to mount our defense of Formosa until we have lost all these [offshore] islands, and much of our prestige as well," Dulles advised the NSC, "we would be fighting at a terrible disadvantage."[19]

The assumption that the Chinese would sooner or later turn against Taiwan if they forcefully dislodged the Nationalists from the offshore islands grew out of a worst-case analysis of their intentions. Evidence was lacking at this time that the Chinese were even massing their forces for an assault on Quemoy or Matsu let alone preparing to invade Taiwan.[20] Indeed, Chinese sources now available indicate that the PLA was to cease its current campaign after securing the Tachens. Further, the military liberation of Taiwan was still only a long-range goal for the PRC, which had neither the immediate intention to invade the Nationalists' main island bastion nor the military capability to do so successfully.[21]

Meeting again on 21 January, the NSC approved a formal directive that authorized American assistance, including the use of the armed forces, for the evacuation of the Tachens and for the defense of Quemoy and Matsu. The decision to include the Matsus in the defensive commitment presumably reflected the fact that the main island of Matsu was relatively close to Taiwan and lay directly opposite Foochow, a possible departure point for an invasion of the Nationalist refuge. The commitment was to remain in effect pending either de facto Chinese Communist acceptance of the American position regarding Taiwan or UN action to pacify the area. The language of the directive explicitly tied this new commitment to the protection of Taiwan and the Penghus by stipulating that U.S. forces should assist in the defense of Quemoy and Matsu so long as Chinese Communist attacks on them were the prelude to a presumed offensive against the Nationalist main island possessions.[22]

In a turnabout from his previous intention to publicize the commitment, Eisenhower chose to keep it secret as a concession to the British, who the evening before had conveyed to Dulles through Ambassador Makins their distraught reaction to a proposed defensive guarantee for Quemoy, which they regarded as ill advised and dangerous. Told by Makins that London would proceed with Oracle only if Washington withheld the guarantee, the secretary granted that it might be possible to "be less specific than now planned in our public statement." It was in the belief that the British would go along with this compromise that Eisenhower elected at the NSC meeting the next day to keep the commitment under wraps.[23] In actuality, London wanted Washington to scotch the commitment entirely but failed to so inform Dulles before the meeting. To add to the confusion, Makins, perhaps out of his zeal for Anglo-American harmony, subsequently misinformed London that Washington had "abandoned the notion of a provisional guarantee" and would make "no additional *public or private* [emphasis added] commitment to the Nationalists." London therefore went forward with Oracle under the misapprehension that Washington had given up its proposed defensive commitment.[24]

Having gained the cooperation of the British, Dulles awaited word of Taipei's reaction to the paired proposals for an evacuation of the Tachens and the joint defense of Quemoy and Matsu. The Nationalist government communicated its acceptance on 22 January, two days before Eisenhower sent his famed message on Formosa to Congress.[25] This approval came despite the fact that Chiang found suspect much of the administration's plan of action. Behind the cease-fire resolution, he saw a British maneuver to bring about a two-China solution; behind the Tachens evacuation, a possible secret deal between Chou En-lai and Hammarskjöld for the release of the imprisoned fliers; and behind the administration's request for a congressional resolution, a device to pigeonhole the mutual defense treaty.[26] For all that, the Generalissimo apparently concluded that a stated American intent to assist militarily in the defense of Quemoy and Matsu represented a major policy reversal that he could ill afford to throw away. Agreeing to leave the Tachens was distasteful, but he was aware of their vulnerability and their marginal value as defensive sentinels, and he recognized that their evacuation was part of a tacit quid pro quo without which he could not count on U.S. assistance to protect Quemoy and Matsu.

With Chiang on board, the White House and State Department put the finishing touches on the president's message and on what would soon become the Formosa Resolution. Empowering the president to employ the armed forces to defend Formosa and the Pescadores, the finalized resolution included in that authority the "securing and protection of such related positions and territories of that area now in friendly hands and the taking of such other measures as he [the president] judges to be required or appropriate in assuring the Defense of Formosa and the Pescadores."[27] This highly elastic language gave Eisenhower unequivocal authority to take military action as needed throughout the Taiwan area.[28] Despite his broad powers as commander in chief and the flexible language of the defense pact awaiting ratification, he wanted an indisputable mandate from Congress for military operations, particularly if he had to order attacks against Chinese mainland targets. His constitutional scrupulosity, along with his wish to ensure political and popular support for the use of armed force, impressed on him the desirability of such authorization. The resolution served another valuable purpose by notifying the Chinese Communists (and their Soviet allies) that a united and determined America was resolved to stand up for its interests in the Taiwan area.

Eisenhower and Dulles labored painstakingly over the Formosa message.[29] The final text rested the president's request for congressional authorization on the strategic necessity to screen Taiwan and the Penghus against attack. Without mentioning Quemoy and Matsu or divulging the administration's intentions regarding them, the message underlined the need "to take into account closely related localities and actions which, under current conditions, might determine the failure or the success of such an attack." Without referring specifically to the Tachens, it stated that the United States was ready to assist in the redeployment of Nationalist forces. The message gave assurance that the president would utilize the requested authority "only in situations which are recognizable as parts of, or definite preliminaries to, an attack against the main positions of Formosa and the Pescadores." This caveat was similar to the one in the NSC directive adopted three days before. The message encouraged prompt ratification of the mutual defense treaty and looked forward to UN action to end the hostilities in the offshore islands. Charging that Peking's political and military provocations since September, together with its proclaimed intent to conquer Taiwan, posed a "serious danger to the security of our country and of the entire Pacific area and indeed to the peace of the world," it depicted the joint resolution as an expression of unified American purpose that would lessen the likelihood of Chinese Communist miscalculations possibly resulting in war.[30]

Though highly effective as a rationale for congressional approval of the joint resolution, the Formosa message was more than a little misleading. It concealed the defensive commitment to Quemoy and Matsu and inflated the present danger of an assault on Taiwan. Focusing on U.S. strategic interests in the Taiwan area, it passed over in silence the connection between the offshore islands and Nationalist morale and American credibility.

A few days later, Peking radio reviled the message as a "barefaced war cry."[31] In truth, Eisenhower and Dulles did not want a military encounter.

Still, they were unquestionably prepared to run the risk of one rather than sacrifice Quemoy and Matsu in the face of Chinese manifestoes to deliver Taiwan from Nationalist rule. Intelligence analysts divided over whether the Chinese would continue their probes against the major offshore islands after the passage of the Formosa Resolution.[32] Just the same, Eisenhower and Dulles hoped that the resolution, the evacuation of the Tachens, and the initiation of Oracle, along with early ratification of the defense pact, would dissuade the Chinese from further advances and calm the situation in the Taiwan area. If deterrence failed, the president could use military force as necessary with a secure congressional mandate behind him. Depending on how the Chinese responded, then, the strategy initiated in January could be a prescription for peace or war.

Congress Backs the President

From the start of the offshore islands crisis, Eisenhower and Dulles tried to sculpt a policy that would sustain essential American security interests while retaining congressional and public backing.[33] They had managed on the whole to keep Congress and the country on their side in the period from September to January, despite uncertainty and division among lawmakers and citizens about the American military role in the islands. As the pulse of the crisis quickened in the new year, public attentiveness and anxiety spiked upwards. After the Formosa message, Congress became directly involved in the application of critical elements of the administration's new strategy. As a result, the domestic leadership of the president and secretary of state faced a more challenging test.

The first task before the two men was to obtain swift and decisive approval of the Formosa Resolution. The longer debate on the resolution stretched out, the greater the potential for divisiveness and partisanship that would detract from the resolution's usefulness as a consensus builder and deterrent. Administration officials also desired to have the congressional mandate in place before raising the curtain on Oracle in the Security Council.[34]

Media commentators generally hailed the president's Formosa message, even while acknowledging the riskiness of the course it proposed. Some pro-Nationalist spokesmen objected to the relinquishment of KMT-held territory adumbrated in the message, while some skeptics, such as influential journalist Walter Lippmann, wanted the president's authority explicitly restricted to Taiwan and the Penghus.[35] On Capitol Hill, no more than a handful of legislators was prepared to deny the president his requested authority. Only one day after the introduction of the Formosa Resolution, the House after an abbreviated debate tendered its approval by a whopping 410–3 margin.[36] The

Senate was less perfunctory in its deliberations. Sitting jointly in secret executive session over a period of three days, the Foreign Relations and Armed Services Committees heard testimony from Dulles and the JCS. Going beyond the president's message, the secretary stressed the politico-psychological, rather than just the military, reasons for a firm and united stand against Chinese probing operations in the offshore islands. Although less than crystal clear in his testimony, he strongly suggested that in present circumstances the United States would protect Quemoy and Matsu.

Testifying in the company of the rest of the JCS, Radford admitted that the proposed resolution could sanction military ripostes ranging "almost from a small defensive action all the way up to World War III" depending on Chinese moves. He disclosed the majority view of the JCS that Quemoy and Matsu were important, but not indispensable, to the defense of Taiwan and the Penghus. The only other JCS member to present his views was Ridgway. Though he placed less military value on Quemoy and Matsu and insisted (unlike Radford) that their successful defense would entail the use of American ground forces, he too supported the Formosa Resolution.[37] On 27 January, after easily rejecting several attempts to limit the geographic scope of the president's authority to Taiwan and the Penghus, the joint committee voted 27–2 to report the resolution favorably without amendment.[38] The next day, after a warm debate and the defeat by large majorities of several more efforts to circumscribe the president's authority, the upper chamber approved the resolution by a resounding 85–3 vote.[39]

In spite of overwhelming assent in both houses, Congress was not free of discomfort or doubts about the Formosa Resolution. As elsewhere in the nation, memories of the Korean War were still fresh on Capitol Hill. Though antagonism toward the Chinese was much in evidence among legislators, they showed little inclination to court a violent clash or to subscribe to Chiang Kai-shek's bellicose program for mainland recovery. A British embassy report accurately concluded that the congressional discussions provided a "clear demonstration of the pacific mood of the country."[40]

That Congress would give the president his unprecedented grant of authority was never in question. The top echelon of both parties lined up solidly behind the resolution. Especially pivotal was the backing of Georgia Democrat Walter George, now chairman of the Foreign Relations Committee.[41] Both Democratic and Republican proponents trumpeted the need to rise above party in complying with the president's bidding. They took as their starting point that the protection of Taiwan and the Penghus was essential to the nation's security interests, a proposition not even the critics of an unrestricted resolution denied.[42] The administration smoothed the resolution's path by cooperating with congressional leaders and doing its best to allay uneasiness and trepidation.[43]

In the end, Walter George best framed the basic question confronting Congress: "What is the alternative?" Few congressmen saw any choice but to follow the lead of the White House. To reject or modify the resolution meant repudiating the president in a time of emergency and conveying an image of disunity to the Chinese Communists that would increase the odds for war. Only a corporal's guard of legislators were willing to dissent from the resolution, whose precedent-setting significance would become more vivid in future crises.

Less than two weeks after the resolution's passage, the Senate on 9 February consented to the mutual defense treaty by a vote of 65–6.[44] Appearing before the Foreign Relations Committee, Dulles predicted the "gravest consequences" for the anticommunist position throughout Asia and beyond if the Senate failed to ratify the pact. He characterized approval of the resolution and the treaty as "two complimentary acts" that together might restrain the Chinese Communists and reassure the Nationalists.[45] To relieve disquiet within the committee about some aspects of the treaty and to expedite its unencumbered ratification, Dulles agreed to three understandings that the committee included in its report to the Senate.[46] The treaty sailed through the upper chamber, the only resistance coming from a half dozen opponents who shared an utter disdain for Chiang's regime.[47]

Ratification of the mutual security pact completed the administration's legislative agenda. In concert with the hierarchy of the two parties, Eisenhower and Dulles had organized a bipartisan coalition and made Congress an accomplice in their offshore islands strategy. Support for the Formosa Resolution and for the defense treaty extended beyond Capitol Hill as well. A majority of commentators in the press applauded both initiatives, though controversy still surrounded the issue of whether or not to defend Quemoy and Matsu.[48] An opinion poll conducted in March showed that 73 percent of a national sampling approved the resolution.[49] All in all, broad political and popular support had coalesced around the president's leadership following the Formosa message. But other currents in domestic opinion, particularly the fear of war and continuing disagreement over the most desirable policy in the offshore islands, made this a brittle consensus.

Trouble with Taipei

At the very moment when the Formosa Resolution and the mutual defense treaty validated the American guardianship of Taiwan, two other developments soured the outlook of Chiang Kai-shek and his compatriots toward Washington. The first was the administration's insistence on going ahead with the UN initiative; the second, its refusal to publicize the defensive commitment to Quemoy and Matsu. In both instances, Chiang had to resign himself unhappily to disagreeable decisions that nourished his doubts about the trustworthiness of his American allies.

Tension between the Nationalists and their American patrons over the UN initiative increased as the administration marched ahead in late January with its new strategy, which included the implementation of Oracle. Despite their somewhat more acquiescent frame of mind following the signing of the mutual defense treaty, the Nationalists still disapproved of a UN-sanctioned cessation of hostilities in the offshore islands, and they lodged energetic objections at the State Department—all of which proved bootless.[50] At the heart of their protests were the two-China implications of a formal cease-fire. George Yeh was convinced that the two-China idea was gaining ground in influential quarters in the United States and that even Dulles was receptive to it.[51]

Two public statements by the secretary of state and the president in mid-January no doubt intensified Nationalist disquiet that the two-China heresy had infiltrated the highest levels of the Eisenhower administration. At a press conference on 18 January, Dulles for the first time mentioned the possibility of a renunciation of force by both the Communists and the Nationalists in the Taiwan Strait.[52] In the following months he made the renunciation-of-force principle, in which was implicit the creation of a de facto two-China situation, a centerpiece of his diplomatic quest for stabilization of the Taiwan area. The next day, when a reporter asked Eisenhower for his opinion of a proposal envisaging Taiwan and Communist China as separate independent states that disavowed aggression against each other, he replied that this was "one of the possibilities that is constantly studied, but you can see that both sides to it might be very reluctant to have that proposal seriously considered."[53] Despite his disclaimer about the practicality of this two-China solution, Eisenhower's admission that such an idea was even under theoretical consideration most certainly discomfited the Nationalists. Both his and Dulles's statements would only have made Taipei more restive about the administration's support for a UN cease-fire in the offshore islands.

Distressing as was the administration's position on a UN cease-fire, Chiang reacted with the most visible anger to its unwillingness to announce its defensive commitment to Quemoy and Matsu. His rage stemmed from a mistaken belief that the firm understanding existed that a public revelation of the commitment went hand in hand with the evacuation of the Tachens.[54] In all events, when the administration refused open disclosure following passage of the Formosa Resolution, Chiang began to carry on about a betrayal of America's word, and he declined to authorize an announcement requesting Washington's assistance for a withdrawal from the Tachens unless the United States "clarified" its position on Quemoy and Matsu.[55]

Chiang's demand placed administration officials in a tight spot. Broadcasting the existence of the commitment would violate the presumed understanding with Britain, was wholly at odds with the ambiguous language employed in the Formosa Resolution to shroud American intentions toward Quemoy and Matsu, and could disrupt the delicate popular and political consensus that had formed around the president's leadership. At the same time, however, the Tachens evacuation would remain in suspension until Taipei formally asked for American assistance. In anticipation of this request, the Pentagon had assembled a massive task force to remove the some 20,000 civilians and 10,000 troops residing on the islands.[56]

In the absence of Dulles, who was holidaying in the Bahamas, Chiang's demand fell directly into Eisenhower's lap. Without hesitation, the president flatly ruled out an announcement of American intentions regarding Quemoy and Matsu. Equally important, he and a small group of civilian and military advisers defined more precisely for their own and Chiang's benefit the exact terms of the secret defensive commitment. In conversations with Yeh, Dulles had simply indicated that the United States' present intention was to join in the defense of Quemoy and Matsu and that this did not represent a formal agreement or commitment between the two governments.[57] The NSC directive the president approved on 21 January had, however, explicitly coupled American intervention to the presumption of an assault on Taiwan and the Penghus. Similarly, the Formosa message and the Formosa Resolution had established a linkage between an actual or presumptive attack on these two main Nationalist positions and the president's authority to protect other KMT-held territories. The assurances about the joint defense of Quemoy and Matsu initially transmitted to Chiang therefore lacked the specificity and conditionality of the American commitment as it acquired a more concrete definition in Washington.

In discussing the commitment with his advisers, Eisenhower revealed his determination to remain as untrammeled as possible. Reluctant to tie down the United States indefinitely "in what was only one incident of the great over-all struggle of freedom against Communist expansion," he was anxious that the Nationalists not construe the commitment as permanent. Neither did he want to order American forces into action against anything less than a major Chinese offensive against Quemoy and Matsu.[58] The president accordingly approved a top secret personal message to Chiang that conformed with his desire to maximize his freedom of action. Explaining that his purpose "in present circumstances" was to assist in the protection of Quemoy and Matsu if he judged that an assault against them was "of a character which shows that it is in fact in aid of and in preparation for an armed attack on Formosa and the Pescadores and dangerous to their defense," he added that he would "at this time" consider any attack which "seriously threatened" the surrender of Quemoy and Matsu as having such a character.[59] This significant communication harmonized earlier, less precise assurances to Chiang with the 21 January NSC directive and with the Formosa message and Formosa Resolution. Linking U.S. military intervention in the offshore islands to the protection of Taiwan and the Penghus from armed assault, the missive registered the president's present intention to defend Quemoy and Matsu against serious attack but left a final decision about such armed action exclusively in his own hands and allowed him to withdraw this assurance at any time. At bottom, what Chiang got was a hedged and provisional defensive commitment that implied no formal obligation and left much to Eisenhower's discretion.

In spite of the president's opposition to a public declaration, Chiang still stalled the announcement needed by Washington to commence the Tachens evacuation. His foot-dragging strained the patience of the White House and State Department, particularly since the huge task force awaiting the start of its mission could not remain on station indefinitely. Finally, on 5 February, under heavy pressure from the Washington, Taipei agreed to make the announcement without disclosure of the defensive commitment.[60]

Once underway, the evacuation went smoothly, except for the loss of a single American aircraft shot down when it accidently strayed over Chinese territory.[61] By 11 February the withdrawal was complete, and soon thereafter the Communists peacefully occupied the Tachens. Later that month, they also took possession of Nanchi, a small island 150 miles north of Taiwan, which the Nationalists had abandoned after removal of some 6,000 troops and civilians.[62]

As the Tachens withdrawal wound down, George Yeh prepared to return to Taiwan after his prolonged sojourn in the United States. In a parting homily to the foreign minister also meant for Chiang's ears, Dulles once again extolled the virtues of a strategy of opportunism for the recovery of the mainland. As a model for Chiang, he held up German chancellor Konrad Adenauer, who remained true to the goal of national reunification without predicting when it would come to pass or asserting that West Germany would achieve it through force of arms.[63]

Regrettably for Dulles, Chiang was no Adenauer. The Nationalist leader had no appetite for a strategy that amounted to de facto acquiescence in a two-China arrangement for the indefinite future. As he reiterated during an interview on the national television program "See It Now" broadcast early in

March, his goal was to free the mainland by means of a counterattack for which he expected the support of his American ally.[64] The next day, Eisenhower reassured the country that the United States was "not going to be party to an aggressive war."[65]

That Chiang had a mind of his own was hardly news to the president or Dulles. The Generalissimo and his associates were experts at gauging how far they had to bend to accommodate their American patrons while serving their own preferences. So it was that despite being thwarted in their desire to have Washington publicize the defensive commitment, the Nationalists tried to get the word out in their own fashion. A front-page article in the *New York Times* on 11 February broke the story, based on Yeh's response to a newsman's question, that the foreign minister had revealed an American pledge to defend the two islands. Administration officials immediately denied the existence of a pledge and Yeh hastily retreated, claiming that the reporter misquoted him.[66] Five days later well-known journalist Joseph Alsop, citing a "high and undoubted authority" in Taiwan (most probably Chiang himself) as his source, alleged in his column that Washington had reneged on a promise to coordinate the evacuation of the Tachens with public revelation of a guarantee for Quemoy and Matsu.[67]

As these news stories stirred public and congressional speculation about American intentions toward the islands, administration officials played a game of peek-a-boo with the British over the existence of a defensive commitment. In a letter to Prime Minister Churchill on 10 February, Eisenhower revealed that his government had "for the moment and under existing conditions" given "certain assurances" to the Nationalists with respect to the coastal islands. Asked by Makins about the meaning of these "assurances," Dulles took refuge in lawyerly obfuscation.[68] When the secretary of state forwarded to Eden a draft of a major speech on Asian policy that he was to deliver on 16 February in New York, the British statesman took umbrage at language that seemed to suggest active support for the Nationalists on Quemoy and Matsu. Shaken by Eden's sharp reaction, Dulles excised the disturbing language, finally settling on a statement that the United States had "no commitment and no purpose to defend the coastal positions as such."[69]

While suggestive of possible military action, Dulles's phraseology maintained the ambiguity in which the administration had swathed its intentions toward Quemoy and Matsu. On 23 February Congressman James Richards, chairman of the House Foreign Affairs Committee and a cosponsor of the Formosa Resolution, berated the secretary for his lack of clarity and candor. Speaking on the House floor, the South Carolina Democrat claimed that it was his understanding from what legislative leaders had ascertained when the resolution came before Congress that the United States would defend

Quemoy and Matsu—a recollection that House majority leader John Mc-Cormick of Massachusetts confirmed.[70] Richards's outburst was far from spontaneous. An ardent pro-Nationalist, he had learned firsthand from Ambassador Koo that the administration had refused to permit an announcement of the defensive commitment.[71] Disappointed with the absence of an open declaration in Dulles's speech, he attempted himself to tear the veil of mystery from the administration's Quemoy-Matsu policy. The episode was a reminder of how the administration's troubles with Taipei in the diplomatic realm could translate into political difficulties at home and how frangible was the congressional consensus constructed a month earlier.

Oracle Checkmated

As the contest over Quemoy and Matsu churned with menacing volatility in late January, rousing worldwide fears of a clash of arms between the United States and China, American diplomatic activity accelerated and broadened to cope with the expanding international dimension of the crisis. Consistent with the strategy set in motion in late January, Dulles wanted to proceed immediately with the long-simmering Oracle project. Expecting that the Chinese (and their Soviet allies) would proscribe such an arrangement, Dulles continued to view Oracle not as a key to a prospective diplomatic solution but as a deterrent against further Chinese encroachment on the islands and as a moral cover for possible American military intervention. Even in the absence of such intervention, by supporting UN action Washington could generate favorable domestic and international publicity for its handling of the Quemoy-Matsu dispute. Eisenhower's approval of UN action in his Formosa message won the plaudits of a solid majority of articulate American opinion, with skepticism and opposition concentrated among pro-Nationalist loyalists who frowned on a formal truce in the Taiwan area.[72]

Despite having given its go-ahead to Oracle, London remained extremely wary of the venture, still fearing that it could entrap Britain in a cold war gambit and anticipating that the Chinese or Soviets would likely refuse to cooperate.[73] However dim its prospects, Oracle was the only diplomatic mechanism that London had at hand for peaceful adjustment of the nerve-racking situation off the coast of China, and it still retained value as an instrument of leverage over Washington. So London went ahead with the finalization of an agreed memorandum with its two Oracle partners setting out the ground rules for the UN exercise. The memorandum activated the first stage of the exercise by means of a letter from the New Zealand representative on the Security Council to the president of that body calling attention to a condition in the coastal islands that was "likely to endanger the maintenance of international peace and security" and requesting an early meeting of the council to consider the matter. Peking, Moscow, and other interested governments were to receive advance notice of the letter, which would make no reference to a cease-fire. The secretary-general was to invite the Chinese to attend the deliberations of the Security Council.[74]

Two days after submission of the New Zealand letter on 28 January, the Soviet Union inserted itself into the diplomatic maneuvering at the United Nations by officially requesting that the Security Council meet to consider "acts of aggression" against the People's Republic by the United States and demanding the withdrawal of American forces from Taiwan and "other territories belonging to China." On the surface, this counterproposal seemed intended to forestall or confuse the New Zealand initiative. Questioning this view, the British ambassador in Moscow, Sir William Hayter, speculated that its actual purpose might be to make participation in the Security Council's deliberations more attractive to Peking, which would be more inclined to attend if the Soviet item were on the agenda. It is pertinent to note that Kremlin leaders around this time were in fact attempting to tutor the Chinese in the necessity, given American power, of resolving international disputes by peaceful negotiations.[75]

In a series of votes the next day, the Security Council launched the New Zealand initiative without scuttling the Soviet counterproposal. Placing both the New Zealand and Soviet item on its agenda, the council then invited a representative of the PRC to participate in its discussion of the former.[76]

Three days later Chou En-lai categorically rejected this invitation. Imputing that the purpose of the New Zealand item was to intrude in internal Chinese affairs and to "cover up" American aggression against the PRC, he proclaimed that his government would send a representative to the Security Council only after it expelled the "representative of the Chiang Kai-shek clique" and only to talk about the Soviet item.[77] In a private message to Secretary-General Hammarskjöld, he elaborated that the goal of the New Zealand item was to legitimate the existence of two Chinas.[78] Though Chou's rebuff did not surprise Washington, it still maddened Eisenhower, who in a private burst of temper snapped that the Chinese were going to all lengths to "try our patience" and that he sometimes thought "it would be best all around to go after them right now without letting them pick their time and the place of their own choosing." He speculated that the Chinese were "acting on their own on this and that it is considerably disturbing to the Russians."[79]

Exactly what Soviet intentions and probable actions were in the struggle over the offshore islands was a question that increasingly claimed the attention of the Eisenhower administration as the Kremlin became actively involved in the crisis. One historian of the Quemoy-Matsu crisis has argued that the administration took Moscow's restraint in the crisis for granted and virtually disregarded its potential involvement in an armed conflict between the United States and China.[80] In actuality, there was more variety and complexity in the views of government officials and intelligence analysts than this conclusion allows. A close examination of these views shows that two different strains of opinion existed about Soviet aims and probable conduct: the first was that Moscow did not want, and would do its best to avoid direct involvement in, a Sino-American military collision; the second was that under certain conditions it could benefit from such a bout and might even want to instigate one. Judgments about Soviet restraint during the crisis varied depending on whether an observer hewed to one strain of opinion rather than another, fluctuated between the two, or remained undecided.

One proponent of the view that Kremlin leaders were unlikely to relish a major military conflict between the United States and China was Ambassador Charles Bohlen. Reporting from his diplomatic perch in Moscow, the veteran Soviet expert conjectured that such a conflict would present the USSR with a "terrible dilemma" — a choice between entanglement in a war in which it had no direct interest or the abandonment of its chief ally. Without trying to predict its choice, he did observe that Moscow lacked a "controlling influence" over Chinese behavior and that even the "degree of [its] influence" was "problematical."[81]

Both strains of opinion appeared in the appraisals of intelligence experts at this time. Analysts held that the USSR would come to the defense of its ally only in dire circumstances, but they also contended that it might find profit in a "limited and localized" Sino-American military conflict that would estrange the United States from its allies and world opinion as well as obstruct its progress toward West German rearmament and other objectives.[82]

The two strains also appeared in a NSC discussion two days before Congress legislated the Formosa Resolution. A cocksure Radford pontificated that "Russia and China were bluffing" about the offshore islands and that neither wanted war with a militarily superior United States. Agreeing that the Russians did not want a general war, Eisenhower nevertheless took the view that they were bent on fomenting an armed fray between the United States and China. Also voicing mistrust of Soviet motives, Dulles pointed out that Moscow stood to benefit from a Sino-American clash that could alienate the European allies and block American plans for western Europe. So leery was Dulles of the Soviets that he questioned whether they even wanted to eschew a general war or the risk of such a war.[83] The next day the secretary of state told British ambassador Makins that the assumption that the Soviets were trying to exercise moderation in Peking needed rethinking.[84]

To some extent, then, Eisenhower and Dulles did clearly place credence in a sinister interpretation of Soviet intentions. At the same time, in letters to NATO commander Gen. Alfred Gruenther and to Churchill in February, the president sounded very much like Bohlen, contending that a Sino-American war would present the Kremlin with a hard choice between an unwanted military conflict with the United States or a repudiation of its alliance with Peking.[85] As for Dulles, his private remarks later in the crisis indicate uncertainty about what the Soviets were thinking or doing with respect to Chinese actions in the Taiwan area.[86]

Though suspicions existed within the administration that the Kremlin might want to encourage Chinese militancy in the offshore islands and though the realization was present that Soviet military involvement was at least possible if large-scale fighting broke out between the United States and the People's Republic, these considerations failed to deflect policymakers from a risk-taking strategy aimed at meeting the Chinese challenge in the Taiwan area through a demonstration of strength and will. Eisenhower and Dulles were convinced that there was nothing to gain in the existing situation by "meekness and weakness," as the president wrote to Churchill.[87] They believed that their strategy, while not without peril, might moderate the aggressive rhetoric and conduct of the Chinese and perhaps lead to at least a tacit cease-fire in the outlying islands. So it was that Dulles, after Chou En-lai's rejection of the Security Council invitation, saw advantage "in bringing the fire a little closer to the feet of the Chinese Communists."[88]

Diplomatic Dead Ends

The bumptious attitude expressed by Dulles left little leeway for talks with the PRC outside the restrictive framework of Oracle. The secretary had, in any case, never felt that the issue of who should control the islands was resolvable through negotiations, and he was disinclined without good cause and protective precautions to have any official dealings with the Chinese. Any move toward discussions with them about problems in the Taiwan area would also have to take into account the sensibilities and interests of the Nationalists as well as domestic reaction. Adding to these considerations, the administration was intolerant of any concessions that smelled of capitulation to China's defiant claims in the offshore islands.

In the aftermath of the PRC's abrupt dismissal of the Security Council invitation, the administration spurned two overtures for discussions outside the UN, one from Peking and the other from Moscow. The first came in the form of a revelation by Hammarskjöld that Chou En-lai had informed him that China was ready to enter into direct negotiations with the United States to alleviate tension in the Taiwan area.[89] There is no evidence that the State Department gave serious thought to following up on this arresting development. The documentary record does indicate that Dulles resented Hammarskjöld's diplomatic freelancing and that he was opposed to having the United States conduct negotiations with the Communists "behind the backs" of the Nationalists on matters that concerned them.[90]

In retrospect, the administration may have bypassed an auspicious opportunity to dissipate the crisis by failing to explore the avenue of direct talks. No one can, of course, say with certainty what the outcome would have been if Dulles had been more open-minded at this juncture; however, it is entirely conceivable that he might have set in motion a process that would have led to an earlier abatement of the crisis or at least averted further escalation. The timing of Chou's indirect overture supports the contention of a number of Western and Chinese historians that the PRC was by this point looking to ease the confrontation with the United States.[91] On the American side no insurmountable obstacles existed to face-to-face talks at this time. What was absent was the political will to engage in such discussions.

Another less promising diplomatic opening appeared when on 4 February the Soviet government transmitted to Britain a proposal for a ten-nation conference that the USSR would convene along with Britain and India and to which they would summon the United States and the PRC together with Burma, Pakistan, Ceylon, and Indonesia. Although Eden doubted that Washington would accept the proposal as it stood, he took it as a sincere gesture and as a sign that the Kremlin too was worried about the drift of events in the Taiwan area. Shortly after Moscow advanced the proposal, the foreign secretary learned that Peking was "more or less" in agreement with it.[92] As he anticipated, though, Washington gave it a frosty reception. A Geneva-style conference attended by the Chinese Communists and excluding the Nationalists did not set Dulles's heart aflutter.[93]

The Soviet proposal came to Eden's attention during a Commonwealth prime ministers conference that started in London on 31 January and extended over the next eight days. The disquieting situation in the offshore islands was near the top of the docket during this assembly. Alarmed by the potentiality for a major conflict over the islands, British, Indian, Canadian, and Australian representatives nervously looked for ways to loosen the knot of controversy; none of them could find any convincing reason that the United States should hazard war over Quemoy and Matsu.[94] China's refusal of the Security Council's invitation further raised the level of anxiety among them. Eden immediately lost interest in moving to the next stage of Oracle, because any expectation that the UN venture might abet a peaceful settlement had disappeared; he obtained the agreement of a disappointed Dulles to put the exercise on hold.[95]

Casting about for a way to prevent a blowup in the offshore islands, Lester Pearson came up with a scheme (which Eden and Nehru approved) for a secret approach through diplomatic channels to the Americans and Chinese. Canada would seek assurance from Washington that its objective was a Nationalist withdrawal from the islands while Britain and India would solicit an assurance from Peking that it would refrain from interference with the evacuation. If each side gave such warrants, the intermediaries would then inform each one of the other's intentions.[96] Behind this scheme lay the hope that Washington might privately give an assurance about a Nationalist pullout that it would not reveal publicly because of domestic constraints. Dulles had recently suggested to Makins that at some unspecified future date the United States might want the Nationalists to give up the islands but that the timing was now wrong because a withdrawal would sap the morale of the Nationalists and other Asian allies.[97] Pursuant to Pearson's scheme, Makins probed Dulles for a more firm and explicit statement of U.S. long-term objectives toward the islands, hoping to elicit a forthright declaration that Washington would seek the eventual departure of Chiang's forces. Dulles would say no more than that the islands would lose much of their importance for his own government if the Communists disavowed any intention to attack Taiwan or use the islands for this purpose.[98] In his view, then, the United States could consider Nationalist retirement from the offshore islands only in conditions where the safety of Taiwan was not at stake. In effect, he was making acceptance of the renunciation-of-force principle, or at least the establishment of a durable de facto cease-fire, a precondition for such a retreat.

The consensus at the close of the Commonwealth conference was that a Nationalist disengagement from the islands was the soundest policy for the United States and the safest way out of the crisis. There was broad agreement that by securing the evacuation of Quemoy and Matsu, as it already had the Tachens, the administration could unilaterally achieve its declared goals to keep Taiwan in friendly hands and bring about a cease-fire in the strait. This line of thought began with the premise that Quemoy and Matsu, like the Tachens, were strategic and political liabilities, indefensible except at the risk of general war. Strategically, the administration's most reasonable course was to liquidate a position of weakness and fall back on Taiwan. Politically, the administration's advantage lay in standing behind a defensive line that had the support of America's allies. The practical effect of a Nationalist withdrawal would be a cease-fire, because the Communists lacked the naval capability to invade Taiwan. In this altered situation, Chiang Kai-shek and his followers could also no longer deceive themselves that the United States might back a war for the reconquest of the mainland.[99]

Following the London meeting, Churchill recommended in a personal letter to Eisenhower—part of a correspondence between the two about the crisis that lasted until the aged prime minister's departure from office in April—that the United States announce its intention to evacuate the Nationalists from all the coastal islands within a few months, indicating to the Chinese that it would use whatever conventional force was necessary to prevent a major disruption of the withdrawal. The present American posture toward the islands might, he forecast, require the president and his colleagues to choose between "standing by while their [Nationalist] allies were butchered or becoming embroiled in a war for no strategic or political purpose."[100]

Churchill's letter promptly drew a stiff rejoinder from Eisenhower, who rejected both its analysis and recommendation. The United States, the president replied, could not coerce Chiang into a retreat from the coastal islands without grave risk of losing the Nationalist army, whose morale and cohesion would deteriorate, causing defections to the Communists and making Taiwan vulnerable to an amphibious operation. Regardless of American air and naval power, the effective defense of Taiwan required loyal and dependable Nationalist troops. Removing Chiang's forces from the coastal islands would not, in any event, solve the problem of the Chinese threat to Taiwan itself. To assume that the Communists would be satisfied only with the islands was mistaken; their real objective was Taiwan and the elimination of the Nationalist army—and later on the takeover of Japan. Invoking the memory of Munich, Eisenhower reminded Churchill that at a certain point "constantly giving in only encourages further belligerency." Additionally, America's own reputation among the noncommunist nations of the western Pacific would suffer if it forced Chiang into further retreat.[101]

In spite of the contention of their alliance partners that Taiwan remained secure behind the shield of American military might and the absence of evidence that the Communists could mount a large-scale invasion, Eisenhower and Dulles saw a clear and present danger to the Nationalist keep. They took Peking's liberationist rhetoric seriously, refracting it through the prism of their ingrained animus against the Communists (in which were intermixed stereotypes of Chinese "fanaticism" and "irrationality") as well as their vivid memories of earlier costly failures to correctly predict China's intervention in Korea or to take Hitler's expansionist pronouncements at face value.[102]

Though the Eisenhower administration gave more weight than did the allies to the military utility of the coastal islands, it justified the need to retain them primarily in politico-psychological terms. In a mantra that the allies came to know well, Eisenhower and Dulles repeatedly claimed that their capture would dangerously dispirit America's friends on Taiwan and elsewhere in the Far East.[103] As the coils of crisis tightened in the new year, the preservation of Nationalist morale became an increasingly acute concern among leading decision makers, who worried that the loss of Quemoy and Matsu as a result of military defeat or forced withdrawal would so severely demoralize Chiang's army and followers that Taiwan might succumb to the Communists through subversion and defection or because of a feeble defense against an invasion. The greatest immediate fear then was not so much that Chinese seizure of Quemoy and Matsu would clear a pathway for an all-out assault on Taiwan as that it would result in a Communist takeover through internal breakdown and a disintegration of the fighting spirit of Chiang's military.[104] The Nationalists themselves fed this fear. Before leaving for Taiwan, Yeh had warned Dulles that the forfeiture of the islands could jeopardize his government's popular support and control over its own military.[105] Dulles was himself uncertain about the loyalty to the United States of Chiang Ching-kuo, the Generalissimo's powerful eldest son, who had been educated and trained in the Soviet Union.[106] Behind anxiety about a collapse of morale hovered the specter of the process of disillusionment and defection that had contributed to the KMT's downfall on the mainland.[107]

Although Britain and other concerned allies felt that the optimum solution to the crisis was to pry Chiang's troops loose from the offshore islands, they continued to search for other remedies to keep the Americans and Chinese from coming to blows. One possibility emerged from a meeting in New York on 16 February between Pearson and Dulles. To end the immediate crisis the secretary of state expressed a willingness to, in effect, accept an unformalized cease-fire that kept the islands under Nationalist control on the tacit understanding that the United States would prevent their use as offensive bases and ultimately seek their evacuation.[108] This modus vivendi offered no guarantee, however, that the Nationalists would agree to depart from the islands and set no timetable for their doing so. For this reason alone, it was unlikely to appeal to the Chinese.

Under the impression that Dulles expected him to pass on his remarks (which also included the revelation that the administration in present circumstances would assist in the defense of the islands) so that they reached Peking, Pearson reported their substance to London and New Delhi for possible transmission to the Chinese. The British deferred to the Indians as the more suitable messengers but, as far as Ottawa could determine, New Delhi never conveyed the secretary's remarks to the PRC. Dulles himself made no effort to follow up on his modus vivendi after his meeting with Pearson in New York.[109]

In late February the secretary of state embarked on a two-week excursion to Southeast Asia and the western Pacific that included stops in Bangkok for a meeting of the new SEATO Council and in Taipei. Discussions with Eden at Bangkok about the offshore islands failed to narrow Anglo-American differences. Advised by Dulles that the United States might intervene in the islands under certain conditions and that it might permit the Nationalists to bomb a Chinese military buildup then underway near Quemoy and Matsu unless a cease-fire soon materialized, Eden concluded that the situation was so ominous that he had to immediately make a direct personal approach to Peking.[110] In a message to Chou En-lai, he asked whether the Chinese government would disavow, either publicly or privately, the forceful prosecution of its claims to KMT-held territory. If Peking gave such assurances, Britain would inform the United States with a "good hope" of finding a peaceful settlement to the problem of the coastal islands. Eden indicated a readiness, if progress seemed possible along these lines, to consult in person with Chou.[111]

This proposal, made with Dulles's approval, stood no chance of acceptance by Peking. In exchange for the vague prospect of an undefined peaceful settlement in the islands (presumably Eden had in mind a Nationalist evacuation), it asked the Chinese to renounce the use of force to complete the process of national unification, a right that they would refuse to bargain away under any circumstances. Denouncing the proposal, Chou berated Britain for supporting Washington in bullying China and insisted that the United States must cease its aggression and agree to negotiations.[112]

On his return to London, Eden went beyond previous public statements of British policy in a speech before the House of Commons on 8 March. Even though its views were fairly widely known, the Conservative government, for the sake of solidarity with Washington, had deliberately downplayed its public disagreement with the Eisenhower administration over a Nationalist pullout from Quemoy and Matsu.[113] All the while, it had to contend with the unsettling impact of the crisis on its own home front. Faultfinding with Washington's high-wire act over the islands, which had ballooned throughout western Europe after Eisenhower's Formosa message, was most pronounced and general in Britain, where the Labourites remained in the vanguard of the naysayers.[114] Outlining the requisites for a peaceful resolution of the crisis to the Commons, Eden for the first time openly advocated a Nationalist withdrawal from Quemoy and Matsu on the condition that the Chinese abstain from an assault against either these islands or Taiwan. Borrowing from Dulles's songbook, he proposed that both the Communists and Nationalists forebear from offensive military action and from any use of force to make good their territorial claims.[115] However, as Eden knew from Chou's brusque treatment of his Bangkok proposal, the Chinese would refuse to renounce the use of force to realize their claims; for that reason alone, aside from the certain unwillingness of the Nationalists to participate in his proposed mutual accommodation, his guidelines fell well short of a practical formula for peace in the Taiwan Strait. Their greatest value was in pacifying the political scene in Britain while avoiding irreconcilable discord with Washington.[116]

The Voluntary Withdrawal Ploy

Despite the inability of Britain and other close allies to persuade the administration to shake Chiang loose from the islands, an eventual voluntary Nationalist pullback was far from repugnant to Eisenhower and Dulles under the right conditions. What the two men rejected was a forced retreat that would tarnish American credibility in Asia, demoralize the Nationalists, and leave Taiwan more susceptible to a Communist takeover — not to mention foment domestic criticism.

Before Dulles departed for Asia, he and Eisenhower spoke about planting the idea of voluntary withdrawal in Chiang's mind while skillfully avoiding any hint of compulsion.[117] The president even privately commissioned pro-Nationalist newspaper czar Roy Howard to try discreetly to redirect the Generalissimo's attention away from his forward bases when he met with him on a planned visit to Taiwan.[118] One can easily comprehend why Eisenhower, who clearly did not relish a military encounter with China and its accompanying undesirable repercussions at home and abroad, found appealing the notion that gentle persuasion might induce Chiang to remove, or at least substantially to scale down, his forces on the coastal islands. If Chiang were not to invest so much military and symbolic importance in his forward positions, their loss would be considerably less costly to the Nationalists. As a consequence, their occupation by the Communists would be unlikely to undermine the political stability of the KMT government or the fighting spirit of its armed forces, nor would it reflect adversely on American credibility. Under these circumstances, the administration would have much less cause to concern itself with the defense of the islands, because their intrinsic military value was insufficient to justify intervention. As an added bonus, their fate would have less political salience for pro-Nationalist partisans.

It was apparently left to Dulles to decide whether and how to pursue the voluntary withdrawal ploy with Chiang while in Taipei during his Asian trip. The secretary's brief visit to the Nationalist capital on 3 March was the occasion for his first conference with the Generalissimo since the ratification of the mutual defense treaty had bonded their governments in a formal alliance. The two men conducted their talks in an amicable manner even when they disagreed, as was the case regarding the introduction of a UN cease-fire resolution, which Chiang still resisted. In terms similar to those he had used with George Yeh in Washington, the secretary rehearsed his catechism for a strategy of opportunism without, however, making any noticeable headway with the Nationalist president.[119]

Though Dulles's appeal for a more realistic strategy of mainland recovery had unspoken implications for the offshore islands, because the Nationalists saw these possessions as stepping stones back to the continent, the secretary did not advance the idea of withdrawal. It must have been evident that the ground was far from fertile to plant the idea. A special mission headed by Adm. Robert Carney, chief of naval operations, had just arrived to commence consultation about accelerated military assistance and improved coordination for joint defense in the Taiwan area. In his interview with Dulles, Chiang made a special point that these consultations should also include Quemoy and Matsu. The Nationalist president's own plans for the islands were clearly incompatible with further retreat.[120] What is more, Dulles himself was in a militant temper when he arrived in Taipei. His trip to Asia convinced him of the existence of an elevated Chinese threat that, in his judgment, required two-fisted counteraction; this would have indisposed him to pursue the approach he and Eisenhower had talked about in Washington. Temporarily set aside, the approach retained its appeal for the president, who would later return to it — but only after the crisis had entered its last and most dangerous phase.

10

Dulles arrived in Washington from his swing through Southeast Asia and the western Pacific in a grim mood. The trip had further energized his animosity toward the Chinese Communists, deepened his foreboding about their designs on the offshore islands and Taiwan, and caused him to reconsider once again the requirements of an effective counterstrategy. After his return, the crisis in the Taiwan Strait entered its climactic phase. In the midst of heightened fears of a military conflict, Washington issued a nuclear warning to Peking and stepped up its political offensive. In a significant reversal, Eisenhower then sanctioned an abortive attempt to lure Chiang into a voluntary withdrawal from his forward islands. The crisis finally ended when the American government responded positively to an offer of direct talks from Chou En-lai in late April 1955 at the conference of Asian-African nations in Bandung, Indonesia.

Turning the Screw

Dulles's sojourn in Asia convinced him that the Chinese threat in the Taiwan area was more serious than ever, demanding more forceful counteraction. On his way to Bangkok, he stopped in Honolulu at CINCPAC headquarters for consultation with Admiral Stump. The admiral's briefing on Chinese military preparations near Quemoy and Matsu greatly disturbed the secretary, who cabled Eisenhower that it might prove necessary to lift the prohibition against Nationalist bombing of mainland targets in order to stem this military buildup before the islands became indefensible except with massive American intervention, perhaps with nuclear weapons.[1] Informing Eden at Bangkok that Washington would consider a removal of the bombing ban if a cease-fire did not soon materialize, Dulles declared that his government was convinced that it was in "a battle for Taiwan" and that the Chinese wanted to capture the island, probably by a combination of attempted invasion and subversion, or that at the least they were feeling out the United States to determine whether it would fight.[2] The failure of Eden's ill-starred post-Bangkok direct approach to Chou En-lai reinforced Dulles's glum appraisal of China's aggressive plans. So too did a conversation with Burmese premier U Nu, who had visited Peking the past December.[3]

Upon his arrival in Washington, Dulles began to sound the tocsin within the administration. Meeting with the president on 6 March 1955, he insisted that the U.S. could not remain aloof while the Communists smashed the Nationalist forces on Quemoy and Matsu. Concurring in this assessment and anticipating that the defense of the islands would dictate the use of "atomic missiles," Eisenhower suggested that Dulles indicate "that we would use atomic weapons as interchangeable with the conventional weapons" in an upcoming report to the nation on his Asian trip.[4] It was the president, then, who took the initiative in planning a nuclear warning to Peking.

Briefing the NSC four days later, Dulles painted a dark picture of a "critical and acute" situation in the Taiwan area. The United States, he warned, might have to "shoot off a gun" in the area before the Chinese would relent; "at least an even chance" existed that American forces would have to fight. Dulles brought up the problem of the loyalty of Chiang's armed forces in his bleak portrayal. Morale on Taiwan was "not too good," he attested, and Nationalist generals were susceptible to Communist bribery and to defection. It was conceivable that one or more of Chiang's armies might switch sides if even a small Communist invading force secured a foothold on the island. The CIA shared (and probably helped to inspire) the secretary's anxieties about potential internal instability.[5]

Calling for immediate steps to prepare national and world opinion for the use of tactical nuclear weapons in the event of American intervention, Dulles also recommended that the administration "temporize" in order to avert an armed clash while the European allies completed their ratification of the Paris accords. The conclusion of that process, after which West Germany would attain full sovereignty and enter NATO, was not expected for another four to six weeks.[6] The participation of an independent and armed West German state in NATO was a paramount American goal, and Eisenhower and Dulles did not want to imperil its attainment by engaging in a brawl with the Chinese that could well cause a falling out between the United States and its alliance partners. By the same token, the two men were unprepared either to insist upon Chiang's withdrawal from Quemoy and Matsu or watch from the sidelines as the Communists overwhelmed the islands.[7]

On 11 March the president and Dulles scrummed with a handful of high-level civilian and military officials to finalize a military course of action. Not wanting to lose either the islands or the accords, Eisenhower emphasized the need to avoid intervention while the latter were still pending, but he kept open the option for American armed action, using nuclear weapons as a last resort, if the Nationalists were unable to repel an assault on their coastal positions.[8]

Dissatisfied with available intelligence on the defensibility of Quemoy and Matsu, Eisenhower delegated his staff secretary and trusted aide, Col. Andrew Goodpaster, to make a quick information-gathering trip to Admiral Stump's Pearl Harbor headquarters. As was his practice throughout the crisis, the president paid close attention to military detail. In this instance, he was especially interested in knowing how soon and in what manner the Communists could attack and how long the Nationalists could hold out alone or with only logistical assistance.[9]

Goodpaster was back in the White House on 15 March to report that Stump believed that the islands would be in the greatest danger during the next ten days because Nationalist defenses were still unfinished. The Pacific commander estimated that after this ten-day period Nationalist forces alone could repulse anything less than an all-out invasion. He judged that an onslaught on this scale would not occur against Quemoy for at least eight weeks and no sooner than four in the case of Matsu. He thought the Nationalists would stand a good chance of fending off an assault by themselves unless the Communists hurled their air force into battle; so far, the Communists had not deployed their air power in strength in the area.[10]

The president also had available to him at this time a national intelligence estimate of Chinese intentions and capabilities that held out only slight expectation that the Communists would stop their probes in the offshore islands without a threat of counteraction by the United States. Barring American intervention, analysts believed that the Chinese had enough forces already in place or conveniently at hand to crush any Nationalist resistance; however, they saw no sign of an imminent Chinese offensive.[11]

Over the entire month or so prior to the opening of the Bandung conference on 18 April neither the intelligence community in Washington nor Stump's headquarters detected any definite evidence that an attack was in the offing.[12] But Stump rated his information on the buildup of assault forces as poor; it was particularly hard to tell whether concentrations of fishing junks were for amphibious operations or the vessels were simply engaged in their normal pursuits.[13] The intelligence community reckoned that the Chinese had the capability to fall upon the islands with little warning. An intense suspicion of the Communists, as well as worst-case thinking, led Admiral Radford to advise that it was safest to assume that preparations for an assault were moving ahead as rapidly as possible, despite the paucity of corroborating evidence.[14]

With the danger flag flying high after Dulles's return, the administration orchestrated a nuclear warning to Peking. Reporting on his Asian junket in a nationwide radio and television broadcast on 8 March, the secretary stated that the United States possessed "new and powerful weapons of precision" that could "utterly destroy military targets without endangering unrelated civilian centers."[15] At a press conference on 15 March, he observed that the United States was prepared to use tactical nuclear weapons in response to a major Communist move in the Taiwan area.[16] The next day, Eisenhower himself confirmed that he would use tactical atomic weapons in the event of war in the Far East, and he deliberately blurred the distinction between nuclear and conventional armaments.[17] Two days later, in a Chicago speech bluntly warning against any new Chinese Communist aggression, Vice President Nixon took the same line, saying that tactical atomic weapons were now "conventional."[18]

Responding to these admonitory signals, Peking radio accused the American government of "atomic diplomacy."[19] This was undeniably an accurate characterization. The administration not only wanted to create a "stop-gap" deterrent during the period of greatest danger before 25 March, as nuclear scholar McGeorge Bundy has contended, but also to keep the Chinese at bay over a longer term, particularly in the delicate stretch of time before the final ratification of the Paris agreements.[20] More broadly, the administration wanted to foster the conditions for an enduring stabilization of the Taiwan area based on at least a de facto cease-fire.

Another reason for the fusillade of nuclear rhetoric, as historian H. W. Brands, Jr., has argued, was to demonstrate the plausibility of the New Look doctrine of nuclear retaliation.[21] Dulles had made this very point in his briefing of the NSC, commenting that the administration had to "educate" American and world opinion "as to the necessity for the tactical use of nuclear weapons." A reluctance to employ such weapons because of popular disapproval or squeamishness could, as he and other NSC members recognized, erode the administration's military posture under the New Look, which depended heavily on a perceived readiness to have recourse to America's varied nuclear arsenal. That consideration aside, Dulles wanted the administration to have a free hand to use tactical nuclear weapons in the Taiwan area "perhaps within the next month or two."[22]

To deter the Chinese, as well as to prepare the ground for possible intervention, Dulles and the State Department also conducted a more vigorous political offensive. In addition to encouraging Chinese self-restraint through international pressure, they sought to seize as much of the moral and political high ground as possible in case the United States had no alternative except to fight. In Dulles's reading of Chinese intentions, the unprecedented gathering at Bandung of twenty-nine Asian and African nations, including Communist China, loomed as a potentially determinative event. He anticipated that Peking's decision for peace or war might pivot on whether or not the other governments in attendance condoned its use of force to make good its claims in the Taiwan area.[23] The State Department accordingly conducted a campaign of persuasion and education among pro-American governments invited to the conference to sensitize them to Washington's viewpoint and to enlist their cooperation in urging a peaceful accommodation.[24]

Dulles also took the offensive in several speeches aimed at domestic and foreign audiences. Describing China's goals in the Far East in luridly malevolent terms and comparing its aggressiveness to that of Hitler's Germany, he held out the prospect of peace in the Taiwan area based on acceptance of the renunciation-of-force principle. In an address on 21 March, he contrasted the "aggressive fanaticism" of the Chinese with the more calculating designs of the Soviets.[25] Besides demonizing the Chinese the better to justify American conduct, Dulles's fervid rhetoric played upon possible differences between Moscow and Peking over the offshore islands by vividly juxtaposing Chinese zealotry with Soviet cool realism. At the very outset of the crisis in the Taiwan Strait, as already seen, the secretary had perceived an opportunity to employ a UN cease-fire initiative to exacerbate tensions in the Sino-Soviet alliance, a basic goal of the policy of pressure toward China. His contrasting depiction of Chinese and Soviet modus operandi in his 21 March speech indicates that he still had in sight this wedge-driving objective. But the documentary record fails to support the view of some scholars that this goal was a major motivation for the administration's stiff line on Quemoy and Matsu during the crisis.[26] Only scattered evidence exists that a desire to attenuate the Sino-Soviet relationship entered into the administration's calculations, which were dominated by other considerations. Further, intelligence experts early in the confrontation gauged that whatever friction was present between Peking and Moscow over the recovery of Chinese Nationalist territories was insufficient to undermine the effectiveness of the circumscribed yet closely knit alliance between the two.[27] Not only that, uncertainty about the Soviet role in the crisis, manifested not just by intelligence experts but by both Eisenhower and Dulles, complicated the pursuit of a wedge strategy.

As part of the administration's political offensive, Dulles tried to restart Oracle, having already failed several times since February to convince Eden to agree to the submission of the New Zealand cease-fire resolution to the Security Council.[28] Ever since the Chinese had rejected the Council's invitation, the British foreign secretary had seen no present benefit either for Britain or for the cause of peace in resuming the UN initiative.[29] He still refused to budge when, on 23 March, Dulles made a strong bid for the immediate introduction of the cease-fire resolution.[30]

Capitalizing on the thickened air of crisis within the administration, the JCS hawks put forward recommendations in late March for more robust counteraction against the Chinese. Replying to a request from Defense Secretary Wilson that the JCS suggest measures to "clarify the seriousness" of American intentions in the Taiwan area, the hawks responded with a three-pronged proposal: first, that the administration privately inform the PRC and USSR that the U.S. would defend the offshore islands "with all means available"; second, that it announce an indefinite suspension of reductions in the armed forces due to the instability in the Far East; third, that it publicly authorize the joint chiefs "to take all steps necessary to *protect* Formosa." The obvious thrust of the proposal (which only Ridgway disapproved) was to intensify the confrontation with China and to put a brake on cutbacks in the armed services resulting from budgetary constraints. On 26 March Wilson and Dulles, together with several of their subordinates, went over the proposal with Radford. Wilson disapproved of the first two recommendations whereas Dulles found fault only with the first. The pugnacious Radford opined that the Far East would remain unstable until the Chinese had suffered a "bloody nose."[31]

While Dulles was not itching for a scrap as was Radford, he was ready to consider extreme measures to bring the Chinese to heel in the strait. Two days later, at a conclave with a few close advisers in which Allen Dulles joined, he talked about putting a marine division on Taiwan and about a partial blockade of the China coast. He also spoke about notifying Peking that an attack on the coastal islands would result in a "severe punitive action across the length and breadth of China." Applying the calculus of the New Look's nuclear retaliatory strategy, he asserted that any time the "enemy wished to attain X" the United States "would exact a cost of 2X from them."[32]

As war jitters spread through the upper levels of his administration, Eisenhower kept a cool head. He recorded in his diary that he did not expect an imminent conflict, despite the fact that the Chinese appeared to be "completely reckless, arrogant, possibly over-confident, and completely indifferent as to human losses." As a veteran of many previous periods of strain, he had learned that "most of the calamities that we anticipate really never occur."[33]

At an NSC meeting on 31 March, Radford presented a somewhat altered version of the proposal discussed earlier with Wilson and Dulles. He also detailed the military's war plan in case of an all-out Chinese attack on the Nationalist forward positions. Specifying initial localized retaliation with nuclear weapons against airfields and POL (petroleum-oil-lubricants) storage sites, the plan provided for the contingency of a "broadening of the scope of operations" that would include expanded air bombardment, a naval blockade, and the mining of Chinese waters.

Radford's exposition left NSC members nearly speechless. Apparently having lost some of his zest for nuclear retaliation, Dulles expressed considerable concern about the political repercussions of the use of atomic weapons. Radford's far from reassuring rejoinder was that the counterattack would employ only "precision atomic weapons" and that "except in one or two instances no large cities or concentrations of civilian population were involved in the targets." Eisenhower, while abstaining from direct comment on the admiral's presentation, did caution against "underestimating the sanity of the Chinese Communists," whose awareness of American military prowess would cause them to think twice before making a grab for the offshore islands.[34]

Even as the president and the NSC came to grips with the implications of Radford's sobering presentation, a critical shift was taking place in the mood of the country and Congress as a result of a full-blown war scare that had erupted a few days earlier. The scare followed a rash of front-page newspaper stories on 26 March that the administration expected a showdown over the offshore islands soon after 15 April and that the president was under pressure from militant advisers not just to safeguard the islands but to destroy Communist China's war-making capacity in an atomic blitz. It quickly became known that the stories had originated in comments made by Chief of Naval Operations Adm. Robert Carney at a private dinner with journalists.[35] Furious with Carney and irate at the press for its sensation mindedness, Eisenhower immediately moved to muzzle him and to correct the impression of an impending showdown.[36] He apparently did not pause to consider how the nuclear warnings issued by him and other top officials might have contributed to the scare headlines he now deplored.

Despite the scramble by the White House to calm war fears, the Carney-inspired stories threw a fright into the country that failed to subside. Reports that Senators Knowland and Bridges wanted Eisenhower to pledge a no-holds-barred defense of Quemoy and Matsu added fuel to the fire. In an exchange with Knowland on the floor of the Senate, Democratic majority leader Lyndon B. Johnson accused the right-wing Republicans of "talking war."

The apparent drift toward war likewise disturbed other powerful Democrats, including Walter George.[37] At a luncheon with the congressional leadership on 31 March, Eisenhower and Dulles tried to patch up the splintering bipartisan front.[38] Even so, marked differences of opinion persisted on the offshore islands issue, both on Capitol Hill and in the country at large. Informed American and foreign observers sensed that the public mood was against intervention to protect the islands.[39] Though the Democratic leadership did not break with the White House, many party members were restive and fearful.[40] On 18 April George lamented to Dulles that Quemoy and Matsu had become a political football and a cause of public division.[41] As Dulles also knew, even some pro-Nationalist stalwarts, such as H. Alexander Smith and Judd, disagreed with the extreme position of Knowland and Bridges.[42]

The war scare undercut the fragile popular and political consensus fashioned by Eisenhower and Dulles after the Formosa message. The administration's nuclear warnings, coupled with the Carney-inspired stories, had stimulated widespread apprehension and controversy. The Formosa Resolution notwithstanding, the president could not now commit American military power to defend the islands without dividing the public and Congress.

As March drew to a close, the distance between the United States and the Commonwealth trio of Britain, Canada, and Australia, which had been active in consulting with Washington about how to end the crisis, was also greater than ever. In a message to Dulles on 16 March, Eden reiterated Britain's desire for an evacuation of the islands. Taking issue with the secretary of state's opinion (expressed a few days earlier to Makins) that the Chinese wanted a showdown both in Taiwan and Southeast Asia, he counseled that moderation was the most effective response to a Chinese strategy whose likely purpose was to isolate the United States and consolidate Asian and world opinion on Peking's side.[43] America's northern neighbors were similarly on edge about Washington's hawkish disposition. On 24 March Pearson delivered a major address in the Canadian House of Commons in which he barred his nation's involvement in a conflict over Quemoy and Matsu and voiced his worry that even limited defensive intervention by the United States might "have a chain reaction with unforseen consequences." Pearson's speech came less than a week after Dulles in a visit to the Canadian cabinet had emoted on the Chinese bogey in Asia.[44]

Also disquieted by American policy, Australia put forward a proposal that combined a Nationalist withdrawal from the coastal islands with a multilateral security guarantee for Taiwan. Outlined to Dulles by Prime Minister Robert Menzies during a visit to Washington on 14 March, the proposal called for various Commonwealth states to join with the United States to collectively guarantee the safety of Taiwan.[45] Though Dulles professed to find merit in the proposal, he was dubious that the British would go along. In point of fact, the next month Eden did tactfully deflect Australian feelers about the collective guarantee. For the British, the disadvantages of undertaking a long-term commitment to the defense of Taiwan far outweighed the short-term gain from the removal of the Nationalists from the coastal islands. More than that, Eden anticipated that British opinion would react unfavorably to such a commitment.[46] His succession to the office of prime minister on 6 April, following Churchill's retirement, and his decision to call a general election for the next month disinclined him to adopt a position that the British electorate would spurn.

Even if Britain had proven more amenable, the Nationalist government would have strenuously resisted, if not entirely rejected, the relinquishment of the islands in return for a collective guarantee that would not have added materially to Taiwan's security and, paired with a retreat from the islands, would have given a boost to the idea of two-Chinas. Soon after they learned of the Australian formula through press leaks in late March, the Nationalists made known their uneasiness at the State Department.[47]

By the end of March, both international and domestic trends ran counter to the momentum toward sharpened confrontation that Dulles set in motion within the administration after his return from Asia. That momentum had already resulted in a nuclear warning and in an invigorated political offensive. Whether it would also sweep the administration toward the more drastic action favored by the JCS hawks was up to Eisenhower to decide.

Proposals for Voluntary Withdrawal

As the offshore islands crisis entered its eighth month in early April, the "horrible dilemma" that had first presented itself to Eisenhower and Dulles the previous September seemed more daunting than ever. The president confessed to congressional leaders that the Quemoy-Matsu issue was the most difficult he had faced since taking office.[48] His bafflement and frustration were understandable. Since the outset of the crisis, he and his secretary of state had struggled to craft a strategy that would forestall the undesirable military and politico-psychological consequences of a Communist takeover of the most important of the offshore islands while simultaneously averting a military intervention that would fail to find approval with the nation's closest allies, world opinion, and many of its own citizens. So far, events had not forced a choice between these grim options; yet the horns of the dilemma were sharper than ever.

On 1 April, the day after Radford briefed the NSC on the confrontational strategy of the JCS hawks as well as the Pentagon's war plan, Eisenhower caucused with a small group of civilian and military advisers. In attendance were John Foster Dulles, Admiral Radford, Colonel Goodpaster, Defense Secretary Wilson, Treasury Secretary Humphrey, Deputy Secretary of Defense Robert Anderson, and Undersecretary of State Herbert Hoover, Jr. The purpose of the meeting was to scrutinize a proposal (apparently originating with Admiral Carney) to station 10,000 American military personnel on Taiwan to man recently arrived antiaircraft and aircraft-warning equipment and to instruct the Nationalists in their use. Radford, who presented the proposal, called attention to ongoing Communist construction of a net of airfields in the Taiwan area that could endanger both the offshore islands and the Nationalist haven.

Once the JCS chairman had completed his recitation, the meeting took an unexpected and significant turn. Objecting to the size of the proposed 10,000-man contingent, Eisenhower then opened the floor to a discussion of the entire situation in the Taiwan Strait. Lamentably, the minutes are silent on the ensuing exchange among the president and his councillors, some of whom like Wilson and Humphrey had for months harbored misgivings about a military engagement over Chiang's forward islands. What the minutes do contain is Eisenhower's summation of a new course of action that tacitly rejected the confrontational strategy of the JCS hawks and resurrected the idea of voluntary withdrawal that he and Dulles had earlier shelved.

The president's summation captured his dismay at having to choose between doing nothing to save Quemoy and Matsu and waging war for them. The first choice, he predicted, would probably result in the breakdown or subversion of Chiang's armed forces and could impair the American security position throughout the region. The second would rend American opinion, leave the United States at loggerheads with its allies, and (so Humphrey had argued) throw the domestic economy into a tailspin. In addition, the islands were difficult to defend and the ultimate objective of any American military operations against the Chinese remained obscure. A preferable course of action, the president concluded, was to persuade Chiang to draw back from his advance positions, perhaps by offering him inducements such as stationing a U.S. marine division on Taiwan.[49]

Even though he reserved a final decision on this proposed strategy, Eisenhower was obviously more than a little attracted to it, as he had been before Dulles's Asian trip. In spite of American military might, he was loathe to do battle with the Chinese over Quemoy and Matsu, explaining to his press secretary that "no force on earth" could hold these positions against a protracted and massive assault in which the Chinese were willing to take enormous casualties. Atomic weapons might slow down such an offensive, but he hesitated to use them unless he had no other choice. What he preferred was that

Chiang treat the islands as dispensable outposts, protected by small contingents of crack troops that the Communists could overcome only at a bloody price. Seen merely as outposts, the islands would not become "another Dienbienphu" and their fall would not devastate Nationalist morale.[50]

The lesson of Dienbienphu — the mistaken overcommitment of military resources and prestige to an isolated and vulnerable military bulwark — had weighed on Eisenhower's mind since the beginning of the crisis. Despite the truculence he had recently exhibited in administration councils, Secretary Dulles, too, still recalled that lesson. In a draft statement to the Nationalist government proposing the outpost concept, which he showed to the president on 4 April, he advised Taipei not to elevate Quemoy and Matsu into a potent symbol as the French citadel had been. He also cautioned that the radioactive fallout from the use of atomic weapons against mainland military targets could cause large numbers of civilian casualties, thereby undermining the Nationalist government's long-term interests on the continent. Under certain atmospheric and wind conditions, the fallout could even affect the inhabitants of Quemoy.[51]

Their nuclear rhetoric to the contrary, Eisenhower and Dulles did not treat atomic weapons as if they had conventional status during this critical stage of the crisis. In considering their actual use to ward off an invasion of Quemoy and Matsu, the two leaders found compelling reasons for restraint.[52] These reasons went beyond those mentioned by the secretary of state in his draft statement. They also included a recognition that the administration's nuclear bravado in March far from stimulating a favorable domestic environment for atomic retaliation had done quite the opposite, as the war scare testified. The secretary and president similarly realized that the employment of nuclear weapons would shock much of world opinion, especially in noncommunist Asia, and rattle the Western allies.[53] Dulles speculated that the Soviets might welcome a resort to such weapons for the propaganda bonanza it would give them. On top of this, he apparently worried that expending too many of these weapons in a conflict with China would diminish the nation's nuclear stockpile.[54]

The uninviting scenario of a nuclear response to an all-out assault on Quemoy and Matsu gave Eisenhower a powerful incentive to turn away from a fracas with China and to win Chiang over to the outpost concept. In an impressive ten-page, single-spaced memorandum completed on 5 April, the president personally spelled out the rationale and modalities of this approach. The crux of his closely reasoned statement was that the "only logical course" was to try to alter the existing situation in the islands "rather than to remain inert awaiting the inevitable moment of decision between two unacceptable choices." Even if successfully beaten back militarily, Eisenhower did not expect that the Chinese would stop threatening the islands; this meant that the U.S. would have to invest its prestige and a disproportionate share of its available mobile forces in their defense for the indefinite future. The islands would remain a political and military albatross around the neck of the United States.

Eisenhower argued that the islands would best serve Nationalist and American interests as expendable outposts. By withdrawing his "excess personnel" from the islands and leaving only enough troops for a valiant defense, the Generalissimo could husband his military prestige and strength on Taiwan, awaiting his opportunity to regain the mainland. In these altered conditions, the United States could solidify domestic and free world opinion behind itself without impairing Nationalist morale or the confidence of its friends in Southeast Asia and elsewhere in the region. The president insisted, as he had all along, that Chiang had to embrace willingly the notion of voluntary withdrawal. As a fillip, he was ready to pledge accelerated military assistance and training for the Generalissimo's forces along with a larger American military presence on Taiwan, including several marine regiments and a wing of combat aircraft.[55]

By putting his personal authority behind the outpost approach, Eisenhower altered the direction of the administration's deliberations. Showing prudence and a sense of proportion, he backed away from a more acute confrontation and an ill-advised overcommitment. He again acted with moderation on 11 April when he refused to extend permission for Nationalist air strikes against the buildup of airfields opposite Taiwan, despite pressure from Admiral Stump and the Nationalists to raid the facilities while they were still in the development stage. He and Dulles agreed that bombing the airfields would weaken the hand of pro-American delegates at the Bandung conference scheduled to convene in a week's time. More fundamentally, the president was apprehensive that this preventive measure could incite Chinese Communist retaliation, perhaps triggering a chain reaction leading to American intervention, and so lay open Nationalist China and the United States to a charge of war instigation or aggression.[56]

To convert Chiang to the outpost approach, Eisenhower decided to send Walter Robertson and Admiral Radford, the Nationalist leader's two staunchest supporters within the administration, on a secret mission to Taiwan.[57] Although the president did not foresee an imminent attack on the coastal islands, he agreed with Dulles that haste was in order. The secretary of state fretted that the relative calm in the islands might turn into a tempest after the Bandung conference.[58]

Before Robertson and Radford left, the purpose of their mission took a startling turn. In a private two-hour session with Dulles on 17 August at the presidential getaway in Augusta, Georgia, Eisenhower consented to a radical new proposal for Chiang. The secretary had drafted it only the previous day together with Robertson, Radford, Hoover, and Anderson and had then shown it to Allen Dulles. The new proposal recommended that the Nationalist leader agree to an American-assisted *total* evacuation of his troops and civilians from Quemoy and Matsu. If he went along, the United States, in collaboration with the Nationalists, would institute a maritime "interdiction"—in other words, a blockade—of the China coast from Swatow in the south to approximately Wenchow in the north (a distance of about 500 miles) in order to cut off the seaborne flow of military supplies to that area. In addition, the United States would dispatch more antiaircraft equipment to Taiwan and locate there a contingent of marines and a combat air wing plus "atomic capabilities in the hands of U.S. units." The interdiction would remain in effect until Peking renounced the use of force against Taiwan. To avoid any inference of an erosion of political support for the Nationalist government, the president would reaffirm that the United States would continue to refuse recognition to the PRC and oppose its representation in the UN. Eisenhower was prepared to ratify this agreement personally with Chiang, perhaps in San Francisco or Honolulu.[59]

The prime mover behind this remarkable evacuation-blockade plan was clearly Secretary Dulles. He had been turning the idea of a blockade over in his mind since at least mid-March; at that time he had pondered whether to warn the Communists they would face a blockade if they struck at Quemoy and Matsu or, alternatively, offer Chiang a blockade in return for the withdrawal of his troops.[60] The secretary, who was less smitten with the outpost approach than Eisenhower, would have known that Radford considered the president's stratagem impractical and doubted that Chiang would accept it.[61] Within the State Department, two of Dulles's intimate advisers, PPS director Robert R. Bowie and Assistant Secretary of State for European Affairs Livingston Merchant, favored a complete Nationalist evacuation.[62]

The purpose of the evacuation-blockade proposal was to get the administration off the hook in the offshore islands under conditions that would save face for Chiang and the United States and undergird the security of Taiwan. The removal of the Generalissimo's forces would eliminate the islands as a locus of conflict between the CCP and KMT and as a potential casus belli for the United States. With the protection afforded by the strait and the Seventh Fleet, the transplanted forces would be much safer on Taiwan. American prestige and military power would no longer remain handcuffed to the defense of militarily unessential territory that was constantly exposed to attack or intrusion from the nearby mainland. The islands were not indispensable stepping stones for a Communist invasion of Taiwan nor vital obstacles to one. Back in September, the JCS hawks had concluded that their possession by the Nationalists only limited "to some degree the fullest use" of the Fukien-Chekiang coast as a launching area for an invasion; Ridgway judged that the islands had no value at all for this purpose and that an invading force could bypass them with "little difficulty."[63] By letting the islands fall under Communist control and inscribing a clear-cut dividing line between Taiwan and the mainland, the U.S. would appease its concerned allies and define a policy that was much more acceptable to American and world opinion. Morally, legally, and politically, a defensive policy that encompassed only Taiwan and the Penghus was far easier to justify. In the short term, the shift to such a policy would remove any chance that a battle with the Chinese in the offshore islands would frustrate the consummation of the administration's European program.

Further, as Eisenhower and Dulles realized, a line of demarcation between KMT- and Communist-controlled territory running through the Taiwan Strait rather than just off the coast of China was conducive to stabilization of the area through a de facto two-China arrangement. The United States was already in a position to guarantee the safety of the Nationalists on Taiwan itself and to block any military excursions by them against the mainland. Eisenhower and Dulles did not ask that the Nationalists forsake their goal of mainland recovery, only that they adopt a more realistic strategy emphasizing patient opportunism rather than military reconquest. A retreat from the offshore islands, which the Nationalists saw as the advance stations for a counteroffensive, would greatly facilitate a reorientation to a less bellicose strategy. Such a retreat would represent at least a tacit accommodation for the foreseeable future by Chiang and his followers to the continued existence of two rival Chinese regimes. What is more, though a strategy of opportunism still held out hope to the Nationalists of an eventual return to the mainland, the president and secretary of state understood that, barring some unpredictable turn of events, they would likely wait in vain for a restoration of their authority on the continent and that ultimately the United States might want to move toward a formal two-China policy. So it was that Eisenhower predicted that "in the long run, unless the unexpected happened, it might be necessary to accept the 'Two Chinas' concept" and that this might come to pass in "5–10 or 12 years."[64]

The planned blockade, paired with a reinforced American military presence on Taiwan, represented both compensation for Chiang's agreement to a Tachens-style withdrawal from the rest of the offshore islands and the counterbalance to the military and politico-psychological ill effects of such a fallback. Washington could present the package proposal to the Nationalist leader as a means of safely removing his valuable troops and equipment from their exposed positions without losing prestige or weakening the defenses of Taiwan. Both the blockade and strengthened American military presence on Taiwan would manifest the administration's resolve to take strong measures to shelter the Nationalist bastion. With a blockade in place, the retention of Quemoy and Matsu as defensive obstacles to obstruct the use of the ports of Amoy and Foochow as staging areas for an invasion would no longer be necessary. A blockade would also impede the seaborne supply of military materials, particularly petroleum products, to the airfields under construction opposite Taiwan. Located in a mountainous region poorly served by surface transportation, the airfields were not easily provisioned by land.[65] A blockade was an alternative to the Nationalist air attacks against the airfield buildup that Eisenhower refused to approve. Lastly, it could give the U.S. leverage to extract a pledge from Peking to abstain from the use of force against Taiwan.

Still enamored of the outpost concept, the president found it difficult to summon enthusiasm for the evacuation-blockade proposal. In presenting the proposal to him at Augusta, Dulles posited that a clean break from the islands combined with a defensive naval interdiction were preferable if the United States was going to refuse either to allow the Nationalists to bomb the airfield buildup or to assist them against a Communist assault after the buildup was complete. If the Nationalists did nothing to hamper the buildup, he estimated that the Communists might possibly achieve air superiority over Quemoy and Matsu as early as June. Brought around by Dulles's persuasion, Eisenhower consented to the new proposal with a few revisions, though he did so hesitantly and without giving up on the outpost approach. He did agree with his secretary of state that the proposal would "immeasurably serve to consolidate world opinion" in favor of the United States.[66]

That a Nationalist pullout from the islands would have garnered kudos from most of the world community was certain; that American participation in a blockade of the southeast China coast would have met with similar approbation was highly questionable. It is similarly hard to visualize how the evacuation-blockade scheme would have united the American public and the Congress behind the administration. Whatever euphemism was substituted for the term "blockade," the administration could hardly conceal the reality of what it was doing or avoid accusations that it was engaged in what was legally an act of war.[67] The previous fall Eisenhower himself had poured scorn on Knowland's suggestion of a blockade to compel the release of the imprisoned American airmen.

Any expectation on the part of the chief executive and secretary of state that a blockade might serve to muscle the Chinese into abjuring the use of force against Taiwan was illusory. Chinese Communist Party leaders would have rejected any such renunciation of their right to take armed action to unify their territory. Too, Chinese military retaliation against a blockade was a real possibility. American naval plans prepared in conjunction with the evacuation-blockade proposal allowed for a military response by the Chinese in the form of minor surface operations and submarine and air attacks. Though these plans called for interdiction only of ocean shipping because search and seizure of coastal junk traffic was unfeasible, Radford intended to mine coastal waters so as to force this traffic out to sea, where it was easier to intercept and control. The JCS chief anticipated that the blockade would result in war, and he had told Eisenhower as much. After learning of the proposed blockade, Ambassador Rankin predicted that the Chinese would refuse to acquiesce in such an affront, if only for reasons of face.[68] Even had the Chinese refrained from a military challenge, the implementation of the blockade would still have saddled American air and naval forces with a burdensome operation of indefinite duration. Furthermore, naval planners recognized that the Chinese could unload seaborne cargoes at ports outside the blockaded area for distribution by overland methods to their destinations.[69]

There is no evidence that senior decision makers or naval planners expected any Soviet military retaliation to a blockade. This is understandable in view of the widely held belief that only in extreme circumstances would the Kremlin consider direct intervention in the Taiwan area in support of its Asian ally. One reason that a blockade first appealed to Dulles was its reduced risk of Soviet counteraction.[70]

The Robertson-Radford Mission

Three days after the Augusta meeting, Assistant Secretary Robertson and Admiral Radford departed for Taiwan on their top secret mission. No record exists of their receiving any oral and written instructions before they left. They evidently did carry with them the evacuation-blockade paper that Eisenhower had approved at Augusta along with a draft policy statement prepared earlier in the State Department embodying the outpost approach.[71] Upon arrival in Taipei, they found waiting for them a message from Washington conveying instructions from the president (Dulles was then at his isolated vacation retreat on Duck Island in eastern Lake Ontario, where he remained until 25 April). The message broadly directed them to seek a solution to the problem in the Taiwan area that was acceptable both to Chiang and the United States. Under no circumstances were they to attempt to impose a solution on the Nationalist president or permit an adversarial atmosphere to develop; they were, however, to tell Chiang that the American public would refuse to countenance American intervention merely to save Quemoy and

Matsu. The message left unmentioned the evacuation-blockade proposal but did contain a favorable reference to the outpost approach.[72]

Despite the president's manifest interest in the outpost approach, his two emissaries put forward only the evacuation-blockade proposal in their sessions with the Generalissimo and his attendants. Robertson, in describing the particulars of this proposal at the crucial initial meeting with Chiang, unaccountably even failed to bring up the reinforced U.S. military presence on Taiwan included in the Augusta plan as an inducement for him to leave the islands. The assistant secretary did inform the Nationalist leader that the president no longer intended, in prevailing circumstances, to come to the defense of Quemoy and Matsu against a major assault. What Robertson left unsaid was that the president still possessed the authority under existing NSC policy and the Formosa Resolution to use armed force to protect the islands in the event of an actual or presumptive attack against Taiwan or the Penghus. The retraction of the defensive commitment meant only that Chiang no longer had Eisenhower's assurance that he would "in present circumstances" respond militarily to *any* seriously threatening offensive against Quemoy and Matsu.

After giving the matter some thought, Chiang unequivocally rejected the evacuation-blockade proposal. The abandonment of Quemoy and Matsu, he protested, would result in an unacceptable loss of respect for his government on Taiwan and throughout Asia. If he deserted the islands, he would jeopardize his leadership, and foreign pressure would build to place Taiwan under an international trusteeship. What is more, he queried the effectiveness of the proposed maritime interdiction.[73]

A second meeting produced no change of heart. Chiang questioned whether Washington would follow through decisively with an interdiction in the face of opposition from Britain and other like-minded nations. Recalling the checkered history of American relations with his government, specifically the secret Yalta agreement on the Far East and the postwar mission of Gen. George Marshall to China, he declared with visible emotion that he could not abide any further concessions to American expediency, however well intentioned.[74]

That Robertson and Radford failed to sway the Generalissimo was predictable. The islands were symbolically too precious for him to relinquish willingly to his despised Communist foes. Once off the islands, the KMT would no longer be camped at the doorstep of the mainland or control any territory that was indisputably Chinese in the eyes of the rest of the world. In such conditions, Chiang knew it would be harder to sustain confidence among his followers in the military reconquest of the mainland and to squelch an attempted two-China solution. As long as the islands stayed under Nationalist authority, they would also remain flash points for a military clash with the Communists that might ensnarl the United States and perhaps bring his dream of mainland recovery closer to reality. Adding to all this, Chiang suspected that Washington would find a reason to withdraw from the blockade after he pulled out of Quemoy and Matsu.[75] Recent events—Washington's advocacy of a cease-fire, its refusal to announce the defensive commitment, and now the abrupt withdrawal of its protective assurances—would only have given fodder to an inbred distrust of the Americans that was steeped in long-standing grievances.

Later, Eisenhower professed that he had not expected Chiang to assent to the evacuation-blockade proposal, and he expressed disappointment that his two envoys declined to introduce the outpost approach.[76] Given his persistent gravitation toward that approach, one wonders why the president was not more emphatic in insisting that they take it up with Chiang; that he failed to do so showed an uncharacteristic hesitation and irresolution on his part. As for Robertson and Radford, they showed scant conviction in pursuing this approach, choosing to keep it under wraps after Chiang dismissed the evacuation-blockade proposal.[77] Yet their decision to hold back on the outpost approach made no real difference to the final outcome of their mission. Chiang would almost certainly have turned thumbs down on a significant reduction of his forces on the islands just as he did their total withdrawal. A scaled-down fight for Quemoy and Matsu ending in their surrender would likely have had no more, and perhaps less, appeal to him than an uncontested retreat.

In retrospect, Chiang's stubborn resistance was a blessing in disguise for the administration. Regardless of the undeniable advantages for the United States of a voluntary evacuation of the islands, the blockade offered as a trade-off was fraught with difficulty and danger. The Robertson-Radford mission was proof of how intensely Eisenhower and Dulles yearned to extricate themselves from their quandary in the offshore islands. Fortunately for them, they found a means of escape not through the ill-conceived evacuation-blockade scheme but an unexpected offer from the Chinese Communists.

The Crisis Winds Down

On 23 April, the day before Robertson and Radford arrived in Taipei, Chou En-lai created a sensation at the Bandung conference by announcing that China was willing to begin direct talks with the United States to relax tensions in the Far East and especially in the Taiwan area. Repeating this statement the next day as the conference came to a close, the Chinese premier and foreign minister appended the qualification that negotiations would not "in the slightest degree affect the just demands of the Chinese people to exercise their sovereign rights in liberating Taiwan."[78] Chinese sources now available indicate that Chou's offer of bilateral discussions, while consistent with his understanding of current Chinese policy, was an impromptu response to the concerns expressed to him by other Asian delegates about the tense situation in the Taiwan Strait.[79] The Chinese statesman's dramatic tender of an olive branch to Washington capped a virtuoso personal performance at the conference, contributing to the aura of flexibility, moderation, and peaceableness that surrounded the PRC's diplomacy there and lending impetus to its proclaimed policy of peaceful coexistence.[80]

The State Department's initial public comment on Chou's offer, issued while Dulles was still on holiday, was discouragingly tepid.[81] Three days later, having returned to Washington and consulted with Eisenhower, the secretary responded more warmly.[82] Besides the fact that the Chinese diplomat's conciliatory gesture occurred in the glare of international publicity, other considerations now made direct discussions more acceptable to the administration than at the time of his earlier oblique overture in February. The crisis had since taken a turn for the worse, and the need for a satisfactory remedy had become all the more pressing. The failure of the Robertson-Radford mission eliminated voluntary withdrawal as a solution, leaving the administration still entrapped by its dilemma. It was hardly coincidental that Eisenhower and Dulles agreed to respond accommodatingly to Chou's offer on the same day that the news arrived from Taipei that Chiang had snubbed the evacuation-blockade proposal. Then too, Dulles credited the Chinese démarche to the efforts of pro-American governments represented at Bandung to infuse a mood into the conference that would divert Peking from armed action in the Taiwan area. He and the president felt that these friendly governments would expect a receptive reaction from Washington to Chou's offer.[83] Further, the two men realized that the Western allies and world opinion generally would rejoice at the vista of peace in the strait. In the light of the war scare, it was also a safe assumption that a relieved American public and Congress would welcome talks. As word of Chou's announcement circulated around Capitol Hill, several prominent Democrats headed by Senator George petitioned the administration to follow up on the offer. Dulles was more inclined to heed them than he was Knowland, who derided the offer as an "invitation to another Munich."[84]

It soon became obvious that the opinion voiced by the California senator was far from popular among his fellow countrymen and congressional colleagues. The administration's affirmative attitude toward a dialogue with the Chinese won the applause of the great majority of the citizenry and the legislative branch. Except for a minority of die-hard pro-Nationalist spokesmen in the media and in Congress, the administration experienced no substantial criticism from any quarter; even some well-known Nationalist devotees such as H. Alexander Smith and Walter Judd stood behind it.[85] The political isolation of Knowland and a few other right-wing Republicans on this question betokened their declining influence over the administration's conduct of foreign policy.[86]

In the aftermath of Bandung, the overheated situation in the Taiwan Strait quickly cooled down. Refraining from actions that might aggravate the situation, Eisenhower formally confirmed a decision not to send large numbers of military personnel to Taiwan to operate antiaircraft batteries.[87] More importantly, he stuck to his earlier decision to deny permission to the Nationalists to bomb the airfields being built across the strait. When Chiang claimed that his government could exercise its right of self-defense to blast the airfields after they became operational, Dulles immediately set him right, insisting that any unprovoked air strikes against them would violate the restrictive provision in the December 1954 exchange of notes.[88] Despite causing distress in Taipei and among high-ranking American military officials, the airfield construction actually posed no immediate serious danger to Taiwan.[89]

Although the wheels of diplomacy would continue to turn as the United States and China inched toward direct talks, Washington's openhanded response to Chou's offer for all practical purposes brought an end to the Taiwan Strait crisis. Eisenhower and Dulles, in retrospect, would pat themselves on the backs for their deft management of this trying encounter. In a celebrated interview for *Life* magazine in January 1956, Dulles gave wide circulation to his controversial claim that he had successfully gone "to the brink" of war to ensure peace in the strait and other contested areas. Eisenhower boasted in his memoirs that his administration had navigated a steady course between appeasement and war during the crisis. Neither man ever publicly revealed the defensive commitment for Quemoy and Matsu or the evacuation-blockade proposal.[90]

The president and his secretary of state had maintained a close working relationship throughout the months of struggle with the Chinese. Conferring frequently, each was attentive to the opinions and recommendations of the other. In partnership, they dominated decision making during the crisis. For the most part, it was Dulles who devised the succession of strategies and tactics employed by the administration. However, Eisenhower, who possessed an astute understanding of the domestic and international dimensions of the crisis and was well versed in essential diplomatic and military details, did not give his secretary a free hand. Not only did he reserve to himself final decisions on important issues, he was an active participant in the policymaking process. His preference for an "institutional presidency," with its reliance on formal advisory bodies such as the National Security Council, allowed for the presentation of diverse opinions and for collective consideration of most major decisions during the crisis.[91] Still, it was often the case that Eisenhower and Dulles had determined their course of action in advance of NSC meetings. As well, in the three weeks or so prior to the Robertson-Radford mission, a period during which the administration's strategy underwent a momentous transformation, they entirely bypassed the NSC.

Although Dulles's instincts were sometimes more belligerent than Eisenhower's and his attraction to the outpost approach less keen, the two men largely saw eye-to-eye during the crisis. They were in accord that their foremost objective was an honorable and peaceful resolution that avoided serious injury to the nation's credibility in Asia or its interests on Taiwan. They wanted to negotiate a course toward peaceful accommodation that skirted the shoals of war and diplomatic, and possibly strategic, defeat. In mapping that course, they and their subordinates had to take into account a multitude of operational, international, and domestic factors.

Historians of the Eisenhower era have not achieved consensus concerning the handling of the crisis by the president and his chief foreign policy adviser. Eisenhower revisionists, notably Stephen Ambrose and Robert Divine, have lauded the president for adroitly keeping his own goals intact and the Chinese off balance by his cleverly calculated strategy of ambiguity with regard to the defense of Quemoy and Matsu. Some later scholars have questioned whether he was as prudent or effective during the crisis as revisionists have asserted. Dulles's performance, too, has elicited differing judgments. Whether the secretary of state was an injudicious brinksman or an astute operator during the crisis remains a point of contention.[92]

On close examination, one finds more to fault than to praise in Eisenhower and Dulles's leadership during this stressful episode. To their credit, they did in a variety of ways exhibit restraint and moderation: they recognized the need to monitor American and Nationalist military actions so as not to unnecessarily aggravate the crisis; deflected some of the more extreme recommendations of the JCS hawks; tried to dampen the emotionally charged imprisoned fliers issue; attempted to create conditions for a de facto ceasefire and long-term stabilization of the Taiwan Strait; and had the good sense to take up the opportunity for direct talks presented at Bandung. On the other hand, overreaction, inflexibility, and immoderate risk-taking too frequently marred the leadership of these two key policymakers. More often than not, their words and actions made the situation in the Taiwan area more frightening and dangerous. As well, flawed perceptions distorted their outlook and decisions. In large measure, the "horrible dilemma" that framed the administration's outlook at the outset of the crisis was an offshoot of its own animus and militancy toward the People's Republic, its quasi commitment to the offshore islands, and a misunderstanding of its adversary's limited political and territorial objectives.

During the first phase of the crisis, Eisenhower and Dulles took a generally cautious tack. Still, the administration's posture of ambiguity, while giving Mao pause, failed to deter the assault on Yikiangshan in January 1955; that event prompted Dulles to recommend a shift to a more forthright strategy. During the second phase of the crisis, the balance in the administration's decisions tilted toward excessive risk-taking and rigidity. Although the evacuation of the Tachens was a prudent move, reducing the area of conflict in the outlying islands, Eisenhower and Dulles unfortunately paired it with an ill-considered secret defensive commitment for Quemoy and Matsu that circumscribed American freedom of action and appeared to increase the danger that the United States and China would come to blows. In this period the two statesmen basically tried to spook the Chinese into a retreat through an assertion of American might and will. The Formosa message and the Formosa Resolution, both of which cranked up the intensity of the crisis, were central to this purpose. The two leaders were unreceptive at this time to talks with the Chinese outside the framework of Oracle. It was not the United States but Britain and other Western allies that exerted the greatest efforts to defuse the crisis by exploring diplomatic avenues to a peaceful accommodation. Though Eisenhower and Dulles discussed a voluntary Nationalist withdrawal from the islands, the secretary declined to test this idea with Chiang during a visit to Taipei in early March.

The final phase of the crisis witnessed an erratic fluctuation between restraint and risk-taking and between flexibility and firmness in the administration's decisions, punctuated by a number of eye-catching turnabouts. In the end, Eisenhower and Dulles succeeded in extracting themselves from their painful predicament in the offshore islands only because of the timely offer of direct talks from Chou En-lai at Bandung. That offer was not a response to the administration's nuclear threats, though likely prompted in part by the political work done by the State Department with friendly Asian-African governments prior to the Indonesian conference.[93]

Underlying the administration's decision making during the crisis were two erroneous conclusions about the scope of the Chinese military campaign in the Taiwan area. One, shared by intelligence analysts and policymakers alike, was that the campaign was aimed at all the offshore islands and could well result in an attempt to seize Quemoy and Matsu if the Chinese did not judge the cost too high. In actuality, CCP leaders, as already seen, had no approved plans or ready capability to carry their military operations beyond the occupation of the Tachens and other territory off the Chekiang coast. At no time did American intelligence spot any preparations for an invasion of Quemoy or Matsu. The airfields across from Taiwan that so preoccupied decision makers in the final two months of the crisis did not become operational until May 1956.[94] The vehemence of Chinese propaganda and official statements, doubts about the adequacy of available intelligence, difficulties in deciphering Chinese intentions and military activities, and worst-case analysis, all contributed to a misinterpretation of Peking's military objectives in the coastal islands.

A second conclusion, accepted by Eisenhower, Dulles and other high-level policymakers from January onward, was that the PRC's main target was Taiwan itself. This view, which Britain and other Western allies rightly questioned, was unduly alarmist, to say the least. Though various intelligence evaluations did underscore the Chinese commitment eventually to join Taiwan to the mainland, none predicted a military assault in the near future.[95] There were no signs of preparations for an invasion at any time during the crisis, and the dominance of the Seventh Fleet in the Taiwan Strait remained undisputed throughout. Policymakers vastly overestimated the military capability of the Chinese to mount an assault on Chiang's redoubt.[96]

It is true that anxiety about the security of Taiwan interlaced in the minds of policymakers with a fear that the loss of the islands would cause a collapse of morale among the Nationalists, perhaps resulting in a Communist take-over through internal instability or a dispirited defense against an invasion. Still classified intelligence reports may tell a different story, but available documents indicate that this fear was overblown. Karl Rankin, whose solicitude for the Nationalists was well honed and who strongly favored the retention of Quemoy and Matsu, did not reckon that the forfeiture of these coastal possessions would have disastrous consequences for Chiang Kai-shek's government.[97] A survey of thirty key Americans on Taiwan conducted by the Taipei embassy in March tended to support this conclusion. The embassy failed to detect any increased vulnerability to subversive activity; the Generalissimo and the KMT seemed in secure control.[98] A national intelligence report in mid-April minimized the danger of subversion and judged the existing state of morale as "fairly good." Acknowledging that the surrender of the coastal islands, whatever the circumstances, would be a "severe blow" to the Nationalists, this report did not foresee a disintegration either of KMT authority or anti-Communist resistance.[99] Eden and the Foreign Office, basing their conclusions in part on the informed assessment of the British consul on Taiwan, were unconvinced that the morale and stability of Chiang's tightly controlled regime balanced precariously on the retention of Quemoy and Matsu. After the crisis had passed, the British consul made note of the fact that the Nationalists had discovered that the threat of a collapse of morale was a "highly effective counter" to any objectionable American suggestion.[100]

Concerns among top American officials that the loss of the islands would result in a damaging decline in American credibility among Asian friends and allies were also overwrought. Intelligence evaluations indicated that annexation of the islands by the mainland would neither have sapped confidence in the United States' leadership in Asia nor weakened indigenous opposition to communist expansion as much as upper-echelon officials dreaded. An estimate prepared early in September 1954 concluded that only South Korea would suffer distress if the United States were to permit the offshore islands to fall; the countries of Southeast Asia would place no great importance on the loss of these Nationalist forward positions, while Japan would feel relieved no crisis had developed.[101] A March 1955 assessment predicted that a voluntary evacuation of Chiang's troops would seriously disappoint only South Korea; there would be some unease in the Philippines, a lesser concern in Thailand, Laos, Cambodia, and South Vietnam, and relief among the rest of the noncommunist Asian countries surveyed.[102]

However historians may now judge Eisenhower and Dulles's perceptions and conduct during the offshore islands crisis, the two leaders appeared to have justifiable cause to congratulate themselves as the level of tension subsided after Bandung. They could take satisfaction in the fact that, despite more than a few worrisome moments, they had weathered the storm successfully. The encounter with the Chinese had abated without a major military incident or a costly concession. For better or worse, Chiang's troops remained in possession of Quemoy and Matsu. American credibility in Asia remained unimpaired, and the Western allies were shaken but not alienated. After much commotion and hand-wringing at home and abroad, the administration had ended up on the right side of both national and world opinion.

Nonetheless, the two leaders were not about to succumb to self-satisfied complacency. Realizing that fighting could resume again in the offshore islands and that the Taiwan Strait remained a powder keg, they bent their efforts in the months after Bandung to solidify the stalemate that had resulted from their chilling face-off with the Chinese.

11

The offshore islands crisis and its aftermath subjected the American relationship with the Nationalist government to more stress than at any time since before Washington shifted to a pro-Nationalist policy following the Chinese intervention in Korea. Taipei had objected in vain to Washington's pursuit of a UN cease-fire in the coastal islands, looking upon a formal cessation of hostilities as the thin edge of a two-China wedge. It had gained its prized mutual security pact only after arduous bargaining and by consenting to restrictive provisions in the exchange of notes. Washington's refusal to publicize the defensive commitment for Quemoy and Matsu had enraged Chiang Kai-shek, while the subsequent withdrawal of that commitment and attempt to rope him into abandoning the islands had compounded his doubts about American trustworthiness and dependability.

The already tense relationship grew more strained after Bandung. The Eisenhower administration's post-Bandung strategy was to prolong and cement an informal cease-fire in the Taiwan Strait so as to preserve Nationalist control of the coastal islands and establish a de facto two-China situation. After responding affirmatively to the offer of direct discussions with the Communists, the administration set nerves further on edge in Taipei by agreeing to ambassadorial talks at Geneva. The American representative's vigorous espousal of the renunciation-of-force principle at these talks excited demands from Taipei for their discontinuation. Even as differences over the Geneva

235

parleys came to a head, the United States and Taiwan locked horns at the UN over the admission of Outer Mongolia. Meanwhile, the operation of the American economic and military aid program on Taiwan accentuated the fundamental divergence between the cherished KMT goal of mainland reconquest and Washington's emphasis on securing the future of Chiang and his followers on their island refuge.

Stabilizing the Strait

Given a ladder by Chou En-lai to step down from the Taiwan Strait crisis, Eisenhower and Dulles willingly descended but without any intention to enter into a broad dialogue with the PRC or even to follow up immediately on the Chinese premier's initiative. Though accepting Chou's offer in principle, they did not want the form or scope of any bilateral talks to compromise existing policies toward Peking or Taipei. So far from being in a hurry to start these discussions, they deliberately stalled, playing for time in order to nurture an international climate against Chinese military action and to stabilize the Taiwan area through an unofficial cease-fire.[1]

In their initial public comments on Chou's overture, the president and secretary of state carefully narrowed the scope of any talks, giving priority to the release of American captives in China, to a cease-fire in the Taiwan area, and to Chinese Communist acceptance of the renunciation-of-force principle. Dulles ruled out any deliberations bearing on the rights, claims, and interests of the Nationalist government.[2] Despite this exclusion, the decision to respond favorably to Chou's invitation caused consternation in Taipei, which soothing assurances from Dulles and other State Department officials failed to allay. Especially distressing to the Nationalist government was Washington's support for a peaceful accommodation in the Taiwan Strait based on observance of the renunciation-of-force principle; the slightest suggestion of a formal cease-fire intensified fears of a two-China arrangement.[3]

Similar alarm was present in Peking. Chou En-lai's private and public statements at Bandung revealed no inclination to confer with the United States about a cease-fire or disavowal of force in the Taiwan area. Following established Chinese policy, the premier drew a distinction between the international and domestic dimensions of conflict in the area: only the tension between the PRC and the United States arising from American "intervention" was a proper subject for dialogue between the two sides, not the PRC's rightful claim to domestic territory held by the "Chiang Kai-shek clique."[4] In a report to the National People's Congress on 13 May, Chou did affirm that the Chinese were "willing to strive for the liberation of Taiwan by peaceful means so far as it is possible." This declaration was somewhat comforting to Dulles but still fell conspicuously short of unequivocal approval of the renunciation-of-force principle.[5]

Alive to the strength of Peking's convictions, Dulles entertained no illusion that he could easily overcome its opposition to an official cease-fire or mutual renunciation of force in the Taiwan area. Rather than push hard for formal arrangements that would probably break down and offer an excuse for the Chinese to resume military action, he and Eisenhower agreed to let matters "simmer" for a time.[6] Dulles wanted to transform the breathing spell after Bandung into an enduring though informal cease-fire, with the United States keeping a rein on the Nationalists and the Communists choosing, in their own interest, to desist from warlike moves. Because Washington had now accepted direct talks in principle, the onus for worsening the situation would fall on the Communists; the longer the unofficial cease-fire lasted, the harder it would be for them to upset it.[7]

Despite the winding down of the crisis, Dulles and the president understood all too well that a threatened or actual all-out offensive against Quemoy and Matsu could once again present an unpalatable choice between standing aloof or inserting American forces. Seeing no way to persuade Chiang to give up these islands or any realistic possibility in the near future of a negotiated settlement of Sino-American differences in the Taiwan area, the two leaders essayed to prolong and reinforce the unofficial cease-fire and freeze the status quo. The purpose of this strategy of unformalized stabilization was to keep the two parties in the unfinished civil war from coming to blows, to avert a situation requiring United States intervention, and to foster the coalescence of a de facto two-China arrangement.

An immediate benefit of the informal cease-fire after Bandung was to put to rest fears that a Sino-American conflict in the Taiwan Strait might upend the final ratification of the Paris accords. The triumphant consummation of the accords went off without a hitch on 5 May. Five days later, at a NATO Council meeting in Paris, Dulles received a stern reminder from Paul-Henri Spaak, the respected Belgian foreign minister, that the potential still existed for a rift over Quemoy and Matsu between the United States and its European allies, who saw no point in American protection of these islands and held Chiang Kai-shek in low regard. Unabashed, Dulles retorted that the Communists themselves made no distinction between Taiwan and the outlying islands. As for Chiang, if he was imperfect, this was also true of other Far Eastern statesmen, and he at least had the virtue of being "resolute, loyal, and Christian."[8]

On 15 May Dulles was in Vienna along with the other Big Four foreign ministers for the signing of the long-delayed Austrian peace treaty. The scent of détente was in the air in the Austrian capital; the Kremlin had also just accepted a Western invitation to hold a conference of Big Four leaders in the near future — the first summit since Potsdam.[9] Figuring that the Soviets now had more to lose than to gain from an explosion in the Taiwan area and hoping to put their nascent moderation toward the West to productive use, Dulles in a private meeting with Soviet foreign minister V. M. Molotov urged that Moscow counsel patience and restraint to its Chinese ally. Molotov, playing his cards close to the vest, gave no hint of any differences with the Chinese or of a readiness to act upon Dulles's request. Declaring only that his government wanted peace, he suggested a five-power conference consisting of the Big Four plus Communist China, an idea to which Dulles understandably did not warm.[10] Despite the Soviet diplomat's unhelpful response, the secretary of state plainly saw in the Kremlin's desire for improved relations with the West an opportunity to check Chinese rashness and widen the fracture lines in the Sino-Soviet alliance.

In the absence of an American initiative after Bandung to sound out the Chinese about the modalities for direct talks, several Asian statesmen consulted with Peking on their own, hoping to serve as unofficial intermediaries. One of these was V. K. Krishna Menon, the chairman of India's UN delegation and a close associate of Prime Minister Nehru. On 27 May, following conversations in Peking between Menon and Chou En-lai, Nehru notified Washington that the Communists would release four American airmen recently convicted of violating Chinese airspace and conducting harassing activities.[11] At month's end, Peking freed these four fliers, who did not belong to the group of eleven Americans convicted and imprisoned the previous November on the more serious charge of espionage.[12]

In spite of this conciliatory gesture, Dulles was still in no rush to enter into discussions. What is more, he was reluctant to give Peking the impression that it could blackmail the United States with the remaining imprisoned airmen.[13] Nor would he accept Menon in an intermediary role; both he and Eisenhower scorned the Indian diplomat as anti-American and procommunist and as an egotistical and unscrupulous manipulator.[14] Conferring with him after his return from Peking, they showed no appetite for any of his recommendations to facilitate Sino-American negotiations. To encourage the release of Americans still held captive in China, however, Eisenhower did inform Menon that Washington would not bar any Chinese nationals from leaving the United States. By implication, this meant a lifting of the official travel ban on those few Chinese expatriates who, for security reasons, were prohibited from exiting the country.[15]

Heartened by the post-Bandung lull, the British government tried to keep open a channel of communication between Washington and Peking and to sustain the momentum for peace. Yet London did not exhort Washington to move quickly toward direct talks. British officials saw little common ground for productive bargaining between the Americans and Chinese over issues in the Taiwan area.[16] Harold Macmillan, Eden's successor at the Foreign Office, gained some insight into Dulles's private thoughts about these issues at the San Francisco conference, beginning on 20 June in observance of the tenth anniversary of the United Nations. Dulles told the new British foreign secretary that he did not expect the Chinese to try to scoop up Quemoy and Matsu under present circumstances, still less to take the offensive against Taiwan. Disclosing that the purpose of the Robertson-Radford mission had been to reel in Chiang's troops from the islands, he speculated that the Generalissimo might still be persuaded in the next six months to fall back from his forward positions. (Still unprepared to confide fully in the British, Dulles kept mum about the evacuation-blockade proposal, whose categorical rejection by Chiang had dashed any real hope of a voluntary pullout in the near future.) The secretary of state emphasized that time was needed to obtain the freedom of the imprisoned fliers and to mitigate the current dispute in the Taiwan Strait. The passage of time would also determine the shape of longer-range developments on the Chinese mainland and Taiwan. Another five years might go by, he reflected, before it was known whether the Chinese Communist regime would hold together and whether it would conduct itself as a responsible member of the international community. Similarly, as native Taiwanese (who had no personal stake in a return to the continent) replaced mainlanders in the Nationalist army, Chiang Kai-shek might become less offensive minded. In the long run, Taiwan might evolve some form of self-government.[17] Clearly, Dulles did not think the moment was ripe for a lasting formal settlement in the Taiwan area.

More than two months after Bandung, the secretary finally decided to seek agreement with Peking on the form and scope of direct talks. What inspired him to take the initiative was the need to outflank the Soviets at the Geneva summit scheduled to start on 18 July. He concurred with Macmillan that a countermove was necessary to block anticipated Soviet efforts at the conference either to raise China-related issues or to agitate for a separate high-level gathering on the Far East to include the People's Republic.[18]

So it was that on 13 July Washington proposed to Peking that the two sides elevate to the ambassadorial level the bilateral consular talks begun in Geneva the previous July to deal with the repatriation of American and Chinese civilians. In addition to the as yet unresolved repatriation issue, the ambassadorial discussions were to encompass (in the carefully chosen language of the American offer) "certain other practical matters now at issue between the two of us."[19] In the State Department's view, the words "between the two of us" implicitly excluded all subjects bearing on the rights and interests of the Nationalist government. This exemption, together with a reflexive aversion to opening up any Pandora's boxes at the talks, significantly narrowed the range of questions under the heading of "certain practical matters" that the department thought suitable to take up with the Chinese.[20]

Only one day after learning of Washington's proposal through the British, Peking replied in the affirmative. Chou En-lai suggested that the initial meeting of ambassadors take place on 21 July after the two sides had first agreed on the wording of a simultaneous identical announcement.[21] Mainly because of a squabble over nomenclature, Peking and Washington failed to put the finishing touches on this announcement until 25 July. The authorized statement followed the language of the American proposal in describing the scope of the talks, which were set to begin on 1 August, after the conclusion of the Geneva summit.[22]

Meantime, at the summit itself Eisenhower and Dulles easily deflected a Soviet attempt to place East Asian topics on the agenda.[23] The problems in the Taiwan area did not go unnoticed by the conference participants, however. Eisenhower and Eden privately urged the Soviets to advise Peking to exercise self-control and moderation; they both felt that this message had gotten across to Kremlin leaders.[24] The topic of the offshore islands also came up in Anglo-American conversations. Still "deeply concerned" about Quemoy and Matsu, Eden reminded Eisenhower that the Chinese could put the American government in a difficult fix at any time. Conceding that the United States would be better off if Chiang's troops left the islands, the president groused that the Generalissimo had proven immune to petitions for withdrawal. Describing the purpose of the Robertson-Radford mission, he gave the mistaken impression that his emissaries had been unable to sell Chiang on the outpost approach, while in actual fact they had declined even to present it to the Nationalist president. Eisenhower made no reference at all to the evacuation-blockade proposal.[25]

In a separate meeting with Eden, Dulles remarked that the Chinese Communists were overly impatient to complete national unification and that they would certainly gain admission to the UN if they only behaved reasonably for a year or two. Admitting that the United States was "living over a volcano" in the offshore islands and lamenting the failure to convince Chiang to vacate them, he still refused to exclude their defense by the United States. Predicting that over the next few years they would decline in significance for the Nationalists as more Taiwanese entered the armed forces, he saw no choice but to "just try to carry the baby along" for now.[26]

The commencement of the Geneva ambassadorial talks with China wrought no change in the strategy of unformalized stabilization. Dulles explained to Eisenhower that he did not intend to hurry the talks toward a conclusion, except for the one objective of obtaining the freedom of captive Americans. "Otherwise, we needed time by which to stabilize the situation," he stressed to the president, who was in full agreement with this approach.[27] The secretary accordingly directed U. Alexis Johnson, the career foreign service officer then serving as ambassador to Prague who had been selected to represent the United States at Geneva, to keep the talks going as long as he could.[28] Johnson's written instructions reflected the restricted American agenda at Geneva: they laid emphasis on the repatriation of detained civilian nationals and, in the category of "other practical matters," on the release of the remaining imprisoned airmen and Chinese endorsement of the renunciation-of-force principle in the Taiwan area.[29]

In a similarly reserved public description of the American agenda, Dulles offered the additional assurance that the talks would not prejudice the rights of Nationalist China or imply any official recognition of the Chinese Communist regime.[30] The secretary and president did, however, hint that the talks might have a wider potential; both of them publicly intimated, after Senator Walter George proposed a Dulles-Chou meeting within the next six months, that such a ministerial conference might merit consideration if the Geneva conversations were successful.[31] In reality, such higher level discussions were far from their minds, though, following the "never say never" rule, they made sure that their public remarks left open a crack in the door.[32] They probably also calculated that the possibility of a ministerial colloquy would make the Chinese more forthcoming at Geneva and less likely to cut short the talks.

The administration's decision to participate in ambassadorial talks garnered the approval of an overwhelming majority of the press, the public, and Congress. Legislative leaders either seconded the decision unqualifiedly or fell into line with only a few murmurs of discontent. In reviewing public commentary, State Department analysts detected a moderating trend in opinion toward Communist China that coexisted with hard-line attitudes on recognition, UN admission, and the protection of Taiwan. A greater readiness to consider an eventual reappraisal of existing American policy toward China ran in tandem with opposition to any major concessions until Peking had proven its reliability.[33]

Whereas the administration's decision obviously struck the right note in the United States, the reverse was true on Taiwan. The Nationalist government understandably had profound misgivings about the Geneva talks, insisting, once they were underway, on frequent progress reports from the State Department. Quick to assert its interests, Taipei was sensitive to the slightest indication that Washington might step into a Communist snare or otherwise take a position that would improve Peking's fortunes while damaging those of its ally.[34]

On 1 August, in a blaze of international publicity, the first session of the talks convened in Geneva at the Palais des Nations, the European home of the United Nations. Coming after the hair-raising tension of the Quemoy-Matsu crisis and during a relatively calm interlude in the cold war, as the world basked in the afterglow of Bandung and the Geneva summit, the talks engendered a mood of excited optimism. The Chinese further stimulated this hopeful atmosphere by releasing the remaining eleven imprisoned American airmen on the eve of the first session. At that initial meeting, U. Alexis Johnson and his Chinese counterpart, Wang Ping-nan, agreed on a two-part agenda, the first part dealing with the repatriation of detained civilians, the second with "other practical matters now at issue between the two sides."[35]

Inaugurated amid buoyant international expectations, the Johnson-Wang talks stalemated within six months.[36] A full account of the negotiations during this period is beyond the scope of this study and is available elsewhere.[37] What is pertinent here is the interconnection between the negotiations and the Eisenhower administration's policymaking toward the Taiwan area as well as the impact of the talks on relations with Peking and Taipei.

Two unresolved disputes produced the eventual deadlock at Geneva. The first was an acrimonious altercation over the implementation of an agreement, reached on 10 September, that stipulated that American and Chinese civilian detainees be allowed to return "expeditiously" to their respective homelands. When Peking refused to permit some Americans to leave because they had violated Chinese law, Washington charged it with bad faith.[38]

The other dispute was over American and Chinese acceptance of the renunciation-of-force principle in the Taiwan area. When Johnson and Wang proceeded to the second item on their agreed agenda, the Chinese representative introduced the topics of a ministerial conference and the abolition of the American trade embargo against China. It was evident that Peking regarded the talks as a fulcrum with which to lever the United States toward conversations at a higher level as well as toward a less hostile stance. But Washington was immovable. Insisting that the subject of a Dulles-Chou conference was outside the scope of the talks, Johnson also sought to put off any serious discussion of the trade embargo.[39] Instead, he focused on a reciprocal renunciation of force (except for self-defense) between the United States and the People's Republic that would specifically include the Taiwan area. The State Department intended this mutual disavowal of aggressive force to include the offshore islands.[40] In a series of proposals and counterproposals, Johnson and Wang failed to reconcile basic differences over the specific application of the renunciation-of-force principle to the Taiwan area. In January 1956, after more than three months of acrid negotiations, the two sides released the texts of their various submissions, exchanging volleys of censorious rhetoric. Although this public wrangle did not end all further discussion of this subject at Geneva, it did expose an unbridgeable gap between the two sides. Peking decried the American effort to apply the renunciation-of-force principle to the Taiwan area as a plot to perpetuate the status quo and manufacture a two-China situation.[41]

American advocacy of this principle in the Taiwan area was also a source of discord with Taipei. Indeed, the Nationalist government objected to any form of reciprocal disavowal of force by the United States and the Chinese Communist regime, whether in or outside the Taiwan area.[42] After Washington and Peking publicized the texts of their proposals and counterproposals in January, Taipei flew into a rage, claiming that the Geneva negotiations affected its rights and interests and insisting that the talks cease without delay. In parallel with Peking, Taipei contended that the application of the renunciation-of-force principle to the Taiwan area would give momentum to the two-China idea. The State Department tried to alleviate Nationalist concerns without permitting Taipei to dictate its conduct of the talks.[43]

As both the Communists and Nationalists rightly suspected, the two-China concept did lurk behind Washington's sponsorship of the nonuse of force in the Taiwan area. Putting this principle into practice could ensure an indefinite continuation of the status quo and at least a tacit acceptance of a two-China situation. All the same, Washington did not pursue a formal agreement with the PRC on a mutual disavowal of force in the Taiwan Strait with any real expectation of success. From the start of the Geneva talks, Dulles understood that the Chinese were unlikely to assent to such an agreement or, if they did, would demand unacceptable concessions such as an American military withdrawal from the area.[44]

Nevertheless, the negotiations with the Chinese on this subject served American purposes in two ways. First, they were useful in dragging out the talks and buying time for an informal cease-fire to take firm root. Second, they provided a deterrent against Communist warlike moves. A Chinese refusal to abjure force, the State Department believed, would detract from the credibility of their protestations of peace and would stand against them in the court of world opinion if they should precipitate hostilities. Without an expectation of sympathetic international opinion, they would be less likely to take up the sword in the strait.[45] From Washington's viewpoint, then, the negotiations on the nonuse of force did not have to bear fruit in order to advance the strategy of unformalized stabilization.

The protection of the offshore islands was a major element in this strategy. While Dulles foresaw a time when the islands would hold less value for the Nationalist government, its present commitment to holding them at whatever cost meant that the United States had to retain an interest in their safekeeping. The need to erect diplomatic inhibitions against a renewed Chinese Communist offensive that might require American intervention acquired a special urgency as a result of President Eisenhower's hospitalization for almost seven weeks after a heart attack in late September 1955. Under existing NSC policy and the terms of the Formosa Resolution, only the chief executive could authorize American military action to defend Quemoy and Matsu. Eisenhower's illness made it all the more necessary to spin out the Geneva talks and maintain a diplomatic disincentive against an unexpected aggressive move.[46]

As the talks neared the six month mark at the end of January 1956, an unofficial cease-fire still reigned in the islands and throughout the Taiwan area, disturbed only by Nationalist harassing activities and minor incidents. Although intelligence analysts did not expect the Chinese to gamble on an assault against Taiwan itself in the foreseeable future, they did anticipate probing operations against the coastal outposts and a probable attempt to seize them if the Chinese were convinced that the United States would forbear from intervention.[47]

Depending on Chinese actions, the potential for another confrontation over the offshore islands would remain as long as Chiang Kai-shek insisted that his front line was 100 miles west of Taiwan. To punctuate his opposition to any retreat from his advance posts, Chiang augmented his forces on Quemoy and Matsu after Bandung. Over the objection of the MAAG, he ordered an additional division to Quemoy during the summer, bringing to six the number stationed on the island. After the JCS determined that the transfer did not "substantially" diminish the defensibility of Taiwan, Washington had no grounds to block it as a violation of the December 1954 exchange of notes. In September 1955, again against the wishes of the MAAG, Chiang ordered another two battalions to Matsu.[48] By increasing the proportion of his total forces garrisoned on the islands, the Nationalist leader made it all the more difficult for the United States to stand apart from their defense.

So despite the relative calm that settled over the Taiwan Strait after Bandung, American decision makers could not let down their guard. The post-Bandung easing of tensions and the Geneva talks left unresolved the fundamental issues separating the United States and the People's Republic in the area. An unofficial cease-fire did take hold in the offshore islands, but its duration was uncertain and at the whim of the Chinese. As long as a large number of Nationalist troops resided on Quemoy and Matsu, a "horrible dilemma" could again confront Washington at any time the Communists chose to menace the islands. For all intents and purposes, American policy toward these disputed specks of real estate was hostage to a resolute adversary and a headstrong ally.

In pursuit of its post-Bandung strategy, the Eisenhower administration did not allow the misgivings and protests of Taipei to stand in its way, placing the accomplishment of its own objectives above the maintenance of smooth relations with its ally. For its part, Chiang's government took a progressively more jaundiced view of the administration's actions in the diplomatic arena. The positive response to Chou's offer at Bandung, the agreement to hold ambassadorial talks, the negotiations at Geneva on a mutual renunciation of force, all these events visibly grated on Taipei, contributing to a more contentious and stressful relationship between Washington and the Nationalist regime.

Barring the Gate at the UN

In striving to stabilize the Taiwan area by means of a de facto two-China arrangement, Eisenhower and Dulles remained fixed in their opposition to Chinese Communist representation in the United Nations. In spite of their personal openness to seating Peking at some future date, the two men recognized that any deviation from their present opposition ran counter to existing U.S. China policy and to dominant American opinion. In contrast, as the prestige and acceptance of the People's Republic rose in the aftermath of Bandung, international opinion looked with mounting favor on its representation in the world organization, with the result that the administration had once more to contend with restive allies and friends. To the dismay of American officials, the Nationalists themselves, by an unpopular veto in the Security Council, weakened the ability of the United States to command international support for the exclusion of the PRC.

As the opening of the tenth session of the General Assembly appeared on the horizon in September 1955, the State Department began to prod the British government to renew the moratorium agreement that for the past four years had kept the representation issue dormant in the UN. Sensitive to trends in international opinion, London recommended an alteration of the moratorium resolution passed at the previous session of the assembly. By having the upcoming assembly decide "not yet" to consider the issue, the proposed change softened the old resolution by implicitly ruling out indefinite postponement. Convinced that the new formula nearly guaranteed the seating of the Chinese Communists in the near term, the State Department rejected it outright.[49]

Having run up against a stone wall, London agreed to recycle the old resolution. Assured of British cooperation, the State Department successfully exercised its concerted efforts to obtain the passage of this resolution by a large majority, clinching the continuation of the moratorium at least to the scheduled termination of the session at the end of 1955. In going along with Washington, London expressed its impatience with protracted postponement.[50]

Before this new moratorium expired at the end of December, the Nationalist government jeopardized its occupancy of the China seat by a veto in the Security Council, cast in defiance of American wishes and bringing on it the opprobrium of many UN members. The ROC used its veto to bar membership in the world body for Outer Mongolia, one of eighteen nations slated for entry as part of a package deal put together under Canadian auspices to overcome a cold war impasse that since 1950 had prevented the admission of any new members. In a game of tit for tat over the previous half decade, the United States had mobilized majority support in the UN to thwart the entry of communist bloc nations, while the Soviet Union employed its veto to quash the applications of noncommunist nations. By late 1955 a long lineup of applicants awaited affirmative action by the UN. The United States and like-minded UN members favored the admission of thirteen of the candidate nations, including Italy, Spain, and Japan, whereas the Soviet Union backed the admission of five of its satellites, four from Eastern Europe along with Outer Mongolia. The package solution proposed by Canada in cooperation with twenty-seven cosponsors aimed at breaking the logjam by simultaneous admission of all eighteen applicants.[51]

Still caught up in the "spirit of Geneva," both the United States and USSR were receptive to a reciprocal arrangement. But while Washington was prepared to tolerate the admission of the East European satellites, it was less willing to swallow the inclusion of Outer Mongolia in the Canadian package. It was not ready, however, to veto Outer Mongolia's application because this might unravel the entire deal, bringing down on its own head both blame for prolonging the impasse and the resentment of those noncommunist nations stuck in the queue at the entrance of the UN. Furthermore, the American government had never before vetoed the admission of a new member. In point of fact, the State Department held that a veto for this purpose would violate the spirit of the Vandenburg Resolution of June 1948, in which the Senate had taken a stand against such obstructive action. The department also took the position that the question of the admission of a new member was unrelated to the Chinese representation issue, inasmuch as the latter involved the separate question of accreditation to an existing seat.[52]

While unwilling to resort to a veto, the United States did lobby against the inclusion of Outer Mongolia in the package solution, mainly because the Nationalist government bristled at the prospect of UN membership for this Asian satellite of the Soviet Union. Contending that Outer Mongolia was historically Chinese territory, Taipei claimed sovereignty over it and refused to accept its independent status. Outer Mongolia's admission would also, from Taipei's perspective, pave the way for the later entry of the illegitimate Chinese Communist regime, another Soviet dependency lacking the qualifications for UN membership.[53] Unlike Washington, the Nationalist government had no qualms about using its veto power to keep out Outer Mongolia. To the State Department's way of thinking, such action was laden with undesirable consequences. If the veto should kill the package deal, the United States would share the blame, because many UN members assumed that Washington exercised a dominating influence over Taipei.[54] Worse, the Nationalist government would rouse so much ill feeling against itself that it might lose its seat in the international organization. Henry Cabot Lodge, Jr., the chief United States delegate at the UN, predicted that a Nationalist veto resulting in a failure to resolve the impasse over new admissions would "raise the issue of Chinese representation in a more acute and difficult form than we have ever known."[55]

Unable to excise Outer Mongolia from the package deal, Washington did its best to dissuade Taipei from resorting to a veto. In two personal letters to Chiang, Eisenhower earnestly requested that his government simply abstain on the vote on the Outer Mongolian application.[56] Dulles gravely warned the Generalissimo that a veto could have "disastrous consequences" for Nationalist China's position in the UN.[57]

Refusing to relent despite intense pressure from Washington, the Nationalist government on 13 December cast its veto against the application of Outer Mongolia. This blocking action set in motion a series of vetoes by the Soviet Union and the Western permanent members that sank the entire package deal. After frantic behind-the-scenes negotiations, a compromise approved the next day permitted the admission of all the candidate nations except for Outer Mongolia and Japan—the rejection of the latter being the levy exacted by the Soviet Union for the exclusion of its own favored Asian applicant. By salvaging most of the package, the UN ended the long deadlock over new admissions and facilitated a rapid increase in membership in succeeding years.[58]

The membership dispute aggravated Washington's already troubled relationship with Taipei. It demonstrated once again the limits of American influence over the Nationalists and the underlying lack of confidence of Chiang and other KMT officials in the reliability of their ally. Later, Ambassador Rankin reported that the Nationalists had suspected that the United States was conniving behind their backs to engineer the package deal. Already pessimistic about holding on to their place in the UN if existing trends in international opinion continued, they saw nothing to be gained by acceding to Outer Mongolia's admission.[59]

The issue of the disputed China seat, together with the broader problem of differing Anglo-American approaches to the People's Republic, were on the agenda when Prime Minister Eden and Selwyn Lloyd (who had replaced Macmillan at the Foreign Office) met in Washington with Eisenhower and Dulles at the end of January 1956. At one session, Dulles and Lloyd squared off over how best to wean the Chinese from the Soviet Union. Arguing that the natural rivalries between the two communist partners would remain latent for a long period, Dulles insisted that it was safest under present conditions in the Asia-Pacific region to resist rather than coddle the Chinese, while Lloyd took the approach that present hard-line policies strengthened the Sino-Soviet relationship. This exchange only confirmed the persistence of a basic difference over China policy that had afflicted Anglo-American relations since 1950. On the Chinese representation issue, Dulles was insistent that the United States would not stomach Peking's admission. The president was similarly unyielding in a separate session with Eden.[60]

In spite of a promise from Eden that he would inform Washington as soon as possible if his government would reinstate the moratorium (which had again expired), London procrastinated for many months. Only in October 1956, by which time the Suez crisis had erupted and the American presidential election was in full swing, did Britain finally give its consent to a renewal.[61] Despite declining support in the UN, the moratorium procedure remained in force for the remainder of the Eisenhower administration.[62]

From the vantage of high officials in the administration early in 1956, the tides of international opinion seemed to be running strongly in favor of the PRC's entry into the world body. Just the same, Eisenhower, Dulles, and their subordinates were determined to uphold the diplomacy of postponement. The Nationalist veto of Outer Mongolia's admission had not made that task any easier. Although the "disastrous consequences" for Nationalist China in the UN against which Dulles had ominously forewarned Chiang failed to come to pass, the episode further soured the relationship between the United States and Taiwan.

Holding the Line on Taiwan

Another point of friction between Washington and Taipei was the scope and implementation of the American aid program for Taiwan. By 1955 expenditures had reached considerable proportions; combined spending for economic and military assistance had averaged about $300 million since 1951.

The delivery of military equipment rapidly accelerated during the offshore islands crisis while the number of MAAG personnel leaped from nearly 800 to more than 2,000.[63] Disagreement between the Americans and Nationalists over the aid program stemmed mainly from a divergence in basic goals. American officialdom saw the program's essential purpose as the security and economic development of Taiwan itself, whereas the Nationalists viewed it primarily as a means to gird themselves to regain the mainland.

Such disagreement was not new in the operation of the aid program, but it had noticeably sharpened by the fall of 1955. Walter McConaughy, the State Department's chief China officer, compared the progress of the program to the construction of the same building by two different crews, one working toward a ten-story structure and the other toward a taller edifice; not until the two crews had completed the eighth or ninth floor would they have a serious quarrel. "This stage has been approximately reached in our program on Taiwan," he concluded, "and we now have to start planning on how we are going to put a roof on the structure. For their part, the Chinese [Nationalists] are going to keep on pushing for a penthouse."[64]

That "penthouse" was the recovery of the mainland, the raison d'être and the rallying slogan of the Nationalist government. Despite Dulles's efforts to convert Chiang to a strategy of opportunism, the Generalissimo and his loyalists still advocated a military campaign to retake the KMT's lost territory.[65] According to Rankin, no "intelligent Chinese [Nationalist] personages" he knew truly expected the United States to undertake a commitment to reinstate the Nationalist government on the continent in present conditions; however, the hope was that future events might cause a change of heart.[66]

The emphasis on mainland reconquest was, in American eyes, an impediment to the achievement of economic self-reliance, a central objective of United States economic assistance to Taiwan. The Nationalist government had in late 1953 prepared a four-year plan for a self-supporting economy but had given it little backing in practice. Though Taiwan had almost completed its postwar recovery by the end of 1955, it remained an American dependency with persistent economic and financial problems, including a trade imbalance, budgetary deficits, and a failure to generate adequate levels of private and public investment.[67]

The military establishment placed a tremendous burden on the economy and was a major obstacle to self-sufficiency. The lion's share of Washington's economic aid went to offset the indirect costs of this establishment, and more than 80 percent of the Nationalist government's budget was military related.[68] In the latter months of 1955 American officials on Taiwan responsible for overseeing the economic assistance program bridled at the unwillingness of the Ministry of Finance either to control its spending or to spur the armed forces to cut their expenditures. These aid officials viewed the absence of financial discipline as symptomatic of a more fundamental difference between the American desire for a more productive, self-reliant Taiwanese economy and the determination of some senior KMT leaders to funnel as much funding from Washington as possible into creating the military forces necessary for a return to the mainland.[69]

The Nationalist concentration on mainland reconquest also stoked disagreement between Taipei and the Pentagon over the size of the army directly supported by American military aid. Only two-thirds of Chiang's military establishment, which in its entirety numbered about 600,000, received direct assistance. The JCS plans then in place called for the development of armed forces totalling just over 400,000, consisting of twenty-one infantry divisions, two armored divisions, and marine, air, and naval units.[70] These supported forces were to be equipped and trained to defend KMT-held territory, to "contribute to collective non-Communist strength in the Far East," and to participate in "such other action as may be mutually agreed upon under the terms of the Mutual Defense Treaty."[71] Despite being earmarked as a strategic reserve with a limited offensive capability, Nationalist forces were primarily intended to perform a defensive role. Moreover, the Pentagon still counted on American air and naval power as the principal bulwark against a major Chinese assault in the Taiwan area.

During most of the last half of 1955 the Defense Department and the Nationalist government engaged in a tug-of-war over the implementation of an agreement reached by Adm. Radford and Chiang Kai-shek in April 1955 to establish nine new reserve infantry divisions. Wanting to enlarge the pool of U.S. equipped and trained manpower, the Nationalists insisted on enough additional military hardware for all nine divisions. The Defense Department was prepared to furnish only enough for one division to use in training exercises. The JCS did not want the reserve program to become a backdoor for the expansion of the regular standing army beyond the twenty-one infantry divisions already directly supported by American aid. In December 1955 the Pentagon and the Nationalist Ministry of Defense finally reached agreement on a nine-division reserve plan that required supplying only enough equipment for one division. The mission of the Nationalist forces remained primarily defensive.[72]

At the end of 1955 the fighting prowess of these forces was still distinctly limited. They could not stand up on their own to a sustained large-scale Communist assault against either Taiwan or the offshore islands. Nor could they contribute to "collective defense" elsewhere in the region unless Taiwan itself were not threatened. They lacked the capability to undertake effective independent offensive action against the mainland on anything more than a minor scale. Only with American air, naval, and logistical support could Chiang Kai-shek and his exiled cohorts establish the military foothold across the strait that was their ambition. Given the unlikelihood of such support and the unwillingness of Washington to tailor its economic and military aid program to a strategy of counterattack, the realization of that aspiration would remain an unattainable dream. For all this, Taiwan had become a major recipient of American economic and military largesse and a valued bastion in the network of anticommunist alliances and alignments stretching across the Asia-Pacific region that the United States had constructed by mid-decade.

The level of stress in Washington's relationship with Taipei, already on the rise during the offshore islands crisis, moved steeply upwards in the post-Bandung period. Yet powerful vested interests on both sides militated against a serious breach. Without its American protector and patron, the Nationalist government could not survive on Taiwan or maintain its international position. Without at least the hope of future American assistance, it could not keep alive its goal to reconquer the mainland. For the United States, the co-operation of Chiang's government was a necessity for the security of Taiwan and for other valuable military and political purposes. So despite their evident differences, Washington and Taipei remained firmly locked together, and the fundamental American commitment to Taiwan was unimpaired.

Between 1950 and 1955 American decision makers hammered out the major features of the U.S. military and political commitment to Taiwan on an anvil of crisis. After North Korean units crossed the 38th parallel in June 1950, President Truman placed the Seventh Fleet between Taiwan and mainland China, thereby reversing the nonmilitary policy toward the island that his administration had pursued since early 1949 and the noninterventionist position he had proclaimed on 5 January 1950. Truman's decision to neutralize the Taiwan Strait followed a reappraisal of the nonmilitary policy begun about two months earlier within the State and Defense Departments. Though wobbly on the eve of the Korean crisis, this policy was by no means fated to topple. By further energizing existing incentives for intervention and generating new ones, the Korean emergency functioned as a major cause for the neutralization.

The decision for intervention did not entail a long-term military commitment to the defense of Taiwan or a revitalized political commitment to Chiang Kai-shek's Nationalist government. American decision makers were undoubtedly intent on keeping Taiwan from the control of a hostile, Kremlin-oriented China. The United States was far from the disinterested policeman in the Taiwan Strait that official statements alleged. All the same, the mission of the Seventh Fleet as a buffer between the island and the mainland was only provisional, and the United States maintained an arm's-length relationship with the Nationalist regime. Washington dispensed only modest amounts of economic and military aid to the Kuomintang and while continuing to recognize the Republic of China as the de jure government of China and stepping up efforts to safeguard the Nationalist seat in the United Nations, refrained from any long-range commitments to Taipei with respect to either recognition or UN representation. In the late summer of 1950 the State Department embarked on a plan to have the UN General Assembly mandate a military standstill in the Taiwan Strait and establish a commission that would analyze and report on Taiwan's future political status. State Department officials wanted to legitimize the U.S. neutralization, create an international deterrent against a Chinese Communist attack, and lay the groundwork for the possible establishment through the United Nations of an autonomous or independent Taiwan. As the Truman administration pursued its objectives toward the Nationalist haven, it had to deal with the controversy caused by the independent-minded Gen. Douglas MacArthur, who wanted the island and its KMT masters securely incorporated within the U.S. defense system in the western Pacific.

The all-out Chinese intervention in Korea in late November 1950 precipitated a new crisis that drove the administration into a fixed defensive commitment to Taiwan and a reinvigorated political relationship with the Nationalists. At the same time, the administration rejected both MacArthur's recommendations for an expanded war against China and Peking's attempts to wed agreement on a Korean cease-fire to a U.S. military withdrawal from Taiwan and the PRC's admittance to the United Nations. By the spring of 1951 Washington had inaugurated large-scale economic and military aid programs for Taiwan, assigned a Military Advisory Assistance Group to the island, and commenced a limited covert war against China utilizing Nationalist territory and manpower. The MacArthur hearings that began in May 1951 gave Secretary of State Dean Acheson a forum in which to enunciate a firm policy of military protection and diplomatic support for Taiwan. About the same time, the State Department worked out with the British Foreign Office a moratorium arrangement in the United Nations that postponed substantive votes or discussion on the question of Chinese representation. This procedural device became the instrument by which the Truman and Eisenhower administrations, practicing a diplomacy of postponement, ensured that the Nationalist government, rather than its Communist rival, occupied the China seat.

The 1954–55 offshore islands crisis further deepened the U.S. commitment to Taiwan. That crisis partially stemmed from the informal American quasi commitment to those Nationalist-occupied coastal islands that was itself an outgrowth of the Taiwan commitment. Originating in the Truman administration, the quasi commitment crystallized after President Eisenhower and his Republican administration took office. The Sino-American fray over the offshore islands subsequently spawned both the mutual defense treaty between the United States and the Republic of China, signed in December 1954, and the Formosa Resolution, overwhelmingly approved by Congress in January 1955. The treaty solemnized the military commitment to Taiwan and anointed the Nationalist government as a formal ally, while the congressional resolution reinforced the authority of the chief executive to use American armed forces to guard Taiwan and the coastal islands. Prior to the passage of the resolution, Eisenhower consented to a secret provisional defensive guarantee for Quemoy and Matsu. The following April, having had second thoughts about its desirability, the president retracted this assurance.

Even so, he still retained authority under existing U.S. policy and the Formosa Resolution to employ military force to shield the islands in the event of a presumptive or actual attack on Taiwan.

The decisive impetus for the evolving commitment to Taiwan came not from any sentimental attachment to Chiang Kai-shek and the Nationalists, nor from a concern for the well-being of the people of Taiwan, nor from an appreciation of the importance of the island's past and prospective trading relationship with Japan — though these considerations were present in the minds of some policymakers — but rather from the pursuit of American national security interests, which were defined in military-strategic and politico-psychological terms and enmeshed with images of an aggressive Communist China linked to the Soviet Union. The principal reasons for the June 1950 interposition were the strategic value of Taiwan in relation to the U.S. offshore defense perimeter in the western Pacific, the diversionary value of the Nationalist military presence on the island in reducing Chinese pressure in Southeast Asia, the military necessity to insulate the island from the Korean conflict, and the determination to flex American might in Asia.

The Chinese intervention in Korea both confirmed American officials in their belief that China was subservient to the Kremlin and infused their policymaking toward the Asian communist giant with an acute animosity and militancy. Decision makers were more determined than ever to keep Taiwan out of the clutches of Mao and his pro-Soviet comrades. The island acquired increased value as a base for covert warfare against China, as a reservoir of military manpower for possible offensive operations outside Nationalist territory, and, at least potentially, as a site for the development of a noncommunist political alternative that could attract disaffected mainland Chinese. The military and political commitment to Taiwan complemented a policy of pressure against the People's Republic. Formalized in NSC 48/5 in May 1951, this policy aimed at splitting China from the Soviet Union through the reorientation, fragmentation, or replacement of the Peking government. Although NSC 48/5 did not necessarily envision the reestablishment of the Nationalists on the mainland and did not endorse their strategy of counterattack, it did prescribe measures that transformed Taiwan into a client state that could serve the purposes of a coercive policy against China.

The Eisenhower administration carried forward the policy of pressure and the commitment to Taiwan, adding its own wrinkles to each, and further embedded the U.S. military-strategic and politico-psychological stake in the island. National security interests were pivotal in the reluctance of President Eisenhower and Secretary of State Dulles to give the Chinese free rein in the offshore islands during the Taiwan Strait crisis. The two Republican statesmen were convinced that, under existing circumstances, to yield any of the more valuable coastal islands by defeat or default would have undesirable, though not fatal, military consequences for the defense of Taiwan; more importantly, they felt that such a loss would dangerously subvert Nationalist morale (whose preservation they considered vital to the stability and security of Taiwan) as well as undermine American credibility in Asia. Further, as the confrontation worsened in January 1955, they were persuaded that Chinese ambitions extended beyond the offshore islands to the capture of Taiwan itself. In an attempt near the climax of the crisis to reduce or eliminate the military-strategic and politico-psychological costs of a forfeiture of the islands, they looked to entice Chiang into either treating these possessions as disposable outposts or vacating them entirely in conjunction with a joint blockade along the southeast China coast and a strengthened U.S. military presence on Taiwan.

Even as the commitment to Taiwan expanded in scope between 1950 and 1955, American decision makers placed limits on it. In framing and carrying it out, they intermixed restraint with assertiveness and aggressiveness; in significant respects, they offered only guarded military and political support to the Nationalists. At no time did they place an American seal of approval on the Kuomintang's strategy for military reconquest of the mainland. Although in late 1951 and early 1952, as frustration with the stalemated war in Korea swelled, some high officials did entertain the possibility of American backing for the forcible return of the Nationalists to the continent, this idea failed to catch fire within policymaking circles. Overall, the bellicose liberationist rhetoric of Chiang Kai-shek and his compatriots fell on deaf ears among decision makers in both the Truman and Eisenhower administrations. During the Taiwan Strait crisis, Dulles prodded Chiang to replace the KMT's strategy of counterattack with a less belligerent strategy of opportunism.

In refusing to involve the United States with illusory schemes to dislodge the Communists from power through a Nationalist counteroffensive, decision makers did not exclude limited KMT military operations against China, either covert or overt. Coastal raids carried out by the Nationalists with American clandestine assistance were part of the secret war against the People's Republic that got into full swing in 1951. Generally ineffective, these forays were virtually suspended by the summer of 1953 and were finally terminated by the National Security Council in December 1954. Also as part of the secret war, the Central Intelligence Agency in 1951–52 organized several incursions into Yunnan province by Kuomintang irregulars based in northern Burma, all of them repulsed by the Chinese. After the CIA subsequently liquidated its involvement with the irregulars, Washington in 1953 prevailed upon Chiang Kai-shek to repatriate about half of them to Taiwan. On various occasions during the Korean War, decision makers also gave consideration to

Nationalist troop landings on Chinese territory, but authorization for such assaults was never forthcoming. As well, neither Truman nor Eisenhower saw fit to employ Chiang's forces on the Korean battlefield. The two presidents did consent to a number of National Security Council policy papers for China, Taiwan, and Southeast Asia that sanctioned Nationalist offensive military operations outside Taiwan under certain conditions, though in practice such operations remained remote contingencies.

Both the Truman and Eisenhower administrations did equip and train the Nationalists for limited offensive missions in China or in various danger spots in Asia. The large sums allocated to the modernization of Chiang Kai-shek's armed forces exceeded purely defensive requirements. Nonetheless, at no time did Washington supply the Nationalists with sufficient military resources to conduct ground operations on any significant scale outside their own territory without U.S. assistance. Not only that, but it was always understood that the primary mission of the KMT forces was to protect Taiwan and that even this role merely supplemented that of the Seventh Fleet. Washington refused to subscribe to inflated Nationalist proposals for military aid, devised with a future counteroffensive against the mainland in mind. For all the money and training that Washington did invest to upgrade the Nationalist forces, their actual fighting capability remained relatively modest at the end of 1955.

To avoid being dragged into an unwanted conflict with China, Washington placed specific restrictions on Nationalist forces that banned military action against the mainland without U.S. approval. Despite being applied asymmetrically to the advantage of the Nationalists, the June 1950 neutralization order did provide a safeguard against Kuomintang provocations that might incite Communist retaliation against Taiwan. After Eisenhower revoked this order in February 1953, Washington insisted that the Nationalists accept new constraints on offensive activities against the continent. In similar fashion, the exchange of notes that accompanied the mutual defense treaty broadly pledged Taipei to refrain from offensive military action against the mainland without Washington's prior consent.

Washington bound its commitment to Taiwan in the political as well as the military realm. Despite their vocal opposition to the admission of the People's Republic to the UN, American leaders never declared that its entry was permanently beyond the pale. Eisenhower and Dulles, for instance, left the door ajar for the Chinese Communists to enter the world organization if they conducted their foreign affairs in a nonaggressive manner and respected the UN Charter. The two men even privately reflected on a scheme for representation by both rival Chinese governments in the General Assembly. On balance, however, the requirements of a hard-line China policy, along with domestic constraints, severely limited the flexibility of both the Truman and Eisenhower administrations on the representation question.

After the political commitment to Chiang Kai-shek's regime coalesced, Washington did its best to uphold the international position of Nationalist China outside as well as inside the United Nations. Yet this support was by no means unstinting. Washington acquiesced in the exclusion of the Nationalist government from the multilateral peace treaty with Japan in 1951, resigned itself to the participation of the People's Republic in the 1954 Geneva conference on Indochina, responded positively to Chinese Premier Chou En-lai's bid for direct talks made at the Bandung conference in April 1955, entered into ambassadorial-level discussions with Communist China at Geneva the following August, and in December 1955 was prepared to tolerate the entry of Outer Mongolia into the United Nations in order to break the logjam over the admission of new members. In each instance, Washington's conduct offended and dismayed the Nationalists.

In an ironic twist, the United States, even while recognizing the Republic of China as the de jure government of China, refused to accept its legal claim to Taiwan and the Penghu Islands, the only territory (apart from the offshore islands) that was actually under its authority. President Truman, in asserting at the time of the June 1950 intervention that a determination of Taiwan's final status would have to await appropriate international action, in effect subscribed to the position that the island's legal status was indeterminate, reverting to the view that had prevailed within the government before his 5 January announcement stating that Taiwan belonged to "China." After the onset of the Korean War, the United States consistently held to the position that the island's status was legally undecided. With the collapse in November 1950 of the Anglo-American plan to have the General Assembly resolve the Taiwan question, the possibility of a formal determination of this status through the United Nations vanished. On Washington's insistence, the multilateral Japanese peace treaty concluded in September 1951 left the island's status ambiguous by merely providing for Japan's renunciation of sovereignty.

Additional evidence of the limited political commitment to the Nationalist government lies in the covert support extended to Chinese elements whose allegiance was neither to the CCP nor KMT. The NSC 48/5 policy statement authorized clandestine aid and assistance to such elements, envisioning as one possible scenario for China the emergence of a "third force" around which dissenters could unite and within which the Nationalists might ultimately find a role. In reality, any notion that an effective "third force" might materialize proved a mirage. Tellingly, NSC 146/2, approved by

Eisenhower in November 1953, prescribed encouragement, but no commitment of support, for "third force" elements.

At various times after the United States assumed the guardianship of Taiwan, the two-China concept, which first surfaced in policy planning for the island in 1949, entered into the deliberations of decision makers and affected American actions toward the Nationalist refuge. Still, this concept did not consistently inform U.S. policy from the June 1950 interposition to the start of the Geneva ambassadorial talks, as some historians have argued.[1] That it was the American goal during this period to segregate Taiwan from China is undeniable. Just the same, the isolation of Taiwan from the rest of China was only the indispensable condition for the application of the two-China concept, not its defining characteristic; in its most common forms, the concept envisaged either an autonomous or independent Taiwan or the acceptance of the entrenched existence of two rival Chinese governments, one in Peking and the other in Taipei. This concept did loom large in the calculations of upper-echelon State Department officials when they planned to address the Taiwan question through the UN after the June 1950 intervention. Yet NSC 48/5, ratified the following spring, even while decreeing the indefinite protection of Taiwan by the Seventh Fleet, manifested uncertainty about the durability of the CCP government and allowed for the island's eventual reversion to a friendly China. At the same time, however, the two-China idea very likely influenced John Foster Dulles when he insisted, during diplomatic preliminaries leading to the separate peace treaty between Tokyo and Taipei in April 1952, that the Nationalist government accept a scope of application provision reflecting its lack of effective authority over the mainland. The concept turned up again in the dual representation scheme in the United Nations to which he and Eisenhower later gave thought. More significantly, it was an essential ingredient in the diplomatic strategy devised by Dulles during the offshore islands crisis, when one of his cardinal, though undeclared, objectives was to stabilize the Taiwan Strait through the creation of a de facto two-China situation.

To the extent that decision makers adopted a two-China approach after June 1950, they did so indirectly and evasively. More an unspoken than an articulated goal, the idea was never formalized as an officially sanctioned policy objective within the government. Not only was the idea unpalatable in some quarters of the foreign affairs bureaucracy, such as the military, it was unacceptable to many pro-Nationalist partisans, both on and off Capitol Hill, and to other Americans who wanted an unyielding stance against Communist China. In addition, it was hemlock to Taipei and Peking, and only gradually found favor in London.

The White House and State Department commanded the policymaking process that shaped the U.S. commitment to Taiwan. Truman, though less actively involved in policy formulation than Eisenhower would be, retained ultimate authority over major decisions. Serving as the chief foreign affairs advisers for their respective presidents, the formidable Dean Acheson and John Foster Dulles each left a large imprint on relations with Taiwan. On critical Taiwan-related issues the State Department generally held sway over other units in the national security apparatus. The Defense Department exercised lesser but still considerable influence. The embittered competition over Taiwan policy between the State Department and the Pentagon prior to the Korean War abated after Truman's neutralization order. The president's dismissal of Secretary of Defense Louis Johnson in September 1950 removed from the government Acheson's arch-rival and an ardent Kuomintang proponent. Under Truman's two succeeding secretaries of defense, George Marshall and Robert Lovett, Taiwan was not a major node of conflict between civilian Pentagon officials and the State Department, though differences existed over specific issues. Eisenhower's Defense Secretary Charles Wilson took a back seat to Dulles in fashioning Taiwan policy but did stand out as a plain-speaking opponent of a defensive commitment to the offshore islands during the Taiwan Strait crisis.

The sharpest differences over Taiwan within the foreign affairs bureaucracy were between the State Department and the JCS. In a number of instances between the summer of 1950 and the spring of 1955, the State Department was instrumental in blocking overly provocative or belligerent recommendations from the joint chiefs (or a hawkish majority) for military action by American or Nationalist forces. Despite oftentimes having their more combative impulses held in check, the joint chiefs contributed significantly to the definition of U.S. national security interests on Taiwan and to the interpretation and implementation of the military commitment.

The domestic environment had an important but intermittent and secondary influence on government actions relating to Taiwan. Because China policy was so politically sensitive, the White House and State Department could not easily afford to overlook public and congressional viewpoints. Domestic calculations did have a perceptible impact on some policies relating to Taiwan during the 1950–55 period; this was certainly the case, to cite a noteworthy example, during the offshore islands crisis. Even when popular and legislative viewpoints did impinge on decision making, however, they were nearly always subordinated to national security considerations. Also, policymakers guided and manipulated domestic and congressional opinion through their public statements and actions or, in some instances, by cloaking their intentions and activities in secrecy. With a few notable exceptions, majority popular opinion from 1950 to 1955 was in tune with declaratory policy on matters relating to Taiwan. Congress, though sometimes balky and quarrelsome, likewise usually followed the lead of the executive branch.

Some scholars have assigned predominant influence over China policy during this period to the pro-Nationalist zealots belonging to the China bloc and China lobby, many associated directly or indirectly with the McCarthyite reign of terror.[2] Such pro-Chiang partisans did undeniably have a disproportionate impact on popular opinion and the political climate, particularly during the Korean War. Yet for all their outspokenness and ample capacity for troublemaking, they were by no measure the arbiters of U.S. China policy. They did not trap decision makers unwillingly in the commitment to Taiwan or a hard-line policy against the People's Republic. As time passed, moreover, decision makers stole most of their thunder on Taiwan-related issues. After the Truman administration publicized its military and political commitment to Taiwan in the spring of 1951, pro-Nationalist spokesmen had less reason and opportunity to fault current policy toward Chiang Kai-shek's regime. The Eisenhower administration immediately bent its efforts upon taking office to preempt the sallies of the Generalissimo's advocates. Then too, political incentives for criticism by pro-Nationalist enthusiasts, most of whom were Republicans, faded after the GOP recaptured the White House. The Eisenhower administration did have to contend with obstreperous congressional Republican right-wingers, who included prominent pro-Nationalist advocates such as California senator William Knowland. But by the fall of 1954 this contingent did not carry as much weight in foreign affairs as earlier; pro-Nationalist partisans exerted only limited influence on the administration during the confrontation over the offshore islands.

Circumstances sometimes compelled decision makers to take heed of international as well as domestic opinion. At several junctures between 1950 and 1955, U.S. officials showed particular concern for the viewpoints of allies and other friendly governments who were disturbed by the negative repercussions, actual or potential, of American involvement with the island and its Nationalist rulers. Although the opinions of anxious or dissenting friendly governments did not take precedence over the advancement of American interests, such sentiments did enter into the policymaking equation, providing an incentive for Washington to act with moderation and restraint, or at least to give the appearance of doing so. It was partially to mollify nervous partners within the Korean coalition in the wake of the Taiwan intervention that Washington vigorously denied any ulterior motives for its unilateral action, tried to bring the troublesome General MacArthur into line with its declared objectives, and set out to internationalize the Taiwan question through UN action. During the crisis that followed the Chinese intervention in Korea,

Washington took into consideration the opposition of its UN partners when deciding against the employment of Nationalist troops in the peninsular conflict or against China. Secretary Acheson, mindful of the necessity to maintain American leadership in the UN, reluctantly endorsed the five-principle peace plan of the UN Cease-fire Group, in spite of the proposal's distasteful provision for Chinese Communist participation in a postarmistice conference to discuss Far Eastern issues, including Taiwan and the contested Chinese seat. During the Taiwan Strait crisis, Eisenhower and Dulles were sensitive to the effect that their actions would have on close allies, as well as other apprehensive friendly governments, and particularly on the delicate European situation.

No nation was more active in attempting to temper Washington's policies toward the two Chinas than Britain. Under both the Labour government of Clement Attlee and the Conservative governments of Winston Churchill and Anthony Eden, Britain tried to steer the United States away from extreme measures regarding Taiwan and toward greater forbearance and flexibility in its relations with Communist China. Unlike their American counterparts, British officials, while also wanting to contain aggressive Chinese Communist expansion, never perceived Mao and his comrades as mere acolytes of the Kremlin, or harbored a deep-seated antagonism toward Peking, or believed that only unrelenting pressure would hasten China's departure from the Soviet camp. They worried that American opposition to China or support for Taiwan, if carried too far, could result in a direct contest of arms between their transatlantic partner and its Chinese Communist adversary. The influence of British officials over their American confreres was limited in most matters relating to China and Taiwan. Washington was more disposed to bend London to its will than to do the opposite, and it sometimes chose not to take London fully into its confidence. On their side, British officials were aware of the attitudinal, institutional, and domestic constraints on American policymaking toward the two Chinas and were unwilling to risk a major breach over China-related issues. Anglo-Chinese relations mattered far less to these officials than the preservation of the "special relationship" with the United States, a main pillar of post–World War II British policy. The Far East was an area in which the United States held sway and that ranked lower in strategic importance for Britain than Europe and the Middle East. Despite all this, London maintained a measure of independence from Washington in its relations with China, and it managed at times to have a moderating impact on its ally.[3]

If Britain endeavored to play a restraining and mediating role, it also often gave way, willingly or not, to American positions and preferences. Through its participation in the moratorium arrangement, it was a partner in the diplomacy of postponement that preserved the China seat in the UN for the Nationalist government. While keeping fluid the arrangement by confining it to specified time periods, officials in London understood full well that any departure from it would raise the ire of Washington and antagonize American popular and congressional opinion. Britain similarly bowed to the American wish that the Japanese peace treaty remain silent about Taiwan's status, other than for a relinquishment of sovereignty by the defeated enemy. In the case of the separate peace treaty between Japan and Nationalist China, London acquiesced in the fait accompli engineered by John Foster Dulles, despite its own preference for a bilateral peace accord between Tokyo and Peking and the ill feeling within the Churchill government over the perceived double-dealing of the American diplomat.

Over the span of the 1950–55 period, Britain came to accept and value American protection of Taiwan. Prior to the June 1950 intervention, the Attlee government was scornful of Chiang Kai-shek's failed regime and in wholehearted agreement with Washington's announced policy of military disengagement. By the fall of 1951, when it went down to defeat at the hands of the Conservatives, the Labour government had for all practical purposes assented to American guardianship of the Nationalist bastion. Taking this process of accommodation one step further, Churchill openly extolled America's self-appointed mission as the guarantor of Taiwan's security. During the crisis over the coastal islands, he and Eden did not question Washington's defensive commitment to the Nationalist stronghold. The two-China idea beckoned London during the confrontation as it did Washington, despite differences over Nationalist retention of Quemoy and Matsu. The British, too, wanted to regularize the situation in the Taiwan Strait, leaving China and Taiwan safe from attack by each other.

Central to the U.S. commitment to Taiwan was Washington's relationship with Chiang Kai-shek's exiled regime. That relationship underwent a startling transformation between 1950 and 1955: treated as a castoff by Washington in early 1950, the Nationalist government had become an essential Asian asset by 1955. The American commitment welded together the United States and the truncated Republic of China in a binding association that each side found necessary and advantageous. For all that, the interests and objectives of the two were far from identical, differing most fundamentally over the proclaimed Nationalist goal to retake the mainland by force. Washington always approached its dealings with Chiang and the Kuomintang with a measure of wariness and distrust, despite the fact that with the passage of time disdain for the Generalissimo and his regime gave way to relatively more positive attitudes. For his part, the watchful and cunning Nationalist leader placed less than complete confidence in his U.S. protector and patron. In spite of the bonds that united Washington and Taipei by the end of 1955, friction between them was more severe than at any time since before the reversal of the policy of military disengagement more than five years earlier.

Because of its dominant position, the United States was able to set the basic terms of its association with Taiwan: Washington exercised effective control over Nationalist offensive military operations, maintained oversight and supervision over the use of economic and military aid, employed pressure in various forms and degrees to bring Taipei into compliance with its wishes, kept Chiang Kai-shek in the dark when necessary about its military plans and diplomatic ventures relating to Taiwan, and involved itself in diplomatic initiatives affecting Nationalist interests that Taipei found objectionable. All the same, American influence and control over the Nationalists was restricted. In part, this was by deliberate choice. Washington preferred to avoid unnecessary supervision or dictation that would incite resistance and resentment, impede the development of a spirit of self-help and self-reliance, and, by giving the appearance that Taiwan was a mere American pawn, undermine the Nationalist regime's international stature and its usefulness as a rallying symbol for anticommunist Chinese throughout Asia. In part, the Nationalists themselves circumscribed American influence and control. In spite of the preponderance of power enjoyed by Washington, Chiang Kai-shek was by no means a pliant cold war proxy. From long experience in dealing with Washington, he and his associates knew how to parry, obstruct, and circumvent unwanted intrusions and initiatives as well as how to exploit their dependency to extract the maximum benefit. To these ends, they utilized the leverage afforded them by the presence of well-placed sympathizers within the American government and of vociferous partisans in Congress and among the articulate public.

The June 1950 intervention and the metamorphosis of Taiwan into an American client state touched a highly sensitive nerve within the CCP leadership and constituted a fundamental source of conflict between the People's Republic and the United States. By its actions, the United States had once again interjected itself into the Chinese civil war, preventing the PRC from fulfilling its goal of national reunification and breathing new life into the shattered Kuomintang, its hated enemy. More than this, American actions intensified fears that Taiwan might serve as a launching pad for an armed offensive against China. For CCP leaders, the involvement of the United States with Taiwan impacted both China's national sovereignty and its security. Their grave concern over that involvement figured in the PRC's decisions to enter the Korean War, to insist on preconditions for a cease-fire during the initial phase of its intervention, to raise the temperature in the Taiwan Strait in 1954, and to participate in the Geneva ambassadorial-level talks.

During the years after 1955 in which the United States and the People's Republic remained hardened adversaries, deep-felt differences over Taiwan endured as a cause of acrimonious dispute and periodic confrontation. These differences proved insuperable until the 1970s, when the two antagonists entered into an improved relationship that culminated in the establishment of diplomatic relations in January 1979, after Washington agreed to break relations with the Republic of China, abrogate the mutual security pact, and withdraw U.S. forces and military installations from Taiwan. Even as the United States ended its formal political and military commitment to its long-time Nationalist ally, Congress, disregarding the objections of the PRC, passed the Taiwan Relations Act in April 1979, creating a new and unique framework for the U.S.-Taiwan connection and ensuring the continuation of strong political, security, and economic ties.

Taiwan itself, despite its humiliating derecognition by the United States and its diplomatic isolation within the global community by the end of the 1970s, rallied to meet the challenge of a precarious future. In succeeding years, it has emerged as one of Asia's richest economies and as a budding democracy. At the same time, its leaders have moderated the Nationalist government's once harsh policy toward the People's Republic and have striven to alter its status as an international pariah.

Until the early 1980s, ongoing American support for Taiwan, particularly arms sales, remained a bone of contention with the PRC; however, divisive disagreement subsided in the years that followed. American and Chinese Communist leaders arrived at a modus vivendi regarding Taiwan while the Communists and Nationalists showed greater adaptability toward each other even while holding differing visions of a unified China.[4] But in June 1995, after a period of relative quiescence, the Taiwan issue erupted once again as a result of Washington's decision to allow Taiwan president Lee Teng-hui to make a private visit to the United States. A veil of uncertainty conceals the direction that future relations will take among the United States, the People's Republic, and Taiwan. What stands out conspicuously is the vivid imprint left on the history of these relations since mid-century by the American commitment to Taiwan forged between 1950 and 1955.

Abbreviations

In addition to the abbreviations used in the text, the following source abbreviations are used in the notes.

AWF	Ann Whitman File, Dwight D. Eisenhower Library, Abilene, Kans.
CA	Records, Office of Chinese Affairs, Record Group 59, National Archives, Washington, D.C.
CAB	Cabinet Papers, Public Record Office, London (Kew), England
CGSID	Chief, General Staff Intelligence Division, United States Army
CHMAAG	Military Advisory Assistance Group, China
CINCFE	Commander in Chief, Far East
CJCS	Records, Chairman, Joint Chiefs of Staff, Record Group 218, National Archives
CNO	Chief of Naval Operations
COHC	Columbia University Oral History Collection, Butler Library, N.Y.
Cong. Rec.	*Congressional Record*
DDEL	Dwight D. Eisenhower Library, Abilene, Kans.
DEA	Department of External Affairs, Ottawa, Canada
DOD	Department of Defense
DOHC	John Foster Dulles Oral History Collection, Seeley Mudd Library, Princeton, N.J.
DOS	Department of State
DSB	*Department of State Bulletin*
Exec. Sess.	*Executive Sessions*
FEA	Records, Bureau of Far Eastern Affairs, Record Group 59, National Archives
FO	Foreign Office, Great Britain
FO 371	Foreign Office Files, Public Record Office
FOI	Freedom of Information Act
FRUS	*Foreign Relations of the United States*
FSPR	Records, Foreign Service Posts of the Department of State, Record Group 84, National Archives, Suitland, Md.
G-3	Records, Assistant Chief of Staff of the United States Army, G-3, Operations, Record Group 319, National Archives
GRC	Government of the Republic of China

JCS	Records, Joint Chiefs of Staff, Record Group 218, National Archives
JSPC	Joint Strategic Plans Committee
Nav Hist Center	Operational Archives, Naval Historical Center, Washington, D.C.
NIE	National Intelligence Estimate
NSC	Records, National Security Council, Record Group 273, National Archives
NYT	*New York Times*
OES	Records of the Office of the Executive Secretariat, 1949–52, Record Group 59, National Archives
ORE	Office of Research Evaluation
OSD	Records, Office of the Secretary of Defense, Record Group 330, National Archives
PAC	Public Archives of Canada, Ottawa, Canada
POS	Records, Office of Public Opinion Studies, 1943–75, Record Group 59, National Archives
PPS	Records, Policy Planning Staff, Record Group 59, National Archives
PREM	Prime Minister's Office Files, Public Record Office
PSF	President's Secretary's Files, Harry S. Truman Library, Independence, Mo.
RG	Record Group
SML	Seeley Mudd Library, Princeton, N.J.
SNIE	Special National Intelligence Estimate
UN	United Nations
UNGA	Official Records, United Nations General Assembly
UNSC	Official Records, United Nations Security Council
WHO	White House Office Records, Dwight D. Eisenhower Library, Abilene, Kans.
WHCF (DDEL)	White House Central Files, Dwight D. Eisenhower Library, Abilene, Kans.
WHCF (HST)	White House Central Files, Harry S. Truman Library, Independence, Mo.

Note: Documents in the Department of State Decimal Files, Record Group 59, National Archives, are cited by decimal file number (for example, 611.94A/1-650).

Preface

1. The wide scope of Nancy Bernkopf Tucker's splendid *Taiwan, Hong Kong, and the United States* precludes a thorough treatment of this formative half decade in U.S.-Taiwan relations. Both June M. Grasso, *Truman's Two-China Policy*, and David M. Finkelstein, *Washington's Taiwan Dilemma*, conclude with the Korean War or shortly thereafter. Other scholars have explored particular aspects of American policy toward Taiwan during the 1950–55 period but very often in studies whose primary focus lies elsewhere.

Chapter One

1. Clough, *Island China*, pp. 6, 38, 69.

2. A classic eyewitness account of the 28 February uprising and its aftermath, scathing in its condemnation of the Nationalists, can be found in Kerr, *Formosa Betrayed*, chaps. 5–14. A more measured scholarly assessment of the rebellion is Lai, Myers, and Wou, *Tragic Beginning*.

3. Hsieh, *Strategy for Survival*, p. 29; Crozier with Chou, *Man Who Lost China*, pp. 325–28.

4. Payne, *Chiang Kai-shek*, p. 294; Crozier, *Man Who Lost China*, p. 351; Hsieh, *Strategy for Survival*, pp. 78–79; Tucker, "Nationalist China's Decline," pp. 131–71; Rao, "Kuomintang Government's Policy toward the United States," p. 58.

5. Pogue, *Statesman, 1945–1959*, chap. 16; Stueck, *Road to Confrontation*, chap. 2.

6. Tucker, *Patterns in the Dust*, pp. 174–76, 187–88; Donovan, *Tumultuous Years*, pp. 34–36, 68, 78; Warren I. Cohen, "Acheson, His Advisers, and China," pp. 15–16.

7. Scholars have disagreed sharply in their interpretations of the Truman administration's China policy from January 1949 to the start of the Korean War. For convenient reviews of this debate, consult McMahon, "Cold War in Asia," pp. 310–14, and Munro-Leighton, "Postrevisionist Scrutiny of America's Role in the Cold War in Asia," pp. 74–77.

My description of China policy in 1949 draws on the following works: Cohen, "Acheson, His Advisers, and China," pp. 13–52; Tucker, *Patterns in the Dust*, chap. 10, and "China's Place in the Cold War," pp. 109–32; Stueck, *Road to Confrontation*, chap. 4; Blum, *Drawing the Line*; McLean, "American Nationalism, the China Myth, and the Truman Doctrine," pp. 25–42; McGlothlen, *Controlling the Waves*, pp. 135–55.

For an understanding of the "wedge" strategy, I have relied on Gaddis, "Dividing Adversaries," pp. 161–64; Mayers, *Cracking the Monolith*, pp. 33–82; Gordon H. Chang, *Friends and Enemies*, pp. 29–76; Finkelstein, *Washington's Taiwan Dilemma*, chap. 3.

8. Blum, *Drawing the Line*, pp. 16–17, 37.

9. Tucker, "Nationalist China's Decline," pp. 166–67; Cumings, *Roaring of the Cataract*, pp. 159–60.

10. Tucker, *Patterns in the Dust*, pp. 165–67; Blum, *Drawing the Line*, chaps. 3, 5, 8; Kepley, *Collapse of the Middle Way*, chap. 3.

11. Tucker, *Patterns in the Dust*, pp. 80–99; Koen, *China Lobby in American Politics*, p. 97. For an excellent brief overview of the lobby, see Warren I. Cohen, "China Lobby," pp. 104–10.

12. Tucker, *Patterns in the Dust*, pp. 155–61; Kusnitz, *Public Opinion and Foreign Policy*, pp. 24–30.

13. NSC 37, "Strategic Importance of Formosa," 1 December 1948, FRUS, 1949, 9:261–62; memorandum of conversation, 7 December 1948, ibid., pp. 263–65.

14. Schaller, *Douglas MacArthur*, pp. 158–60.

15. Gordon, "American Planning for Taiwan," pp. 203–4.

16. Gaddis, "Strategic Perspective," pp. 61–79.

17. McGlothlen, *Controlling the Waves*, pp. 88, 134. In trying to demonstrate that

Acheson's Taiwan policy was driven by a Japan-centered Asian strategy, McGlothlen overstates his case and overlooks compelling contrary evidence; CIA Intelligence Memorandum No. 111, 3 January 1949, box 2, NSC Meetings, Subject File, PSF.

18. NSC 37/3, "Strategic Importance of Formosa," 11 February 1949, FRUS, 1949, 9:284–86.

19. Secretary of Defense to NSC, 2 April 1949, ibid., pp. 307–8.

20. Statement by secretary of state at the 35th NSC Meeting, 3 March 1949, ibid., pp. 294–96.

21. NSC 37/2, "Current Position of the United States with Respect to Formosa," 3 February 1949, ibid., pp. 281–82; NSC 37/5, "Supplementary Measures with Respect to Formosa," 1 March 1949, ibid., pp. 290–92; Acheson to Livingston T. Merchant, 2 March 1949, ibid., pp. 293–94. See also Grasso, Truman's Two-China Policy, chap. 1, and Finkelstein, Washington's Taiwan Dilemma, chap. 4.

22. Grasso, Truman's Two-China Policy, chap. 3; Finkelstein, Washington's Taiwan Dilemma, chap. 5.

23. Walton Butterworth to Dean Rusk, 9 June 1949, FRUS, 1949, 9:346–49; PPS 53, "United States Policy toward Formosa and the Pescadores," 6 July 1949, ibid., pp. 356–59; Finkelstein, Washington's Taiwan Dilemma, pp. 172–81. Among the drawbacks of a UN solution noted in the State Department was that the United States would have to bear the responsibility for enforcing any decision by the world organization. Su-ya Chang, "Pragmatism and Opportunism," p. 26.

24. For a discussion of the contested issue of Taiwan's status, consult Chiu, "China, the United States, and the Question of Taiwan," pp. 112–76.

25. Wolf, "'To Secure a Convenience,'" pp. 299–326; Martin, Divided Counsel, pp. 54–55, 96.

26. Memorandum of conversation, 9 September 1949, FRUS, 1949, 9:388; Martin, Divided Counsel, pp. 61–70; "Discussion of Far Eastern Affairs in Preparation for Conversations with Mr. Bevin," 13 September 1949, box 14, CA, 1944–50.

27. ORE 76-49, "Survival Potential of Non-Communist Regimes in China," 19 October 1949, box 257, Intelligence File, PSF.

28. NSC 37/8, "The Position of the United States with Respect to Formosa," 6 October 1949, FRUS, 1949, 9:392–97; Acheson to MacDonald, 28 October 1949, ibid., pp. 401–3; summary of discussion, 47th NSC Meeting, 20 October 1949, box 220, Subject File, PSF; Finkelstein, Washington's Taiwan Dilemma, pp. 190–99.

29. Reminiscences of Wu Kuo-chen, pp. 113, 140–42, Chinese Oral History Project. A biographical sketch of Wu appears in Biographical Dictionary of Republican China, ed. Boorman with Howard, 3:438–40.

30. Finkelstein, "From Abandonment to Salvation," pp. 367–81; Su-ya Chang, "Pragmatism and Opportunism," pp. 37–40.

31. Rotter, Path to Vietnam, pp. 103–8; Blum, Drawing the Line, chaps. 9–10; Schaller, American Occupation of Japan, chap. 11.

32. MacArthur allowed veteran Japanese pilots to go to Taiwan to assist the Nationalists, blessed the efforts of pro-KMT freelancers to sell weapons to them, and dispatched a close aide to sound out Chiang about having an SCAP staff officer act as his adviser. The general may also have hinted to the Generalissimo that he step aside for K. C. Wu. Schaller, Douglas MacArthur, pp. 170–71.

33. NSC 37/9, "Possible United States Military Action toward Taiwan Not Involving Major Military Forces," 27 December 1949, FRUS, 1949, 9:460–61.

34. Blum, *Drawing the Line*, pp. 168–74; Schaller, *American Occupation of Japan*, pp. 200–209.

35. Memorandum of conversation, 29 December 1949, FRUS, 1949, 9:463–67.

36. NSC 48/2, "The Position of the United States with Respect to Asia," 30 December 1949, FRUS, 1949, 7:1215–20.

37. Tsou, *America's Failure in China*, pp. 529–30; Finkelstein, "From Abandonment to Salvation," pp. 381–94.

38. Kepley, *Collapse of the Middle Way*, pp. 60–63.

39. Summary of daily meeting with the secretary, 3 January 1950, box 1, Summaries of the Secretary's Daily Meetings, 1949–50, OES.

40. Statement by President Truman, 5 January 1950, DSB 12 (16 January 1950): 79; memorandum, 6 January 1950, box 59, Elsey Papers; meeting with the president, 5 January 1950, FRUS, *Secretary's Memoranda: Visits of Foreign Dignitaries, 1949–52*. For a summary of the maneuvering and confusion that accompanied the issuance of the presidential statement, see Gordon H. Chang, *Friends and Enemies*, p. 310 n. 47.

41. Remarks by Secretary Acheson, DSB 12 (16 January 1950): 79–81.

42. Tsou, *America's Failure in China*, p. 481; Acheson to Johnson, 14 April 1950, FRUS, 1950, 6:326.

43. For the Chinese Communist accusation, see NYT, 4 January 1950, 16:2–3. Whereas Mao found assurance in Washington's announced intention not to come to the defense of Taiwan, Stalin had reason to look askance at it because of his strong desire to thwart any possible normalization of relations between the United States and the PRC. For an analysis that links the Soviet leader's views on a Chinese invasion of Taiwan to his objective of sharpening discord between Peking and the West, see Goncharov, Lewis, and Xue, *Uncertain Partners*, pp. 97–104.

44. Koo Memoirs, VI, J 235.

45. Senate Committee, *Reviews of the World Situation*, pp. 229–45.

46. Memorandum of conversation, 5 January 1950, FRUS, 1950, 6:258–63.

47. China Telegram, 5–11 January 1950, POS. The China Telegram was a compilation and analysis of American opinion on Far Eastern questions prepared weekly by the State Department's Office of Public Opinion Studies.

48. Finkelstein, "From Abandonment to Salvation," p. 467; Senate Committee, *Reviews of the World Situation*, pp. 131–47; Blum, *Drawing the Line*, pp. 182–83; "Crisis in Asia—An Examination of U.S. Policy," DSB 12 (23 January 1950): 113–16.

49. Dobbs, "Limiting Room to Maneuver," pp. 525–38.

50. China Telegram, 9–15 February 1950, POS; "A Summary of Current American Attitudes on U.S. Policy toward the Far East," 13 February 1950, box 33, ibid.

51. Kepley, *Collapse of the Middle Way*, pp. 68–76, 83; Fried, *Nightmare in Red*, pp. 120–29.

52. Kepley, *Collapse of the Middle Way*, pp. 77–80; Schoenbaum, *Waging Peace and War*, pp. 199–200.

53. Acheson to Johnson, 7 March 1950, FRUS, 1950, 6:316–17; Acheson to Johnson, 14 April 1950, ibid., pp. 325–26. The Nationalist government had for some time obtained military material in the open market through Commerce International China

(CIC), which served as its purchasing agent. A subsidiary of World Commerce Corporation, a multinational company combining business and intelligence enterprises, CIC also contracted the services of the American Technical and Military Group, a private military advisory team of more than thirty inactive U.S. armed services personnel headed by retired Adm. Charles M. Cooke, a former commander of the Seventh Fleet and an ardent pro-Nationalist partisan. Cooke, besides supervising this group and acting as a military adviser to Chiang Kai-shek, put to good use his contacts with the China bloc and the American military establishment. He supplied Senator William Knowland and Congressman Walter Judd as well as the Navy Department with reports on Nationalist military needs and capabilities together with other intelligence. He also established an unofficial liaison between Taipei and General MacArthur's headquarters.

"How Formosa Was Dropped but Did Not Fall," [undated memorandum], box 11, Cooke Papers; Cooke to Albert Wedemeyer, 15 September 1950, box 9, ibid.; JCS 1967/27, May 1950, CCS 381 Formosa (11-8-48) Sec. 3, JCS, 1948–50; Cooke to Knowland, 23 May 1950, box 96, Judd Papers.

For further discussion of the activities of Admiral Cooke and a fascinating array of Americans involved in private assistance to Taiwan during this period, see Cumings, *Roaring of the Cataract*, pp. 508–25. A provocative piece of detective work, Cumings's account of these activities contains considerable speculation and guesswork.

Cooke, in his pro-Nationalist sympathies and confrontationist attitude toward the new order in China, mirrored the outlook of many of his senior navy colleagues, who were unreconciled to Chiang's expulsion from the mainland. For the views of navy leaders during this period, consult Marolda, "U.S. Navy and the Chinese Civil War," pp. 108–15.

54. Senate Committee, *Reviews of the World Situation*, pp. 272–76. In light of the later reconsideration of Taiwan policy, it is interesting to note that Acheson acknowledged that he had not irrevocably written off the island. "You can say that you can assume a whole lot of things might happen, and they might happen," he cryptically observed, "and if they did we would reconsider this thing, but they are not happening and the thing is now marching down this road" (277).

In condemning "purely provocative" Nationalist bombing of the mainland, Acheson no doubt had particularly in mind an air raid on Shanghai on 6 February in which American-supplied Nationalist planes had inflicted heavy civilian casualties and destroyed American-owned property. The air raid had elicited a stern note of protest to Taipei from the outraged secretary of state. For the details of this episode, see Finkelstein, *Washington's Taiwan Dilemma*, pp. 292–94.

55. ORE 7-50, "Probable Developments in Taiwan," 20 March 1950, box 257, Intelligence Files, PSF.

56. He, "Last Campaign to Unify China," pp. 1–12. See also Zhang, *Deterrence and Strategic Culture*, pp. 64–73. Huebner, "Abortive Liberation of Taiwan," pp. 256–75, is instructive but appeared before new Chinese sources became available.

57. James Webb to U.S. Embassy Taipei, 19 May 1950, FRUS, 1950, 6:342–43; Webb to U.S. Embassy Taipei, 26 May 1950, ibid., pp. 344–46; ibid., p. 346 n. 2.

58. Leffler, *Preponderance of Power*, pp. 341–44.

59. NSC 68, 14 April 1950, *FRUS*, 1950, 1:234–92. For appraisals of this policy paper, see especially Gaddis, *Strategies of Containment*, pp. 89–106; Leffler, *Preponderance of Power*, pp. 355–60. Mayers, *Cracking the Monolith*, p. 80, and Gordon H. Chang, *Friends and Enemies*, pp. 69–70, comment on the paper's bearing on China policy.

60. Schaller, *American Occupation of Japan*, pp. 234–45.

61. Stueck, *Road to Confrontation*, pp. 146–51; Schaller, *American Occupation of Japan*, pp. 245–51; Gordon H. Chang, *Friends and Enemies*, pp. 63–72; Mayers, *Cracking the Monolith*, pp. 40, 66–70.

62. Julius Holmes to Acheson, 6 January 1950, 611.94A/1-650.

63. Memorandum for the prime minister, 14 April 1950, file 42, vol. 7, Wrong Papers.

64. Minute, 3 May 1950, F 1022/15, FO 371/83013. Merchant's views appear to have reflected those of the State Department. See U.S.-U.K. memorandum on ministerial talks agenda (China item), 6 May 1950, FC 1022/15B, FO 371/83013.

65. Records of Ministerial Talks, U.S.-U.K., 9 May 1950, PREM 8/1204; memorandum by secretary of state for Foreign Affairs, 19 May 1950, C.P. (50) 114, CAB 129/40. In spite of Britain's official recognition of the People's Republic, the two governments had failed to establish formal diplomatic relations, and conditions for British businessmen in China had deteriorated. Martin, *Divided Counsel*, pp. 139–45; Tang, *Britain's Encounter with Revolutionary China, 1949–54*, pp. 71–83.

66. Schoenbaum, *Waging Peace and War*, pp. 193–95, 198–202.

67. Rusk to Acheson, 26 April 1950, *FRUS*, 1950, 6:333–35.

68. Merchant to Rusk, 27 April 1950, box 22, CA, 1948–56.

69. JCS to Johnson, 2 May 1950, CD 9-4-29, OSD, 1950; Bradley to Johnson, 5 May 1950, CD 6-4-6, ibid.

70. Philip Sprouse to Rusk, 11 May 1950, box 18, CA, 1944–50.

71. McGlothlen, *Controlling the Waves*, pp. 96–101. A biographical sketch of Sun can be found in *Biographical Dictionary of Republican China*, ed. Boorman with Howard, 3:165–67.

72. "Hypothetical Development of the Formosan Situation," 3 May 1950, 793.00/5-350.

73. Military attaché Taipei to CSGID [CGSID], 3 January 1950, box 18, CA, 1944–50. Significantly, sometime in December 1949 or thereabouts, Sun apparently rejected an offer from a U.S. official for full American backing if he took control of the Nationalist government. Cumings, *Roaring of the Cataract*, p. 534.

74. Finkelstein, "From Abandonment to Salvation," pp. 510–11.

75. ORE 7-50, "Probable Developments in Taiwan," 20 March 1950, box 257, Intelligence File, PSF.

76. Strong to Sprouse, 11 May 1950, box 18, CA, 1944–50.

77. Dulles had privately found fault in the 5 January announcement for claiming that the island was Chinese territory and disregarding a moral obligation to the Taiwanese, who would be "subjected to the cruel fate of being the final battleground between the Red Regime and the Nationalist Army." Dulles to Arthur Vandenberg, 6 January 1950, box 48, J. F. Dulles Papers (SML).

78. Dulles to Webb, 19 May 1950, box 17, CA, 1944–50.

79. Extract from draft memorandum, Rusk to Acheson, 30 May 1950, *FRUS, 1950*, 6:349–51. It is not clear that Acheson actually saw this memorandum.

80. Burns to Rusk, 29 May 1950, ibid., pp. 346–47.

81. Robert Barnett to Merchant, 15 June 1950, 794A.5-MAP/6-1550; McGlothlen, *Controlling the Waves*, pp. 119, 127.

82. "U.S. Policy toward Formosa," box 18, CA, 1944–50.

83. Fisher Howe to W. Park Armstrong, 31 May 1950, *FRUS, 1950*, 6:347–49.

84. Franks to Sir Maberly E. Dening, 7 June 1950, FC 10345/9, FO 371/83320.

85. Rusk to Acheson, 9 June 1950, box 17, CA, 1944–50.

86. Chen Chih-mai to Koo, 15 June 1950, box 180, Koo Papers. A few weeks earlier Dulles had privately assured H. Alexander Smith and five other pro-KMT Republican Senators that he was on their side on the Taiwan issue. The legislators came away from their meeting with Dulles with an understanding "that we would start no 'fireworks' until Dulles has a chance to move in on this with Acheson." Smith Diary, 22 May 1950, Smith Papers.

87. Memorandum of conversation, 12 June 1950, box 180, Koo Papers; Koo Diary, 12 June 1950, ibid.

88. Clubb to Rusk, 16 June 1950, box 17, CA, 1944–50.

89. Memorandum, circa 15 June 1950, box 18, ibid.

90. MacArthur to JCS, 29 May 1950, box 8, RG 6, MacArthur Papers.

91. Poole, 1950–1952, pp. 385–86. Summary of meeting, 14 June 1950, box 19, G-3.

92. Kusnitz, *Public Opinion and Foreign Policy*, pp. 33–35.

93. Cumings, *Roaring of the Cataract*, pp. 531–44.

94. Schoenbaum, *Waging Peace and War*, p. 209.

95. Nix to Mrs. Harry S. Truman, 17 January 1951, box 1768, General File, PSF. Truman divulged the existence of the letter at a Blair House meeting with his advisers after the start of the Korean War. Memorandum of conversation, 26 June 1950, *FRUS, 1950*, 7:180.

96. For the report that a coup was in preparation, see Cohen, "Acheson, His Advisers, and China," p. 32. When queried in later years about his knowledge of any U.S. covert efforts to replace Chiang Kai-shek prior to the Korean War, Rusk wrote that "talk of a military coup came a dime a dozen during this period. We did not permit the United States to be drawn into any such discussions." Dean Rusk to author, 8 July 1993.

97. Arrangements were made for Defense Secretary Johnson to meet with Hollington Tong, Chiang's personal adviser. Koo Diary, 7 June 1950, Koo Papers. On MacArthur's recommendation, Adm. Charles Cooke, the Generalissimo's personal military consultant, flew in from Taipei to petition the visiting Americans. What Cooke wanted from Washington was a positive declaration of policy, U.S. advisers, and economic and military assistance. Cooke to Judd, 16 June 1950, box 96, Judd Papers.

98. Charles Willoughby to MacArthur, 15 June 1950, box 1, RG 6, MacArthur Papers.

99. Schaller, *Douglas MacArthur*, pp. 177–79. Schaller suggests that the general might have wanted to link a Taiwan command to the Pentagon's agreement to an early Japanese peace treaty that he also desired.

100. MacArthur memorandum on Formosa, 14 June 1950, *FRUS*, *1950*, 7:161–65.

101. Oral History of Ambassador William J. Sebald, p. 10, DOHC; Bradley to JCS, 25 June 1950, 091 (China) 1950, CJCS/7321, CJCS, 1949–53.

102. Merchant to Rusk, 23 June 1950, 694.001/6-2350.

103. *NYT*, 25 June 1950, 18:5.

104. Looking back, Rusk believed that the attitude of the United States toward Taiwan "would have proved very difficult" in the absence of a North Korean attack, without which he doubted intervention to defend the island would have occurred. Dean Rusk to author, 8 July 1993.

Chapter Two

1. For viewpoints that question the causal influence of the crisis, see Buhite, *Soviet-American Relations in Asia*, pp. 100–101; Lowe, *Origins of the Korean War*, p. 154; Cumings, *Roaring of the Cataract*, pp. 625–27.

2. Acheson, *Present at the Creation*, p. 405; Paige, *Korean Decision*, pp. 109, 125–27; Webb to John W. Snyder, 25 April 1975, Webb Papers.

3. Bradley and Blair, *A General's Life*, pp. 532–34.

4. Acheson, *Present at the Creation*, pp. 405–6.

5. Memorandum of conversation, 25 June 1950, *FRUS*, *1950*, 7:158–59. Ronald McGlothlen has suggested that Acheson wanted to hold off on an immediate insertion of the Seventh Fleet in the Taiwan Strait so as not to give Chiang Kai-shek an opportunity to further solidify his position in the absence of a coup d'état. According to McGlothlen, Undersecretary of State James Webb privately informed Truman at the first Blair House meeting that Acheson only wished the fleet to move toward the Strait but not enter it, at least not for the moment. McGlothlen, *Controlling the Waves*, p. 128. There is no mention of such a conversation in a letter cited by McGlothlen containing Webb's recollection many years later of the Blair House meeting. Webb to Snyder, 25 April 1975, Webb Papers. Moreover, the official memorandum of conversation for this meeting records Acheson's recommendation that the president order the fleet (then in the Philippines) to "proceed to Formosa and [to] prevent an attack on Formosa from the mainland" and from the reverse direction.

6. Memorandum of conversation, 26 June 1950, *FRUS*, *1950*, 7:179–81.

7. Tucker, *Patterns in the Dust*, p. 195.

8. Daily Staff Summary, 26 June 1950, OES.

9. Kaufman, *Korean War*, pp. 34–35.

10. Donovan, *Tumultuous Years*, p. 206.

11. Memorandum of conversation, 25 June 1950, *FRUS*, *1950*, 7:158.

12. Memorandum of conversation, 26 June 1950, ibid., p. 180.

13. Schaller, *Douglas MacArthur*, p. 192, presents evidence of a continuing official interest in Chiang's removal. However, State Department papers contain no record of deliberations, analyses, or recommendations on the subject of the Generalissimo's replacement after 25 June. One intriguing memorandum authored by Edmund Clubb on 7 July refers to the "current project of Representative Walter Judd to proceed to Formosa to induce the Generalissimo to resign his post." Clubb to Fulton

Freeman and Wallace Stuart, 7 July 1950, 794A.00/7-750. Years later, Judd categorically denied any knowledge of such an undertaking. Judd to Strong, 10 March 1982, box 139, Judd Papers.

14. President's statement, 27 June 1950, FRUS, 1950, 7:202–3.

15. Transcript of Princeton Seminars, 13 February 1954, box 76, Acheson Papers.

16. Chiu, "China, the United States, and the Question of Taiwan," pp. 122, 171–72.

17. China Telegram, 22–28 June, 29 June–5 July, 1950, POS; Cong. Rec., Senate, 27 June 1950, pp. 9228–34. "It was all very wonderful and an answer to prayer," rejoiced New Jersey Republican H. Alexander Smith. "The saving of Formosa was clearly God guided." Smith Diary, 28 June 1950, Smith Papers.

18. Chou En-lai Statement, 28 June 1950, Important Documents Concerning the Question of Taiwan, pp. 13–15; Mao Tse-tung Address, 8th Meeting of Central People's Government Council, 28 June 1950, ibid., p. 12; Whiting, China Crosses the Yalu, p. 80.

19. Zhang, Deterrence and Strategic Culture, p. 74; He, "'Last Campaign to Unify China,'" pp. 14–15.

20. Field, History of United States Naval Operations, pp. 67, 128, 396. An account of the operations of Task Force 72 (the official designator of the Formosa Patrol Force) appears in Marolda, "U.S. Navy and the Chinese Civil War," pp. 183, 309–13. Four destroyers were initially assigned to patrol duties, but this number often fell to three because of naval losses in Korean waters.

21. JCS to Johnson, 28 July 1950, FRUS, 1950, 6:395; Acheson to Johnson, 31 July 1950, ibid., pp. 404–5.

22. Address by Vice Adm. Arthur D. Struble, 7 June 1951, Drawer 1, Safe C, Radford Papers.

23. Dingman, "Atomic Diplomacy," pp. 60–65.

24. JCS to MacArthur, 26 July 1950, box 8, RG 6, MacArthur Papers; Poole, 1950–1952, p. 391.

25. DOS to Loy Henderson, 16 August 1950, FRUS, 1950, 6:441–42.

26. Henderson to DOS, 9 July 1950, FRUS, 1950, 7:371–72; Lewis Douglas to DOS, 14 July 1950, ibid., p. 384; Strong to DOS, 14 July 1950, ibid., p. 375.

27. CIA memorandum no. 36, 17 July 1950, box 3, NSC Records, Subject File, PSF.

28. Memorandum, 22 July 1950, box 18, CA, 1944–50; JCS to CINCFE, 29 July 1950, box 8, RG 6, MacArthur Papers.

29. CIA 8-50, "Review of the World Situation," 16 August 1950, box 209, NSC Meetings, Subject File, PSF; Clubb to Merchant, 29 August 1950, box 18, CA, 1944–50.

30. Clubb to Rusk, 27 September 1950, FRUS, 1950, 7:795–96; Walter Bedell Smith memorandum for the president, 12 October 1950, CIA Cold War Records: The CIA under Harry Truman, p. 360.

31. Stueck, Road to Confrontation, p. 210.

32. Henderson to Acheson, 29 June 1950, FRUS, 1950, 7:218.

33. Stairs, Diplomacy of Constraint, pp. 52–53, 93.

34. Arnold Heeney to Hume Wrong, 6 July 1950, file K-10 (July 1950), vol. 167, Records of the Privy Council, RG 2 (B1), PAC; memorandum for the minister, 11 July 1950, file 1, 50056-A-40, DEA.

35. Memorandum by chiefs of staff, 28 June 1950, D.O. (50), PREM 8/1405.

36. Memorandum on Formosa by the minister of state, 3 July 1950, C.P. (50) 156, PREM 8/1408.

37. Minute, 14 July 1950, D.O. (50) 14th Meeting, PREM 8/1405; note to the prime minister, 19 July 1950, FC 1024/47, FO 371/83298.

38. NYT, 11 July 1950, 7:4.

39. Bevin to Franks, 7 July 1950, FRUS, 1950, 7:329–30.

40. Acheson to Bevin, 10 July 1950, ibid., pp. 347–51; Lowe, *Origins of the Korean War*, pp. 165–66.

41. George McGhee to Acheson, 13 July 1950, FRUS, 1950, 7:372–73; Acheson to Nehru, ibid., p. 913; Acheson, *Present at the Creation*, pp. 416–20.

42. Douglas to DOS, 8 July 1950, FRUS, 1950, 7:331.

43. Bevin to Acheson, 15 July 1950, ibid., pp. 395–99.

44. Editorial note, ibid., p. 430.

45. Acheson to Nehru, 25 July 1950, ibid., pp. 466–68.

46. JCS to Acheson, 27 July 1950, FRUS, 1950, 6:391–94.

47. Rusk to Karl Rankin, 14 August 1950, ibid., p. 438.

48. Statement of Foreign Minister Yeh, 28 June 1950, 795.00/7-150.

49. On a visit to Taiwan in August, Nationalist ambassador Wellington Koo found that the imminence of another world war was a common expectation within the KMT. Koo Memoir, VII, A 123–26.

50. Memorandum of conversation, 29 June 1950, box 18, CA, 1944–50. In later years a high Nationalist official told Rusk that Chiang had made the troop offer in the confident expectation that Washington would reject it. Schoenbaum, *Waging Peace and War*, p. 213. There was unquestionably disagreement among Chiang's military and civilian advisers over the troop contribution. George Yeh told Wellington Koo that during a four-hour debate he and his civilian colleagues won approval for the contribution over the objections of the military, who were reluctant to divert scarce equipment to Korea. Koo Diary, 29 June 1950, Koo Papers. Admiral Cooke later claimed that he planted the idea of the troop offer in Chiang's mind and that the Nationalist leader had accepted it over the opposition of many of his advisers. Cooke to Chiang Kai-shek, 17 February 1953, box 2, Cooke Papers; Cooke to Walter Robertson, 20 January 1954, box 7, ibid.

51. Truman, *Years of Trial and Hope*, p. 343.

52. MacArthur to Department of Army, 3 July 1950, box 8, RG 6, MacArthur Papers; Johnson to Acheson, 17 July 1950, FRUS, 1950, 6:379–80.

53. Acheson to Strong, 22 July 1950, FRUS, 1950, 6:387.

54. Strong to DOS, 23 July 1950, ibid., p. 388.

55. DOS to Strong, 24 July 1950, ibid., p. 391; Acheson to Johnson, 29 July 1950, ibid., pp. 399–400; Johnson to Acheson, 2 August 1950, ibid., p. 406; Webb to Marshall, 28 September 1950, ibid., pp. 522–24.

56. Strong to DOS, 14 July 1950, ibid., p. 375.

57. DOS to Strong, 14 July 1950, 793.00/7-1450; JCS to MacArthur, 17 July 1950, box 18, CA, 1944–50.

58. Johnson to Acheson, 29 July 1950, FRUS, 1950, 6:401.

59. Acheson to Johnson, 31 July 1950, ibid., pp. 402–4.

60. Johnson to MacArthur, 4 August 1950, ibid., p. 423.

61. Summary of discussion, 62nd NSC Meeting, 27 July 1950, box 220, NSC Meetings, Subject File, PSF; NSC 37/10, FRUS, 1950, 6:414. Acheson had earlier removed preneutralization restrictions on the sale of U.S. military equipment to the Nationalists, including tanks and jet aircraft. Acheson to Johnson, 24 July 1950, box 17, CA, 1944–50.

62. Strong to DOS, 3 August 1950, FRUS, 1950, 6:412–13.

63. Rusk to Acheson, 3 August 1950, box 18, CA, 1944–50; MacArthur to JCS, 4 August 1950, box 8, RG 6, MacArthur Papers; Bradley and Blair, A General's Life, p. 549; JCS to MacArthur, 14 August 1950, FRUS, 1950, 6:439.

64. NYT, 2 August 1950, 6:3.

65. D. Clayton James, Triumph and Disaster, p. 456.

66. Extracts of conversation, 6 and 8 August 1950, FRUS, 1950, 6:427–30.

67. D. Clayton James, Triumph and Disaster, pp. 457–58. No evidence exists that MacArthur's talks with Chiang and other Nationalist officials encroached on political affairs.

68. Koo Diary, 2 July 1950, Koo Papers.

69. The China Mail, 12 June 1950, box 14, Rankin Papers. The Nationalist government, for reasons of prestige and symbolism, would have preferred the appointment of an ambassador to replace the ailing John Leighton Stuart, who had left China for the United States in 1949. Koo Memoir, VII, A 111.

70. Rankin to Rusk, 14 April 1950, box 14, Rankin Papers; Rankin to Rusk, 18 August 1950, FRUS, 1950, 6:443; Rankin to Rusk, 25 August 1950, box 2, Taipei (1950–54), FSPR; Rankin, China Assignment, p. 68.

71. Report of Far East Command Survey Group to Formosa, 11 September 1950, box 8, RG 6, MacArthur Papers; DOS to Rankin, 21 November 1950, FRUS, 1950, 6:579.

72. Clubb to John H. Ohly, 8 September 1950, box 17, CA, 1944–50; Bell to Lemnitzer, 15 September 1950, FRUS, 1950, 6:501–2.

73. John O. Bell to Lemnitzer, 18 September 1950, FRUS, 1950, 6:509; Chang, "Pragmatism and Opportunism," p. 186.

74. Barnett to Clubb, 17 November 1950, 894A.00R/11-1450.

75. U.K. High Commissioner, Ottawa, to Commonwealth Relations Office, 5 August 1950, FC 1024/53, FO 371/83298; Pearson to Acheson, 15 August 1950, box 18, CA, 1944–50.

76. B. A. B. Burrows to J. S. H. Shattock, 17 August 1950, FC 10345/26, FO 371/83320.

77. Bevin to U.K. Delegation to UN, 25 August 1950, FC 1195/15, FO 371/83401; Dening to Burrows, 26 August 1950, with memorandum on Formosa, FC 1016/125, FO 371/83237.

78. Grasso, Truman's Two-China Policy, pp. 142–54.

79. FO to U.K. Delegation to UN, 10 March 1950, UP 213/63, FO 371/88504; Acheson to Franks, 4 August 1950, box 18, CA, 1944–50; Bevin to Franks, 11 August 1950, FRUS, 1950, 2:259–62. A convenient discussion of Anglo-American differences over the representation question during this period appears in Tang, Britain's Encounter with Revolutionary China, pp. 130–37.

80. Ruth Bacon to Freeman, 29 June 1950, FRUS, 1950, 2:246; DOS to Austin, 31 July

1950, ibid., pp. 251–52; DOS to Austin, 4 August 1950, ibid., pp. 251–52; Erskine, "The Polls," p. 125.

81. Rusk to Rankin, 14 August 1950, FRUS, 1950, 6:438.

82. Meeting with the president, 3 August 1950, box 65, Acheson Papers.

83. Chou En-lai to President of UN Security Council and UN Secretary-General, 24 August 1950, *Important Documents Concerning the Question of Taiwan*, pp. 21–22.

84. NYT, 26 August 1950, 4:2–3; *Yearbook of the United Nations, 1950*, p. 289.

85. MacArthur to Clyde A. Lewis, 20 August 1950, box 8, RG 9, MacArthur Papers.

86. Accounts of this episode are numerous. See, for example, D. Clayton James, *Triumph and Disaster*, pp. 460–64.

87. Foreign Policy Aspects of the MacArthur Statement, 26 August 1950, box 65, Acheson Papers.

88. *Public Papers of the Presidents of the United States: Harry S. Truman, 1950*, p. 607. In a radio and television report on Korea the next day, Truman called for a peaceful settlement of the Taiwan question through "international action." Ibid., p. 613.

89. Summary of daily meeting with the president, 1 September 1950, box 1, Summaries of the Secretary's Daily Meetings, 1949–1950, OES.

90. Caridi, *Korean War and American Politics*, pp. 51–55, 63–64; Kepley, *Collapse of the Middle Way*, pp. 94–95.

91. "Public Attitudes Concerning Formosa," 26 September 1950, box 33, POS.

92. "Chinese Representation in the United Nations," 24 August 1950, FRUS, 1950, 3:1121–25; "Chinese Representation in the United Nations," 6 September 1950, ibid., pp. 1184–85.

93. Preliminary Tripartite Meetings, 1 September 1950, FRUS, 1950, 6:478.

94. State Department Position Paper on Formosa, 28 August 1950, enclosed with JCS 1966/47, 1 September 1950, box 8, RG 6, MacArthur Papers; Clubb to Robbins Gilman, 31 August 1950, box 18, CA, 1950–54.

95. Nakatsuji, "Short Life of the Official 'Two China' Policy," pp. 33–49.

96. Memorandum of conversation, 28 August 1950, FRUS, 1950, 6:464–66; ibid., p. 467 n. 1; H. Freeman Matthews to Acheson, 30 August 1950, box 19, CA, 1944–50.

97. Bradley to Johnson, 8 September 1950, FRUS, 1950, 6:491; Webb to Johnson, 13 September 1950, ibid., p. 497.

98. Memorandum of conversation, 19 September 1950, box 180, Koo Papers; Koo Memoir, VII, A 210–13.

99. Pogue, *Statesman, 1945–1959*, pp. 420–37; NYT, 21 September 1950, 5:3.

100. U.S. Delegation Minutes, Fourth Meeting of the Foreign Ministers, 14 September 1950, FRUS, 1950, 3:1225–27.

101. UNGA, Fifth Session, 277th Plenary Meeting, 19 September 1950, pp. 1–16.

102. Acheson to Truman, 20 September 1950, FRUS, 1950, 3:1247; meeting with the president, 14 September 1950, FRUS, *Secretary's Memoranda: Visits of Foreign Dignitaries*.

103. *Yearbook of the United Nations, 1950*, p. 298.

104. UNSC, 1950, 506th Meeting, 29 September 1950, pp. 1–15.

105. James, *Triumph and Disaster*, p. 515; Wiltz, "Truman and MacArthur," pp. 168–75; FRUS, 1950, 6:533–34.

106. Meeting with the president, 9 October 1950, FRUS, *Secretary's Memoranda: Visits of Foreign Dignitaries.*

107. Chou En-lai to President of UN General Assembly and UN Secretary-General, 17 October 1950, *Important Documents Concerning Taiwan,* pp. 23–24.

108. MacDonald, *Korea,* pp. 62–68.

109. Acheson to Marshall, 11 November 1950, FRUS, *1950,* 6:555–56.

110. Austin to DOS, 11 October 1950, ibid., pp. 528–29; DOS to Austin, 11 October 1950, ibid., p. 532.

111. Sir Gladwyn Jebb to FO, 13 November 1950, FC 1024/116, FO 371/83300; Jebb to FO, 15 November 1950, FC 1024/123, FO 371/83300; Jebb to FO, FC 1024/125, FO 371/83301.

112. Minutes, 20th Meeting of the U.S. Delegation to the UN General Assembly, 15 November 1950, FRUS, *1950,* 6:563–72.

113. Reeves, *Life and Times of Joe McCarthy,* pp. 331–32, 343–45.

114. Dulles to Acheson, 15 November 1950, FRUS, *1950,* 6:572–73. Dulles had prepared, but did not introduce, an alternate resolution that would ultimately have restored Taiwan to China but not as long as the island might "become a base for a new aggression in the Pacific and the object of a bloody civil struggle" and only if the inhabitants of Taiwan were granted a satisfactory measure of autonomy. Memorandum of conversation, 16 November 1950, ibid., pp. 574–76. Acheson had previously indicated that he approved such an arrangement for Taiwan. Dulles memorandum on Formosa, 25 October 1950, box 18, CA, 1944–50. The arrangement would obviously have kept Taiwan separate from the Communist mainland for the indefinite future.

115. Robert Lovett to Acheson, 24 November 1950, FRUS, *1950,* 6:579–80.

116. Zhang, *Deterrence and Strategic Culture,* pp. 73–74, 89–90, 115; Xiaolu Chen, "China's Policy toward the United States," pp. 189–91; Hao and Zhai, "China's Decision to Enter the Korean War," pp. 101–4; Christensen, "Threats, Assurances, and the Last Chance for Peace," p. 136; Goncharov, Lewis, and Xue, *Uncertain Partners,* pp. 157–59, 180–81. For the view that the revolutionary nationalism of Mao and the CCP leadership as well as their security concerns played a crucial role in China's entry, see Jian Chen, "China's Changing Aims during the Korean War," pp. 8–41. Hunt, "Beijing and the Korean Crisis," pp. 463–65, also regards revolutionary nationalism as a motivating factor.

Chapter Three

1. Foot, *Wrong War,* pp. 101–3; DOS to Certain Diplomatic Missions, 12 December 1950, FRUS, *1950,* 7:1532–34.

2. Hsieh, *Strategy for Survival,* pp. 78–79, 90–91, 106–7.

3. Robert Rinden to DOS, 2 February 1951, box 16, Rankin Papers; minutes of undersecretary's meeting, 21 February 1951, box 2, Minutes of the Undersecretary's Meetings, 1951–1952, OES.

4. Koo Memoir, VII, A 310.

5. MacArthur to JCS, 29 November 1950, box 9, RG 6, MacArthur Papers.

6. JCS to MacArthur, 29 November 1950, FRUS, *1950,* 7:1253–54; Poole, *1950–1952,* pp. 397–98.

7. MacDonald, *Korea*, pp. 69–70, 87–90; Foot, *Wrong War*, pp. 113–30.

8. An excellent account of the administration's deliberations over an expanded war can be found in Foot, *Wrong War*, chap. 4.

9. Kusnitz, *Public Opinion and Foreign Policy*, pp. 51–53; Caridi, *Korean War and American Politics*, pp. 108–20.

10. MacDonald, *Korea*, pp. 79–87; Foot, "Anglo-American Relations in the Korean Crisis," pp. 43–57.

11. "Strategic Importance of Formosa," 2 January 1951, FRUS, 1951, 7:1474–76.

12. NSC 101, "Courses of Action Relative to Communist China and Korea," 12 January 1951, ibid., pp. 70–72; Ridgway to Gen. J. Lawton Collins, 29 December 1950, box 20, Ridgway Papers; Foot, *Wrong War*, p. 118.

13. NSC 101/1, "U.S. Action to Counter Chinese Communist Aggression," 15 January 1951, FRUS, 1951, 7:79–81.

14. "U.S. Action to Counter Chinese Communist Aggression," 17 January 1951, ibid., pp. 1515–17.

15. Summary of discussion, 80th NSC Meeting, 18 January 1951, box 220, NSC Meetings, Subject File, PSF.

16. JCS 2118/15, "Courses of Action Relative to Communist China and Korea — Chinese Nationalists," 29 January 1951, CCS 381 Far East (11-28-50) Sec. 3, JCS, 1951–53.

17. "Report on the Effect within China and Other Eastern Countries of United States Backing of Chiang Kai-shek," 9 February 1951, FRUS, 1951, 7:1574–75.

18. Merchant to Rankin, 23 January 1951, 793.00/12-2050; Strong to Clubb, 22 January 1951, CA, 1948–56; memorandum of conversation, 6 February 1951, FRUS, *Secretary's Memoranda of Conversations*.

19. Memorandum for the record, DOS-JCS Meeting, 6 February 1951, FRUS, 1951, 7:1566–68; James, *Triumph and Disaster*, p. 559.

20. Rusk to Merchant, 7 February 1951, FRUS, 1951, 7:1569.

21. Pollack, "Korean War and Sino-American Relations," pp. 224–29; Jian Chen, "China's Changing Aims during the Korean War," pp. 26–39; Hunt, "Beijing and the Korean Crisis," pp. 465–67; Christensen, "Threats, Assurances, and the Last Chance for Peace," p. 145.

22. MacDonald, *Korea*, pp. 79–87; Stairs, *Diplomacy of Constraint*, pp. 165–76; Foot, "Anglo-American Relations in the Korean Crisis," pp. 45–55.

23. Speech at UN Security Council, 28 November 1950, *Important Documents Concerning the Question of Taiwan*, pp. 26–70.

24. Austin to DOS, 4 December 1950, FRUS, 1950, 7:1355–56. Additional proof of the considerable importance the Chinese delegation placed on the Taiwan question appears in the Oral History of Ernest A. Gross, pp. 819–20, 839–40, COHC.

25. Henderson to DOS, 13 December 1950, FRUS, 1950, 7:1538–39.

26. Brief for the prime minister's visit to Washington, 2 December 1950, PREM 8/1202.

27. U.S. Delegation Minutes, First Meeting of the Truman-Attlee Talks, FRUS, 1950, 7:1365–69; memorandum of conversation, 5 December 1950, ibid., pp. 1391–92; U.S. Delegation Minutes, Second Meeting of the Truman-Attlee Talks, 5 December 1950, ibid., p. 1398.

28. U.S. Delegation Minutes, Fifth Meeting of the Truman-Attlee Talks, ibid., p. 1451.

29. U.S. Delegation Minutes, Second Meeting of the Truman-Attlee Talks, 5 December 1950, ibid., p. 1402.

30. "The Prime Minister's Visit to Washington, New York, and Ottawa," December 1950, Annex 2, Record of Second [Truman-Attlee] Meeting, 5 December 1950, PREM 8/1202; memorandum of conversation, 7 December 1950, FRUS, 1950, 7:1437.

31. "U.S. Position on Two Principal Alternative Courses in Korea," 7 December 1950, FRUS, 1950, 7:1439, 1441.

32. Truman-Attlee Talks Communiqué, 7 December 1950, ibid., p. 1477.

33. Stairs, Diplomacy of Constraint, pp. 160–61; Foot, Wrong War, pp. 111–13.

34. Extract from P.M.M. (51), 4th Meeting, 5 January 1951, PREM 8/1408; extract from P.M.M. (51), 5th Meeting, 8 January 1951, ibid.; note for the secretary's use, 4 January 1951, PREM 4/1405.

35. "Policy in Regard to Korea and the Far East," 5 January 1951, P.M.M. (51) 7, CAB 133/90.

36. Stairs, Diplomacy of Constraint, pp. 161–63.

37. Acheson, Present at the Creation, p. 513.

38. Koo Diary, 11 January 1951, 15 January 1951, Koo Papers.

39. NYT, 18 January 1951, 3:2. Despite some moderation of the Chinese terms in a later counterproposal from Peking, Washington pushed ahead with the passage of the aggressor resolution. Foot, Substitute for Victory, pp. 30–33.

40. NYT, 16 January 1951, 9:3; China Telegram, 11–17 January 1951, POS.

41. Stairs, Diplomacy of Constraint, pp. 165–76; Dockrill, "Foreign Office, Anglo-American Relations and the Korean War," pp. 469–71.

42. FRUS, 1952–54, 14:1008 n. 7.

43. Leary, Perilous Missions, pp. 103–12.

44. Rankin to Merchant, 20 December 1950, FRUS, 1950, 6:606–8.

45. Poole, 1950–1952, p. 403.

46. "U.S. Action to Counter Chinese Communist Aggression," 17 January 1951, FRUS, 1951, 7:1516.

47. Rusk confided the State Department's views to Canadian ambassador Hume Wrong. Memorandum of conversation, 14 February 1951, file U-2/2-11 (pla), vol. 2141, Interim 78, Access Section, RG 25, PAC.

Rusk was almost certainly aware of the top secret talks that Charles Burton Marshall of the Policy Planning Staff was then conducting through an intermediary with "Third Party," a Chinese national identified with non-Communist and nationalist Communist elements in Peking. The talks, which were taken quite seriously by senior State Department officials, canvassed the possibility of a Korean cease-fire as well as a Sino-Soviet schism or a coup d'état against Mao Tse-tung. The exchanges carried on until May before ending inconclusively. The memoranda of conversation for these talks can be found in FRUS, 1951, 7:1476–1698 passim.

48. Division of Research for Far East [DOS], "Guerillas in Communist China," 7 December 1950, 793.00/1-1251; "Guerilla Activities in China," 15 December 1950, box 257, EF-16 China, Strategic Plans Division Records, Nav Hist Center; CIA to

NSC, 11 January 1951, *FRUS, 1951*, 7:1503–6; Working Paper on Support of China Mainland Resistance, 21 March 1953, box 40, CA, 1948–56.

49. Ranelagh, *The Agency*, pp. 190–93, 198–219.

50. Rankin to Merchant, 31 May 1951, box 16, Rankin Papers.

51. Smith, *Portrait of a Cold Warrior*, p. 77; Leary, *Perilous Missions*, pp. 133, 137–41; Samson, *Chennault*, p. 314.

52. CIA Special Estimate SE-9, 18 June 1952 (released to author through FOI); memorandum of conversation, 1 October 1953, box 187, Koo Papers; Marolda, "U.S. Navy and the Chinese Civil War," pp. 199–202; NYT, 7 December, 1952, 1:7.

53. McCoy, *Politics of Heroin*, pp. 126–31; Prados, *Presidents' Secret Wars*, pp. 73–75. Journalist Bertil Lintner presents new information about the CIA operation on the Burma-Yunnan frontier and its aftermath in "CIA's First Secret War," pp. 56–58.

54. Marolda, "U.S. Navy and the Chinese Civil War," pp. 251–53; CIA Special Estimate SE-9, 18 June 1952 (released to author through FOI); Hunt, "Beijing and the Korean Crisis," p. 471.

55. Memorandum of conversation, 13 November 1952, box 187, Koo Papers.

56. John Allison to Dulles, 24 December 1952, *FRUS, 1952–54*, 14:120.

57. Report on U.S. Economic Assistance to Formosa, 22 May 1952, ibid., p. 55.

58. DOS to U.S. Embassy Taipei, 27 February 1951, *FRUS, 1951*, 7:1584–85; Thomas D. Cabot to Maj. Gen. S. L. Scott, 7 March 1951, ibid., p. 1591; Su-ya Chang, "Pragmatism and Opportunism," p. 192.

59. Yeh to Rankin, 9 February 1951, box 155, Koo Papers.

60. NYT, 21 April 1951, 1:4.

Chapter Four

1. D. Clayton James, *Triumph and Disaster*, pp. 608–11.

2. Rinden to DOS, 2 May 1951, 793.00/5-251.

3. D. Clayton James, *Triumph and Disaster*, pp. 585–90; Schaller, *Douglas MacArthur*, pp. 232–38.

4. Memorandum on Substance of Discussions, Joint DOS-JCS Meeting, 4 April 1951, *FRUS, 1951*, 7:1616–19.

5. High Commissioner for Canada, London, to Ottawa, 13 April 1951, and Wrong to Ottawa, 21 April 1951, file 2, 50056-A-40, DEA.

6. Summary of discussion, 90th NSC Meeting, 3 May 1951, box 220, NSC Meetings, Subject File, PSF.

7. NSC 48/5, "United States Objectives, Policies and Courses of Action in Asia," 17 May 1951, *FRUS, 1951*, 6:33–57.

8. "Chinese-American Friendship," DSB 24 (28 May 1951): 846–48.

9. China Telegram, 17–23, 24–29 May 1951, POS.

10. FO to U.K. Embassy Washington, 22 May 1951, FC 10345/4, and Franks to FO, 24 May 1951, FC 10345/5, FO 371/92246.

11. U.K. Embassy Washington to FO, 21 May 1951, FC 10345/4, FO 371/92246.

12. Warren I. Cohen, *Dean Rusk*, p. 60.

13. Rusk, *As I Saw It*, p. 173.

14. Rusk to author, 8 July 1993.

15. D. Clayton James, *Triumph and Disaster*, pp. 627–37; Schaller, *Douglas MacArthur*, pp. 246–50; Wiltz, "The MacArthur Inquiry," pp. 3593–636.

16. Senate Committee, *Military Situation in the Far East*, 1:23–24, 42–44, 178, and 2:886, 1260, 1326, 1584, 1653. An uncensored copy of the hearings is available at the Legislative Branch, National Archives. For testimony by Marshall and Bradley on the combat capabilities of Nationalist troops, see pp. 928, 1733, 1811–12, 2394, 2642 of this copy. An analysis of censored portions of the hearings appears in Wiltz, "The MacArthur Hearings of 1951," pp. 167–73.

17. Senate Committee, *Military Situation in the Far East*, 1:52 (MacArthur quotation), 616, and 2:882, 984.

18. Ibid., 3:1671–763.

19. Ibid., 4:2578–81, 2640.

20. Ibid., 3:1820, 1967–69, 1983, 2001, 2057, 2142. Acheson was now willing to let the World Court decide, if necessary, whether an American vote against Chinese Communist representation in the Security Council constituted a veto.

21. D. Clayton James, *Triumph and Disaster*, pp. 638–40; Schaller, *Douglas MacArthur*, pp. 249–50.

22. China Telegram, 26 April–2 May 1951, POS.

23. Senate Committee, *Military Situation in the Far East*, 5:3588–89.

24. Ibid., 3:2116–18, 2206–7.

25. Koen, *China Lobby in American Politics*, p. 27; China Telegram, 4–10 May 1950, POS.

26. NYT, 10 June 1951, 9:1, 11 June 1951, 24:2 (Kohlberg quotation), 14 June 1951, 3:6.

27. Fried, *Nightmare in Red*, pp. 130–31; Reeves, *Life and Times of Joe McCarthy*, pp. 370–75; Kahn, *China Hands*, pp. 227–43.

28. Rankin Diary, 6 March 1951, box 1, Rankin Papers; for evidence of Chinese Nationalist secret assistance to McCarthyites, see Newman, "Clandestine Chinese Nationalist Efforts," pp. 205–22.

29. Elsey to Truman, 28 March 1951, box 59, Elsey Papers.

30. Memorandum of discussion at Blair House, 8 June 1951, ibid.

31. Truman's postpresidential indictment of the lobby appears in Miller, *Plain Speaking*, p. 289.

32. J. Howard McGrath to Secretary of Commerce, 27 July 1951, box 635, Official File, WHCF (HST).

33. James Lanigan to Theodore Tannenwald, Jr., 9 October 1951, box 161, Subject File, PSF.

34. Robert Joyce to Fisher, 10 May 1951, 793.00/5-1051; Tannenwald Diary, 6, 17 July and 20, 23, 30 August 1951, Tannenwald Papers. Tannenwald, the chief of staff to the director for mutual security, took on the China lobby investigation as a special assignment.

35. Wertenbaker, "The China Lobby," pp. 4–24; Horton, "The China Lobby— Part II," pp. 5–22.

36. Chinese Embassy Press Release, 18 April 1952, box 186, Koo Papers.

37. China Telegram, 10–16, 17–23 April 1952, POS.

38. See, for example, Geraldine Fitch, "China Lob-Lolly," (N.Y., n.d.), box 3, Utley Papers.

39. MacDonald, *Korea*, pp. 107–10; Porter, *Britain and the Rise of Communist China*, p. 64; Tang, *Britain's Encounter with Revolutionary China*, pp. 107–12.

40. Acheson to U.S. Embassy, London, 25 May 1951, FRUS, 1951, 2:247–48; memorandum of conversation, 1 June 1951, ibid., pp. 251–53.

41. Tang, *Britain's Encounter with Revolutionary China*, pp. 138–43; Zhai, *The Dragon, the Lion, and the Eagle*, p. 104.

42. Appleton, *The Eternal Triangle?*, p. 180.

43. *Parliamentary Debates*, 23 April 1951, House of Commons, 5th ser., vol. 487 (1951), cols. 2301–2.

44. Cabinet Minutes, C.M. 34 (51) (3), 7 May 1951, CAB 128/9.

45. Extract from Pearson's statement in House of Commons, 7 May 1951, file 2, 50056-A-40, DEA.

46. Pruessen, *John Foster Dulles*, pp. 461–84; Schonberger, *Aftermath of War*, pp. 236–60.

47. "Japanese Peace Treaty, Chinese Participation and Disposal of Formosa," 20 March 1950, C.P. (51) 78, CAB 129/45; C.M. (51) (22) (3), 22 March 1951, CAB 128/19; memorandum of conversation, 30 March 1951, FRUS, 1951, 6:954.

48. Schonberger, "Peacemaking in Asia," pp. 61–62.

49. U.S. Aide-Mémoire, 12 April 1951, FRUS, 1951, 6:977 n. 1.

50. Provisional Draft of a Japanese Peace Treaty, 23 March 1951, ibid., p. 945.

51. Memorandum of conversation, 12 April 1951, ibid., p. 978. By this time Japan had regained its prewar position as Taiwan's largest trading partner, taking one-third of the island's exports and supplying about the same proportion of its imports (except for those financed by U.S. aid). Report on U.S. Economic Assistance to Formosa, 22 May 1952, FRUS, 1952–54, 14:56.

52. Su-ya Chang, "United States and the Long-term Disposition of Taiwan," pp. 459–61.

53. Joint United States–United Kingdom Draft, April–May 1951, FRUS, 1951, 6:1025.

54. Dulles to Acheson, 5 June 1951, ibid., p. 1106; C.P. (51) 155, 7 June 1951, CAB 129/46.

55. Draft Joint Statement of the United Kingdom and the United States, 19 June 1951, FRUS, 1951, 6:1134.

56. Schonberger, *Aftermath of War*, p. 270.

57. C.P. (51) 155, 7 June 1951, CAB 129/46; FRUS, 1951, 6:1109 n. 4; Schonberger, *Aftermath of War*, p. 271.

58. William Sebald to Dulles, 19 May 1951, FRUS, 1951, 6:1050.

59. Schonberger, *Aftermath of War*, pp. 271–72.

60. Pruessen, *John Foster Dulles*, pp. 491–92; Bernard Cohen, *Political Process and Foreign Policy*, pp. 21–22, 142–52.

61. Yoshida to Dulles, 6 August 1951, FRUS, 1951, 6:1242.

62. Yoshitsu, *Japan and the San Francisco Peace Settlement*, pp. 67–69; Dower, *Empire and Aftermath*, pp. 393–94, 410–12.

63. Schonberger, "Peacemaking in Asia," pp. 67–68; Warren I. Cohen, "China in Japanese-American Relations," pp. 39–40.

64. Koo Memoir, VII, D 15–16, 30, 44–46.

65. The text of Chiang Kai-shek's statement is printed in ibid., sec. 3, app. I; for popular reaction, see Rankin to DOS, 7 August 1951, 793.00/8-751.

66. Memoranda of conversations, 15, 21 (Dulles quotation), and 28 June 1951, box 184, Koo Papers; Koo Memoir, VII, D 183–86.

67. Memorandum of conversation, 3 July 1951, box 184, Koo Papers.

68. Su-ya Chang, "United States and the Long-term Disposition of Taiwan," pp. 459–70.

69. Koo Memoir, VII, D 325–28.

70. Acheson to U.S. Embassy Taipei, 21 August 1951, FRUS, 1951, 6:1279.

71. Koo Memoir, VII, D 183–84, 281; U.S. Embassy Taipei to DOS, 3 March 1952, box 5, Taipei (1950–55), FSPR.

72. Memorandum of conversation, 2 November 1951, 693.94/11-251.

73. Memorandum of conversation, 29 November 1951, box 184, Koo Papers.

74. Yoshitsu, *Japan and the San Francisco Peace Settlement*, pp. 75–77; Dower, *Empire and Aftermath*, pp. 405–9.

75. Yoshida to Dulles, 24 December 1951, FRUS, 1951, 6:1466–67.

76. Dening to FO, 14 December 1951, FJ 10310/37, FO 371/92605; Acheson to Dulles and Sebald, 18 December 1951, FRUS, 1951, 6:1448–50.

77. Memorandum of conversation, 27 December 1951, box 184, Koo Papers.

78. Adamthwaite, "Foreign Office and Policy-making," pp. 12–15; Tang, *Britain's Encounter with Revolutionary China*, pp. 112–15; Zhai, *The Dragon, the Lion, and the Eagle*, pp. 113–16; Carlton, *Anthony Eden*, pp. 295–96, 299, 305; Robert R. James, *Anthony Eden*, pp. 345, 352–53.

79. Acheson, *Present at the Creation*, p. 596.

80. Minutes of Truman-Churchill Talks, Third Session, 8 January 1952, box 116, General File, PSF.

81. NYT, 18 January 1952, 1:8.

82. Memorandum of conversation, 10 January 1952, FRUS, 1952–54, 14:1078–80; FO to U.K. Embassy Washington, 10 January 1952, FJ 10310/4, FO 371/99403.

83. Schonberger, *Aftermath of War*, pp. 275–77; Carlton, *Anthony Eden*, pp. 303–4. By his own account, Eden did not see or read the Yoshida letter before its publication nor understand the significance of Dulles's reference to it in Washington. Eden, *Full Circle*, pp. 20–22.

84. Koo Memoir, VII, D 377–79, 382.

85. Schonberger, "Peacemaking in Asia," pp. 71–72.

86. Niles Bond to DOS, 7 April 1952, FRUS, 1952–54, 14:1234–35.

87. Yoshitsu, *Japan and the San Francisco Peace Settlement*, pp. 78–83.

88. "Conclusion of the Sino-Japanese Treaty," 7 May 1952, box 34, CA, 1948–56.

89. E. H. Jacobs-Larkcom to FO, 7 May 1952, FJ 10310, FO 371/99405.

Chapter Five

1. Rankin to DOS, 25 June 1951, 793.00/6-2551.

2. Rankin to DOS, 25 June 1951, 793.00/7-1951; Rankin to Maj. Gen. William

Chase, 9 October 1951, box 16, Rankin Papers; Office of the Chief, Army Section, MAAG Formosa, to Chief, MAAG Formosa, 17 September 1951, box 89, G-3.

3. Making no secret that he believed he deserved the rank of ambassador, Rankin also contended that his promotion would signal American confidence in the Nationalist government. Rankin to Allison, 2 August 1952, box 19, Rankin Papers. Acheson was, however, reluctant to ask for the resignation of Ambassador John Leighton Stuart, whose health was precarious. Memorandum of discussion, 24 July 1952, box 67, Acheson Papers.

4. Rankin, *China Assignment*, pp. 126–27.

5. Rankin to Rusk, 24 November 1951, box 16, Rankin Papers.

6. Rankin Diary, 9 September 1951, Rankin Papers.

7. Jacoby, *U.S. Aid to Taiwan*, pp. 71–84; Ho, "Economics," p. 237; Ravenholt, "Formosa Today," pp. 616–17.

8. Ho, "Economics," pp. 233–36, 241; Ravenholt, "Formosa Today," p. 618.

9. Rusk to R. Allen Griffin, 19 March 1951, FRUS, 1951, 7:1596–97.

10. Acheson to U.S. Embassy Taipei, 13 July 1951, ibid., pp. 1750–51.

11. Merchant to Cabot, 13 August 1951, 893.10/8-351; Rankin to DOS, 7 August 1951, 793.00/8-751.

12. Rankin to DOS, 13 October 1951, FRUS, 1951, 7:1832–33; Acheson to U.S. Embassy Taipei, 24 October 1951, ibid., p. 1837; Rankin to DOS, 31 October 1951, ibid., p. 1841.

13. Rankin to DOS, 9 January 1953, 794A.5-MSP/1-953; A. Guy Hope to Walter McConaughy, 12 January 1953, 893.00/1-1253.

14. Memorandum of conversation, 30 August 1951, included with Barnett to Allison, 1 February 1952, 611.94A/1-1152; McConaughy to Allison, 16 December 1952, box 2, Economic Affairs, 1948–58, FEA.

15. Chase, *Front Line General*, pp. 163–65; a capsule biography appeared in NYT, 21 April 1951, 1:4.

16. Chase, *Front Line General*, pp. 169–70.

17. Memorandum of conversation, 30 August 1951, attached to Barnett to Allison, 1 February 1952, 611.94A/2-1152.

18. Barnett to Rusk, 3 October 1951, FRUS, 1951, 7:1820; Report on Military Advisory and Assistance Program for Formosa, 13 June 1952, FRUS, 1952–54, 14:67.

19. Chase, *Front Line General*, p. 178.

20. Ibid., p. 180.

21. Memorandum of conversation, 30 August 1951, attached to Barnett to Allison, 1 February 1952, 611.94A/2-1152; Chase, *Front Line General*, p. 181.

One of the effects of the political commissar system was to circumscribe the authority of Gen. Sun Li-jen, who remained an American favorite. An outspoken proponent of military and political reform, Sun was particularly critical of this system. The general eventually lost all power on Taiwan. In 1954 he was removed from his post as commander in chief of the army and appointed personal chief of staff to Chiang Kai-shek, a position without any real responsibility. In August 1955 he was relieved of that post after charges were laid against him in connection with the activities of a trusted subordinate who confessed to being a Communist agent. In October, a commission of inquiry judged him guilty of gross negligence. Spared any further punishment, he was not reappointed to any other position. A U.S. diplomatic representative in Taipei, reflecting a widespread suspicion in American official circles, speculated that the entire affair was a "put-up job" to strip Sun of all remaining authority and influence. "Sun Li-jen and 'Authoritarianism' in the GRC," 22 September 1955, box 1, Miscellaneous Subject Files, 1951–54, FEA; William Cochran, Jr., to McConaughy, 7 September 1955, box 53, CA, 1948–56; Koo Memoir, VII, K 305–6.

22. Chase, *Front Line General*, p. 175; Rankin to DOS, 4 February 1952, FRUS, 1952–54, 14:4–5.

23. Rankin to DOS, 9 January 1953, 794A.5/1-953.

24. Chase, *Front Line General*, p. 175.

25. Summary of Problems Related to China Policy, 20 November 1952, box 33, CA, 1948–56; memorandum, 20 March 1953, box 4, Miscellaneous Subject Files, 1951–54, FEA.

26. Memorandum, 20 March 1953, box 4, Miscellaneous Subject Files, 1951–54, FEA.

27. NSC 48/5, "United States Objectives, Policies and Courses of Action in Asia," 17 May 1951, FRUS, 1951, 6:38.

28. Martin to McConaughy, 2 September 1952, 611.94A/9-252.

29. Rankin to Perkins, 23 June 1952, 794A.00/6-2352. Rankin's tolerant view of political conditions on Taiwan was not shared by an unidentified prominent Nationalist official who secretly visited the Office of Chinese Affairs in October 1952. Warning that the power of Chiang Ching-kuo was on the rise and that his reactionary views and high-handed methods had alienated not just the Taiwanese but some mainland functionaries, he claimed that the U.S. mission was not in a position to construct an accurate picture of the political situation because its representatives dealt professionally only with National authorities who were either pro–Chiang Kai-shek and pro–Chiang Ching-kuo or were frightened into appearing so. Memorandum of conversation, 8 October 1952, box 35, CA, 1948–56.

30. Jacobs-Larkcom to Shattock, 2 November 1951, FC 1018/88, FO 371/92210; Ravenholt, "Formosa Today," pp. 620–22.

31. Following an unofficial week-long visit to Taiwan in the fall of 1952, the Australian minister to the Philippines concluded that the "Nationalist regime as it exists in Formosa to-day is a vastly improved regime from what it was reputed to be when it had control of the mainland." Dispatch of Australian minister, 22 September 1952, file 2, 50056-A-40, DEA.

32. Allison, *Ambassador from the Prairie*, p. 208.

33. Koo to Yeh, 16 May 1952, box 169, Koo Papers.

34. Memoranda of conversations, 20 October 1952 and 12 November 1952, box 187, ibid. No doubt exemplifying the positive newspaper opinion to which Acheson made reference in his meeting with Koo, the *New York Times* editorialized shortly beforehand that "Formosa is blooming into a garden spot in the troubled Far East. Though many problems are still to be ironed out, it is being well-governed by a popular government." NYT, 10 October 1952, 24:2.

35. NIE 25, 2 August 1951, FRUS, 1951, 1:123; NIE 27/1, 1 April 1952, FRUS, 1952–54, 14:23–25.

36. While naval patrol vessels ventured no closer than twelve miles to Chinese territory, surveillance aircraft sometimes penetrated Communist air space, drawing antiaircraft fire and sometimes attacks by MIG-15 jets. Marolda, "U.S. Navy and the Chinese Civil War," pp. 308–10.

37. Field, *History of United States Naval Operations*, p. 442; FRUS, 1952–54, 14:79 n. 1.

38. The show of force took place in the midst of an escalated air war in Korea begun a month earlier with the first bombing of North Korean power plants along the Yalu River. Kaufman, *Korean War*, pp. 276–77.

39. NYT, 14 March 1952, 1:4; Marolda, "U.S. Navy and the Chinese Civil War," pp. 301–2.

40. Radford, *From Pearl Harbor to Vietnam*, pp. 247, 249–50, 255; memorandum of conversation, 12 June 1952, box 187, Koo Papers.

41. Briefing Paper, 26 February 1953, box 3, Miscellaneous Subject Files, 1951–54, FEA; Marolda, "U.S. Navy and the Chinese Civil War," pp. 263–65.

42. Martin to McConaughy, 2 September 1952, 611.94A/9-252.

43. Rankin to Acheson, 11 April 1952, FRUS, 1952–54, 14:42–43.

44. Acheson to U.S. Embassy Taipei, 9 May 1952, ibid., pp. 49–50.

45. Chase, *Front Line General*, p. 197.

46. For an example of Chiang's views, see "Report of Discussions between Gen. Frank Merrill and Generalissimo Chiang Kai-shek," undated, enclosed in Allen Dulles to Allison, 4 April 1952, 611.94A/4-452.

47. Rankin to DOS, 25 April 1952, 793.00/4-2552.

48. CNO to JCS, 22 August 1952, CCS 381 Far East (11-28-50) Sec. 11, JCS, 1951–53.

49. Nonetheless, as historian Rosemary Foot has documented, the Nationalists were in a position to exert an indirect influence on progress toward a Korean armistice because of the Truman administration's insistence on nonforcible repatriation of prisoners of war, which was then the biggest roadblock to a Korean settlement. Conditions in the compounds for captured North Korean and Chinese soldiers badly compromised the policy of nonforcible repatriation by making it nearly impossible for POWs to decide freely whether or not to return to their homelands. The majority of Chinese POWs were in pro-Nationalist compounds dominated by POW "trusties" who were typically ex-KMT army officers drafted into the People's Liberation Army. With the acquiescence or approval of camp administrators, some of them from Taiwan, these trusties exercised control by means of misinformation, terror, and control of essential supplies. As well, instructors recruited from Taiwan and selected by the Nationalist Ministry of Defense were involved in a psychological warfare program for prisoners. The anti-Communist compounds were in close contact with the Nationalist government.

Screening of Chinese POWs by the UN Command indicated that only one-quarter wanted to return to China, and Taipei let it be known that Chinese nonrepatriates were welcome on Taiwan. Chinese Communist negotiators at Panmunjom thus faced a situation where many Chinese prisoners would reject repatriation and choose the despised Nationalist regime instead. This unpalatable prospect made nonforcible repatriation hard for the PRC to accept and contributed to the lack of progress at the armistice talks at Panmunjom. Foot, *Substitute for Victory*, pp. 87–102, 108–21, 124–29.

It is safe to assume that the PRC's predicament gratified Chiang, who had ample cause to want to prolong a war that had already proven a boon to him and that might yet offer still more rewards. Even if an armistice did transpire, he could anticipate a propaganda coup if his mainland enemy accepted nonforcible repatriation and large numbers of Chinese POWs opted for Taiwan.

50. Foot, *Wrong War*, chap. 6.

51. Short, *Origins of the Vietnam War*, pp. 87, 92–96, 104, 109.

52. Foot, *Wrong War*, pp. 189–90.

53. China Telegram, 14–20 February 1952, POS.

54. NYT, 7 February 1952, 8:4.

55. Brendon, *Ike, His Life and Times*, pp. 217, 222, 226.

56. Lovett to Acheson, 1 November 1951, FRUS, 1951, 7:1841–45.

57. Poole, 1950–1952, pp. 407–8; JCS to Lovett, 4 March 1952, FRUS, 1952–54, 14:15–18. E. J. Kahn, Jr., has claimed from personal knowledge that at the end of 1951 the CIA was preparing to construct a secret installation on Saipan to train Nationalist forces for an invasion of the mainland. Kahn, *China Hands*, p. 240.

58. Report on Military Advisory and Assistance Program for Formosa, 13 June 1952, FRUS, 1952–54, 14:69.

59. Memorandum of conversation, 27 December 1951, box 184, Koo Papers.

60. Paper prepared by John Foster Dulles, 30 November 1950, FRUS, 1950, 6:162–64.

61. NYT, 17 February 1952, 63:1, 16 March 1952, 3:7.

62. Allison, *Ambassador from the Prairie*, pp. 177–80.

63. Conversation with John Allison, 4 January 1952, box 227, Judd Papers.

64. Kahn, *China Hands*, pp. 212–44; Koen, *China Lobby in American Politics*, pp. 173–90; Acheson, *Present at the Creation*, pp. 573–75.

65. JCS to Lovett, 4 March 1952, FRUS, 1952–54, 14:15–18.

66. NSC 128, 22 March 1952, ibid., pp. 20–21.

67. Summary of discussion, 114th NSC Meeting, 2 April 1952, ibid., pp. 26–27. State Department officials who had scrutinized NSC 128 before the meeting had been puzzled by what the JCS had in mind. Were the chiefs recommending that the Seventh Fleet no longer restrain Nationalist incursions against the mainland? That the United States beef up the "military potential" of Nationalist forces with a view to their early employment against the mainland? That the United States now commit itself to the return of the Nationalists to their lost territory? If so, such recommendations obviously involved "serious policy issues." Acheson's advisers warned that, even though Nationalist forces were now incapable of major operations across the Taiwan Strait, they could, if the Seventh Fleet no longer stood in their way, cause enough disturbance to provoke a major Chinese Communist reaction. The Nationalists would not be averse to provoking hostilities between the United States and China in order to advance their goal of mainland recovery. Nitze to Acheson, 1 April 1952, box 33, CA, 1948–56.

68. In a conversation with China Office director Walter McConaughy in the fall, Acheson opined that the moment was inopportune for deneutralization because it might alienate the UN allies whose support was badly needed in the General Assembly on the Korean issue. McConaughy replied that the time might be ripe to

review the question after the adjournment of the assembly. Memorandum of conversation, 20 October 1952, 793.00/10-2052.

69. Memorandum of substance of discussion, 9 April 1952, FRUS, 1952–54, 14: 31–42.

70. The participants in the meeting did instruct a working group of senior NSC staff members to study long-range measures to preserve Taiwan as an "asset." This group appears never to have completed a report. Ibid., p. 54 n. 1.

71. MAAG Program for Formosa, 13 June 1952, FRUS, 1952–54, 14:69; Rearden, *The Formative Years*, p. 184.

72. JSPC 752/19, 24 April 1952, CCS 381 Far East (11-28-50) Sec. 14, JCS, 1951–53; JSPC to JCS, 2 May 1952, ibid., Sec. 15; Schnabel and Watson, *The Korean War*, p. 857.

73. NSC 124/2, 25 June 1952, FRUS, 1952–54, 12:125–34.

74. Marolda, "U.S. Navy and the Chinese Civil War," pp. 291–92, 297–98.

75. Report of discussion between Gen. Frank Merrill and Generalissimo Chiang Kai-shek, undated, enclosed in Allen Dulles to Allison, 4 April 1952, 611.94A/4-452; Rankin to DOS, 27 October 1952, 793.001/10-2752.

76. Mark W. Clark, *From the Danube to the Yalu*, pp. 68–75, 79–82, 117; Blair, *Forgotten War*, p. 969.

77. Schnabel and Watson, *The Korean War*, pp. 857–58.

78. JCS to Lovett, 5 August 1952, CD 092 (Korea) June–August 1952, box 318, OSD, 1952.

79. Schnabel and Watson, *The Korean War*, pp. 860–61.

80. Memorandum for the record, 14 August 1952, CD 092 (Korea) June–August 1952, box 318, OSD, 1952; Truman, *Years of Trial and Hope*, p. 463.

81. Memorandum for the record, 14 August 1952, CD 092 (Korea) June–August 1952, box 318, OSD, 1952; memorandum of discussion, DOS-DOD Meeting, 19 August 1952, FRUS, 1952–54, 14:89–90; memorandum of conversation, 20 October 1952, 793.00/10-2052.

82. Memorandum of discussion, 24 September 1952, FRUS, 1952–54, 15:537–38.

83. Memorandum for the record, 14 August 1952, CD 092 (Korea) June–August 1952, box 318, OSD, 1952; memorandum of discussion, DOS-DOD Meeting, 19 August 1952, FRUS, 1952–54, 14:88–94.

84. Memorandum for the secretary of state, [23 August 1952], CD 092 (Korea) June–August 1952, OSD, 1952.

85. Martin to McConaughy, 2 September 1952, 611.94A/9-252.

Chapter Six

1. Hoopes, *Devil and John Foster Dulles*, chap. 9; Caridi, *Korean War and American Politics*, pp. 224–45.

2. Memorandum of conversation, 2 January 1953, box 187, Koo Papers.

3. Memorandum of conversation [Dulles and Koo], 2 January 1953, ibid.

4. Extract, State of the Union Message, 2 February 1953, FRUS, 1952–54, 14:140.

5. Rankin, *China Assignment*, p. 159; Rankin Diary, 3 September 1951, Rankin Papers.

6. Koo Diary, 9 March 1953, Koo Papers.

7. Hoopes, *Devil and John Foster Dulles*, pp. 146–47, 153–54; Tucker, "A House Divided," pp. 37–41.

8. Watson, *1953–1954*, p. 15; Hoopes, *Devil and John Foster Dulles*, p. 194.

9. For Eisenhower and Dulles's views on Asia, China, and Chiang Kai-shek, see Tucker, "John Foster Dulles," pp. 236–39; Gordon H. Chang, *Friends and Enemies*, pp. 80–88, 170–174; Gaddis, "American 'Wedge Strategy,'" pp. 167–75; introduction to *Great Powers in East Asia*, ed. Cohen and Iriye, pp. 1–11.

The issue of who was in charge of foreign policy during the Eisenhower years has exercised scholars since the "Eisenhower revisionists" successfully demolished the myth that Dulles was the prime mover and the president little more than a figurehead. Scholars now assign Eisenhower a central role but have not agreed on the extent of Dulles's influence. My own research confirms Richard H. Immerman's conclusion that the two "were in a real sense a team." See introduction to *Dulles and the Diplomacy of the Cold War*, ed. Immerman, p. 9. The literature generated by Eisenhower revisionism is too large to cite here. Useful reviews of this scholarship are McMahon, "Eisenhower and Third World Nationalism," pp. 453–73; Joes, "Eisenhower Revisionism," pp. 283–96; Burk, "Eisenhower Revisionism Revisited," pp. 196–209; Rabe, "Eisenhower Revisionism," pp. 97–115.

10. Kusnitz, *Public Opinion and Foreign Policy*, p. 63.

11. Reinhard, *Republican Right since 1945*, pp. 108, 115–17, 125–29; Reichard, *Reaffirmation of Republicanism*, chap. 3.

12. Hoopes, *Devil and John Foster Dulles*, pp. 148–49, 152–56, 160; Brands, *Cold Warriors*, pp. 3, 7–9, 13.

13. Rourke, *Congress and the Presidency*, pp. 83–93; Nelson, "Dulles and the Bipartisan Congress," pp. 43–64.

14. Oral History of U. Alexis Johnson, DOHC.

15. Memorandum of conversation, 15 March 1952, file 2, 50293-40, DEA; "Formosan Decision," p. 30.

16. China Telegram, 29 January–4 February, 4–11 February 1953, POS; NYT, 3 February 1953, 1:7, 5 February 1953, 1:1, 7 February 1953, 1:2.

17. Foot, *Wrong War*, p. 209; Kaufman, *Korean War*, p. 305.

18. Eisenhower, *White House Years*, p. 123.

19. Memorandum of conversation, 15 February 1953, file 3, 50293-40, DEA. In private conversations with State Department advisers, Dulles observed that "to make more likely success both in Korea and in Indo-China it would be necessary to consider how the Formosa potential can be used to create uncertainty on the mainland of China." The deneutralization announcement was intended as a first step in this direction. "United States Foreign Policy," 3 February 1955, box 26, PPS, 1947–1953.

20. Arnold, *First Domino*, pp. 101, 114–15; Spector, *Advice and Support*, pp. 167–72.

21. NYT, 4 February 1953, 4:4.

22. Zhai, *The Dragon, the Lion, and the Eagle*, p. 128.

23. For Bradley's public statement, see NYT, 3 February 1953, 12:3; his "eyewash" comment was made to a member of the military staff in the British embassy. Canadian Embassy Washington to Pearson, 6 February 1953, file 3, 50293-40, DEA.

24. Memorandum of conversation, 30 January 1953, box 2, Miscellaneous Subject Files, FEA, 1951–54.

25. The official French response, for example, was restrained but not critical, while the Canadian was nonjudgmental and the Australian supportive. Foreign reaction was summarized in Allison to Dulles, 11 February 1953, 793.00/2-1153.

26. NYT, 2 February 1953, 5:1, 9 February 1953, 3:1.

27. For Eden's comments before the House of Commons, see *Parliamentary Debates*, 3 February and 5 February 1953, House of Commons, 5th ser., vol. 510 (1952–53), cols. 1672, 2058, 2062. London had first learned of the proposed announcement early in January when Dulles told Churchill. The Foreign Office subsequently let it be known at the State Department that the British government frowned on any alteration of the neutralization order. Excerpt from memorandum ("Formosa"), undated, *FRUS*, 1952–54, 14:126; memorandum of conversation, 28 January 1953, ibid., pp. 129–30.

28. Matthews to U.S. Embassy Taipei, 30 January 1953, *FRUS*, 1952–54, 14:132.

29. Statement by Chiang Kai-shek, 3 February 1953, box 145, Koo Papers; Koo Memoir, VII, F 35; Koo Diary, 8 March 1953, Koo Papers. The Nationalists airdropped two million leaflets over the mainland containing the passage in the State of the Union address announcing deneutralization. Allison to Dulles, 11 February 1955, 793.00/2-1153.

30. Schnabel and Watson, *The Korean War*, pp. 934–35.

31. Allison to Dulles, 24 December 1952, *FRUS*, 1952–54, 14:118–20.

32. Dulles to Eisenhower, 2 January 1953, ibid., pp. 125–26.

33. Clark, *From the Danube to the Yalu*, pp. 322–33.

34. NSC 147, "Analysis of Possible Courses of Action in Korea," 2 April 1953, *FRUS*, 1952–54, 15:838–50; Schnabel and Watson, *The Korean War*, pp. 928–34, 949, 952–54; Keefer, "Eisenhower and the End of the Korean War," pp. 277–79.

35. Charles Stelle to Matthews, 28 March 1953, 611.93/3-2853.

36. Excerpt from Dulles to Matthews, 4 April 1953, *FRUS*, 1952–54, 14:170 n. 2; memorandum of discussion, 139th NSC Meeting, 8 April 1953, ibid., pp. 180–82.

37. Jones to DOS, 23 April 1953, ibid., p. 193; editorial note, ibid., p. 194. The existence of the secret understanding was publicly revealed as a result of a press leak. Memorandum of conversation, 19 August 1953, ibid., pp. 245–46.

38. Memorandum of discussion, DOS-JCS Meeting, 27 March 1953, ibid., pp. 164–69; memorandum of discussion, DOS-JCS Meeting, 3 April 1953, ibid., pp. 170–72; JCS to CINCPAC (Radford), 6 April 1953, ibid., pp. 172–75.

39. CINCPAC to CHMAAG FORMOSA, 7 May 1953, CCS 381 Formosa (11-8-48) Sec. 10, JCS, 1951–53.

40. NSC 154/1, "United States Tactics Immediately Following an Armistice in Korea," 7 July 1953, *FRUS*, 1952–54, 15:1341–44.

41. Chiang Kai-shek to Eisenhower, 15 April 1953, ibid., pp. 188–89; Chiang Kai-shek to Eisenhower, 7 June 1953, ibid., pp. 203–4; Jones to DOS, 24 June 1953, ibid., p. 213.

42. Kaufman, *Korean War*, pp. 326–32.

43. Dulles to Rankin, 24 June 1953, *FRUS*, 1952–54, 14:214.

44. Memorandum of conversation, 29 June 1953, ibid., p. 216.

45. Koo Memoir, VII, F 227–29.

46. Memorandum of conversation, 1 July 1953, *FRUS*, 1952–54, 14:223; excerpt from Rankin to Robertson, 18 January 1954, ibid., p. 349 n. 3.

47. Watson, 1953–1954, pp. 203–8.

48. Memorandum of conversation, 1 June 1953, FRUS, 1952–54, 14:199–201.

49. Rankin, *China Assignment*, p. 172. In an August 1953 dispatch examining the "Prerequisites to a Return to the Chinese Mainland," Rankin suggested that over the next year the United States increase from twenty-one to thirty-six the number of divisions it financed directly. This would, he argued, lift the morale of the Nationalists and afford sufficient offensive power for a variety of options, including major military campaigns south of the Yangtze River. Rankin to DOS, 20 August 1953, 793.00/8-2053.

50. NSC 146/2, "United States Objectives and Courses of Action with Respect to Formosa and the Chinese National Government," 6 November 1953, FRUS, 1952–54, 14:307–8.

51. Gaddis, *Strategies of Containment*, chaps. 5–6; Kinnard, *Eisenhower and Strategy Management*, pp. 1–10, 23–25; Weigley, *American Way of War*, pp. 399–402.

52. Memorandum of discussion, 169th NSC Meeting, 5 November 1953, FRUS, 1952–54, 14:273–77.

53. Memorandum of conversation, 19 March 1953, box 187, Koo Papers.

54. Dobbs, *Unwanted Symbol*, pp. 171–74.

55. Koo Memoir, VII, F 224–25, H 50–62.

56. Memorandum of conversation, 21 August 1952, FRUS, 1952–54, 12:212; NSC Staff Study on NSC 146/2, 6 November 1953, FRUS, 1952–54, 14:315.

57. Rankin to DOS [Yeh to Nixon], 19 December 1953, FRUS, 1952–54, 14:344–45.

58. Rankin to DOS, 19 December 1953, ibid., pp. 343–44.

59. Matthews to U.S. Embassy Taipei, 6 February 1953, ibid., pp. 145–46.

60. He, "Evolution of the People's Republic of China's Policy," p. 223; Li, "Chinese Intentions," p. 48.

61. Summary of CINCPAC to CNO, 26 June 1953, FRUS, 1952–54, 14:227 n. 2.

62. Summary of DOS to U.S. Embassy Taipei, 26 July 1953, ibid., p. 232 n. 2.

63. CINCPAC (Stump) to CNO, 23 July 1953, ibid., pp. 237–38.

64. Rankin to DOS, 22 July 1953, FRUS, 1952–54, 14:233–35; Rankin to DOS, 24 July 1953, 793.00/7-2453.

65. U. Alexis Johnson to Walter Bedell Smith, 3 August 1953, FRUS, 1952–54, 14:240–41.

66. Summary of JCS to CINCPAC, 23 September 1953, ibid., p. 238 n. 3.

67. Rankin to DOS, 19 July 1953, 793.00/7-1553; for Chase's views, see memorandum of conversation, 20 July 1953, 794A./7-2053 (released to author through FOI).

68. Charles E. Wilson to Dulles, 7 December 1953, FRUS, 1952–54, 14:339–40.

69. Dulles to Wilson, 17 August 1953, ibid., p. 244.

70. Sebald to DOS, 3 September 1953, FRUS, 1952–54, 12:29; McCoy, *Politics of Heroin*, pp. 131–32; Kenneth Ray Young, "Nationalist Chinese Troops in Burma," pp. 66–67. CIA aircraft supplying Li Mi's forces during Operation Paper had transported opium on their outbound flights from Mong Hsat, the main KMT base in Burma. Lintner, "CIA's First Secret War," pp. 57–58.

71. Kenneth Ray Young, "Nationalist Chinese Troops in Burma," pp. 60–63, 80–81; Clubb, "Effect of Chinese Nationalist Military Activities in Burma," pp. 38–39.

72. Memorandum, "Chinese Nationalist Irregular Troops in Burma," 8 April 1953, box 4, FEA, 1953; Burma Diary, pp. 92, 103–4, 153, 202, Sebald Papers.

73. Sebald to DOS, 19 March 1953, FRUS, 1952–54, 12:77; Burma Diary, p. 150, Sebald Papers.

74. Allison to Bruce, 18 November 1953, FRUS, 1952–54, 12:36–39.

75. Matthews to U.S. Embassy Taipei, 30 January 1953, ibid., pp. 48–49.

76. Dulles to U.S. Embassy Taipei, 19 February 1953, ibid., p. 53; Dulles to U.S. Embassy Taipei, 24 February 1953, ibid., pp. 58–59; Dulles to U.S. Embassy Taipei, 27 February 1953, ibid., p. 60; Dulles to U.S. Embassy Taipei, 4 March 1953, ibid., pp. 63–64.

77. Koo Diary, 10 March 1953, Koo Papers; Koo Memoir, VII, F 282.

78. Rankin to DOS, 22 February 1953, FRUS, 1952–54, 12:56–58.

79. Rankin to DOS, 12 March 1953, ibid., p. 70.

80. Dulles to U.S. Embassy Taipei, 13 March 1953, ibid., p. 72; excerpt from DOS to U.S. Embassy Taipei, 18 March 1953, ibid., p. 73 n. 3.

81. Summary of U.S. Embassy Taipei to DOS, 27 March 1953, ibid., p. 85 n. 2; Dulles to U.S. Embassy Rangoon, 27 March 1953, ibid., pp. 85–86.

82. Kenneth Ray Young, "Nationalist Chinese Troops in Burma," p. 93.

83. "Chinese Nationalist Irregular Troops in Burma," 8 April 1953, box 4, FEA, 1953. Columnists Joseph and Stewart Alsop disclosed in a story on 11 February 1953 that the CIA had supported an attempted invasion of Yunnan by Li Mi's forces in the summer of 1951. FRUS, 1952–54, 12:52 n. 4.

84. U.K. UN Delegation to Foreign Office, 22 April 1953, FB 1041/106, FO 371/106687; Kenneth Ray Young, "Nationalist Chinese Troops in Burma," pp. 110–11. Though officially uninformed, the British had known for some time about American clandestine operations in Burma.

85. Kenneth Ray Young, "Nationalist Chinese Troops in Burma," pp. 113–24.

86. U.S. Embassy Taipei to DOS, 25 May 1953, FRUS, 1952–54, 12:105–6; U.S. Embassy Taipei to DOS, 8 June 1953, 793.00/6-853.

87. Sebald to DOS, 24 July 1953, FRUS, 1952–54, 12:120; Sebald to DOS, 31 August 1953, ibid., p. 131.

88. Kenneth Ray Young, "Nationalist Chinese Troops in Burma," p. 126; Clubb, "Effect of Chinese Nationalist Military Activities in Burma," p. 32.

89. Eisenhower to Chiang Kai-shek, 28 February 1953, FRUS, 1952–54, 12:152–53.

90. The full text of Chiang's reply to Eisenhower on 9 October is printed in Koo Memoir, VII, G 141–42.

91. Sebald to DOS, 13 October 1953, FRUS, 1952–54, 12:159.

92. Memorandum of conversation, 24 November 1953, box 187, Koo Papers.

93. Sebald to DOS, 23 November 1953, FRUS, 1952–54, 12:173.

94. Rankin to William Donovan, 25 November 1953, box 41, CA, 1948–56.

95. Recording that a limited removal of "foreign forces" had occurred (but not mentioning the KMT or Taiwan), the resolution registered concern that these troops had turned over few arms, and it urged further efforts toward evacuation and relinquishment of all weapons. UNGA, Eighth Session, 470th Meeting, 8 December 1953, pp. 447–49.

96. Kenneth Ray Young, "Nationalist Chinese Troops in Burma," pp. 134–36.

97. Ibid., chap. 6; Tucker, Taiwan, Hong Kong, and the United States, pp. 66–67.

98. Rankin to Donovan, 25 November 1953, box 41, CA, 1948–56.

99. Excerpt from U.S. Embassy Taipei to DOS, 6 April 1954, FRUS, 1952–54, 12:220 n. 1; Sebald to Philip Bonsal, 29 April 1954, ibid., p. 221.

100. Bacon to McConaughy, 26 May 1953, FRUS, 1952–54, 3:641–51; Dulles to U.S. Embassies in London and Paris, 12 June 1953, ibid., pp. 670–71; NSC 154, "United States Tactics Following an Armistice in Korea," 15 June 1953, FRUS, 1952–54, 15:1173.

101. Bacon to McConaughy, 26 May 1953, FRUS, 1952–54, 3:644; Koo Memoir, VII, F 122–23, 165; memorandum of conversation, 29 July 1953, box 187, Koo Papers.

102. Gallup, *The Gallup Poll*, 2:1153.

103. NYT, 9 April 1953, 1:6; memorandum of telephone conversation, 9 April 1953, box 2, chronological series, John Foster Dulles File — Eisenhower Library, SML. Originating in a background interview given by Dulles, the *New York Times* story was seen in some quarters as a trial balloon. Dulles reacted angrily to the story, contending that its author had misconstrued his casual remark that the UN had considered a trusteeship for Taiwan in the past and might again in the future. There is no collateral evidence that the secretary of state or anyone else in the State Department was then actively examining a trusteeship. Telephone conversation regarding *New York Times* story, 9 April 1953, box 1, Telephone Call Series, Dulles Papers (DDEL).

104. Ambrose, *The President*, p. 99.

105. Eisenhower to Dulles, 2 June 1953, FRUS, 1952–54, 3:656.

106. Press and Radio News Conference, 20 October 1953, box 68, J. F. Dulles Papers (SML); FRUS, 1952–54, 14:330 n. 4.

107. Notes of a conference, 7 June 1953, box 1, Subject Series, Dulles Papers (DDEL). The dual representation idea appears to have originated with Dean Rusk. Synder, "Dean Rusk to John Foster Dulles," pp. 84–86.

108. NSC 154, "United States Tactics Following an Armistice in Korea," 15 June 1953, FRUS, 1952–54, 15:1170–73.

109. Brief for the U.K. Delegation, "Korea and Other Far Eastern Problems," Cabinet, Preparations for Meetings of Commonwealth Prime Ministers, GEN 433/7 (Revise), 26 May 1953, CAB 130/86; Churchill to Jebb, 2 May 1953, FC 10345/6, FO 371/105221.

110. Porter, *Britain and the Rise of Communist China*, pp. 64–65, 130–31.

111. Minutes of Meetings and Memoranda, Meeting of Commonwealth Prime Ministers, June 1953, CAB 133/135.

112. Seldon, *Churchill's Indian Summer*, pp. 396–404; Fish, "After Stalin's Death," pp. 333–55.

113. "United Nations General Assembly, Chinese Representation," 4 September 1955, C. (53) 247, CAB 129/62.

114. Position Paper, "Question of Chinese Representation," 29 August 1953, FRUS, 1952–54, 3:692; Winthrop Aldrich to DOS, 2 September 1953, ibid., pp. 694–95; Dulles to U.S. Embassy London, 11 September 1953, ibid., p. 703.

115. Second Restricted Tripartite Meeting, Heads of Governments, 7 December 1953, FRUS, 1952–54, 5:1808–10, 1814–15.

116. Memorandum by the secretary of state for Foreign Affairs, Policy in the Far East, 24 November 1953, C. (53) 330, CAB 129/64.

117. Eisenhower, *White House Years*, p. 249.

118. Memorandum of conversation, 23 January 1953, *FRUS, 1952–54*, 3:719.

119. NSC 162/2, "Basic National Security Policy," 30 October 1953, *FRUS, 1952–54*, 2:580–82.

120. NSC 166/1, "U.S. Policy towards Communist China," 6 November 1953, *FRUS, 1952–54*, 14:279–306.

121. NSC 146/2, "United States Objectives and Courses of Action with Respect to Formosa and the Chinese Nationalist Government," 6 November 1953, ibid., pp. 307–30; NSC Staff Study on NSC 146/2, 6 November 1953, ibid., pp. 311–30; Howard Jones to DOS, 18 June 1953, ibid., p. 206; Johnson to Dulles, 3 July 1953, 793.00/6-2053.

122. Rankin to DOS, 22 December 1953, 793.00/12-2253.

Chapter Seven

1. For the Eisenhower administration's policies in Indochina in 1953–54, see Anderson, *Trapped by Success*, chaps. 2–4; Billings-Yun, *Decision against War*; Kaplan, Artaud, and Rubin, *Dien Bien Phu*.

2. Memorandum of conversation, 24 March 1954, *FRUS, 1952–54*, 14:396; memorandum of conversation, 19 May 1954, *FRUS, 1952–54*, 13:1584.

3. A failed assault in July 1953 by 5,000 commandos and paratroopers against the Communist-held island of Tungshan, about 50 miles northeast of Swatow, resulted in a virtual suspension of forays against the south China coast. NYT, 8 February 1954, 5:2–3. The CIA as well as top civilian and military authorities in the Taiwan embassy were in agreement that the raids had been largely unsuccessful. Memorandum of conversation, 6 November 1953, box 110, Rankin Papers.

4. Koo Memoir, VII, G 97–98.

5. Director, Strategic Plans Division, to CNO, 21 July 1954, EG-16, box 306, Strategic Plans Division Records, Nav Hist Center; Secretary of Navy to Secretary of Defense, 6 April 1955, ibid.

6. NSC 5405, "United States Objectives and Courses of Action with Respect to Southeast Asia," 16 January 1954, *FRUS, 1952–54*, 12:374.

7. Ferrell, *Diary of James C. Hagerty*, p. 15; memorandum by assistant staff secretary to the president, [undated], *FRUS, 1952–54*, 13:1024.

8. Historical Division of the Joint Secretariat, *History of the Indochina Incident*, vol. 1, pp. 420–21.

9. Draft of message to State Department, 22 April 1954, box 23, Rankin Papers.

10. U.S. Embassy Taipei to DOS, 15 June 1954, 793.00/6-1554.

11. Yeh to Radford, 4 January 1954, enclosed in Rankin to DOS, 8 March 1954, 794A.5-MSP/3-854. The Kai plan called for the creation by the end of 1955 of a strategic force of forty-one divisions, an air force to include 500 jet fighters and bombers, and a navy to include fourteen large transport ships and a tripling of the existing number of destroyers and destroyer escorts. Rinden to DOS, 12 January 1954, 794A.5-MSP/1-1254.

12. Yeh to Radford, 23 March 1954, box 169, Koo Papers. The twenty-four divisions were to be maintained at only 80 percent of authorized strength and would be supplemented with reserves once actual mobilization began.

13. JCS 1966/86, 31 August 1954, CCS 381 Formosa (11-8-48) Sec. 15, JCS, 1954–56; Watson, 1953–1954, p. 260.

14. Watson, 1953–1954, pp. 258–59; JCS 2099/381, Report by the Ad Hoc Committee on Programs for Military Assistance, 2 June 1954, 092 (8-22-96) Sec. 11, JCS, 1954–56.

15. Watson, 1953–1954, pp. 236, 250, 260; Report of the Van Fleet Mission to the Far East, 26 April–7 August 1954, submitted to the president on 4 October 1954, box 2, Presidential Subseries, Special Assistant Series, Office of the Special Assistant for National Security Affairs, WHO; Robertson to Dulles, 25 October 1954, FRUS, 1952–54, 12:953–55.

16. FRUS, 1952–54, 12:955 n. 4.

17. Annex to NSC 5441, "U.S. Policy toward Formosa and the Government of the Republic of China," 28 December 1954, FRUS, 1952–54, 14:1054–55.

18. Memorandum of discussion, 186th NSC Meeting, 26 February 1954, FRUS, 1952–54, 7:1224–25.

19. NYT, 21 March 1954, 2:4.

20. "The Threat of a Red Asia," DSB 30 (12 April 1954): 539–42.

21. Koo Memoir, VII, H 4–5, 12, 28–29.

22. Gurtov, First Vietnam Crisis, pp. 128, 163; Hinton, Communist China in World Politics, p. 254.

23. Johnson with McAllister, Right Hand of Power, pp. 233–36.

24. Memorandum of conversation, 27 June 1954, UP 122/70, FO 371/112337.

25. Memorandum of conversation, 17 August 1954, box 1, White House Memoranda Series, Dulles Papers (DDEL).

26. The Foreign Office believed that not just Britain but a majority of UN members would oppose continuation of the moratorium until the Charter review and that the Soviet Union would veto any Charter amendment embodying a two-China arrangement. J. C. Ward to Pierson Dixon, 7 August 1954, UP 122/91, FO 371/1123338.

27. Jia, "Unmaterialized Rapprochement," pp. 165–69; China Telegram, 1–8 July 1954, POS.

28. NYT, 9 July 1954, 2:2–4.

29. Eisenhower's comment appears in the entry for 6 July 1954, Ferrell, Diary of James C. Hagerty, p. 84.

30. Eisenhower to Churchill, 8 July 1954, box 17, International Series, AWF; Churchill to Eisenhower, 9 July 1954, ibid.

31. Moran, Winston Churchill, pp. 576–78. For Anglo-American differences over Indochina, consult Warner, "Britain and the Crisis over Dien Bien Phu," and "From Geneva to Manila," pp. 55–167.

32. Denise Artaud, "France between the Indochina War and the European Defense Community," p. 263.

33. Memorandum of conversation, 18 August 1954, FRUS, 1952–54, 3:755.

34. Bacon to Robertson, 14 September 1954, ibid., pp. 785–86; memorandum of conversation, 14 September 1954, ibid., p. 786.

Although still unwilling to commit themselves to the moratorium for more than a limited time period, the British did accept new language in the resolution coauthored by them and the Americans and subsequently approved by the General Assembly. The revised language eliminated the word "postponement" that had been present in earlier resolutions—a modification proposed by the State Department at the behest of the Nationalist government, which found the concept of postponement offensive because it implied that the General Assembly was merely waiting for the opportune moment to seat the Communists. Ideally, the Nationalists would have preferred to meet the representation issue head on with a straight yes or no vote on a substantive resolution. The State Department saw more merit in deferment, however. Henry Cabot Lodge, Jr., to DOS, 16 August 1954, ibid., pp. 752–53; Cochran to DOS, 19 August 1954, ibid., pp. 757–60.

35. Memorandum of discussion, 216th NSC Meeting, 6 October 1954, FRUS, 1952–54, 12:932.

36. Jones to DOS, 24 February 1954, FRUS, 1952–54, 14:367; memorandum of conversation, 2 March 1954, box 154, Koo Papers.

37. Robertson to Dulles, 25 February 1954, FRUS, 1952–54, 14:367–68.

38. Memorandum for the file, 27 February 1954, ibid., pp. 368–70.

39. The Bureau of European Affairs, the Bureau of United Nations Affairs, and the Policy Planning Staff counseled that to start negotiations in advance of Geneva would sow discord with Britain and France and would hand the Soviets an issue to use for divisive and propagandistic purposes. The PPS also worried that a treaty might implicate the United States in the defense of the offshore islands. The Bureau of Near Eastern, South Asian, and African Affairs warned that a pact would further antagonize India, already alienated because of U.S. military aid to Pakistan. The Office of Philippine and Southeast Asian Affairs opined that a treaty would produce no significant benefits in its region and would offend neutralist opinion. Merchant to Robertson, 20 March 1954, 793.5/3-2054; David Wainhouse to Robertson, 23 March 1954, 793.5/3-2054; Robert Bowie to Robertson, 22 March 1954, 793.5/3-2054; Donald Kennedy to John Jernegan, 18 March 1954, 793.5/3-1854; Bonsal to McConaughy, 17 March 1954, 793.5/3-1754.

40. Memorandum of conversation, 19 May 1954, box 191, Koo Papers.

41. Memorandum of conversation, 30 April 1954, FRUS, 1952–54, 16:622; Eden to FO, 30 April 1954, FC 1042/1, FO 371/110231.

42. Warner, "From Geneva to Manila," pp. 149–63; Dingman, "Dulles and the Creation of the South-East Asia Treaty Organization," pp. 457–77.

43. Dulles to Everett Drumwright, 18 June 1954, 611.94A/6-1854.

44. Ambrose, *The President*, pp. 186–89, 202; Greenstein, *Hidden-Hand Presidency*, pp. 182–216.

45. For Judd's support for a treaty, see memorandum of telephone conversation, 24 February 1954, box 2, Telephone Call Series, Dulles Papers (DDEL). One reason that the China bloc did not agitate more vigorously for a treaty, as Knowland confided to Koo in July, was that this might stir a messy debate about the political situation on Taiwan. The California senator pointed out that there was much talk within the administration and in congressional circles about the existence of a police state on the island because of charges leveled by K. C. Wu, the former provincial governor. Memorandum of conversation, 14 July 1954, box 191, Koo Papers. Wu, who had resigned his post in 1953 and moved to the United States, had recently authored an article for *Look* magazine in which he detailed from his own personal experience

the system of political controls and indoctrination, secret police, and illegal activities overseen by Chiang Ching-kuo in the name of his father. Wu, "Your Money Has Built a Police State in Formosa," pp. 39–45. For Wu's own retrospective account of his estrangement from Chiang Kai-shek, consult "Reminiscences of Wu Kuo-chen," Chinese Oral History Project.

Wu's charges and his appeal for genuine political reform were bound to draw attention because he had been recognized as the outstanding advocate on Taiwan of democracy and cooperation with the U.S., had been popular with the American press and officialdom, and had for a time enjoyed a close relationship with the Generalissimo and Madame Chiang Kai-shek. Disturbed by Wu's exposé, Taipei tried to discredit his character and motives and to rebut his accusations. Koo Memoir, VII, H 158–60, 193. The ex-governor found few sympathizers among pro-Nationalist partisans who knew and once admired him. Judd to Richard Raines, 31 May 1954, box 252, Judd Papers; Knowland to R. G. McFarlane, 12 August 1954, Knowland Papers; Smith Diary, Smith Papers, 6 April, 8 April, 9 April, and 16 June 1954. The State Department maintained a self-professed "attitude of sympathetic silence" toward the entire matter; without implying agreement with Wu's indictment, it acknowledged that the Nationalist government needed to make more progress toward representative government. Progress Report on NSC 146/2, 14 July 1954, 237th NSC Meeting (released to author through FOI).

46. Robertson to Dulles, 25 August 1954, FRUS, 1952–54, 14:548–50.

47. MacArthur to Harold Waddell, 27 August 1954, ibid., p. 552; Jernegan to Robertson, 27 August 1954, ibid., p. 551; Bowie to Robertson, 27 August 1954, ibid., pp. 552–53; Merchant to Robertson, 30 August 1954, ibid., p. 553. The principal objections came from State Department Counselor Douglas MacArthur II and the Bureau of Near Eastern, South Asia, and African Affairs (which still fretted about adverse Indian opinion).

48. Smith to Robertson, 1 September 1954, ibid., p. 555.

49. Memorandum of telephone conversation, 20 August 1954, box 2, Telephone Call Series, Dulles Papers (DDEL).

50. Translation of Record of Conversation, 9 September 1954, 611.93/9-2154.

51. Rankin, China Assignment, p. 192; NIE 10-2-54, "Communist Courses of Action in Asia through Mid-1955," 15 March 1954, FRUS, 1952–54, 14:396.

52. Rankin to Drumwright, 20 February 1954, FRUS, 1952–54, 14:364; Rankin to Richard Berry, 21 April 1954, ibid., pp. 412–14.

53. Kalicki, Pattern of Sino-American Crises, pp. 126, 131; George and Smoke, Deterrence in American Foreign Policy, p. 277.

54. Li, "Chinese Intentions," p. 49; He, "Evolution of the People's Republic of China's Policy," pp. 223–24; Zhang, Deterrence and Strategic Culture, pp. 195–99.

55. Memorandum of discussion, 199th NSC Meeting, 27 May 1954, FRUS, 1952–54, 14:433.

56. Memorandum of conversation, 22 May 1954, ibid., pp. 428–29.

57. Drumwright to Dulles, 19 May 1954, 611.93/5-1754.

58. Memorandum of conversation, 22 May 1954, box 1, White House Memoranda Series, Dulles Papers (DDEL); memorandum of conversation, 22 May 1954, FRUS, 1952–54, 14:428–29; Robertson to Dulles, 19 August 1954, ibid., p. 542.

59. It is noteworthy that in authorizing periodic visits by the Seventh Fleet to the Tachens and other islands, the president consented to rules of military engagement that permitted carrier-based planes to strike in self-defense at the Chinese mainland if the fleet, while on routine patrol *"or if engaged in defending outlying islands against attack* [emphasis added]," were to clash with Chinese forces assaulting the islands. These rules represented a potential breach of the no-defense policy. Memorandum of conversation, 22 May 1954, FRUS, 1952–54, 14:429.

60. Memorandum of conversation, 1 July 1954, ibid., pp. 487–88.

61. Dulles outlined this strategy in a letter to Allison, 20 August 1954, ibid., pp. 545–46.

62. Robertson to Dulles, 19 August 1954, ibid., p. 541.

63. Ibid., p. 488 n. 5.

64. Memorandum of telephone conversation, 16 June 1954, ibid., pp. 472–74.

65. Schwartz to Bowie, 20 August 1954, ibid., pp. 543–44.

66. Dulles to U.S. Embassy Taipei, 5 August 1954, ibid., p. 519; Cochran to DOS, 16 August 1954, ibid., p. 524; Rankin to McConaughy, 13 September 1954, ibid., pp. 625–27.

67. Ibid., p. 505 n. 3; NYT, 26 July 1954, 1:3. The taut climate resulting from the *Tuapse* incident may have contributed to the shooting down of the airliner. Allen Dulles told the NSC that apparently a "trigger happy" pilot thought the downed plane had intended to bomb a Soviet tanker. Excerpt from memorandum of discussion of NSC meeting, 29 July 1954, FRUS, 1952–54, 14:512.

68. State Department Press Release No. 406, 26 July 1954, box 79, J. F. Dulles Papers (SML); FRUS, 1952–54, 14:511 n. 3.

69. Recalling the incident in later years, Admiral Radford related that, when asked by Secretary Dulles to send some carriers to the area, he had said, "Yes, we could put them in, but we are going to have some shooting there." "It's okay with me," Dulles had replied. It was also apparently all right with Eisenhower. Upon hearing news of the incident from the secretary, the president had exclaimed, "Well Foster, it didn't take long for something to happen over there, did it?" "John Foster Dulles and the Far East," pp. 12–13, Transcript of a Special Conference Meeting of the Advisory Committee of the Dulles History Project, 17 July 1964, DOHC; entry for 26 July 1954, Ferrell, *Diary of James C. Hagerty*, p. 98.

70. China Telegram, 22–28 July 1954, POS.

71. Stolper, "China, Taiwan, and the Offshore Islands," pp. 35–36.

72. My analysis of PRC policy toward Taiwan and the offshore islands during this period draws on the following: Jia, "Searching for Peaceful Coexistence," pp. 267–71; He, "Evolution of the People's Republic of China's Policy," pp. 225–26; Tsai, "Taiwan Straits Crises," p. 127; Stolper, "China, Taiwan, and the Offshore Islands," pp. 3–4, 10, 15–38; Lewis and Xue, *China Builds the Bomb*, pp. 21–22; Zhang, *Deterrence and Strategic Culture*, pp. 189–99; Chang and He, "Absence of War in the U.S.-China Confrontation over Quemoy and Matsu," pp. 1500–1524.

73. Zhang, *Deterrence and Strategic Culture*, p. 192.

74. Transcript of Press and Radio News Conference, 3 August 1954, box 79, J. F. Dulles Papers (SML); Stolper, "China, Taiwan, and the Offshore Islands," p. 40. The Bureau of Far Eastern Affairs did investigate the feasibility of a western Pacific pact

(Taiwan, South Korea, Japan, and the Philippines) following Dulles's press conference remark but concluded that most of the prospective members were opposed or unenthusiastic. Charlton Ogburn, Jr., to Drumwright, 12 August 1954, box 48, CA, 1948–56. Taipei, believing that such a pact was unattainable because of ill feeling toward Japan on the part of South Korea and the Philippines, proposed instead that Washington negotiate a series of trilateral pacts in which the United States together with Nationalist China would join in separate treaties with South Korea, the Philippines, and Japan respectively. Rankin to DOS, 24 May 1954, FRUS, 1952–54, 12:511–12.

75. Zhang, *Deterrence and Strategic Culture*, pp. 189–90, 194 (Mao quotation), 222–23; Li, "Chinese Intentions," pp. 49–52; Chang and He, "Absence of War in the U.S.-China Confrontation over Quemoy and Matsu," pp. 1507–10. Chang and He stress the essential difference in purpose between the shelling of Quemoy and the military campaign in the Tachens.

76. NSC 5429, "Review of U.S. Policy in the Far East," 4 August 1954, FRUS, 1952–54, 12:696–703.

77. JCS to Charles Wilson, 11 August 1954, ibid., pp. 719–23.

78. Memorandum of discussion, 18 August 1954, FRUS, 1952–54, 14:526–40.

79. President's News Conference, 17 August 1954, *Public Papers of the Presidents: Dwight D. Eisenhower, 1954*, p. 719.

80. NYT, 20 August 1954, 3:5.

81. Ibid., 25 August 1954, 1:1.

82. Eden to U.K. Embassy Washington, 30 August 1954, FC 1094/11, FO 371/110257.

83. Memorandum for the record, 31 August 1954, FRUS, 1952–54, 14:554–55.

Chapter Eight

1. Although Eisenhower administration officials most certainly viewed the 1954–55 confrontation as a "crisis," Chinese leaders apparently did not. Chang and He, "Absence of War in the U.S.-China Confrontation over Quemoy and Matsu," p. 1502 n. 5. My characterization of the encounter as a "crisis" is consistent with common usage in Western scholarship and with my own focus on American perceptions and actions.

2. SNIE 100-4-54, "The Situation with Respect to Certain Islands off the Coast of Mainland China," 4 September 1954, FRUS, 1952–54, 14:563–71; SNIE 100-4/1-54, "The Situation with Respect to the Nationalist Occupied Islands off the Coast of Mainland China," 10 September 1954, ibid., pp. 595–97; CIA Report No. 50318, "The Chinese Offshore Islands," 8 September 1954, box 9, International Series, AWF; memorandum of discussion, 215th NSC Meeting, 24 September 1954, FRUS, 1952–54, 14:659.

3. He, "Evolution of the People's Republic of China's Policy," p. 224; Li, "Chinese Intentions," pp. 45–46, 50–51; Zhang, *Deterrence and Strategic Culture*, p. 199.

4. Radford to Wilson, 2 September 1954, CCS 381 Far East (11-28-50) Sec. 22, JCS, 1954–56.

5. Memorandum of discussion, 213th NSC Meeting, 9 September 1954, FRUS, 1952–54, 14:585–95.

6. Radford to Wilson, 2 September 1954, CCS 381 Far East (11-28-50) Sec. 22, JCS,

1954–56; Ridgway to Deputy Secretary of Defense, 3 September 1954, ibid.; memorandum of discussion, 213th NSC Meeting, 9 September 1954, FRUS, 1952–54, 14:590.

7. Ambrose, *The President*, p. 23; Kinnard, *Eisenhower and Strategy Management*, pp. 20–21.

8. Memorandum of discussion, 213th NSC Meeting, 9 September 1954, FRUS, 1952–54, 14:586–93.

9. Dulles to Smith, 4 September 1954, ibid., p. 560; Dulles to Smith, 5 September 1954, ibid., p. 572.

10. Memorandum of telephone conversation, 6 September 1954, ibid., pp. 573–74; Smith to Dulles, 6 September 1954, ibid., p. 574.

11. China Telegram, 2–8, 9–15 September 1954, POS.

12. Radford to Wilson, 11 September 1954, FRUS, 1952–54, 14:598–610.

13. Brands, *Cold Warriors*, p. 117.

14. Memorandum of discussion, 214th NSC Meeting, 12 September 1954, FRUS, 1952–54, 14:616–18.

15. Ibid., pp. 615–18, 621.

16. Ibid., pp. 619–22.

17. Dulles memorandum, 12 September 1954, ibid., p. 612.

18. Ulam, *Expansion and Coexistence*, pp. 554–55; Sutter, *China-Watch*, pp. 40–43.

19. Memorandum of discussion, 216th NSC Meeting, 6 October 1954, FRUS, 1952–54, 14:690.

20. Bohlen to DOS, 9 October 1954, ibid., pp. 720–21.

21. CINCPAC to CHMAAG, 14 September 1954, CCS 381 Formosa (11-8-48) Sec. 10, JCS, 1951–53.

22. G. C. Stewart to Frederick Nolting, Jr., 1 October 1954, FRUS, 1952–54, 14:673.

23. Gerald Stryker to Edwin Martin, 22 September 1954, ibid., pp. 655–58.

24. NYT, 8 October 1954, 8:2; memorandum of conversation, 12 October 1954, box 191, Koo Papers.

25. Robert Cutler to Dulles, 26 September 1954, FRUS, 1952–54, 14:661–62.

26. Kalicki, *Pattern of Sino-American Crises*, p. 124; Pach and Richardson, *Presidency of Dwight D. Eisenhower*, p. 100.

27. A Gallup poll in September revealed that 41 percent of a national sample favored using U.S. air and naval power to resist a Communist invasion of Taiwan, whereas 31 percent would merely provide military supplies and 21 percent would give no assistance at all. China Telegram, 16–22, 23–29 September and 30 September–6 October 1954 (Gallup poll), POS.

28. Reinhard, *Republican Right since 1945*, pp. 121–25; Ambrose, *The President*, pp. 217–21.

29. Carlton, *Anthony Eden*, pp. 362–63; Stebbins, *United States in World Affairs*, pp. 146–67.

30. Dulles memorandum, 12 September 1954, FRUS, 1952–54, 14:611–12.

31. Stolper, "China, Taiwan, and the Offshore Islands," pp. 42–43; memorandum of discussion, 216th NSC Meeting, 6 October 1954, FRUS, 1952–54, 14:689; memorandum of conversation, 18 October 1954, ibid., p. 774; Paris to FO, 17 December 1954, FC 1042/246, FO 371/110242.

32. Record of meeting, 17 September 1954, FC 1042/10, FO 371/110231.

33. Minute, 16 September 1954, FC 1042/8, FO 371/110231.

34. Cabinet Minutes, 21 September 1954, C.C. 61 (54) (2), CAB 128/27.

35. Martin, *Divided Counsel*, pp. 222–23; Zhai, *The Dragon, the Lion, and the Eagle*, pp. 146–47, 152.

36. Memorandum of conversation, 22 September 1954, FRUS, 1952–54, 14:653; Dulles to Smith, 27 September 1954, ibid., p. 663; Dulles to Smith, 27 September 1954, ibid., pp. 663–64.

37. Roger Makins to FO, 15 September 1954, FC 1042/6G, FO 371/110231; record of meeting, 17 September 1954, FC 1042/10, FO 371/110231.

38. Memorandum of conversation, 4 October 1954, FRUS, 1952–54, 14:679; memorandum of conversation, 8 October 1954, ibid., pp. 710–13; memorandum of conversation, 9 October 1954, ibid., pp. 716–18.

39. Memorandum of conversation, 6 October 1954, ibid., pp. 703–4.

40. The cease-fire resolution applied only to the offshore islands rather than to the entire Taiwan Strait as the British had suggested. The agreed minute contained restrictions confining the discussion in the Security Council to the narrow terms of the resolution and excluding consideration of broader issues such as the China seat or the disposition of Taiwan. Ibid., p. 716 n. 1, 719 n. 3, 726 n. 3.

41. Ambassador Rankin predicted a "violently unfavorable reaction" to the initiative by the Nationalist leadership. Rankin to Robertson and Drumwright, 5 October 1954, ibid., p. 682.

42. Robertson to Dulles, 7 October 1954, ibid., pp. 706–7.

43. Dulles to Robertson, 7 October 1954, ibid., p. 708; memorandum of conversation, 7 October 1954, ibid., p. 708 n. 2.

44. MacArthur to Herbert Hoover, Jr., 14 October 1954, ibid., p. 757.

45. Memorandum of conversation, 13 October 1954, ibid., pp. 732–52; Rankin to Dulles, 14 October 1954, ibid., pp. 754–55.

46. Cabinet Minute, 15 October 1954, C.C. (54) 66, CAB 128/27; FO to U.K. Embassy Washington, 15 October 1954, FC 1042/68G, FO 371/110234.

47. Memorandum of conversation, 18 October 1954, FRUS, 1952–54, 14:771–75.

48. Eden to FO, 20 October 1954, FC 1042/96G, FO 371/110235.

49. Dulles memorandum, 12 September 1954, FRUS, 1952–54, 14:613.

50. Cabinet Minute, 22 October 1954, C.C. (54) (69) (2), CAB 128/27; Makins to FO, 14 October 1954, FC 1042/68G, FO 371/110234.

51. FO to Humphrey Trevelyan, 12 October 1954, FC 1042/56G, FO 371/11023; minute, 19 October 1954, FC 1042/96G, FO 371/11023; Canadian High Commissioner, London, to Pearson, 18 October 1954, file 1, 50056-B-40, DEA. A report from Trevelyan, the British chargé d'affaires in Peking, offered little promise that the Chinese would cooperate in the UN exercise if a treaty announcement prefaced it, whatever military restrictions a pact imposed on the Nationalists. Trevelyan predicted that CCP leaders would scorn the treaty and the UN initiative as devices to uncouple Taiwan from the mainland. Trevelyan to FO, 29 October 1954, FC 1042/115, FO 371/110236.

52. Commonwealth Relations Office to U.K. High Commissioner, New Delhi, 2 November 1954, FC 1042/117, FO 371/110236.

53. Makins to FO, 5 November 1954, FC 1042/135, FO 371/110237.

54. Lodge to Dulles, 19 October 1954, FRUS, 1952–54, 14:778–79; extracts of memorandum of conversation, 20 October 1954, ibid., pp. 780–87.

55. Memorandum of discussion, 214th NSC Meeting, 12 September 1954, FRUS, 1952–54, 12:906.

56. Memorandum of conversation, 27 October 1954, ibid., p. 801.

57. Memorandum of conference, 18 October 1954, box 9, Chronological Series, Dulles Papers (DDEL); Hoover to Dulles, 19 October 1954, FRUS, 1952–54, 14:779.

58. Memorandum of discussion, 220th NSC Meeting, 28 October 1954, FRUS, 1952–54, 14:803–9; Report by secretary of state to NSC, 28 October 1954, ibid., pp. 809–12.

59. JCS Secretaries to JCS, 22 October 1954, ibid., p. 754 n. 3.

60. JSSC Report, 29 October 1954, ibid., pp. 819–20.

61. Radford memorandum, 29 October 1954, ibid., pp. 817–19.

62. Memorandum of discussion, 221st NSC Meeting, 2 November 1954, ibid., pp. 827–39.

63. Jia, "Searching for Peaceful Coexistence," p. 273; He, "Evolution of the People's Republic of China's Policy," p. 226.

64. Dulles to Rankin, 3 November 1954, FRUS, 1952–54, 14:854–55.

65. The *Washington Post* divulged the existence of the talks soon after they commenced, much to the chagrin of Dulles, who wanted to keep them under wraps until a formal announcement so as not to prejudice the chances for proceeding with Oracle. Memorandum of conversation, 5 November 1954, ibid., p. 866.

66. Dulles to Eisenhower, 23 November 1954, ibid., p. 929.

67. The texts of the treaty and exchange of notes are in *United States Treaties and Other International Agreements*, pt. 1, 6:435–38, 450.

68. Hoopes, *Devil and John Foster Dulles*, pp. 271–72.

69. Memorandum of discussion, 221st NSC Meeting, 2 November 1954, FRUS, 1952–54, 14:835.

70. Memorandum of discussion, 229th NSC Meeting, FRUS, 1952–54, 2:841.

71. Memorandum of conversation, 6 November 1954, FRUS, 1952–54, 14:871, 875–76, 879–80.

72. Memorandum of conversation, 9 November 1954, ibid., pp. 881–82; memorandum of conversation, 22 November 1954, ibid., p. 925.

73. Memorandum of conversation, 22 November 1954, ibid., pp. 922–24; memorandum of conversation, 23 November 1954, ibid., pp. 927–28.

74. Memorandum of conversation, 19 November 1954, ibid., pp. 904–9; Ge, "'A Horrible Dilemma,'" p. 256.

75. Memorandum of conversation, 23 November 1954, box 192, Koo Papers.

76. Makins to FO, 23 November 1954, FC 1042/178, FO 371/110238.

77. W. D. Allen to Dening, 16 November 1954, FC 1042/108G, FO 371/110238; Eden to U.K. Embassy Washington, 20 November 1954, FC 1042/174G, FO 371/110238.

78. Cabinet Minutes, 24 November 1954, C.C. (54) (79) (2), CAB 128/27.

79. Cabinet Minutes, 29 November 1954, C.C. (54) (80) (7), CAB 128/27; FO to U.K. Embassy Washington, 29 November 1954, FC 1042/192G, FO 371/110239; record of meeting, 30 November 1954, FC 1042/202, FO 371/110239.

80. Memorandum of conversation, 30 November 1954, FRUS, 1952–54, 14:965.

81. *FRUS, 1955–57*, 2:6–7 n. 4. The Chinese alleged that the B-29, which they shot down over Liaoning province, belonged to an air wing whose task included evacuation and recovery of underground personnel. Allen to DOS, 30 November 1954, ibid., p. 961. In a conversation with Canadian ambassador A. D. P. Heeney, Deputy Undersecretary of State for Political Affairs Robert D. Murphy acknowledged that several of the personnel on the flight had specialized training beyond leaflet dropping and that the plane might have had special equipment not pertinent to its mission. Memorandum of conversation, 14 December 1954, ibid., p. 1032.

The Public Security Ministry in Peking claimed that 106 American and National-ist agents who had entered China since 1951 had been killed and another 124 captured. The Nationalists had sent most of the agents, but some were under the authority of the CIA or of the "Free China Movement" subordinated to the CIA. NYT, 25 November 1954, 1:8.

82. Trevelyan, *World's Apart*, p. 155; Trevelyan to Allen, 22 January 1955, FC 1041/445, FO 371/115038.

83. China Telegram, 25 November–1 December 1954, POS.

84. JCS 2118/74, 1 December 1954, 093 Asia (6-25-48), JCS, 1954–56.

85. Summary of report of Ad Hoc Working Group, 30 November 1954, *FRUS, 1952–54*, 14:950 n. 3; memorandum, 26 November 1954, ibid., p. 951.

86. SNIE 100-6-54, "World Reactions to Certain Possible U.S. Courses of Action against Communist China," 28 November 1954, ibid., pp. 951–56.

87. Ferrell, *Diary of James C. Hagerty*, p. 117.

88. *Public Papers of the Presidents: Dwight D. Eisenhower, 1954*, pp. 1074–77; Ferrell, *Diary of James C. Hagerty*, pp. 123–24.

89. China Telegram, 2–8 December 1954, POS.

90. *FRUS, 1952–54*, 14:1003 n. 3; Lodge to DOS, 6 December 1954, ibid., pp. 994–96; Lodge to DOS, 17 December 1954, ibid., pp. 1037–38.

91. "Foreign Minister Chou En-lai's Statement on U.S.-Chiang Kai-shek 'Mutual Security Treaty,'" *Important Documents Concerning the Question of Taiwan*, pp. 161–70.

92. China Telegram, 2–8, 9–15 December 1954, POS.

93. Ge, "'A Horrible Dilemma,'" pp. 285–86.

94. Memorandum of conversation, 6 December 1954, *FRUS, 1952–54*, 14:988–93.

95. Cabinet Minutes, 14 December 1954, C.C. (54) (86) (1), CAB 128/27; minute, 15 December 1954, FC 1042/281, FO 371/110242.

96. Dulles to Hoover and Robertson, 17 December 1954, *FRUS, 1952–54*, 14:1035.

97. NSC 5429/5, "Current U.S. Policy toward the Far East," 22 December 1954, *FRUS, 1952–54*, 12:1062–72.

98. Memorandum of discussion, 230th NSC Meeting, 5 January 1955, *FRUS, 1955–57*, 2:5.

99. Memorandum of discussion, 229th NSC Meeting, 21 December 1954, *FRUS, 1952–54*, 14:1045–47.

100. NSC 5503, "U.S. Policy toward Formosa and the Government of the Republic of China," 15 January 1955, *FRUS, 1955–57*, 2:30–35.

101. NIE 43-54, "Probable Developments in Taiwan through Mid-1956," 14 September 1954, *FRUS, 1952–54*, 14:628–45.

Chapter Nine

1. Ferrell, *Diary of James C. Hagerty*, p. 197.

2. A brief account of Hammarskjöld's mission appears in *Hammarskjöld Public Papers, 1953–56*, pp. 417–21, 436–40.

3. Allison to DOS, 12 January 1955, *FRUS, 1955–57*, 2:12–13; Lodge to DOS, 13 January 1955, ibid., pp. 26–30.

4. Statement by the president, 14 January 1955, *Public Papers of the Presidents: Dwight D. Eisenhower, 1955*, pp. 85–86. The president's temper boiled when Knowland, ignoring his appeal for restraint, gave a speech lashing out at Hammarskjöld for his wasted effort in Peking. Ferrell, *Diary of James C. Hagerty*, p. 16; memorandum of conversation, 17 January 1955, *FRUS, 1955–57*, 2:34.

5. Memorandum of conversation, 19 January 1955, *FRUS, 1955–57*, 2:44–45; Dulles to Hammarskjöld, 28 January 1955, ibid., p. 160. Faulting the secretary-general for being too gullible, Dulles confronted him with a *New York Times* photo showing him standing beneath a banner with a Chinese inscription denouncing American aggression. U.K. Embassy Washington to FO, 29 January 1955, FC 1041/177, FO 371/115029.

6. *Hammarskjöld Public Papers, 1953–1956*, p. 457.

7. U.K. Embassy Washington to FO, 19 January 1955, FC 1691/42, FO 371/115179; U.K. Embassy Washington to FO, 20 January 1955, FC 1041/30, FO 371/115024.

8. Chang and He, "Absence of War in the U.S.-China Confrontation over Quemoy and Matsu," p. 1514.

9. Memorandum of conversation, 19 January 1955, *FRUS, 1955–57*, 2:39; Chase to Stump and Vice Adm. Alfred M. Pride, 19 January 1955, 381 Formosa (11-8-48) Sec. 17, JCS, 1954–56.

10. Memorandum of conversation, 19 January 1955, *FRUS, 1955–57*, 2:41–43; memorandum of conversation, 19 January 1955, ibid., pp. 50–52.

11. He, "Evolution of the People's Republic of China's Policy," p. 227.

12. Memorandum of conversation, 19 January 1955, *FRUS, 1955–57*, 2:49.

13. Billings-Yun, *Decision against War*, pp. 83–84, 90–95.

14. Memorandum of discussion, 233d NSC Meeting, 21 January 1955, *FRUS, 1955–57*, 2:91.

15. Memorandum of discussion, 20 January 1955, ibid., pp. 55–68.

16. Memorandum of discussion, 232d NSC Meeting, 20 January 1955, ibid., p. 82.

17. Ambrose, *The President*, p. 23.

18. Memorandum of discussion, 232d NSC Meeting, 20 January 1955, *FRUS, 1955–57*, 2:69–82.

19. Ibid., p. 76.

20. Dulles told Makins that there was no threat as yet to Quemoy and only a slight one to Matsu. U.K. Embassy Washington to FO, 29 January 1955, FC 1041/1850, FO 371/115029.

21. He, "Evolution of the People's Republic of China's Policy," p. 228; Li, "Chinese Intentions," pp. 52–56; Chang and He, "Absence of War in the U.S.-China Confrontation over Quemoy and Matsu," pp. 1510–11.

22. Memorandum of discussion, 233d NSC Meeting, 21 January 1955, *FRUS, 1955–57*, 2:95–96.

23. Eden to U.K. Embassy Washington, 20 January 1955, FC 1041/21G, FO 371/115023; memorandum of conversation, 20 January 1955, FRUS, 1955–57, 2:86–89; memorandum of discussion, 233d NSC Meeting, 21 January 1955, ibid., p. 91.

24. Memorandum of conversation, 21 January 1955, FRUS, 1955–57, 2:96–99, 97 n. 3; U.K. Embassy Washington to FO, 21 January 1955, FC 1041/37, FO 371/115024; Foot, "Search for a *Modus Vivendi*," p. 155.

25. Memorandum of conversation, 22 January 1955, FRUS, 1955–57, 2:106–7.

26. Koo Memoir, VII, J 106.

27. Joint Resolution of U.S. Congress, FRUS, 1955–57, 2:162–63.

28. Eisenhower later claimed that he and congressional leaders had a clear understanding that the resolution would not mention any of the offshore islands. Memorandum of conversation, 4 February 1955, box 195, Koo Papers.

29. The message went through at least eleven drafts. President's Draft Message to Congress #11, 22 January 1955, box 2, Draft and Correspondence, Dulles Papers (DDEL); released to author through FOI.

30. Message of the president to Congress, 24 January 1955, FRUS, 1955–57, 2:115–19.

31. NYT, 28 January 1955, 1:7.

32. SNIE 100-3-55, "Communist Reactions to Certain Possible U.S. Courses of Action with Respect to the Islands off the Coast of China," 25 January 1955, FRUS, 1955–57, 2:127.

33. For a fuller discussion, see Accinelli, "Eisenhower, Congress, and the 1954–55 Offshore Islands Crisis," pp. 329–48.

34. Memorandum, 28 January 1955, box 2, White House Memoranda Series, Dulles Papers (DDEL).

35. China Telegram, 20–26 January and 27 January–2 February 1955, POS.

36. *Cong. Rec.*, House, 25 June 1955, pp. 680–81.

37. Senate, *Executive Sessions of the Foreign Relations Committee*, 7:68–130, 135–241.

38. Ibid., pp. 275, 279, 281.

39. *Cong. Rec.*, Senate, 28 January 1955, p. 994.

40. U.K. Embassy Washington to FO, Weekly Political Summary, 22–28 January 1955, Policy toward China, file 3, 50056-B-40, DEA. For analysis of the debates in the House and Senate, consult Accinelli, "Eisenhower, Congress, and the 1954–55 Offshore Islands Crisis," pp. 336–37.

41. NYT, 10 April 1955, IV, 7:1; Nelson, "Dulles and the Bipartisan Congress," p. 47.

42. *Cong. Rec.*, 25 January 1955, pp. 660, 663, 668; 27 January 1955, p. 821; 28 January 1955, p. 986.

43. Eisenhower wished to alleviate concern even among proponents that the resolution might authorize preventive war or leave control of American forces in the hands of an impetuous local commander or possibly even Chiang Kai-shek. He therefore issued a statement that the deployment of U.S. naval and air units in the Taiwan Strait was solely for defensive purposes and that he alone would order them into action in all cases except immediate self-defense or a direct attack on Taiwan and the Penghus. The president's impeccable military background and reputation

gave his reassuring statement all the more credence. Diary, 27 January 1955, Hagerty Papers; NYT, 28 January 1955, 1:8.

44. *Cong. Rec.*, Senate, 9 February 1955, pp. 1415–16.

45. Senate, *Executive Sessions of the Foreign Relations Committee*, 7:309–53.

46. Senate Committee, Executive Report No. 2, "Mutual Defense Treaty with the Republic of China." The understandings provided that: 1) the American defense commitment under the treaty could not be extended to [Nationalist] Chinese-held territory other than Taiwan and the Penghus without the advance consent of the Senate; 2) the treaty had no effect on the legal status of Taiwan and the Penghus; 3) the American defense commitment under the treaty would apply only in the event of external armed attack, and neither signatory could undertake military operations from Nationalist-held territory except by joint agreement.

The second understanding addressed concerns that the treaty might be construed as confirmation of the Republic of China's legal claim to Taiwan and the Penghus. These concerns arose as a result of a memorandum written by Benjamin Cohen, the former New Dealer and counselor in the State Department during the Truman administration, that attracted attention in the American and foreign press. Cohen contended that the treaty, once ratified, would constitute formal recognition of Nationalist China's title to Taiwan and the Penghus and that this was not in the American interest. First circulated among Democrats on the Foreign Relations Committee by the Democratic National Committee, the memorandum had a distinct political coloration. An irate Dulles saw the memorandum as a partisan and legally dubious attempt to galvanize opposition to the treaty in the Senate. In his appearance before the Foreign Relations Committee, he denied that the treaty altered the juridical status of Taiwan and the Penghus and expressed a readiness to accept an understanding to this effect. Benjamin Cohen, "Memorandum on the Proposed Mutual Defense Treaty with the Republic of China," [undated], attached to Arthur Dean to Dulles, 1 February 1955, box 2, White House Memoranda Series, Dulles Papers (DDEL); memorandum of discussion, 231st NSC Meeting, 13 January 1955, FRUS, 1955–57, 2: 20–23; Senate, *Executive Sessions of the Foreign Relations Committee*, 7:316, 324.

47. *Cong. Rec.*, 9 February 1955, Senate, pp. 1388–97, 1404–7, 1413.

48. China Telegram, 3–9 February and 10–16 February 1955, POS.

49. "Recent Opinion Polling Results on U.S.-Chinese Relations," 5 August 1955, box 33, ibid.

50. Memorandum of conversation, 22 January 1955, FRUS, 1955–57, 2:107; Rankin to DOS, 23 January 1955, ibid., pp. 112–13.

51. Koo Memoir, VII, J 59–62, J 147–48; Yeh to O. K. Yui, 15 January 1955, box 169, Koo Papers.

52. NYT, 19 January 1955, 3:6.

53. President's News Conference, 19 January 1955, *Public Papers of the Presidents: Dwight D. Eisenhower*, 1955, p. 190.

54. When Dulles had first informed Yeh of the proposed guarantee of Quemoy, he had in fact planned on a public announcement. But in subsequent conversations with the foreign minister prior to the Formosa message, both he and Assistant Secretary Robertson had backed away from such a declaration because of British ob-

jections (about which they kept the Nationalist diplomat in the dark). For some reason, Yeh did not immediately inform Chiang of this change. Memorandum of conversation, 21 January 1955, FRUS, 1955–57, 2:100–101; memorandum of conversation, 22 January 1955, ibid., p. 107; Koo Memoir, VII, J 177.

55. Rankin to DOS, 30 January 1955, FRUS, 1955–57, 2:167–68.

56. Editorial note, ibid., p. 199; Koo Diary, 7 February 1955, Koo Papers.

57. "U.S. Commitments to GRC," 1 February 1955, box 51, CA, 1948–56.

58. Memorandum of conversation, 30 January 1955, FRUS, 1955–57, 2:175.

59. Hoover to Rankin, 31 January 1955, ibid., p. 183.

60. Memorandum of conversation, 3 February 1955, ibid., pp. 204–7; Hoover to U.S. Embassy Taipei, 4 February 1955, ibid., pp. 215–17; Rankin to DOS, 5 February 1955, ibid., pp. 219–20.

61. Editorial note, ibid., pp. 248–49. To avoid any confusion about guidelines for engagement with Chinese forces or for attacks on Chinese bases, Eisenhower himself personally dictated the orders to the Seventh Fleet. Memorandum for the record, 29 January 1955, ibid., pp. 163–64; Diary, 29 January 1955, Hagerty Papers.

62. The United States had declined to defend Nanchi. Rankin, *China Assignment*, p. 223; memorandum of discussion, 237th NSC Meeting, 17 February 1955, FRUS, 1955–57, 2:282–85.

63. Memorandum of conversation, 10 February 1955, FRUS, 1955–57, 2:251–59.

64. NYT, 2 March 1955, 2:4.

65. President's News Conference, 2 March 1955, *Public Papers of the Presidents: Dwight D. Eisenhower, 1955*, p. 310.

66. NYT, 11 February 1955, 1:6, 12 February 1955, 1:7; Yeh to Robertson, 11 February 1955, box 51, CA, 1948–56.

67. The text of the column appears in Koo Memoirs, VII, pt. I, sec. 4, app. II, i–iii.

68. Eisenhower to Churchill, 10 February 1955, FRUS, 1955–57, 2:260. The "assurances" did not represent in any technical sense an agreement or commitment, Dulles told Makins, but merely meant that "present circumstances were somewhat reassuring" to the Nationalists. Memorandum of conversation, 11 February 1955, box 1, General Correspondence and Memorandum, Dulles Papers (DDEL).

69. Cabinet Minutes, 15 February 1955, C.C. 55 (13) (1), CAB 128/28; Eden to U.K. Embassy Washington, 15 February 1955, FC 1041/383G, FO 371/115036; Makins to FO, 15 February 1955, FC 1041/393, FO 371/115037. The portion of the speech dealing with the offshore islands is printed in FRUS, 1955–57, 2:278–79.

70. *Cong. Rec.*, 23 February 1955, House, pp. 1962–64; Koo Memoir, VII, J 271.

71. Memorandum of conversation, 9 February 1955, box 195, Koo Papers.

72. China Telegram, 27 January–2 February 1955, POS. China bloc leaders such as Knowland were cognizant of the two-China implications of a UN cease-fire. The California senator and several other pro-Chiang stalwarts helped to bottle up in the Foreign Relations Committee a sense of the Senate resolution introduced by Minnesota Democrat Hubert Humphrey and eight cosponsors recommending that the president seek prompt action to secure a cease-fire in the area of the offshore islands and the Taiwan Strait. Senate, *Executive Sessions of the Foreign Relations Committee*, 7:286–304.

73. FO to U.K. Embassy Washington, 25 January 1955, FC 1041/65, FO 371/115025.

74. Memorandum of conversation, 26 January 1955, FRUS, 1955–57, 2:129–32; Re-

port of New Zealand–United Kingdom–United States Working Party, 26 [27] January 1955, ibid., pp. 133–34.

75. Hayter surmised that Kremlin leaders, while keeping a united public front with the Chinese, were behind the scenes probably trying to curb them from pressing their territorial claims to the point of an armed clash with the United States that might suck in the USSR. Eden saw merit in this view. Hayter to FO, 1 February 1955, FC 1041/226, FO 371/1115030; Cabinet Minutes, 31 January 1955, C.C. (55) (8) (2), CAB 128/28. For evidence that the Soviets were urging moderation on the Chinese in dealing with international problems, see Jia, "Searching for Peaceful Coexistence," p. 275.

76. NYT, 31 January 1955, 1:8; UNSC, 690th Meeting, 31 January 1955, pp. 1–23.

77. DSB 32 (14 February 1955): 254–55.

78. D. M. Johnson to Pearson, 8 February 1955, file 4, 50056-B-40, DEA.

79. Ferrell, *Diary of James C. Hagerty*, p. 186.

80. Gordon H. Chang, *Friends and Enemies*, pp. 128–31.

81. Bohlen to DOS, 27 January 1955, FRUS, 1955–57, 2:147–49.

82. SNIE 100-3-55, "Communist Reactions to Certain Possible U.S. Courses of Action with Respect to the Islands off the Coast of China," 25 January 1955, ibid., p. 128; SNIE 11-4-55, "Review of Current Communist Attitudes toward General War," 15 February 1955, ibid., pp. 275–76.

83. Memorandum of conversation, 234th NSC Meeting, 27 January 1955, ibid., pp. 135–40.

84. Makins to FO, 29 January 1955, FC 1041/185G, FO 371/115029.

85. Eisenhower to Gruenther, 1 February 1955, FRUS, 1955–57, 2:192–93; Eisenhower to Churchill, 10 February 1955, ibid., p. 261.

86. Memorandum of conversation, 20 March 1955, ibid., pp. 425–26; memorandum of conversation, 14 April 1955, ibid., p. 478.

87. Eisenhower to Churchill, 25 January 1955, ibid., p. 129.

88. Memorandum of conversation, 7 February 1955, ibid., p. 235.

89. Lodge to DOS, 6 February 1955, ibid., pp. 231–33. During the course of the month, Dulles learned from other sources of China's agreeableness to bilateral talks about the imprisoned fliers and other causes of strain between the two nations. Kenneth Young, *Negotiating with the Chinese Communists*, pp. 43–44.

90. Memorandum of conversation, 7 February 1955, FRUS, 1955–57, 2:237; Johnson to Pearson, 11 February 1955, file 5, 50056-B-40, DEA.

91. Sutter, *China-Watch*, pp. 44–46; Stolper, "China, Taiwan, and the Offshore Islands," pp. 95–98; Jia, "Searching for Peaceful Coexistence," p. 275, He, "Evolution of the People's Republic of China's Policy," p. 228. The fullest account of Chinese attitudes toward diplomatic negotiations at this time appears in Chang and He, "Absence of War in the U.S.-China Confrontation over Quemoy and Matsu," pp. 1514–17, 1521. These authors present fresh evidence that Mao, believing that the United States did not want war and practicing his own version of brinksmanship, wished to keep the heat on Washington through intransigent propaganda and diplomatic stonewalling. Yet they also acknowledge the importance of Chou En-lai's suggestion of bilateral talks, and they speculate that a positive response by the Eisenhower administration might have avoided the later escalation of the crisis.

92. Hayter to FO, 4 February 1955, FC 1041/277, FO 371/1115032; Eden to U.K. Embassy Washington, 5 February 1955, FC 1041/261, FO 371/115032; Trevelyan to FO, 7 February 1955, FC 1041/311, FO 371/115033.

93. Memorandum of conversation, 7 February 1955, FRUS, 1955–57, 2:236.

94. Memorandum on Formosa, 5 February 1955, vol. 32, Correspondence, Pre-1958 Series, Pearson Papers; Pearson to Heeney, 28 January 1955, file 2, 50056-B-40, DEA; High Commissioner for Canada, Canberra, to Pearson, 29 January 1955, ibid.

95. Memorandum of conversation, 7 February 1955, FRUS, 1955–57, 2:234–35.

96. Memorandum on Formosa, 5 February 1955, vol. 32, Correspondence, Pre-1958 Series, Pearson Papers; Pearson Diary, 5 February 1955, ibid.

97. Makins to FO, 29 January 1955, FC 1041/185G, FO 371/115029.

98. Makins to FO, 7 February 1955, FC 1041/307, FO 371/115033; Makins to FO, 9 February 1955, FC 1041/339, FO 371/115035.

99. This summary is based on Walter Lippmann, "Toward a Cease-Fire," *Washington Post and Times Herald*, 8 February 1955, 17:1–3. Eden told the American ambassador in London, Winthrop Aldrich, that Lippmman's column "expressed the consensus of opinion of the Prime Ministers at the Commonwealth conference to an extraordinary degree." Aldrich to Dulles, 11 February 1955, FRUS, 1955–57, 2:265.

100. Churchill to Eisenhower, [15 February 1955], FRUS, 1955–57, 2:270–73.

101. The letter was transmitted in Dulles to Aldrich, 18 February 1955, ibid., pp. 292–95.

102. For images of Chinese unpredictability and recklessness among American officials, see Foot, *Wrong War*, pp. 28, 233–34, and Gordon H. Chang, *Friends and Enemies*, pp. 170–74.

103. See, for example, Hoover to Aldrich, 4 February 1955, FRUS, 1955–57, 2:214–15; memorandum of conversation, 7 February 1955, ibid., pp. 236–37; memorandum of conversation, 11 February 1955, ibid., pp. 262–65.

104. Eisenhower to Wedemeyer, 28 February 1955, box 9, Dwight D. Eisenhower Diary Series, AWF; memorandum of conversation, 17 February 1955, FRUS, 1955–57, 2:88; Eisenhower to Churchill, 29 March 1955, ibid., p. 419; Dulles to Douglas, 29 March 1955, box 2, General Correspondence and Memorandum, Dulles Papers (DDEL).

105. Rankin to Robertson, 13 March 1955, FRUS, 1955–57, 2:360–61.

106. Memorandum of conversation, 14 March 1955, ibid., p. 369.

107. Progress Report on NSC 148/2, 239th NSC Meeting, 16 February 1955 (released to author through FOI).

108. Pearson to High Commissioner for Canada, London, 21 February 1955, FC 1041/486, FO 371/115040.

109. Minute, 18 February 1955, FC 1041/562, FO 371/115042; memorandum, 22 February 1955, file 22, vol. 8, Reid Papers; memorandum, "Formosa and the Coastal Islands," 8 March 1955, file 6, 50056-B-40, DEA.

110. Dulles to Hoover, 25 February 1955, FRUS, 1955–57, 2:308; Eden to FO, 25 February 1955, FC 1041/468, FO 371/115039.

111. For a summary of Eden's message, see FRUS, 1955–57, 2:338 n. 2.

112. Trevelyan to FO, 28 February 1955, FC 1041/504, FO 371/115040.

113. C. T. Crowe to A. H. B. Hermann, 25 February 1955, FC 1041/484G, FO 371/115040.

114. NYT, 30 January 1955, IV, 5:7.

115. Eden, Speech to the House of Commons, 8 March 1955, *Parliamentary Debates*, House of Commons, 5th ser., vol. 538 (1955), cols. 160–61.

116. Memorandum of conversation, 9 March 1955, FRUS, 1955–57, 2:344.

117. Memorandum for the record, 24 March 1955, ibid., p. 300 n. 1.

118. Ferrell, *Diary of James C. Hagerty*, pp. 202–3.

119. Dulles to Hoover, 4 March 1955, FRUS, 1955–57, 2:320–28.

120. Memorandum of record and understanding, 6 March 1955, ibid., pp. 329–30; Dulles to Hoover, 4 March 1955, ibid., p. 324.

Chapter Ten

1. Dulles to Hoover, 21 February 1955, FRUS, 1955–57, 2:299–300.

2. Dulles to Hoover, 25 February 1955, ibid., pp. 307–8; Dulles to Hoover, 25 February 1955, ibid., pp. 310–11.

3. Memorandum of conversation, 9 March 1955, ibid., p. 341; minutes of cabinet meeting, 11 March 1955, ibid., p. 352.

4. Memorandum of conversation, 6 March 1955, ibid., pp. 336–37.

5. Memorandum of discussion, 230th NSC Meeting, 10 March, 1955, ibid., pp. 346, 348–49. Allen Dulles reported to his brother that the Nationalist government's vulnerability to subversion was more serious than generally acknowledged. Allen Dulles to J. F. Dulles, 16 March 1955, ibid., pp. 380–84. The secretary of state still had doubts about the pro-American allegiance of Chiang Ching-kuo, as apparently did the CIA. Perhaps with these suspicions in mind, he rather mysteriously told the cabinet that Chiang Kai-shek was in a "particularly dangerous situation, more dangerous than I can tell you even in this room." Memorandum of conversation, 14 March 1955, ibid., p. 369, and Diary, 11 March 1955, Hagerty Papers.

6. Memorandum of discussion, 230th NSC Meeting, 10 March 1955, FRUS, 1955–57, 2:345–50. For European ratification of the Paris agreements, see Barber, *United States in World Affairs*, pp. 26–32.

7. Memorandum of conversation, 11 March 1955, FRUS, 1955–57, 2:353–55.

8. Memorandum for the record, 11 March 1955, ibid., pp. 357–59.

9. Memorandum for the record, 16 March 1955, ibid., p. 360 n. 9.

10. Memorandum for the president, 15 March 1955, box 9, International Series, AWF.

11. NIE 100-4-55, "Communist Capabilities and Intentions with Respect to the Offshore Islands and Taiwan through 1955, and Communist and Non-Communist Reactions with Respect to the Defense of Taiwan," 16 March 1955, FRUS, 1955–57, 2:376–80.

12. See, for example, memorandum of discussion, 243d NSC Meeting, 31 March 1955, ibid., p. 431; Diary, 12–20 April, Hagerty Papers.

13. Goodpaster to Eisenhower, 15 March 1955, FRUS, 1955–57, 2:367.

14. Memorandum of discussion, 242d NSC Meeting, 24 March 1955, ibid., p. 391.

15. NYT, 9 March 1955, 1:8.

16. Ibid., 16 March 1955, 1:1.

17. President's News Conference, 16 March 1955, *Public Papers of the Presidents: Dwight D. Eisenhower, 1955*, p. 332.

18. NYT, 18 March 1955, 16:7.

19. Ibid., 21 March 1955, 5:5.

20. For Bundy's "stop-gap" interpretation, see *Danger and Survival*, pp. 278–79.

21. Brands, "Testing Massive Retaliation," pp. 124–51. Brands errs, however, in treating the entire crisis as a test of the Eisenhower-Dulles doctrine of "massive retaliation."

22. Memorandum of discussion, 230th NSC Meeting, 10 March 1955, FRUS, 1955–57, 2:347.

23. Memorandum of conversation, 7 April 1955, ibid., pp. 453–55; memorandum of conversation, 8 April 1955, ibid., pp. 463–64.

24. Dulles to U.S. Embassy Turkey, 8 April 1955, ibid., pp. 466–67; Makins to FO, 9 April 1955, FC 1041/693, FO 371/115045.

25. Dulles, "An Estimate of Chinese Communist Intentions," speech before Advertising Club of New York, New York, 21 March 1955, DSB 32 (4 April 1955): 551–52; Dulles, "Some Aspects of Foreign Policy," speech before Associated Church Press, Washington, D.C., 13 April 1955, ibid., 32 (25 April 1955): 675–77.

26. Mayers, *Cracking the Monolith*, pp. 6, 136–42; Gaddis, *Long Peace*, p. 183.

27. NIE 10-7-54, "Communist Courses of Action in Asia through 1957," FRUS, 1952–54, 14:930–31, 934–35. An NSC staffer noted after the crisis that the Soviet response throughout had been "characterized by a withholding of commitment or of official support for the Chinese 'liberation' program," but he detected no sign that the evident differences between the two communist partners had produced unmanageable strain. "The Sino-Soviet Factor in the Soviet Approach to International Security," 23 May 1955, box 99, PPS, 1955.

28. Dulles to Hoover, 25 February 1955, FRUS, 1955–57, 2:312; memorandum of conversation, 9 March 1955, ibid., pp. 344–45.

29. Eden to U.K. Embassy Washington, 12 March 1955, FC 1041/557, FO 371/115042.

30. Dulles to Eden, 23 March 1955, FRUS, 1955–57, 2:387–88; Eden to Dulles, 25 March 1955, ibid., pp. 397–98; Dulles to Eden, 26 March 1955, ibid., pp. 404–5; Eden to Dulles, 28 March 1955, ibid., pp. 416–17. The British did not want a cease-fire resolution introduced unless the Chinese attacked the offshore islands. Tabling a resolution in the absence of an actual assault would, they believed, waste the "one shot in the Anglo-American armoury," because the Soviet Union would veto the resolution. If, following a veto, the Chinese were then to try to seize the islands, the United States would proceed to ask the Security Council to condemn their aggression, a move the Britain could not support. Canadian Embassy Washington to Pearson, 1 April 1955, file 7, 50056-B-40, DEA.

31. Wilson to JCS, 22 March 1955, FRUS, 1955–57, 2:385–86; JCS to Wilson, 27 March 1955, ibid., pp. 406–8; memorandum of conversation, 26 March 1955, ibid., pp. 400–4.

32. Memorandum of conversation, 28 March 1955, ibid., pp. 411–15.

33. Diary entry by the president, 26 March 1955, ibid., pp. 405–6.

34. Memorandum of discussion, 243d NSC Meeting, 31 March 1955, ibid., pp. 431–33; "U.S. Military Courses of Action to Meet a Chinese Communist Attack against the Quemoy or Matsu Island Groups," 31 March 1955, 091 China (Feb–Mar 55), CJCS, 1953–57.

35. Among the elite newspapers in which the Carney-inspired stories appeared were the *New York Times, New York Herald Tribune,* and *Christian Science Monitor.* Clippings can be found in box 9, International Series, AWF. Journalist Marquis Childs, who had arranged the dinner at Carney's request, told a member of the Canadian embassy staff that the admiral made it clear to the invited newsmen that he was speaking with the full concurrence and support of Radford. Carney did not disguise the fact that he and Radford believed that the moment had arrived for a showdown with Communist China. Childs believed that the main purpose of Carney's briefing was to ensure that Eisenhower authorized American intervention if the Communists attacked the offshore islands. Canadian Embassy Washington to Pearson, 29 March 1955, file 54, vol. 5, Le Pan Papers. *New York Times* columnist James Reston told a Canadian diplomat that John Foster Dulles had spoken in almost the same terms as Carney when he called at the offices of the newspaper the day after the dinner. Memorandum (Le Pan) for the Ambassador, 3 May 1955, file 56, vol. 5, ibid.

36. Ferrell, *Diary of James C. Hagerty,* p. 219; President's News Conference, 30 March 1955, *Public Papers of the Presidents: Dwight D. Eisenhower, 1955,* pp. 369–70, 373.

37. NYT, 28 March 1955, 3:5–7, 29 March 1955, 1:6, 30 March, 1955, 1:8.

38. Bipartisan Congressional Luncheon Meeting, 30 March 1955, box 1, Legislative Meeting Series, AWF.

39. Koo Memoir, VII, J 309; NYT, 7 April 1955, 13:3–4; Canadian Embassy Washington to Pearson, 4 April 1955, file 7, 50056-B-40, DEA. "The Carney thing proved a complete boomerang," journalist Stewart Alsop privately observed. "Radford-Carney planned to wake up the country. The net effect was to scare everybody pissless." Stewart Alsop to Joseph Alsop, 9 April 1955, box 215, Alsop Papers.

40. NYT, 10 April 1955, IV, 7:1–5. Nervous Democrats found a spokesman in the titular head of the party, Adlai Stevenson, who in a nationwide radio address on 11 April questioned American military involvement in the coastal islands and advanced a plan to reduce tension in the strait. Stevenson's speech drew favorable comments from Senate Democratic leaders and from much of the nation's press. Ibid., 12 April 1955, 1:8, 13 April 1955, 4:3; China Telegram, 14–20 April 1955, POS.

41. Memorandum of conversation, 18 April 1955, box 5, Subject Series, Dulles Papers (DDEL).

42. Smith to Dulles, 7 April 1955, box 116, Smith Papers; Dulles to Eisenhower, 6 April 1955, FRUS, 1955–57, 2:445 n. 6.

43. "United Kingdom Appreciation of Far Eastern Situation," 16 March 1955, FRUS, 1955–57, 2:374–75. In remarking to Makins on the Chinese desire for a showdown, Dulles maintained that their intentions toward Southeast Asia were even more menacing than toward Taiwan. Makins to FO, 14 March 1955, FC 1041/582, FO 371/115042. During the final phase of the offshore islands confrontation, the Eisen-

hower administration grappled with a concurrent crisis in South Vietnam, where both the political survival and continuation of American support for Prime Minister Ngo Dinh Diem were in question. See Anderson, *Trapped by Success*, pp. 99–116.

44. Lester B. Pearson statement in Canadian House of Commons, 24 March 1955, box 2, White House Memoranda Series, Dulles Papers (DDEL); Cabinet Conclusions, 18 March 1955, vol. 32, Correspondence, Pre-1958 Series, Pearson Papers.

45. Memorandum of conversation, 14 March 1955, FRUS, 1955–57, 2:370–71. Australian government officials felt that their own domestic opinion would favor such a pledge but would disapprove of American involvement in an armed conflict over the offshore islands. Memorandum of conversation, 16 March 1955, file 6, 50056-B-40, DEA.

46. Cabinet Minutes, 12 April 1955, C.M. (55) (2) (3), CAB 128/29.

47. Memorandum of conversation, 23 March 1955, box 195, Koo Papers.

48. Bipartisan Congressional Luncheon Meeting, 31 March 1955, box 1, Legislative Meetings, AWF.

49. Hoover to Dulles, 1 April 1955, FRUS, 1955–57, 2:439–41.

50. Diary, 4 April 1955, Hagerty Papers.

51. Dulles, "Preliminary Draft of Possible Statement of Position for Communication to the Republic of China," 4 April 1955, box 53, CA, 1948–56.

52. On the question of "self-deterrence" in nuclear decision making during the crisis, see Gaddis, *Long Peace*, pp. 130–40. Any explanation for the nonuse of nuclear weapons during the crisis must also take into account Chinese restraint. Had the Chinese intended to invade Quemoy or Matsu and actually done so, Eisenhower would have been hard-pressed to avoid nuclear retaliation.

53. A national intelligence estimate predicted that the predominant reaction to the use of atomic weapons against Communist China would be "shock." The reaction was expected to be especially negative if the weapons were employed to defend Quemoy and Matsu. An emotional and extremely critical response was forecast in noncommunist Asia. NIE 100-4-55, "Communist Capabilities and Intentions with Respect to the Offshore Islands and Taiwan through 1955, and Communist and Non-Communist Reactions with Respect to the Defense of Taiwan," 16 March 1955, FRUS, 1955–57, 2:379.

54. Bipartisan Congressional Luncheon Meeting, 30 March 1955, box 1, Legislative Meeting Series, AWF.

55. Eisenhower to Dulles, 5 April 1955, FRUS, 1955–57, 2:445–50.

56. Chase to CINCPAC [Stump], 8 April 1955, ibid., pp. 465–66; CINCPAC to CNO [Carney], 8 April 1955, ibid., pp. 471–73; memorandum of conversation, 11 April 1955, ibid., pp. 475–76.

57. Eisenhower wanted someone whom Chiang trusted to present the outpost idea to him. He initially considered sending Walter Judd and retired Gen. Albert Wedemeyer as his envoys. Memorandum, 9 April 1955, box 4, Dulles-Herter Series, AWF.

58. Makins to FO, 7 April 1955, FC 1041/69, FO 371/115045.

59. Annex E, enclosed with memorandum of conversation, 17 April 1955, FRUS, 1955–57, 2:493–95. The provision in the proposal for the emplacement of nuclear weapons on Taiwan was most probably Radford's idea. He had already looked into

the suitability and availability of nuclear-capable "Honest John" rockets for the defense of the island. See Ridgway to Radford, 5 April 1955, FRUS, 1955–57, 2:452–53.

60. Dulles had discussed these ideas with both Pearson and Australia's Robert Menzies. Memorandum of conversation, 16 March 1955, file 6, 50056-B-40, DEA.

61. The admiral had spoken to Eisenhower about his reservations a week before Dulles presented the evacuation-blockade proposal to the president. Memorandum of telephone conversation, 11 April 1955, box 9, Eisenhower Diary Series, AWF.

62. Bowie to Dulles, 7 February 1955, FRUS, 1955–57, 2:238–40. Bowie to Dulles, 9 April 1955, ibid., pp. 473–75; Merchant to Dulles, 6 April 1955 (released to author through FOI).

63. Memorandum, Radford to Wilson, 2 September 1954, CCS 381 Far East (11-28-50) Sec. 22, JCS, 1954–56.

64. Memorandum of conversation, 17 April 1955, FRUS, 1955–57, 2:492.

65. Sebald to Hoover, 21 April, ibid., p. 500.

66. Memorandum of conversation, 17 April 1955, ibid., p. 493.

67. Eisenhower preferred the term "maritime zone" to "blockade," recognizing the legal significance of the latter. Memorandum of conversation, 22 April 1955, ibid., p. 503. Legal advisers within the State Department used the term "zone of defense." They found no precedents in international law for such a zone; on the other hand, they did not believe that international law or the UN Charter forbade it. Anderson to Radford, 22 April 1955, ibid., pp. 505–6.

68. Carney to Radford, 22 April 1955, ibid., p. 504.; memorandum for the record, 29 April 1955, ibid., pp. 529–30.

69. Carney to Radford, 22 April 1955, ibid., p. 504.

70. Memorandum of conversation, 16 March 1955, file 6, 50056-B-40, DEA.

71. FRUS, 1955–57, 2:502 n. 2.

72. Hoover to Robertson and Radford, 22 April 1955, ibid., pp. 501–2.

73. Robertson to Dulles, 25 April 1955, ibid., pp. 510–17.

74. Robertson to Dulles, 27 April 1955, ibid., pp. 523–25.

75. Memorandum for the record, 29 April 1955, ibid., p. 530.

76. Eisenhower to Dulles, 26 April 1955, ibid., pp. 522–23.

77. Robertson to Dulles, 27 April 1955, ibid., p. 524.

78. NYT, 24 April 1955, 1:8, 25 April 1955, 7:2.

79. Chang and He, "Absence of War in the U.S.-China Confrontation over Quemoy and Matsu," pp. 1520–21.

80. Kahin, Asian-African Conference, pp. 14–16, 25–29, 35–38; Jia, "Searching for Peaceful Coexistence," pp. 277–78; Hinton, China's Turbulent Quest, pp. 76–77.

81. State Department press release, 23 April 1955, FRUS, 1955–57, 2:507 n. 3.

82. Memorandum of conversation, 25 April 1955, ibid., p. 517; editorial note, ibid., pp. 519–20.

83. Memorandum, 3 May 1955, box 1, L. Arthur Minnich Series, Office of the Staff Secretary, WHO; memorandum of conversation, 25 April 1955, FRUS, 1955–57, 2:517.

84. NYT, 24 April 1955, 1:6, 3:4–5, 26 April 1955, 1:4.

85. "Recent Opinion Polling Results on U.S.-Chinese Relations," 5 August 1955, box 33, POS; China Telegram, 21–27 April and 28 April–4 May 1955, ibid. Smith was

one of a dozen Republican senators who issued a statement in favor of cease-fire negotiations. NYT, 1 May 1955, 1:5.

86. NYT, 8 May 1955, IV, 8:1.

87. Memorandum of conversation, 4 May 1955, FRUS, 1955–57, 2:553.

88. Rankin to DOS, 11 May 1955, ibid., pp. 561–62; Dulles to U.S. Embassy Taipei, 18 May 1955, ibid., pp. 565–66.

89. A well-informed press story, citing the views of the highest American civilian and military representatives on Taiwan, cautioned against acceptance of exaggerated reports on the scope of the buildup to which the Nationalists had given currency. The best available intelligence indicated that construction was still in the preliminary stage and that the string of airfields was not expected to become operational until later in the year. Furthermore, the airfields consisted of little more than landing strips without most of the ancillary facilities of fully developed airbases. NYT, 21 May 1955, 1:1. During a three-day visit to Taiwan in early May, Admiral Stump told Chiang that the airfield buildup might only be defensive. Rankin to DOS, 11 May 1955, FRUS, 1955–57, 2:561.

90. Shepley, "How Dulles Averted War," pp. 72, 78; Eisenhower, *White House Years*, p. 483.

91. For Eisenhower's leadership style, consult Greenstein, *Hidden-Hand Presidency*, pp. 21–23, 30–35, 113–38; Henderson, *Managing the Presidency*, pp. 105–15.

92. Ambrose, *The President*, pp. 244–45; Divine, *Eisenhower and the Cold War*, pp. 64–66. Other complimentary assessments of Eisenhower's leadership during the crisis appear in Hoopes, *Devil and John Foster Dulles*, p. 283, and Rushkoff, "Eisenhower, Dulles and the Quemoy-Matsu Crisis," pp. 465–80. For more critical evaluations of Eisenhower-Dulles diplomacy, see Brands, "Testing Massive Retaliation," pp. 146–48; Gordon H. Chang, "To the Nuclear Brink," pp. 96–123; Graebner, "Eisenhower and Communism," pp. 71–75; Pach and Richardson, *Presidency of Dwight D. Eisenhower*, pp. 102–4; Chang and He, "Absence of War in the U.S.-China Confrontation over Quemoy and Matsu," pp. 1522–23. Diverse appraisals of Dulles's performance during the crisis appear in Immerman, *Dulles and the Diplomacy of the Cold War*; see especially the essays by Ronald Pruessen, Nancy Tucker, and John Lewis Gaddis, and the conclusion by Immerman. Marks, *Power and Peace*, pp. 80–86, offers a flattering but unconvincing appreciation.

93. Chang and He, "Absence of War in the U.S.-China Confrontation over Quemoy and Matsu," p. 1520. The crisis was a proximate cause of China's decision in January 1955, even before Washington's nuclear warnings, to build its own atomic bomb. Lewis and Xue, *China Builds the Bomb*, pp. 35–40.

94. Chang and He, "Absence of War in the U.S.-China Confrontation over Quemoy and Matsu," p. 1518.

95. CINCPAC/Commander in Chief, Pacific Fleet Intelligence Estimate, "Chinese Communist and Chinese Nationalist Capabilities and Probable Courses of Action with Respect to Chin-men, Matsu, and Nan-chi Islands through Mid-1956," 18 February 1955 (released to author through FOI); NIE 100-4-55, 16 March 1955, FRUS, 1955–57, 2:376–77.

96. Chang and He, "Absence of War in the U.S.-China Confrontation over Quemoy and Matsu," pp. 1517–18.

97. Rankin to Roberston, 13 March 1955, FRUS, 1955–57, 2:361.

98. Rankin to DOS, 30 March 1955, box 28, WHCF (DDEL).

99. NIE 100-4/1-55, "Morale on Taiwan," 16 April 1955, FRUS, 1955–57, 2:479–89.

100. Office of High Commissioner for Canada, London, to Pearson, 14 February 1955, file 5, 50056-B-40, DEA; U.K. Consul Tamsui to FO, 26 February 1955, FC 1041/489, FO 371/115040; U.K. Consul Tamsui to FO, 26 October 1955, FC 1015/23, FO 371/114987.

101. SNIE 100-4-54, "The Situation with Respect to Certain Islands off the Coast of Mainland China," 4 September 1954, FRUS, 1952–54, 14:570.

102. NIE 100-4-55, 16 March 1955, FRUS, 1955–57, 2:380.

Chapter Eleven

1. Makins to FO, 3 May 1955, FC 1041/827, FO 371/115049; Australian Embassy Washington to Australian high commissioner, Ottawa, 5 May 1955, file 8, 50056-B-40, DEA.

2. President's News Conference, 27 April 1955, *Public Papers of the Presidents: Dwight D. Eisenhower, 1955*, pp. 425–26; State Department press release, 26 April 1955, box 2, White House Memoranda Series, Dulles Papers, DDEL.

3. Memorandum of conversation, 5 May 1955, FRUS, 1955–57, 2:545–49; Rankin to DOS, 9 May 1955, ibid., pp. 558–59; Koo Memoir, VII, K 10.

4. Memorandum of conversation between Charles Malik and Chou En-lai, 25 April 1955, 793.00/5-655; memorandum of conversation, 6 May 1955, FRUS, 1955–57, 2:555.

5. NYT, 17 May 1955, 1:1; Dulles to Eisenhower, 18 May 1955, FRUS, 1955–57, 2:566–67.

6. Dulles to Robertson, 25 May 1955, FRUS, 1955–57, 2:574.

7. Memorandum of conversation, 19 May 1955, box 51, CA, 1948–56.

8. U.K. Permanent Delegation (NATO), Paris, to FO, 10 May 1955, FC 1034/13, FO 371/115007.

9. Barber, *United States in World Affairs*, pp. 28–29, 41–44, 59–60.

10. Memorandum of conversation, 14 May 1955, FRUS, 1955–57, 2:563–65.

11. G. L. Mehta to Dulles, 27 May 1955, ibid., pp. 574–75.

12. NYT, 31 May 1955, 1:8.

13. Memorandum of phone call, 3 June 1955, box 3, Telephone Call Series, Dulles Papers, DDEL.

14. Dulles to Eisenhower, 14 March 1955, box 4, Dulles-Herter Series, AWF; Eisenhower Diary, 14 August 1955, box 8, Whitman Diary, ibid.

15. Memorandum of conversation, 14 June 1955, FRUS, 1955–57, 2:594–95; memorandum of conversation, 14 June 1955, ibid., pp. 595–602; memorandum of conversation, 10 June 1955, ibid., pp. 588–89. The State Department had already announced in early April that seventy-six Chinese students with technical training, previously denied permission to leave the United States, were now free to depart. Franklin Gowen to Dulles, 8 April 1955, ibid., pp. 467–70; Koo Memoir, VII, J 34. An informative account of the issue of detained Chinese students appears in Han, "An Untold Story," pp. 77–99.

16. Brief for the secretary of state, 22 June 1955, FC 1041/941, FO 371/115054; Cabinet Minutes, 30 June 1955, C.M. (55) (19) (6), CAB 128/29.

17. Record of conversation, 20 June 1955, FC 1041/943, FO 371/115054; record of conversation, 22 June 1955, FC 1041/944, FO 371/115054; memorandum of conversation, 20 June 1955, FRUS, 1955–57, 2:605–7.

By the summer of 1955, Taiwanese were entering the armed forces in larger numbers as younger replacements for demobilized mainlanders. By August 1956 over 80 percent of conscripts were Taiwan-born, and it was expected that within a few years natives of the island would constitute a majority of the Nationalist military. Rankin to DOS, 24 August 1956, 793.4/8-2456.

18. Excerpt from Makins to Dulles, 30 June 1955, FRUS, 1955–57, 2:640 n. 2; Dulles to Aldrich, 8 July 1955, ibid., p. 641. Dulles expected the Soviets to propose a six-power conference on the Far East that would include the People's Republic and India. Memorandum of conversation, 23 June 1955, ibid., p. 610.

19. Dulles to Aldrich, 11 July 1955, ibid., pp. 643–44.

20. Robertson to Dulles, 12 July 1955, ibid., pp. 648–49.

21. Aldrich to DOS, 15 July 1955, ibid., pp. 653–55.

22. Memorandum for file, 15 July 1955, ibid., p. 655; text of identic announcement, 25 July 1955, ibid., p. 678. The tempest over nomenclature is described in Kenneth Young, *Negotiating with the Chinese Communists*, p. 51.

23. Minutes of 3rd Plenary Meeting, 19 July 1955, Record of Plenary Meetings and Meetings of the Foreign Ministers at the Geneva Conference, 18–23 July 1955, box 2, International Trips and Meetings, Office of the Staff Secretary, WHO.

24. Eisenhower spoke with Marshal Georgi Zhukov, his wartime comrade in arms, and with Khrushchev. Memorandum of conversation, 23 July 1955, FRUS, 1955–57, 2:673–74; editorial note, ibid., pp. 681–82. His positive assessment of these conversations appears in Bipartisan Legislative Meeting, 25 July 1955, box 1, Legislative Meeting Series, AWF. For Eden's exchanges with Nikolai A. Bulganin (19 July) and with Khrushchev and Bulganin together (22 July), see Record of Conversations of the Prime Minister at the Geneva Conference, 18–23 July 1955, Annex VI, CAB 133/141. Evidence of the prime minister's belief that the Soviets were receptive to his appeal for Chinese restraint appears in Cabinet Minutes, 26 July 1955, C.M. (55) (26) (4), CAB 128/29.

25. Eden-Eisenhower conversation, 17 July 1955, Record of Conversations of the Prime Minister at the Geneva conference, 18–23 July 1955, Annex VI, CAB 133/141.

26. Eden-Dulles conversation, 22 July 1955, ibid.

27. Memorandum of conversation, 5 August 1955, FRUS, 1955–57, 3:15–16.

28. FRUS, 1955–57, 2:685 n. 1.

29. Dulles to Johnson, 29 July 1955, ibid., pp. 685–87.

30. State Department press release, 26 July 1955, box 90, J. F. Dulles Papers (SML).

31. NYT, 25 July 1955, 1:5, 27 July 1955, 1:1, 28 July 1955, 8:8.

32. Memorandum of conversation, 5 August 1955, FRUS, 1955–57, 3:16.

33. "Recent Press and Congressional Discussion of U.S. China Policy," 30 August 1955, box 33, POS; summary of Hoover to Dulles, 18 July 1955, FRUS, 1955–57, 2:659 n. 4; NYT, 1 August 1955, 3:5. Additional evidence of a moderating trend in public

sentiment toward China appeared in a national opinion poll in late August showing that 82 percent of those surveyed favored a meeting between Dulles and Chou En-lai whereas only 10 percent did not. Kusnitz, *Public Opinion and Foreign Policy*, pp. 74–75.

34. Memorandum of conversation, 28 July 1955, FRUS, 1955–57, 2:382–85; partial text of message from Yeh to Dulles, 28 July 1955, ibid., p. 683 n. 2; memorandum of conversation, 9 August 1955, ibid., 3:22–25; Koo Memoir, VII, K 62–63, 92.

35. Johnson to DOS, 1 August 1955, FRUS, 1955–57, 3:1–3.

36. Johnson with McAllister, *Right Hand of Power*, p. 259.

37. Although written before State Department documentation became available, the best account remains Kenneth Young, *Negotiating with the Chinese Communists*, chaps. 3–4.

38. Ibid., chap. 3.

39. Johnson to DOS, 14 September 1955, FRUS, 1955–57, vol. 3 (Microfiche Supplement); Dulles to Johnson, 19 September 1955, FRUS, 1955–57, 3:93–94; Johnson to DOS, 28 September 1955, ibid., p. 106; Dulles to Johnson, 12 October 1955, ibid., pp. 125–26.

40. McConaughy to Johnson, 13 February 1956, FRUS, 1955–57, vol. 3 (Microfiche Supplement); Johnson to McConaughy, 19 February 1956, ibid.

41. Kenneth Young, *Negotiating with the Chinese Communists*, pp. 95–106, app. C.

42. Koo Memoir, VII, K 234; excerpt from U.S. Embassy Taipei to DOS, 9 November 1955, FRUS, 1955–57, 3:185 n. 3; Rankin to DOS, 17 November 1955, ibid., pp. 175–76.

43. Rankin to DOS, 26 January 1956, FRUS, 1955–57, 3:279–82; Hoover to U.S. Embassy Taipei, 13 February 1956, ibid., pp. 307–8.

44. Dulles to Johnson, 5 August 1955, FRUS, 1955–57, vol. 3 (Microfiche Supplement).

45. Hoover to U.S. Embassy Taipei, 25 November 1955, ibid., pp. 185–87.

46. Excerpt from McConaughy to Johnson, 30 September 1955, ibid., p. 102 n. 3.

47. NIE 13-56, "Chinese Communist Capabilities and Probable Courses of Action through 1960," 5 January 1956, ibid., pp. 232–33.

48. Summary of telegram from Chase to CINCPAC, 15 June 1955, FRUS, 1955–57, 2:616 n. 3; Cochran to DOS, 28 June 1955, ibid., pp. 615–16; Dulles to DOS, 2 July 1955, ibid., p. 628; A. C. Davis to Robertson, 3 August 1955, FRUS, 1955–57, 3:13–14; Maj. Gen. George Smythe to CINCPAC, 18 September 1955, ibid., pp. 91–92.

49. Lodge to Dulles, 7 September 1955, 310.2/9-755; memorandum of conversation, 7 September 1955, FRUS, 1955–57, 11:300–301; Hoover to Stuart, 26 September 1955, 310.2/9-2655.

50. UN Mission to DOS, 10 September 1955, FRUS, 1955–57, 11:302.

51. Luard, 1945–1955, pp. 368–69.

52. UN Mission to DOS, 13 November 1955, FRUS, 1955–57, 11:356–57; memorandum of conversation, 17 November 1955, ibid., p. 374; Lodge to DOS, 1 December 1955, ibid., p. 415; NYT, 14 November 1955, 1:8, 11:4–6, 7 December 1955, 16:8.

53. Rankin to DOS, 22 November 1955, FRUS, 1955–57, 11:390–91; Chiang Kai-shek

to Eisenhower, 26 November 1955, ibid., pp. 401–4; Chiang Kai-shek to Eisenhower, 4 December 1955, ibid., pp. 423–24.

54. C. Burke Elbrick to Francis Wilcox, 16 November 1955, 310.2/11-1655; Murphy to Dulles, 28 November 1955, 310.2/11-2855.

55. Lodge to DOS, 18 November 1955, FRUS, 1955–57, 11:378.

56. Eisenhower to Chiang Kai-shek, 22 November 1955, ibid., p. 388; Eisenhower to Chiang Kai-shek, 28 November 1955, ibid., pp. 408–9.

57. Dulles to Chiang Kai-shek, 22 November 1955, ibid., pp. 389–90.

58. Luard, 1945–1955, pp. 369–72; Yearbook of the United Nations, 1955, pp. 26–29.

59. Rankin to DOS, 23 December 1955, FRUS, 1955–57, 3:463–67.

60. Memorandum of conversation, 31 January 1956, ibid., pp. 290–93; memorandum of conversation, 31 January 1956, ibid., p. 468.

61. Memorandum of conversation, 1 March 1956, FRUS, 1955–57, 11:470; Robertson to Wilcox, 4 June 1956, box 17, CA, 1954–56; memorandum of conversation, 7 October 1956, FRUS, 1955–57, 11:474.

62. Appleton, The Eternal Triangle?, pp. 190–95.

63. Memorandum on Taiwan, 7 September 1956, box 12, CA, 1954–56; "U.S. Military and Economic Aid Programs," March 1956, box 12, ibid; memorandum for the files, 4 October 1956, box 18, ibid.

64. McConaughy to Robertson, 21 November 1955, 611.93/10-2155.

65. Paul Meyer to DOS, 31 January 1956, 793.5/1-3156.

66. Rankin to Bowden, 4 November 1955, FRUS, 1955–57, 3:159.

67. Report on Taiwan by the Interdepartmental Committee on Certain U.S. Aid Programs, 6 July 1956, FRUS, 1955–57, 3:390–92; Progress Report on NSC 5503, 11 April 1956, box 266, NSC.

68. Memorandum on Taiwan, 7 September 1956, box 12, CA, 1954–56; Barnett, "Economy of Formosa," p. 6.

69. "United States–GRC Friction," 21 September 1955, box 1, Miscellaneous Subject File, Records of the Assistant Secretary of State for Far Eastern Affairs, FEA, 1954–56; Cochran to DOS, 21 October 1955, 611.93/10-2155.

70. NSC 5441, "U.S. Policy toward Formosa and the Government of the Republic of China," 28 December 1954, FRUS, 1952–54, 14:1054–55.

71. NSC 5503, "U.S. Policy toward Formosa and the Government of the Republic of China," 15 January 1955, FRUS, 1955–57, 2:31.

72. Memorandum for the Record, 3 October 1955, 091 (Apr–Dec 1955), CJCS, 1953–57; memorandum for the Files, 1 July 1955, box 5, CA, 1954–56; Robertson to Dulles, 8 July 1955, FRUS, 1955–57, 2:639–40; memorandum of conversation, 18 August 1954, box 54, CA, 1948–56; CINCPAC to Rankin, 23 December 1955, box 5, CA, 1954–56.

Conclusion

1. Wang, "Origins of America's 'Two China' Policy," p. 198.

2. This viewpoint appears in Koen, China Lobby in American Politics, and Purifoy, Harry Truman's China Policy.

3. For assessments of the British role similar to my own, consult Tang, *Britain's Encounter with Revolutionary China*, pp. 192–96, and Zhai, *The Dragon, the Lion, and the Eagle*, pp. 208–16.

4. Indispensable for an understanding of the importance of the Taiwan issue in Sino-American relations after 1955 is Tucker, *Taiwan, Hong Kong, and the United States*. Valuable information and analysis for the period after the Sino-American rapprochement is contained in Harding, *A Fragile Relationship*, and Myers, *A Unique Relationship*.

Primary Sources

Manuscripts and Archival Records

Bailey/Howe Library, University of Vermont, Burlington, Vt.
  Warren R. Austin Papers
Bancroft Library, University of California, Berkeley
  William F. Knowland Papers
Butler Library, Columbia University, N.Y.
  V. K. Wellington Koo Papers
Danforth Library, New England College, Henniker, N.H.
  Styles Bridges Papers
Department of External Affairs, Ottawa, Canada
  Records Relating to Communist China, Far East, Formosa and Coastal Islands,
    and Chinese Representation in UN, 1950–55
Dwight D. Eisenhower Library, Abilene, Kans.
  John Foster Dulles Papers
· Dwight D. Eisenhower Presidential Papers (Ann Whitman File, White House
    Central Files)
  James C. Hagerty Papers
  C. D. Jackson Papers
  Walter Bedell Smith Papers
  White House Office Records: Office of the Special Assistant for National Security
    Affairs; Office of the Staff Secretary
Hoover Institution on War, Revolution, and Peace, Stanford, Calif.
  Claire L. Chennault Papers
  Charles M. Cooke Papers
  Everett F. Drumwright Papers
  R. Allen Griffin Papers
  Walter H. Judd Papers
  Marvin Liebman Papers
  Arthur W. Radford Typescript Memoirs
  Hubert G. Schenck Papers
  William J. Sebald Papers
  John Leighton Stuart Diary
  Freda Utley Papers
Lehman Suite, Columbia University, N.Y.
  Herbert H. Lehman Papers

Library of Congress, Washington, D.C.
  Joseph and Stewart Alsop Papers
  Claire L. Chennault Papers
  Philip C. Jessup Papers
  Robert A. Taft Papers
MacArthur Memorial Bureau of Archives, Norfolk, Va.
  Douglas A. MacArthur Papers: RG 5, 6, 9, 10
  Charles A. Willoughby Papers
Seeley Mudd Library, Princeton, N.J.
  Allen Dulles Papers
  John Foster Dulles Files (Eisenhower Library)
  John Foster Dulles Papers
  Emmet J. Hughes Papers
  George F. Kennan Papers
  Arthur Krock Papers
  Livingston T. Merchant Papers
  Karl Rankin Papers
  H. Alexander Smith Papers
  Whiting Willauer Papers
National Archives, Suitland, Md.
  RG 84, Records of the Foreign Service Posts of the Department of State (Taipei),
    1950–55
National Archives, Washington, D.C.
  Civil Reference Branch
  RG 59, General Records of the Department of State, 1950–55
  RG 59, Lot Files:
    Action Summaries of the Undersecretary's Meetings, 1945–52
    Bureau of Far Eastern Affairs, Records of the Officer in Charge of Burma Af-
      fairs, 1948–56
    Bureau of Far Eastern Affairs, Records Relating to Economic Affairs, 1948–58
    Bureau of Far Eastern Affairs, Miscellaneous Subject Files, 1951–54
    Bureau of Far Eastern Affairs, Records of the Deputy Assistant Secretary of
      State for Far Eastern Economic Affairs, 1951–57
    Bureau of Far Eastern Affairs, 1953
    Bureau of Far Eastern Affairs, Office of the Special Assistant for Regional Pro-
      grams, 1953–57
    Bureau of Far Eastern Affairs, Files Relating to Southeast Asia and the Geneva
      Conference, 1954
    Bureau of Far Eastern Affairs, Records of the Assistant Secretary of State for Far
      Eastern Affairs, Miscellaneous Subject Files, 1954–56
    Bureau of Far Eastern Affairs, Subject File, 1955
    Bureau of Intelligence and Research, 1950–54
    Memoranda of Conversations with the President, 1949–52
    Office of Chinese Affairs, 1944–50
    Office of Chinese Affairs, 1948–56
    Office of Chinese Affairs, 1954–56

Office of the Executive Secretariat, 1949–52, Daily Staff Summary, August
1949–December 1951
Office of the Executive Secretariat, 1949–52, Minutes of the Undersecretary's
Meetings, 1951–52
Office of Public Opinion Studies, 1943–75
Policy Planning Staff, 1947–53
Policy Planning Staff, 1954
Policy Planning Staff, 1955
Position Papers and Reports for the Undersecretary's Meetings, 1949–52
Summaries of the Secretary's Daily Meetings, 1949–50
Legislative Branch
RG 46, United States Senate. Committee on Foreign Relations and Committee
on Armed Services. *Military Situation in the Far East.*, 82d Cong., 1st sess.,
3 May–25 June 1951 (uncensored testimony)
RG 273, Records of the National Security Council
Modern Military Branch
RG 218, Records of Joint Chiefs of Staff
Chairman, Joint Chiefs of Staff, 1949–53
Chairman, Joint Chiefs of Staff, 1953–57
Joint Chiefs of Staff, 1948–50
Joint Chiefs of Staff, 1951–53
Joint Chiefs of Staff, 1954–56
RG 263, Central Intelligence Agency
Estimates of the Office of Research Evaluation, 1946–50
National Intelligence Estimates Concerning the Soviet Union, 1950–61
Studies in Intelligence
RG 319, U.S. Army Staff Records, G-3, Operations, 1950–55,
U.S. Army Staff Records, G-3, Operations, Assistant Chief of Staff, 1950–51
RG 330, Records of the Office of Secretary of Defense, 1950–54
Nevada Historical Society, Reno, Nev.
Patrick McCarran Papers
Operational Archives, Naval Historical Center, Washington Navy Yard, Washington, D.C.
Arthur W. Radford Papers
Strategic Plans Division Records
Public Archives of Canada, Ottawa, Canada
Arnold D. Heeney Papers
Douglas V. Le Pan Papers
Lester B. Pearson Papers
Escott Reid Papers
Hume Wrong Papers
RG 2 (B1), Records of the Privy Council
RG 25, Records of the Department of External Affairs
Public Record Office, London (Kew), England
CAB 128, Cabinet Minutes
CAB 129, Cabinet Memoranda
CAB 130, Ad-Hoc Committees

CAB 131, Defense Committee
CAB 133, Commonwealth and International Conferences
CAB 134, Cabinet Committees
FO 371, Foreign Office Files, 1950–55
FO 800, Ernest Bevin Papers
PREM 8, 11, Prime Minister's Office
Harry S. Truman Library, Independence, Mo.
Dean Acheson Papers
Clark M. Clifford Papers
Matthew Connelly Papers
George M. Elsey Papers
Theodore Tannewald, Jr., Papers
Harry S. Truman Presidential Papers: David D. Lloyd Files, Charles S. Murphy
Files, President's Secretary's Files, White House Central Files
James E. Webb Papers
United States Army Military History Institute, Carlisle, Pa.
William J. Donovan Papers
Matthew B. Ridgway Papers

Manuscripts on Microtext

Declassified Documents Reference System. Retrospective Collection. Collections
1983–91. Research Publications, Woodbridge, Conn.
Memoirs of Dr. V. K. Wellington Koo. Chinese Oral History Project, East Asian
Institute, Columbia University, N.Y. (Microfilming Corporation of America,
1978)

Oral Histories

Chinese Oral History Project, East Asian Institute, Columbia University, N.Y.
Tsiang Ting-fu [T. F. Tsiang]
Reminiscences of Wu Kuo-chen [K. C. Wu]
Columbia University Oral History Project, Butler Library, Columbia University, N.Y.
Dwight D. Eisenhower
Andrew J. Goodpaster
Ernest A. Gross
Walter H. Judd
William F. Knowland
Walter S. Robertson
John Foster Dulles Oral History Collection, Seeley Mudd Library, Princeton, N.J.
Sherman Adams
John M. Allison
Dillon Anderson
Robert Bowie
Chiang Kai-shek
Dwight D. Eisenhower
John Foster Dulles and the Far East
Andrew J. Goodpaster
Bourke B. Hickenlooper

U. Alexis Johnson
Sir Thomas MacDonald
Livingston T. Merchant
Sir Leslie Munro
Arthur W. Radford
James P. Richards
Matthew B. Ridgway
William J. Sebald
H. Alexander Smith
George Yeh
Yoshida Shigeru
Dwight D. Eisenhower Oral History Collection, Dwight D. Eisenhower Library, Abilene, Kans.
Dwight D. Eisenhower
Andrew J. Goodpaster
William F. Knowland
Harry S. Truman Library Oral History Interviews, Harry S. Truman Library, Independence, Mo.
Robert W. Barnett
W. Walton Butterworth
O. Edmund Clubb
George M. Elsey
Oliver Franks
Walter H. Judd
Philip D. Sprouse
Senior Officers Debriefing Program, United States Army Military History Institute, Carlisle, Pa.
Mark W. Clark
Richard Collins
Andrew J. Goodpaster
Matthew B. Ridgway

Correspondence and Interviews
Author's telephone interview with former Foreign Service Officer, 3 June 1993
Dean Rusk to author, 8 July 1993

Newspapers and Periodicals
Department of State Bulletin, 1950–55
New York Times, 1950–55

Published Documents and Papers
Great Britain
 United Kingdom. *Parliamentary Debates*. House of Commons. 5th ser. London: His/Her Majesty's Stationery Office.
 Sess. 1950–51, vol. 487.
 Sess. 1952–53, vol. 510.

Sess. 1953–54, vol. 530.

Sess. 1955, vol. 538.

People's Republic of China

   Important Documents Concerning the Question of Taiwan. Peking: Foreign Languages Press, 1955.

United Nations

   Cordier, Andrew W. and Wilder Foote, eds. *Public Papers of the Secretaries-General of the United Nations.* Vol. 2: *Dag Hammarskjöld, 1953–1956.* N.Y.: Columbia University Press, 1972.

   United Nations. *Official Records of the General Assembly.* Plenary Meetings, 1950. Vol. 1.

   United Nations. *Official Records of the Security Council.* 1950.

   United Nations. *Official Records of the Security Council.* 1952.

   United Nations. *Official Records of the General Assembly.* Plenary Meetings, 1953.

   United Nations. *Official Records of the Security Council.* 1955.

U.S. Executive Branch

   U.S. Central Intelligence Agency. Scott A. Koch, ed. *CIA Cold War Records: Selected Estimates on the Soviet Union, 1950–1959.* Washington, D.C., 1993.

   U.S. Central Intelligence Agency. Michael Warner, ed. *CIA Cold War Records: The CIA under Harry Truman.* Washington, D.C., 1994.

   U.S. Department of State. *Foreign Relations of the United States.* Washington, D.C.: Government Printing Office

   1947–1952, Microfiche Supplement: *Secretary's Memoranda of Conversations.* 1988.

   1949–1952, Microfiche Supplement: *Secretary's Memoranda: Visits of Foreign Dignitaries.* 1988.

   1949, vol. 7: *The Far East and Australia.* 1976.

   1949, vol. 9: *The Far East: China.* 1974.

   1950, vol. 1: *National Security Affairs; Foreign Economic Policy.* 1980.

   1950, vol. 2: *The United Nations; The Western Hemisphere.* 1976.

   1950, vol. 3: *Western Europe.* 1977.

   1950, vol. 6: *East Asia and the Pacific.* 1976.

   1950, vol. 7: *Korea.* 1976.

   1951, vol. 1: *National Security Affairs; Foreign Economic Policy.* 1979.

   1951, vol. 2: *The United Nations; The Western Hemisphere.* 1979.

   1951, vol. 6: *Asia and the Pacific* (two parts). 1977.

   1951, vol. 7: *Korea and China* (two parts). 1983.

   November 1952–December 1954, Microfiche Supplement: *Secretary of State's Memoranda of Conversations.* 1992.

   1952–1954, vol. 2: *National Security Affairs* (two parts). 1984.

   1952–1954, vol. 3: *United Nations Affairs.* 1979.

   1952–1954, vol. 5: *Western European Security* (two parts). 1983.

   1952–1954, vol. 7: *Germany and Austria* (two parts). 1986.

   1952–1954, vol. 12: *East Asia and the Pacific* (two parts). 1987.

   1952–1954, vol. 13: *Indochina* (two parts). 1982.

   1952–1954, vol. 14: *China and Japan* (two parts). 1985.

1952–1954, vol. 15: *Korea* (two parts). 1984.

1952–1954, vol. 16: *The Geneva Conference*. 1981.

1955–1957, vol. 2: *China* (two parts). 1986.

1955–1957, vol. 3: Microfiche Supplement: *China*. 1987.

1955–1957, vol. 5: *Austrian State Treaty; Summit and Foreign Ministers Meetings, 1955*. 1988.

1955–1957, vol. 11: *United Nations and General International Matters*. 1988.

1955–1957, vol. 19: *National Security Policy*. 1990.

U.S. Department of State. *United States Treaties and Other International Agreements*. Part I. Vol. 6 (1955). Washington, D.C.: Government Printing Office, 1956.

U.S. President. *Public Papers of the Presidents of the United States: Harry S. Truman* (1950–53). *Dwight D. Eisenhower* (1953–55). Washington, D.C.: Government Printing Office, 1965–66, 1959–61.

U.S. Legislative Branch

U.S. Congress. *Congressional Record*. 81st Cong., 2d sess., 1950. Vol. 96. Washington, D.C.: Government Printing Office, 1950.

U.S. Congress. *Congressional Record*. 84th Cong., 1st sess., 1955. Vol. 101. Washington, D.C.: Government Printing Office, 1955.

U.S. Congress. Senate. Committee on Foreign Relations. *Reviews of the World Situation, 1949–1950*. 81st Cong., 1st and 2d sess., 1949–50. Historical Series. Washington, D.C.: Government Printing Office, 1974.

U.S. Congress. Senate. Committee on Foreign Relations and Committee on Armed Services. *Military Situation in the Far East*. 82d Cong., 1st sess., 3 May–25 June 1951. 5 vols. Washington, D.C.: Government Printing Office, 1951.

U.S. Congress. Senate. *Executive Sessions of the Foreign Relations Committee*. 83d Cong., 1st sess., 1953. Historical Series. Vol. 5. Washington, D.C.: Government Printing Office, 1977.

U.S. Congress. Senate. *Executive Sessions of the Foreign Relations Committee*. 83d Cong., 2d sess., 1954. Historical Series. Vol. 6. Washington, D.C.: Government Printing Office, 1977.

U.S. Congress. Senate. *Executive Sessions of the Foreign Relations Committee*. 84th Cong., 1st sess., 1955. Historical Series. Vol. 7. Washington, D.C.: Government Printing Office, 1978.

U.S. Congress. Senate Committee on Foreign Relations. Executive Report No. 2, "Mutual Defense Treaty with the Republic of China." 8 February 1955. 84th Cong., 1st sess., 1955. Washington, D.C.: Government Printing Office, 1955.

Secondary Works

Books and Dissertations

Acheson, Dean. *Present at the Creation*. New York: W. W. Norton, 1969.

Adams, Sherman. *Firsthand Report: The Story of the Eisenhower Administration*. New York: Harper & Bros., 1961.

Allison, John M. *Ambassador from the Prairie; or Allison Wonderland*. Boston: Houghton Mifflin, 1973.

Ambrose, Stephen E. *The President*. Vol. 2 of *Eisenhower*. New York: Simon & Schuster, 1984.

Anderson, David L. *Trapped by Success: The Eisenhower Administration and Vietnam, 1953–1961*. New York: Columbia University Press, 1991.

Appleton, Sheldon. *The Eternal Triangle? Communist China, the United States and the United Nations*. East Lansing: Michigan State University Press, 1961.

Arnold, James R. *The First Domino: Eisenhower, the Military, and America's Intervention in Vietnam*. New York: William Morrow & Co., 1991.

Attlee, Clement. *Twilight of Empire: Memoirs of Prime Minister Clement Attlee*. New York: A. S. Barnes, 1962.

Bachrack, Stanley D. *The Committee of One Million: "China Lobby" Politics, 1953–1971*. New York: Columbia University Press, 1976.

Barber, Hollis W. *The United States in World Affairs, 1955*. New York: Harper & Row, 1957.

Billings-Yun, Melanie. *Decision against War: Eisenhower and Dien Bien Phu*. New York: Columbia University Press, 1988.

Blair, Clay. *The Forgotten War: America in Korea, 1950–1953*. New York: Times Books, 1987.

Blum, Robert M. *Drawing the Line: The Origin of the American Containment Policy in East Asia*. New York: W. W. Norton, 1982.

Boardman, Robert. *Britain and the People's Republic of China, 1949–1974*. London: The Macmillan Press, 1976.

Boorman, Howard L., with Richard C. Howard, eds. *Biographical Dictionary of Republican China*. 5 vols. New York: Columbia University Press, 1967–79.

Borg, Dorothy, and Waldo Heinrichs, eds. *Uncertain Years: Chinese-American Relations, 1947–1950*. New York: Columbia University Press, 1980.

Bradley, Omar N., and Clay Blair. *A General's Life*. New York: Simon & Schuster, 1983.

Brands, H. W., Jr. *Cold Warriors: Eisenhower's Generation and American Foreign Policy*. New York: Columbia University Press, 1988.

Brendon, Piers. *Ike, His Life and Times*. New York: Harper & Row, 1986.

Brinkley, Douglas, ed. *Dean Acheson and the Making of U.S. Foreign Policy*. New York: St. Martin's, 1993.

Buckley, Roger. *Occupation Diplomacy: Britain, the United States and Japan, 1945–52*. Cambridge: Cambridge University Press, 1982.

Bueler, William M. *U.S. China Policy and the Problem of Taiwan*. Boulder: Colorado Associated University Press, 1971.

Buhite, Russell D. *Soviet-American Relations in Asia, 1945–1954*. Norman: University of Oklahoma Press, 1982.

Bullock, Alan. *Ernest Bevin, Foreign Secretary, 1945–1951*. New York: W. W. Norton, 1983.

Bundy, McGeorge. *Danger and Survival: Choices about the Bomb in the First Fifty Years*. New York: Random House, 1988.

Byrd, Martha. *Chennault: Giving Wings to the Tiger*. Tuscaloosa: University of Alabama Press, 1987.

Camilleri, Joseph. *Chinese Foreign Policy*. Seattle: University of Washington Press, 1981.

Caridi, Ronald J. *The Korean War and American Politics; the Republican Party as a Case Study*. Philadelphia: University of Pennsylvania Press, 1968.

Carlton, David. *Anthony Eden: A Biography*. London: Allen Lane, 1981.

Chang, Gordon H. *Friends and Enemies: The United States, China, and the Soviet Union, 1948–1972*. Stanford, Calif.: Stanford University Press, 1990.

Chang, Su-ya. "Pragmatism and Opportunism: Truman's Policy toward Taiwan, 1949–1952." Ph.D. dissertation, Pennsylvania State University, 1988.

Chase, William C. *Front Line General*. Houston, Tex.: Pacesetter Press, 1975.

Chiu, Hungdah. *China and the Taiwan Issue*. New York: Praeger, 1979.

Clark, Cal. *Taiwan's Development: Implications for Contending Political Economy Paradigms*. Westport, Conn.: Greenwood Press, 1989.

Clark, Mark W. *From the Danube to the Yalu*. New York: Harper & Row, 1954. Reprint, Blue Ridge Summit, Pa.: Tab Books, 1988.

Clough, Ralph N. *Island China*. Cambridge, Mass.: Harvard University Press, 1978.

Clubb, O. Edmund. *The Witness and I*. New York: Columbia University Press, 1974.

Cohen, Bernard. *The Political Process and Foreign Policy, the Making of the Japanese Peace Settlement*. Princeton, N.J.: Princeton University Press, 1957.

Cohen, Warren I. *Dean Rusk*. Totowa, N.J.: Cooper Square Publishers, 1980.

———, ed. *New Frontiers in American-East Asian Relations: Essays Presented to Dorothy Borg*. New York: Columbia University Press, 1983.

Cohen, Warren I., and Akira Iriye. *The Great Powers in East Asia, 1953–1960*. New York: Columbia University Press, 1990.

Condit, Doris M. *The Test of War, 1950–1953*. Vol. 2 of *History of the Office of the Secretary of Defense*. Washington: Historical Office, Office of the Secretary of Defense, 1988.

Cotton, James, and Ian Neary, eds. *The Korean War in History*. Manchester: Manchester University Press, 1989.

Crozier, Brian, with Eric Chou. *The Man Who Lost China: The First Full Biography of Chiang Kai-shek*. New York: Charles Scribner's Sons, 1976.

Cumings, Bruce. *The Roaring of the Cataract, 1947–1950*. Vol. 2 of *The Origins of the Korean War*. Princeton: Princeton University Press, 1990.

Divine, Robert A. *Eisenhower and the Cold War*. New York: Oxford University Press, 1981.

Dobbs, Charles M. *The Unwanted Symbol: American Foreign Policy, the Cold War and Korea, 1945–1950*. Kent, Ohio: Kent State University Press, 1981.

Donoughue, B., and G. W. Jones. *Herbert Morrison: Portrait of a Politician*. London: Weidenfeld and Nicolson, 1973.

Donovan, Robert K. *Tumultuous Years: The Presidency of Harry S. Truman, 1949–1953*. New York: W. W. Norton, 1982.

Dower, John. *Empire and Aftermath: Yoshida Shigeru and the Japanese Experience, 1878–1954*. Cambridge, Mass.: Harvard University Press, 1979.

Dulles, Foster Rhea. *American Foreign Policy toward Communist China, 1949–1969.* New York: Thomas Y. Crowell, 1972.

Dunn, Frederick S. *Peace-Making and the Settlement with Japan.* Princeton, N.J.: Princeton University Press, 1963.

Eden, Anthony. *Full Circle: The Memoirs of Anthony Eden.* Boston: Houghton Mifflin, 1960.

Eisenhower, Dwight D. *The White House Years, Mandate for Change, 1953–1956.* Garden City, N.Y.: Doubleday & Co., 1963.

Ferrell, Robert H., ed. *The Diary of James C. Hagerty: Eisenhower in Mid-Course, 1954–1955.* Bloomington: Indiana University Press, 1983.

————, ed. *The Eisenhower Diaries.* New York: W. W. Norton, 1981.

Field, James A., Jr. *History of United States Naval Operations in Korea.* Washington, D.C.: Government Printing Office, 1962.

Finkelstein, David Michael. "From Abandonment to Salvation: The Evolution of United States Policy toward Taiwan, 1949–1950." Ph.D. dissertation, Princeton University, 1990.

————. *Washington's Taiwan Dilemma, 1949–1950: From Abandonment to Salvation.* Fairfax, Va.: George Mason University Press, 1993.

Finn, Richard B. *Winners in Peace: MacArthur, Yoshida and Postwar Japan.* Berkeley: University of California Press, 1992.

Fitch, Geraldine. *Formosa Beachhead.* Chicago: Henry Regnery, 1953.

Foot, Rosemary. *A Substitute for Victory: The Politics of Peacemaking at the Korean Armistice Talks.* Ithaca, N.Y.: Cornell University Press, 1990.

————. *The Wrong War: American Policy and the Dimensions of the Korean Conflict, 1950–1953.* Ithaca, N.Y.: Cornell University Press, 1985.

Fraser, T. G., and Peter Lowe, eds. *Conflict and Amity in East Asia: Essays in Honour of Ian Nish.* London: Macmillan, 1992.

Fried, Richard M. *Nightmare in Red: The McCarthy Era in Perspective.* New York: Oxford University Press, 1990.

Gaddis, John L. *The Long Peace: Inquiries into the History of the Cold War.* New York: Oxford University Press, 1987.

————. *Strategies of Containment: A Critical Appraisal of Postwar American National Security Policy.* New York: Oxford University Press, 1982.

Gallup, George H., ed. *The Gallup Poll: Public Opinion, 1935–1971.* 3 vols. New York: Random House, 1972.

Garver, John W. *Foreign Relations of the People's Republic of China.* Englewood Cliffs, N.J.: Prentice Hall, 1993.

Ge, Su. "'A Horrible Dilemma' — The Making of the U.S.-Taiwan Mutual Defense Treaty, 1948–1955." Ph.D. dissertation, Brigham Young University, 1987.

George, Alexander L., and Richard Smoke. *Deterrence in American Foreign Policy: Theory and Practice.* New York: Columbia University Press, 1974.

Gibert, Stephen P., and William M. Carpenter. *America and Island China: A Documentary History.* Lanham, Md.: University Press of America, 1989.

Gilbert, Martin. *1945–1965.* Vol. 8 of *Winston Churchill.* London: Heinemann, 1988.

Gittings, John. *The World and China, 1922–1972.* New York: Harper & Row, 1974.

Goncharov, Sergei N., John W. Lewis, and Xue Litai. *Uncertain Partners: Stalin, Mao, and the Korean War.* Stanford, Calif.: Stanford University Press, 1993.

Grasso, June M. *Truman's Two-China Policy, 1948–1950.* Armonk, N.Y.: M. E. Sharpe, 1987.

Greenstein, Fred I. *The Hidden-Hand Presidency: Eisenhower as Leader.* New York: Basic Books, 1982.

Guhin, Michael A. *John Foster Dulles: A Statesman for His Times.* New York: Columbia University Press, 1972.

Gurtov, Melvin. *The First Vietnam Crisis: Chinese Communist Strategy and United States Involvement, 1953–1954.* New York: Columbia University Press, 1967.

Gurtov, Melvin, and Byong-Moo Hwang. *China under Threat: The Policies of Strategy and Diplomacy.* Baltimore, Md.: The Johns Hopkins University Press, 1980.

Han, Nianlong, et al., eds. *Diplomacy of Contemporary China.* Translated by Qiu Ke'an et al. Hong Kong: New Horizon Press, 1990.

Harding, Harry. *A Fragile Relationship: The United States and China since 1972.* Washington, D.C.: The Brookings Institution, 1992.

Harding, Harry, and Yuan Ming, eds. *Sino-American Relations, 1945–1955: A Joint Reassessment of a Critical Decade.* Wilmington, Del.: Scholarly Resources, 1989.

Henderson, Phillip G. *Managing the Presidency: The Eisenhower Legacy—From Kennedy to Reagan.* Boulder, Colo.: Westview Press, 1988.

Hinton, Harold C. *China's Turbulent Quest: An Analysis of China's Foreign Relations since 1949.* Bloomington, Ind.: Indiana University Press, 1970.

———. *Communist China in World Politics.* Boston: Houghton Mifflin, 1966.

Historical Division of the Joint Secretariat. *History of the Indochina Incident, 1940–1954.* Vol. 1 of *The History of the Joint Chiefs of Staff: The Joint Chiefs of Staff and the War in Vietnam.* Wilmington, Del.: Michael Glazier, Inc., 1982.

Ho, Samuel P. S. *Economic Development of Taiwan, 1860–1970.* New Haven, Conn.: Yale University Press, 1978.

Hoopes, Townsend. *The Devil and John Foster Dulles.* Boston: Little, Brown, 1973.

Hsieh, Chiao Chiao. *Strategy for Survival.* London: Sherwood Press, 1985.

Hsiung, James, et al., eds. *Contemporary Republic of China: The Taiwan Experience, 1950–1980.* New York: Praeger, 1981.

Hua, Qingzhao. *From Yalta to Panmunjom: Truman's Diplomacy and the Four Powers, 1945–1953.* Ithaca, N.Y.: East Asia Program, Cornell University, 1993.

Immerman, Richard, ed. *John Foster Dulles and the Diplomacy of the Cold War: A Reappraisal.* Princeton, N.J.: Princeton University Press, 1990.

Jacoby, Neil H. *U.S. Aid to Taiwan: A Study of Foreign Aid, Self-Help, and Development.* New York: Praeger, 1966.

James, D. Clayton. *Triumph and Disaster, 1945–1964.* Vol. 3 of *The Years of MacArthur.* Boston: Houghton Mifflin, 1985.

James, Robert Rhodes. *Anthony Eden: A Biography.* New York: McGraw Hill, 1987.

Jia, Qing-guo. "Unmaterialized Rapprochement: Sino-American Relations in the Mid-1950s." Ph.D. dissertation, Cornell University, 1988.

Johnson, U. Alexis, with Jef McAllister. *The Right Hand of Power: The Memoirs of an American Diplomat.* Englewood Cliffs, N.J.: Prentice Hall, Inc., 1984.

Kahin, George McTurnan. *The Asian-African Conference, Bandung, Indonesia, April 1956*. Ithaca, N.Y.: Cornell University Press, 1956.

Kahn, E. J., Jr. *The China Hands: America's Foreign Service Officers and What Befell Them*. New York: Viking Press, 1977.

Kalicki, J. H. *The Pattern of Sino-American Crises: Political-Military Interactions in the 1950s*. London: Cambridge University Press, 1975.

Kaplan, Lawrence S., Denise Artaud, and Mark R. Rubin, eds. *Dien Bien Phu and the Crisis of Franco-American Relations*. Wilmington, Del.: Scholarly Resources, 1990.

Kaufman, Burton I. *The Korean War: Challenges in Crisis, Credibility, and Command*. New York: Alfred A. Knopf, 1986.

Keeley, Joseph. *The China Lobby Man: The Story of Alfred Kohlberg*. New Rochelle, N.Y.: Arlington House, 1969.

Keith, Ronald C. *The Diplomacy of Zhou Enlai*. New York: St. Martin's Press, 1989.

Kennan, George F. *Memoirs, 1925–1950*. Boston: Little, Brown, 1967.

Kepley, David R. *The Collapse of the Middle Way: Senate Republicans and the Bipartisan Foreign Policy, 1948–1952*. Westport, Conn.: Greenwood Press, 1988.

Kerr, George H. *Formosa Betrayed*. Boston: Houghton Mifflin, 1965.

Kinnard, Douglas. *President Eisenhower and Strategy Management*. Lexington: University of Kentucky Press, 1977.

Koen, Ross Y. *The China Lobby in American Politics*. New York: Harper & Row, 1974.

Krieg, Joann, ed. *Dwight D. Eisenhower, Soldier, President, Statesman*. Westport, Conn.: Greenwood Press, 1987.

Kusnitz, Leonard A. *Public Opinion and Foreign Policy: America's China Policy, 1949–1979*. Westport, Conn.: Greenwood Press, 1984.

Lai, Tse-han, Ramon H. Myers, and Wei Wou. *A Tragic Beginning: The Taiwan Uprising of February 28, 1947*. Stanford, Calif.: Stanford University Press, 1991.

Lasater, Martin L. *The Taiwanese Issue in Sino-American Strategic Relations*. Boulder, Colo.: Westview Press, 1984.

Leary, William M. *Perilous Missions: Civil Air Transport and CIA Covert Operations in Asia, the True Story of the CIA's Secret "Air Force."* University: University of Alabama Press, 1984.

Leffler, Melvyn. *A Preponderance of Power: National Security, the Truman Administration, and the Cold War*. Stanford, Calif.: Stanford University Press, 1992.

Lewis, John Wilson, and Xue Litai. *China Builds the Bomb*. Stanford, Calif.: Stanford University Press, 1988.

Li, Tsung-jen, and Tong Te-kong. *The Memoirs of Li Tsung-jen*. Boulder, Colo.: Westview Press, 1978.

Louis, Wm. Roger, and Hedley Bull, eds. *The 'Special Relationship': Anglo-American Relations since 1945*. Oxford: Clarendon Press, 1986.

Lowe, Peter. *The Origins of the Korean War*. New York: Longman, 1986.

Luard, Evan. *Britain and China*. London: Chatto & Windus, 1962.

———. *1945–1955*. Vol. 1 of *A History of the United Nations*. London: The Macmillan Press, 1982.

Lyon, Peter. *Eisenhower, Portrait of the Hero*. Boston: Little, Brown, 1974.

MacArthur, Douglas. *Reminiscences*. New York: McGraw Hill, 1964.

MacDonald, Callum A. *Korea, the War before Vietnam*. London: The Macmillan Press, 1986.

Macmillan, Harold. *Tides of Fortune, 1945–1955*. New York: Harper & Row, 1969.

Marks, Frederick W., III. *Power and Peace: The Diplomacy of John Foster Dulles*. Westport, Conn.: Praeger, 1993.

Marolda, Edward John. "The U.S. Navy and the Chinese Civil War, 1945–1952." Ph.D. dissertation, George Washington University, 1990.

Martin, Edwin W. *Divided Counsel: The Anglo-American Response to Communist Victory in China*. Lexington: University of Kentucky Press, 1986.

Mayers, David Allen. *Cracking the Monolith: U.S. Policy against the Sino-Soviet Alliance, 1949–1955*. Baton Rouge: Louisiana State University Press, 1986.

McCoy, Alfred W. *The Politics of Heroin in Southeast Asia*. New York: Harper & Row, 1972.

McGlothlen, Ronald. *Controlling the Waves: Dean Acheson and U.S. Foreign Policy in Asia*. New York: W. W. Norton & Co., 1993.

Melanson, Richard A., and David Mayers, eds. *Reevaluating Eisenhower: American Foreign Policy in the Fifties*. Urbana: University of Illinois Press, 1987.

Miller, Merle. *Plain Speaking: An Oral Biography of Harry S. Truman*. New York: Berkley Publishing Corp., 1974.

Moran, Lord. *Winston Churchill: The Struggle for Survival, 1940–1965*. London: Constable and Co., 1966.

Munro, John A., and Alex I. Inglis, eds. *1948–1957*. Vol. 2 of *Mike: The Memoirs of the Right Honourable Lester B. Pearson*. Toronto: University of Toronto Press, 1973.

Myers, Ramon, ed. *A Unique Relationship: The United States and the Republic of China under the Taiwan Relations Act*. Stanford, Calif.: Hoover Institution Press, 1989.

Nakatsuji, Keiji. "The Straits in Crisis: America and the Long-Term Disposition of Taiwan, 1950–1958." Ph.D. dissertation, University of Chicago, 1985.

Oshinsky, David. *A Conspiracy So Immense: The World of Joe McCarthy*. New York: The Free Press, 1982.

Ovendale, Ritchie. *The English-Speaking Alliance: Britain, the United States, the Dominions and the Cold War, 1945–51*. London: Allen Unwin, 1985.

Pach, Chester J., Jr., and Elmo Richardson. *The Presidency of Dwight D. Eisenhower*. Rev. ed. Lawrence: University of Kansas Press, 1991.

Paige, Glenn D. *The Korean Decision, June 24–30, 1950*. New York: The Free Press, 1968.

Panikkar, K. M. *In Two Chinas: Memoirs of a Diplomat*. London: George Allen & Unwin, 1955.

Payne, Robert. *Chiang Kai-shek*. New York: Weybright & Talley, 1969.

Pemberton, William E. *Harry S. Truman: Fair Dealer and Cold Warrior*. Boston: G. K. Hall, 1989.

Pogue, Forrest C. *Statesman, 1945–1959*. Vol. 4 of *George C. Marshall*. New York: Viking Press, 1987.

Poole, Walter S. *1950–1952*. Vol. 4 of *The History of the Joint Chiefs of Staff: The Joint Chiefs of Staff and National Policy*. Wilmington, Del.: Michael Glazier, 1980.

Porter, Brian. *Britain and the Rise of Communist China: A Study of British Attitudes, 1945–1954*. London: Oxford University Press, 1967.

Prados, John. *Presidents' Secret Wars: CIA and Pentagon Covert Operations since World War II*. New York: William Morrow, 1986.

Pruessen, Ronald W. *John Foster Dulles: The Road to Power*. New York: The Free Press, 1982.

Purifoy, Lewis McCarroll. *Harry Truman's China Policy: McCarthyism and the Diplomacy of Hysteria, 1947–1951*. New York: New Viewpoints, 1976.

Radford, Arthur W. *From Pearl Harbor to Vietnam: The Memoirs of Admiral Arthur W. Radford*. Edited by Stephen Jurika, Jr. Stanford, Calif.: Hoover Institution Press, 1980.

Randle, Robert F. *Geneva 1954, the Settlement of the Indochina War*. Princeton, N.J.: Princeton University Press, 1969.

Ranelagh, John. *The Agency: The Rise and Decline of the CIA*. New York: Simon & Schuster, 1986.

Rankin, Karl Lott. *China Assignment*. Seattle: University of Washington Press, 1964.

Rearden, Steven L. *The Formative Years, 1947–1950*. Vol. 1 of *History of the Office of the Secretary of Defense*. Washington, D.C.: Historical Office, Office of the Secretary of Defense, 1984.

Reeves, Thomas C. *The Life and Times of Joe McCarthy: A Biography*. New York: Stein & Day, 1982.

Reichard, Gary W. *The Reaffirmation of Republicanism: Eisenhower and the Eighty-Third Congress*. Knoxville: University of Tennessee Press, 1975.

Reinhard, David W. *The Republican Right since 1945*. Lexington: University of Kentucky Press, 1983.

Ridgway, Matthew B. *Soldier: The Memoirs of Matthew B. Ridgway*. New York: Harper & Bros., 1956.

Roberts, Priscilla, ed. *Sino-American Relations since 1900*. Hong Kong: University of Hong Kong, 1991.

Roper, Elmo. *You and Your Leaders*. New York: William Morrow, 1957.

Rotter, Andrew J. *The Path to Vietnam: Origins of the American Commitment to Southeast Asia*. Ithaca, N.Y.: Cornell University Press, 1987.

Rourke, John. *Congress and the Presidency in U.S. Foreign Policymaking: A Study of Interaction and Influence, 1945–82*. Boulder, Colo.: Westview Press, 1983.

Rusk, Dean. *As I Saw It*. Edited by Daniel S. Papp. New York: W. W. Norton, 1990.

Ryan, Mark A. *Chinese Attitudes toward Nuclear Weapons: China and the United States during the Korean War*. Armonk, N.Y.: M. E. Sharpe, 1989.

Samson, Jack. *Chennault*. New York: Doubleday, 1987.

Schaller, Michael. *The American Occupation of Japan: The Origins of the Cold War in Asia*. New York: Oxford University Press, 1985.

———. *Douglas MacArthur: The Far Eastern General*. New York: Oxford University Press, 1989.

Schnabel, James F., and Robert J. Watson. *The Korean War*. Vol. 3 of *The History of the Joint Chiefs of Staff: The Joint Chiefs of Staff and National Policy*. Wilmington, Del.: Michael Glazier, 1979.

Schoenbaum, Thomas J. *Waging Peace and War: Dean Rusk in the Truman, Kennedy, and Johnson Years*. New York: Simon & Schuster, 1988.

Schonberger, Howard B. *Aftermath of War: Americans and the Remaking of Japan, 1945–1952*. Kent, Ohio: Kent State University Press, 1989.

Seldon, Anthony. *Churchill's Indian Summer: The Conservative Government, 1951–1955*. London: Hodder & Stoughton, 1981.

Short, Anthony. *The Origins of the Vietnam War*. New York: Longman, 1989.

Smith, Joseph B. *Portrait of a Cold Warrior*. New York: Putnam, 1976.

Spanier, John W. *The Truman-MacArthur Controversy and the Korean War*. New York: W. W. Norton, 1965.

Spector, Ronald H. *Advice and Support: The Early Years of the U.S. Army in Vietnam, 1941–1960*. New York: The Free Press, 1985.

Stairs, Denis. *The Diplomacy of Constraint: Canada, the Korean War, and the United States*. Toronto: University of Toronto Press, 1974.

Stebbins, Richard P. *The United States in World Affairs, 1954*. New York: Harper & Bros., 1956.

Stueck, William W., Jr. *The Road to Confrontation: American Policy toward China and Korea, 1947–1950*. Chapel Hill: University of North Carolina Press, 1981.

———. *The Wedemeyer Mission, American Politics and Foreign Policy during the Cold War*. Athens: University of Georgia Press, 1984.

Sutter, Robert G. *China-Watch: Sino-American Reconciliation*. Baltimore, Md.: The Johns Hopkins University Press, 1978.

Tang, James Tuck-Hong. *Britain's Encounter with Revolutionary China, 1949–54*. New York: St. Martin's Press, 1992.

Trevelyan, Humphrey. *Worlds Apart, China, 1953–5; Soviet Union, 1962–5*. London: The Macmillan Press, 1971.

Truman, Harry S. *Years of Trial and Hope*. Vol. 2 of *Memoirs*. Garden City, N.Y.: Doubleday, 1956.

Tsai, George W. "The Taiwan Straits Crises: Analysis of the China, Taiwan, United States Relationship, 1949–1983." Ph.D. dissertation, Northern Arizona University, 1985.

Tsou, Tang. *America's Failure in China, 1941–50*. Chicago: University of Chicago Press, 1963.

Tucker, Nancy Bernkopf. *Patterns in the Dust: Chinese-American Relations and the Recognition Controversy, 1949–1950*. New York: Columbia University Press, 1983.

———. *Taiwan, Hong Kong, and the United States, 1945–1992: Uncertain Friendships*. New York: Twayne Publishers, 1994.

Ulam, Adam B. *Expansion and Coexistence: The History of Soviet Foreign Policy, 1917–1967*. New York: Praeger, 1968.

United Nations. *Yearbook of the United Nations, 1950*. New York: Department of Public Information, United Nations, 1951.

———. *Yearbook of the United Nations, 1951*. New York: Department of Public Information, United Nations, 1952.

———. *Yearbook of the United Nations, 1955*. New York: Department of Public Information, United Nations, 1956.

Watson, Robert J. 1953–1954. Vol. 5 of *The History of the Joint Chiefs of Staff: The Joint Chiefs of Staff and National Policy*. Washington, D.C.: Government Printing Office, 1986.

Weigley, Russell F. *The American Way of War: A History of United States Military Strategy and Policy*. Bloomington: University of Indiana Press, 1977.

Whiting, Allen S. *China Crosses the Yalu: The Decision to Enter the Korean War*. New York: Macmillan, 1960.

Wu, Hsiu-chuan. *Eight Years in the Ministry of Foreign Affairs: Memoirs of a Diplomat*. Peking: New World Press, 1985.

Yoshitsu, Michael M. *Japan and the San Francisco Peace Settlement*. New York: Columbia University Press, 1983.

Young, John W., ed. *The Foreign Policy of Churchill's Peacetime Administration, 1951–1955*. Leicester, U.K.: Leicester University Press, 1988.

Young, Kenneth. *Negotiating with the Chinese Communists: The United States Experience, 1953–1967*. New York: McGraw-Hill, 1968.

Young, Kenneth Ray. "Nationalist Chinese Troops in Burma—Obstacle in Burma's Foreign Relations, 1949–1961." Ph.D. dissertation, New York University, 1970.

Zhai, Qiang. *The Dragon, the Lion, and the Eagle: Chinese-British-American Relations, 1949–1958*. Kent, Ohio: Kent University Press, 1994.

Zhang, Shu Guang. *Deterrence and Strategic Culture: Chinese-American Confrontations, 1949–1958*. Ithaca, N.Y.: Cornell University Press, 1992.

Articles and Essays

Accinelli, Robert. "Eisenhower, Congress, and the 1954–55 Offshore Islands Crisis." *Presidential Studies Quarterly* 20 (Spring 1990): 329–48.

Adamthwaite, Anthony. "The Foreign Office and Policy-making." In *The Foreign Policy of Churchill's Peacetime Administration, 1951–1955*, edited by John W. Young, pp. 1–28. Leicester, U.K.: Leicester University Press, 1988.

Alsop, Stewart. "The Story Behind Quemoy: How We Drifted Close to War." *Saturday Evening Post*, 13 December 1958, pp. 26–27, 86–88.

Artaud, Denise. "France between the Indochina War and the European Defense Community." In *Dien Bien Phu and the Crisis of Franco-American Relations*, edited by Lawrence S. Kaplan, Denise Artaud, and Mark R. Rubin, pp. 251–68. Wilmington, Del.: Scholarly Resources, 1990.

Barnett, A. Doak. "The Economy of Formosa: Progress on a Treadmill." *American Universities Field Staff Reports, East Asian Series* 3 (Hong Kong 1954): 241–51.

Brands, H. W., Jr. "Testing Massive Retaliation, Credibility and Crisis Management in the Taiwan Strait." *International Security* 12 (Spring 1988): 124–51.

Briggs, Philip J. "Congress and the Cold War: U.S.-China Policy, 1955." *China Quarterly* 85 (March 1981): 80–95.

Browne, Blaine T. "'The Very Thing We Feared Most': American Images of China in a Decade of War and Revolution, 1945–1955." *Maryland Historian* 18 (Fall/Winter 1987): 1–21.

Buhite, Russell D. "'Major Interests': American Policy toward China, Taiwan, and Korea, 1945–1950." *Pacific Historical Review* 47 (August 1978): 425–51.

Burk, Robert F. "Eisenhower Revisionism Revisited: Reflections on Eisenhower Scholarship." *The Historian* 50 (February 1988): 196–209.

Chang, David W. "U.S. Aid and Economic Progress in Taiwan." *Asian Survey* 5 (March 1965): 152–60.

Chang, Gordon H. "To the Nuclear Brink: Eisenhower, Dulles, and the Quemoy-Matsu Crisis." *International Security* 12 (Spring 1988): 96–122.

Chang, Gordon H., and He Di. "The Absence of War in the U.S.-China Confrontation over Quemoy and Matsu in 1954–1955: Contingency, Luck, Deterrence?" *American Historical Review* 98 (December 1993): 1500–1524.

Chang, Su-ya. "The United States and the Long-term Disposition of Taiwan in the Making of Peace with Japan, 1950–1952." *Asian Profile* 16 (October 1988): 459–70.

Chen, Jian. "China's Changing Aims during the Korean War, 1950–1951." *The Journal of American-East Asian Relations* 1 (Spring 1992): 8–41.

Chen, Xiaolu. "China's Policy toward the United States, 1949–1955." In *Sino-American Relations, 1945–1955: A Joint Reassessment of a Critical Decade*, edited by Harry Harding and Yuan Ming, pp. 184–97. Wilmington, Del.: Scholarly Resources, 1989.

"The China Lobby: A Case Study." *Congressional Quarterly Weekly Report* 9 (June 29, 1951): 939–58.

Chiu, Hungdah. "China, the United States, and the Question of Taiwan." In *China and the Taiwan Issue*, edited by Hungdah Chiu, pp. 112–91. New York: Praeger, 1979.

Christensen, Thomas J. "Threats, Assurances, and the Last Chance for Peace, the Lessons of Mao's Korean War Telegrams." *International Security* 17 (Summer 1992): 122–50.

Clubb, O. Edmund. "The Effect of Chinese Nationalist Military Activities in Burma on Burmese Foreign Policy." Rand Corporation Study P-1595-RC (January 20, 1959): 1–60.

———. "Formosa and the Offshore Islands in American Policy, 1950–1955." *Political Science Quarterly* 74 (December 1959): 517–31.

Cohen, Warren I. "Acheson, His Advisers, and China, 1949–1950." In *Uncertain Years, Chinese-American Relations, 1947–1950*, edited by Dorothy Borg and Waldo Heinrichs, pp. 13–52. New York: Columbia University Press, 1980.

———. "China in Japanese-American Relations." In *The United States and Japan in the Postwar World*, edited by Warren I. Cohen and Akira Iriye, pp. 36–60. Lexington, Ky: University of Kentucky Press, 1989.

———. "The China Lobby." In *Encyclopedia of American Foreign Policy*, edited by Alexander De Conde. Vol. 1. New York: Scribner, 1978.

———. "Consul General O. Edmund Clubb on the 'Inevitability' of Conflict between the United States and the People's Republic of China, 1949–50." *Diplomatic History* 5 (Spring 1981): 165–68.

Dean, Arthur H. "United States Foreign Policy and Formosa." *Foreign Affairs* 33 (1955): 360–75.

Dingman, Roger. "Atomic Diplomacy during the Korean War." *International Security* 13 (Winter 1988/89): 50–91.

————. "John Foster Dulles and the Creation of the South-East Asia Treaty Organization in 1954." *International History Review* 11 (August 1989): 457–77.

Dobbs, Charles M. "Limiting Room to Maneuver: The Korea Assistance Act of 1949." *The Historian* 48 (August 1986): 525–38.

Dockrill, Michael. "Britain and the First Chinese Off-Shore Islands Crisis, 1954–55." In *British Foreign Policy, 1945–56*, edited by Michael Dockrill and John W. Young, pp. 173–96. London: Macmillan, 1989.

————. "The Foreign Office, Anglo-American Relations and the Korean Truce Negotiations, July 1951–July 1953." In *The Korean War in History*, edited by James Cotton and Ian Neary, pp. 100–119. Manchester: Manchester University Press, 1989.

————. "The Foreign Office, Anglo-American Relations and the Korean War, June 1950–June 1951." *International Affairs* [London] 62 (Summer 1986): 459–76.

Erskine, Hazel. "The Polls: Red China and the U.N." *Public Opinion Quarterly* 35 (Spring 1971): 123–35.

Farrar-Hockley, Anthony. "The China Factor in the Korean War." In *The Korean War in History*, edited by James Cotton and Ian Neary, pp. 4–10. Manchester: Manchester University Press, 1989.

Feaver, John Hansen. "The China Aid Bill of 1948: Limited Assistance as a Cold War Strategy." *Diplomatic History* 5 (Summer 1981): 188–206.

Fetzer, James. "Senator Vandenberg and the American Commitment to China, 1945–1950." *The Historian* 36 (February 1974): 283–303.

Fish, M. Steven. "After Stalin's Death: The Anglo-American Debate Over a New Cold War." *Diplomatic History* 10 (Fall 1986): 333–55.

Foot, Rosemary. "Anglo-American Relations in the Korean Crisis: The British Effort to Avert an Expanded War, December 1950–January 1951." *Diplomatic History* 10 (Winter 1986): 43–57.

————. "Making Known the Unknown War: Policy Analysis of the Korean Conflict in the Last Decade." *Diplomatic History* 15 (Summer 1991): 411–31.

————. "New Light on the Sino-Soviet Alliance: Chinese and American Perspectives." *Journal of Northeast Asian Studies* 10 (Fall 1991): 16–29.

————. "The Search for a *Modus Vivendi*: Anglo-American Relations and China Policy in the Eisenhower Era." In *The Great Powers in East Asia, 1953–1960*, edited by Warren I. Cohen and Akira Iriye, pp. 143–63. New York: Columbia University Press, 1990.

"Formosan Decision First Step 'Asian Fight Asian' Policy." *Newsweek*, 9 February 1953, p. 30.

Gaddis, John Lewis. "The American 'Wedge Strategy,' 1949–1955." In *Sino-American Relations, 1945–1955: A Joint Reassessment of a Critical Decade*, edited by Harry Harding and Yuan Ming, pp. 157–83. Wilmington, Del.: Scholarly Resources, 1989.

————. "Dividing Adversaries: The United States and International Communism, 1945–1958." In *The Long Peace: Inquiries into the History of the Cold War*. New York: Oxford University Press, 1987.

————. "The Strategic Perspective: The Rise and Fall of the 'Defensive Perimeter' Concept, 1947–1951." In *Uncertain Years, Chinese-American Relations, 1947–1950*, edited by Dorothy Borg and Waldo Heinrichs, pp. 61–118. New York: Columbia University Press, 1980.

Gordon, Leonard. "American Planning for Taiwan, 1942–1945." *Pacific Historical Review* 37 (1968): 201–28.

————. "United States Opposition to Use of Force in the Taiwan Strait, 1954–1962." *Journal of American History* 72 (December 1985): 637–60.

Graebner, Norman A. "Eisenhower and Communism: The Public Record of the 1950s." In *Reevaluating Eisenhower: American Foreign Policy in the Fifties*, edited by Richard A. Melanson and David Mayers, pp. 67–87. Urbana: University of Illinois Press, 1987.

Halperin, M. H., and Tang Tsou. "United States Policy toward the Offshore Islands." In vol. 15 of *Public Policy*, edited by John D. Montgomery and Arthur Smithies, pp. 119–38. Cambridge: Harvard University Press, 1966.

Han, Yelong. "The Untold Story: American Policy toward Chinese Students in the United States, 1949–1955." *Journal of American-East Asian Relations* 2 (Spring 1993): 77–99.

Hao, Yufan and Zhai Zhihai. "China's Decision to Enter the Korean War: History Revisited." *China Quarterly* 121 (March 1990): 94–115.

He, Di. "The Evolution of the People's Republic of China's Policy toward the Offshore Islands." In *The Great Powers in East Asia, 1953–1960*, edited by Warren I. Cohen and Akira Iriye, pp. 222–45. New York: Columbia University Press, 1990.

————. "'The Last Campaign to Unify China': The CCP's Unmaterialized Plan to Liberate Taiwan, 1949–1950." *Chinese Historians* 5 (Spring 1992): 1–6.

Ho, Samuel P. S. "Economics, Economic Bureaucracy, and Taiwan's Economic Development." *Pacific Affairs* 60 (Summer 1987): 226–47.

Horton, Philip. "The China Lobby—Part II." *The Reporter* 6 (29 April 1952): 5–24.

Huebner, Jon W. "The Abortive Liberation of Taiwan." *China Quarterly* 110 (June 1987): 256–75.

Hunt, Michael H. "Beijing and the Korean Crisis, June 1950–June 1951." *Political Science Quarterly* 107 (Fall 1992): 453–78.

Immerman, Richard H. "Confessions of an Eisenhower Revisionist." *Diplomatic History* 14 (Summer 1990): 319–42.

————. "Eisenhower and Dulles: Who Made the Decisions?" *Political Psychology* 1 (Autumn 1979): 21–38.

————. "The United States and the Geneva Conference of 1954: A New Look." *Diplomatic History* 14 (Winter 1990): 43–66.

Jia, Qingguo. "Searching for Peaceful Coexistence and Territorial Integrity." In *Sino-American Relations, 1945–1955: A Joint Reassessment of a Critical Decade*, edited by Harry Harding and Yuan Ming, pp. 267–86. Wilmington, Del.: Scholarly Resources, 1989.

Joes, Anthony James. "Eisenhower Revisionism and American Politics." In *Dwight D. Eisenhower: Soldier, President, Statesman*, edited by Joann P. Krieg, pp. 283–96. Westport, Conn.: Greenwood Press, 1987.

"K. C. Wu Story." *The Reporter* 10 (27 April 1954): 18–20.

Keefer, Edward C. "President Dwight D. Eisenhower and the End of the Korean War." *Diplomatic History* 3 (Summer 1986): 267–89.

Kuo, Ting-yee. "History of Taiwan." In *China and the Taiwan Issue*, edited by Hung-dah Chiu, pp. 3–27. New York: Praeger, 1979.

Li, Xiaobing. "Chinese Intentions and [the] 1954–55 Offshore Islands Crisis." *Chinese Historians* 2 (January 1990): 45–59.

Lintner, Bertil. "The CIA's First Secret War." *Far Eastern Economic Review* 156 (16 September 1993): 56–58.

Lippmann, Walter. "Toward a Cease-Fire." *Washington Post and Times Herald*, 8 February 1955, 17:1–3.

Lowe, Peter. "The Frustrations of Alliance: Britain, the United States, and the Korean War, 1950–1951." In *The Korean War in History*, edited by James Cotton and Ian Neary, pp. 80–99. Manchester: Manchester University Press, 1989.

Mabon, David W. "Elusive Agreements: The Pacific Pact Proposals of 1949–1951." *Pacific Historical Review* 57 (May 1988): 147–77.

Matray, James. "America's Reluctant Crusade: Truman's Commitment of Combat Troops in the Korean War." *The Historian* 42 (May 1980): 437–55.

Mayers, David. "Eisenhower's Containment Policy and the Major Communist Powers, 1953–1956." *International History Review* 5 (February 1983): 59–83.

McLean, David. "American Nationalism, the China Myth, and the Truman Doctrine: The Question of Accommodation with Peking, 1949–50." *Diplomatic History* 10 (Winter 1986): 25–42.

McMahon, Robert J. "The Cold War in Asia: Toward a New Synthesis?" *Diplomatic History* 12 (Summer 1988): 307–27.

————. "Credibility and World Power: Exploring the Psychological Dimension in Postwar American Diplomacy." *Diplomatic History* 15 (Fall 1991): 455–71.

————. "Eisenhower and Third World Nationalism: A Critique of the Revisionists." *Political Science Quarterly* 101 (Fall 1986): 453–73.

Munro-Leighton, Judith. "A Postrevisionist Scrutiny of America's Role in the Cold War in Asia, 1945–1950." *Journal of American-East Asian Relations* 1 (Spring 1992): 73–98.

Myers, Ramon H. "The Economic Development of Taiwan." In *China and the Taiwan Issue*, edited by Hungdah Chiu, pp. 28–73. New York: Praeger, 1979.

Nakatsuji, Keiji. "The Short Life of the Official 'Two China' Policy: Improvisation and Postponement in 1950." *UCLA Historical Journal* 6 (1985): 33–49.

Nelson, Anna Kasten. "John Foster Dulles and the Bipartisan Congress." *Political Science Quarterly* 102 (Spring 1987): 43–64.

————. "The 'Top of Policy Hill': President Eisenhower and the National Security Council." *Diplomatic History* 7 (Fall 1973): 307–26.

Newman, Robert P. "Clandestine Chinese Nationalist Efforts to Punish Their Detractors." *Diplomatic History* 7 (Summer 1983): 205–22.

Ovendale, Ritchie. "Britain, the United States, and the Recognition of Communist China." *Historical Journal* 26 (March 1983): 139–58.

Paterson, Thomas G. "If Europe, Why Not China? The Containment Doctrine, 1947–1949." *Prologue* 13 (Spring 1981): 19–38.

Pollack, Jonathan D. "The Korean War and Sino-American Relations." In *Sino-American Relations, 1945–1955: A Joint Reassessment of a Critical Decade*, edited by Harry Harding and Yuan Ming, pp. 213–37. Wilmington, Del.: Scholarly Resources, 1989.

Rabe, Stephen. "Eisenhower Revisionism: A Decade of Scholarship." *Diplomatic History* 17 (Winter 1993): 97–115.

Rao, Geping. "The Kuomintang Government's Policy toward the United States, 1945–1949." In *Sino-American Relations, 1945–1955: A Joint Reassessment of a Critical Decade*, edited by Harry Harding and Yuan Ming, pp. 51–61. Wilmington, Del.: Scholarly Resources, 1989.

Ravenholt, Albert. "Formosa Today." *Foreign Affairs* 30 (July 1952): 612–24.

Rushkoff, Bennett C. "Eisenhower, Dulles and the Quemoy-Matsu Crisis, 1954–1955." *Political Science Quarterly* 96 (Fall 1981): 465–80.

Schaller, Michael. "Consul General O. Edmund Clubb, John P. Davies, and the 'Inevitability' of Conflict between the United States and China, 1949–50: A Comment and New Documentation." *Diplomatic History* 9 (Spring 1985): 149–60.

Schonberger, Howard. "Peacemaking in Asia: The United States, Great Britain, and the Japanese Decision to Recognize Nationalist China, 1951–52." *Diplomatic History* 10 (Winter 1986): 59–73.

Shepley, James. "How Dulles Averted War." *Life*, 16 January 1956, pp. 70–80.

Sigal, Leon V. "The 'Rational Policy' Model and the Formosa Straits Crisis." *International Studies Quarterly* 14 (June 1970): 121–56.

Stolper, Thomas E. "China, Taiwan, and the Offshore Islands." *International Journal of Politics* 15 (Spring–Summer 1985): 1–170.

Stueck, William. "The Limits of Influence: British Policy and American Expansion of the War in Korea." *Pacific Historical Review* 55 (February 1986): 65–95.

Synder, William P. "Dean Rusk to John Foster Dulles, May–June 1953: The Office, the First 100 Days, and Red China." *Diplomatic History* 7 (Winter 1983): 79–86.

Tsou, Tang. "Mao's Limited War in the Taiwan Strait." *Orbis* 3 (Fall 1959): 332–50.

———. "The Quemoy Imbroglio: Chiang Kai-shek and the United States." *Western Political Quarterly* 12 (December 1959): 1075–91.

Tucker, Nancy Bernkopf. "American Policy toward Sino-Japanese Trade in the Postwar Years: Politics and Prosperity." *Diplomatic History* 8 (Summer 1984): 183–208.

———. "China's Place in the Cold War: the Acheson Plan." In *Dean Acheson and the Making of U.S. Foreign Policy*, edited by Douglas Brinkley, pp. 109–32. New York: St. Martin's Press, 1993.

———. "John Foster Dulles and the Taiwan Roots of the 'Two Chinas' Policy." In *John Foster Dulles and the Diplomacy of the Cold War: A Reappraisal*, edited by Richard H. Immerman, pp. 235–62. Princeton, N.J.: Princeton University Press, 1990.

———. "A House Divided: The United States, the Department of State, and China." In *The Great Powers in East Asia, 1953–1960*, edited by Warren I. Cohen and Akira Iriye, pp. 35–62. New York: Columbia University Press, 1990.

———. "Nationalist China's Decline and Its Impact on Sino-American Relations, 1949–1950." In *Uncertain Years, Chinese-American Relations, 1947–1950*, edited by Dorothy Borg and Waldo Heinrichs, pp. 131–71. New York: Columbia University Press, 1980.

Umemoto, Tetsuya. "Congress and the Japanese Peace Settlement." *American Review* [Tokyo] 17 (March 1983): 129–52.

Wang, Jisi. "The Origins of America's 'Two China' Policy." In *Sino-American Relations, 1945–1955: A Joint Reassessment of a Critical Decade*, edited by Harry Harding and Yuan Ming, pp. 198–212. Wilmington, Del.: Scholarly Resources, 1989.

Warner, Geoffrey. "Britain and the Crisis over Dien Bien Phu, April 1954: The Failure of United Action," and "From Geneva to Manila: British Policy toward Indochina and SEATO, May–September 1954." In *Dien Bien Phu and the Crisis of Franco-American Relations*, edited by Lawrence S. Kaplan, Denise Artaud, and Mark R. Rubin, pp. 57–77, 149–67. Wilmington, Del.: Scholarly Resources, 1990.

Wei, Yung, "Political Development in the Republic of China on Taiwan." In *China and the Taiwan Issue*, edited by Hungdah Chiu, pp. 74–111. New York: Praeger, 1979.

Wertenbaker, Charles. "The China Lobby." *The Reporter* 6 (15 April 1952): 2–24.

Wiltz, John E. "The MacArthur Hearings of 1951: The Secret Testimony." *Military Affairs* 39 (December 1975): 167–73.

———. "The MacArthur Inquiry, 1951." In *Congress Investigates*, edited by Arthur M. Schlesinger, Jr., and Roger Burns. Vol. 5, pp. 3593–3636. New York: Chelsea House, 1973.

———. "Truman and MacArthur: The Wake Island Meeting." *Military Affairs* 42 (December 1978): 68–75.

Wolf, David C. "'To Secure a Convenience,' Britain Recognizes China—1950." *Journal of Contemporary History* 18 (April 1983): 299–326.

Wu, K. C. "Your Money Has Built a Police State in Formosa." *Look*, 29 June 1954, pp. 39–45.

Zhai, Qiang. "Britain, the United States, and the Jinmen-Mazu Crises, 1954–55 and 1958." *Chinese Historians* 2 (Fall 1992): 25–48.

———. "Dulles, Wedge, and the Sino-American Ambassadorial Talks, 1955–1957." *Chinese Historians* 2 (December 1988): 29–44.

Zhang, Shuguang. "'Preparedness Eliminates Mishaps': The CCP's Security Concerns in 1949–50 and the Origins of Sino-American Confrontation." *Journal of American-East Asian Relations* 1 (Spring 1992): 42–72.

Chiang Ching-kuo, 94, 207, 288 (n. 29), 299–300 (n. 45), 313 (n. 5)

Chiang Kai-shek, 239, 264; commitment to mainland conquest, xi–xii, 4–5, 42, 99–100, 112, 172, 198–99; refuge on Taiwan, 4; Acheson and, 5, 9, 16, 32, 61; Truman administration and, 5, 100, 256; U.S. aloofness toward, 5–6, 38–39, 53–54, 61–62, 263; MacArthur's support for, 7, 9, 41–42; Britain and, 10, 263; appointment of Wu as governor, 11; and defense of Taiwan against China, 16–17; plots for overthrow of, 20–21, 22, 25–26, 274 (n. 96); Truman and, 26, 32, 61, 92; Seventh Fleet intervention and, 32, 38; Harriman and, 42; and Korean War, 55, 100, 119, 289–90 (n. 49); and Japanese peace treaty, 84; corruption under, 92; and U.S. economic and military aid, 93, 123, 250; Rankin and, 95–96; authoritarianism of, 96; Radford and, 98, 250; offer of troops for Korean War, 106, 116–17, 277 (n. 50); Eisenhower administration and, 111–12, 125, 196–97, 256; Dulles and, 112, 113, 119, 172, 209–10, 230, 237; Eisenhower and, 112–13, 157, 175, 228; and Pacific treaty proposal, 122; and defense of offshore islands, 123–25, 244; and Kuomintang guerrillas in Burma, 125, 127, 128; and French-Indochina War, 139; and U.S.-Taiwan defense treaty, 146, 167–68, 175–76; and captured Soviet tanker, 151; and offshore islands cease-fire proposal, 167–68, 195–96, 209–10; and evacuation of offshore islands, 175, 191, 196–97, 198, 209, 210, 227–28, 244; and U.S. defense of Quemoy and Matsu, 196–97, 235, 244; and "opportunism" strategy of Dulles, 198, 210, 249, 256

Chiang Kai-shek, Madame (May-ling Soong), 66, 113, 126

Childs, Marquis, 315 (n. 35)

China, People's Republic of: and U.S.-Taiwan relationship, ix, xi, 25, 53–54, 151–52, 264–65; intervention in Korean War, x–xi, 53, 55, 56–57, 107, 254, 255; Britain and U.S. relations with, xi, 18, 19, 72, 79, 130–31, 166, 238–39, 262; NSC 48/5 policy and, xi, 70–72, 108, 133–34, 255, 258, 259; Nationalist claim to government of, 3–4, 69, 171–72; Nationalist "mainland recovery" objective, 4–5, 53–54, 171–72, 198–99, 249, 250–51, 256; Roosevelt and, 5; Republicans in Congress and, 6, 31, 73, 75, 114, 129–30; American public opinion and, 7, 75, 129, 241; British relations with, 10, 18, 19, 79, 132, 166, 262; claim to Taiwan, 10, 33, 49, 236; Nationalist blockade of, 10, 36–37; Soviet alliance, 12, 18, 22, 65, 163, 173, 238; seizure of Hainan and Chusan Islands, 16–17; American anticommunism and, 17, 31, 53, 57, 76, 261; U.S. containment doctrine and, 18, 71; U.S. refusal of recognition to, 18–19; and Seventh Fleet intervention in Taiwan Strait, 34, 45, 53–54, 60; Nationalist military actions in, 40, 57–59, 65, 66, 98, 112, 138, 181, 256–57, 272 (n. 54); aggression charge against United States, 43, 45, 51; UN representation issue, 44–45, 48, 79–80, 128–30, 131, 132, 135, 140–44, 169–70, 245, 254, 257, 262–63, 298–99 (n. 34); in Korean War, 52, 53, 59–60, 62, 97, 108; anticommunism in, 58, 71–72; and Korean War cease-fire proposals, 59–61, 63, 68; U.S. aggression charge against, 62, 63; U.S. covert warfare against, 64–67, 254, 256; Rusk's "Slavic Manchukuo" speech and, 72, 73; U.S. hostility toward, 98, 113–14, 151, 153; U.S. deneutralization policy and, 112, 115; military campaigns against offshore islands, 123, 148, 152–53, 155; campaign for "liberation" of Taiwan, 146, 151–52, 155, 158, 236–37; attacks on Tachen Islands, 148, 152, 159, 165,

174, 185, 186, 190; downing of British airliner, 151; bombing of Quemoy, 152, 157, 158, 159, 161, 164; NSC 5429 policy and, 153, 154, 180–81; U.S. threat of war with, 157, 162, 173, 202, 214, 215, 216–17, 232; offshore islands crisis and U.S. relations, 157–59, 255–56; and cease-fire in offshore islands crisis, 167, 203–4, 236–37; capture of American fliers, 177–78, 186, 238, 242, 306 (n. 81); and U.S.-Taiwan defense treaty, 178–79; capture of Yikiangshan, 185, 187; Formosa Resolution and, 192–93, 232; U.S. threat of nuclear weapons use, 211, 212, 214, 217, 221, 316 (nn. 52, 53); military threat to Quemoy and Matsu, 211–12, 213–14, 221–22, 232–33, 244–45; proposed blockade of, 223, 225–26, 317 (n. 67); negotiations in offshore islands crisis, 228–30, 236, 239–44; U.S. trade embargo against, 243; Korean War prisoners, 289–90 (n. 49)

China, Republic of. *See* Taiwan

China Aid Act (1948), 14, 15, 93

China lobby, 7, 69, 75–78

China White Paper, 128

Chinese civil war, 14, 17, 44

Chinese Communist Party (CCP), 5, 34, 53, 60, 65, 180, 225–26, 264

Chinese Revolution, 53, 181

Chou Chih-jou, 98–99

Chou En-lai, 52, 201, 208; and Seventh Fleet in Taiwan Strait, 34, 45; and Korean War cease-fire, 60, 63; and U.S.-Taiwan defense treaty, 178–79; and captured American fliers, 186, 191; and negotiations with United States on offshore islands, 203–4, 211, 228–29, 230, 232, 236, 240, 258

Churchill, Sir Winston S.: and Cairo Declaration, 4; and Japan-China relations, 87; and U.S.-British relations, 87, 131, 132, 143; and Chinese UN seat, 131, 132, 141–42, 143; and U.S.-Taiwan relations, 131, 262, 263; and offshore

islands, 206, 263; retirement of, 219

Chusan Islands, 16–17

CINCPAC, 105–6, 118, 211

Civil Air Transport (CAT), 64, 66

Clark, Mark W., 106, 116–17

Clubb, O. Edmund, 24

Cohen, Benjamin, 309 (n. 46)

Collins, J. Lawton, 106–7

Commerce International China (CIC), 271–72 (n. 53)

Congress (U.S.): and relations with Taiwan, 6–7, 25, 261, 265; and aid to Taiwan, 15, 94–95, 120, 140; elections of 1950, 53; Senate MacArthur hearings, 73–75; Senate ratification of Japan treaty, 82–83, 88; elections of 1952, 111; and Chinese UN seat, 130; and offshore islands crisis, 162; elections of 1954, 164; Eisenhower's Formosa message to, 185, 192, 197, 200; and French-Indochina War, 188; and Formosa Resolution, 193–95, 199–200, 254; Senate ratification of Taiwan treaty, 195; and relations with China, 241

Containment doctrine, 12, 18, 71, 104, 111, 133

Cooke, Charles M., 271–72 (n. 53), 274 (n. 97)

Cutler, Robert, 189

Davies, John Paton, 73, 113

Defense Department (U.S.), 6, 11, 19, 27, 67, 123, 250, 260

Democratic Party, 164, 218

Dening, Sir Maberly E., 86

Dewey, Thomas E., 114

Dickey, John, 142

Dienbienphu, 138, 148, 160, 188, 221

Douglas, Lewis, 37

Drumwright, Everett F., 148

Dulles, Allen, 105, 126, 151, 159, 163, 313 (n. 5)

Dulles, John Foster: and two-China policy, xi, 85, 86, 130, 132, 135, 142,

shore islands, 123, 154, 155, 159, 160, 194; and U.S.-Taiwan defense treaty, 173; and Nationalist evacuation of offshore islands, 188, 223, 228; and Formosa Resolution, 194, 202; plans for war with China, 214, 216, 217; proposed U.S. troops on Taiwan, 220; secret mission to Taiwan, 222, 223, 226, 227, 228; and proposed blockade of China, 226

Rankin, Karl: appointed chargé to Taiwan, 42, 92; and U.S.-Taiwan relations, 42, 92, 135, 247, 249; and covert war on China, 64, 66; and Nationalist government, 92, 95–96; and Chinese threats to offshore islands, 98–99, 147, 233; elevation to ambassadorial rank, 112, 287 (n. 3); and Nationalist military forces, 120, 128, 294 (n. 49); and U.S.-Taiwan defense treaty, 168; and proposed blockade of China, 226

Rau, Sir Benegal, 60

Rayburn, Sam, 188

Red Scare, 57, 113

Reporter, 77

Republican Party: and Truman administration, 6–7, 13, 31–32, 47, 73, 75, 100–101; and MacArthur, 47, 57, 75; and Eisenhower administration, 111, 129, 164, 261

Republic of China. *See* Taiwan

Rhee, Syngman, 119, 122

Richards, James P., 199–200

Ridgway, Matthew B., 41, 58, 98, 153, 160, 161, 194, 224

Robertson, Walter S., 120; appointed Far Eastern Bureau chief, 113; support of Chiang government, 113, 135; and U.S.-Taiwan defense treaty, 144, 146, 147, 167, 168, 174; secret mission to Taiwan, 222, 226, 227, 228

Roosevelt, Franklin D., 4, 5

Rusk, Dean, 49–50; appointed Far Eastern Bureau chief, 16; and Truman's nonmilitary policy, 16, 19, 22–23; and relations with China, 18–19; and pro-

posals for deposing Chiang, 20, 22, 23, 25–26, 274 (n. 96); and Seventh Fleet in Taiwan Strait, 30, 31, 47; and Sino-Soviet alliance, 65, 72–73; "Slavic Manchukuo" speech, 72–73; resignation from government, 96

Schuman, Robert, 50

Sebald, William J., 126, 128

Seventh Fleet, 70, 97, 173; ordered to Taiwan Strait, ix, x, 29, 30, 33, 34, 38, 253; and defense of Taiwan, 22, 32–33, 47, 233; and prevention of Nationalist attack on China, 32, 33, 104, 115; in Korean War, 34, 35; and defense of offshore islands, 40, 301 (n. 59); Nationalist forces as backup to, 42–43, 257; Chinese government and, 53; revision of mission, 59, 104–5, 115, 116

Shanghai, air raid on, 272 (n. 54)

Sherman, Forrest B., 30

Smith, H. Alexander, 13, 14, 218, 230

Smith, Walter Bedell, 65, 101, 103, 106, 126, 160

Southeast Asia, 18, 100, 137, 234

South East Asia Treaty Organization (SEATO), 138, 145, 146

South Korea: U.S. forces in, 30, 31–32; U.S. defense treaty, 119, 122, 145; prisoners of war, 119, 289–90 (n. 49); and Nationalist offshore islands, 234

South Vietnam, 315–16 (n. 43)

Soviet Union, 237–38; in U.S. national security planning, 12, 17, 31; alliance with China, 12, 18, 22, 65, 163, 173, 238; tanker seized by Nationalist navy, 150–51, 301 (n. 67); and Nationalist offshore islands, 163, 201–3, 204, 215–16, 314 (n. 27); and UN membership dispute, 246, 247

Spaak, Paul-Henri, 237

Sprouse, Philip D., 24

Stalin, Joseph V., 14, 132, 163, 271 (n. 43)

Stassen, Harold, 153, 161

State Department (U.S.): and Chiang

government, 5–6, 17; and relations
with China, 6, 18; and Defense
Department, 6, 260; China lobby
and, 7; UN trusteeship plan, 9, 10; and
separation of Taiwan from China, 9,
10, 13–14, 24; and military aid to Taiwan, 12, 14, 43, 67, 93, 116; and Truman's nonmilitary policy, 13–14, 16,
19, 27; McCarthy's attacks on, 15, 76,
114; and Taiwan Strait intervention,
35, 40, 43–44, 45, 47, 79; and Chinese
UN seat, 37, 44, 129, 245–46, 254,
298–99 (n. 34); UN commission plan,
48–49, 52, 79, 253; and Nationalist
invasion of China, 58–59, 105; and
Sino-Soviet alliance, 65; and Japanese peace treaty, 81, 88, 89; and NSC
48/5 policy, 104, 105, 259; and evacuation of Kuomintang guerrillas from
Burma, 127; and French-Indochina
War, 143; and U.S.-Taiwan defense
treaty, 144, 145, 146; and Soviet tanker
incident, 150; and Chinese capture
of U.S. fliers, 177; and Bandung conference, 215; and negotiations with
Chou, 229, 239–40, 242, 243; and
Outer Mongolia UN membership,
246, 247

Stevenson, Adlai E., 315 (n. 40)
Strategic Air Command, 35
Strong, Robert C., 21, 42
Struble, Arthur B., 35
Stuart, John Leighton, 287 (n. 3)
Stuart, W. W., 24
Stump, Felix B., 123, 124, 174, 211–12,
213–14, 222
Sun Li-jen, 20, 21, 22, 25, 32, 287–88
(n. 21)
Sun Yat-sen, 4

Tachen Islands: Nationalist defense of,
124; Chinese attacks on, 148, 152, 159,
165, 174, 185, 186, 190; in security of
Taiwan, 161, 187; Nationalist evacuation of, 190, 191, 193, 196–97, 198, 199,
232

Taft, Robert A., 13, 100, 114
Taiwan (Republic of China): role in
U.S.-Chinese relations, ix, xi, 25,
53–54, 151–52, 264–65; democracy in,
ix, 96; U.S. commitment to, ix–xi, 55,
59, 61–62, 68, 69, 89, 91, 107–9, 155,
174–75, 251, 253, 254–55, 258, 261,
263–64; Korean War and, x–xi, 31–32,
33, 55, 254, 255; U.S. nonmilitary policy and, 3, 8–9, 10, 12, 13–15, 16, 17, 25,
107, 253; claim to government of
China, 3–4, 69, 171–72; Kuomintang
misrule and corruption, 4, 10–11, 92,
96; Nationalist "mainland recovery"
objective, 4–5, 53–54, 171–72, 198–99,
249, 250–51, 256; Truman administration and, 5–6, 7, 29, 37–38, 69, 78–79,
89, 109, 253, 260, 261; Republicans in
Congress and, 6, 13, 15, 48, 75, 261;
China lobby and, 7, 76, 77; strategic
value to United States, 7–9, 30–31,
46, 74, 255; trade with Japan, 8, 285
(n. 51); UN trusteeship proposal, 9–10,
23; legal status of, 9–10, 33, 81, 258,
309 (n. 46); Chinese claim to, 10, 33,
49, 236; blockade of China, 10, 36–37;
British disdain for Nationalist government, 10, 263; U.S. economic and
military aid, 10–11, 14, 41, 43, 67–68,
93, 94–95, 117–18, 120, 236, 248–50,
251; American public opinion and, 15,
47–48, 73, 260–61; self-defense against
China, 16–17, 23–24, 206; Nationalist
armed forces, 16–17, 42–43, 94, 101–6,
121, 139–40, 249–51, 257, 320 (n. 17);
plots against Chiang government,
20–21, 25–26; Seventh Fleet intervention and, 29, 32–33, 38, 40, 47, 59;
U.S. ambivalence toward Chiang
government, 32, 38–39, 43, 53–54, 61,
109, 113, 118, 253, 263–64; U.S. neutralization policy and, 37–40, 41, 57,
97, 137, 253, 257; offer of troops for
Korea, 39, 56, 57–58, 106–7, 116–17,
277 (n. 50); military actions in China,
40, 57–59, 65, 66, 98, 112, 138, 181,

of MacArthur, 67–68, 69, 70, 76; Republican attacks on, 70, 100–101; and China lobby investigation, 77

Truman administration, 7, 114; commitment to Taiwan, x–xi, 59, 78–79, 89, 109, 254, 261; and economic and military aid to Taiwan, 5, 15; and Korean War, 51, 56–57, 63, 254; covert war against China, 64; Asia policy, 69, 77; and Japanese peace treaty, 69–70; China lobby investigation, 77; and Chinese UN seat, 80; and Chiang's mainland ambitions, 100

Tsiang, T. F., 171

Tuapse (Soviet tanker), 150–51, 301 (n. 67)

United Nations: proposed trusteeship for Taiwan, 9–10, 23; Korean War coalition, 34, 36, 50–51, 261–62; Chinese representation, 44–45, 48, 79–80, 129–30, 131, 132, 135, 140–44, 169–70, 245, 254, 257, 262–63, 298–99 (n. 34); proposed commission on Taiwan, 48–49, 50, 253; and aggression charge against United States, 51; Cease-fire Group, 62, 63, 262; and aggression charge against China, 63; condemnation of Kuomintang guerrillas in Burma, 127, 128; ten-year Charter review, 130, 142; cease-fire initiative in offshore islands crisis, 165–69, 170, 196, 200–201, 304 (n. 40), 310 (n. 72); and U.S. fliers captured in China, 178; Outer Mongolia admission dispute, 235–36, 246–48

Vandenburg Resolution (1948), 246

Van Fleet, James A., 140

Veterans of Foreign Wars (VFW): controversy over MacArthur's message to, 46–48, 51

Vietnam, 18, 22

Vincent, John Carter, 113

Wake Island conference (1950), 51

Wang Ping-nan, 242–43

Webb, James, 275 (n. 5)

Western Enterprises, Inc., 66, 138–39

West Germany, 164–65, 198, 212–13

Wilson, Charles E., 160, 161, 189, 216, 220, 260

World Commerce Corporation, 271–72 (n. 53)

Wu, K. C., 11, 22, 299–300 (n. 45)

Wu Hsiu-chuan, 60

Yalta agreement, 227

Yeh, George, 96, 172, 198; and Nationalist operations against China, 39, 66–67; and Japanese peace treaty, 88; and Eisenhower administration, 111–12; and Nationalist offer of troops for Korea, 116, 277 (n. 50); and U.S.-Taiwan defense treaty, 122, 144, 174, 179; and offshore islands crisis, 171, 188, 196, 199, 207

Yikiangshan Island, 185, 187, 232

Yoshida Shigeru, 80, 82, 83, 85–86, 87–88

Young, Kenneth T., 19–20

Younger, Kenneth, 36–37

1954 between the United States and China over Quemoy and Matsu and other Nationalist-held offshore islands.

The commitment that took shape in Washington from 1950 to 1955 was extensive yet also guarded, restraining the Nationalists from taking any provocative military action against the mainland. Nonetheless, Accinelli argues that neither the Korean War nor the Indochina War divided the United States and the People's Republic of China more fundamentally during this period than did the issue of U.S.-Taiwanese relations.

Robert Accinelli is professor of history at the University of Toronto.